STRATEGIC INTERESTS IN THE MIDDLE EAST

To Gina and Tracy

Strategic Interests in the Middle East
Opposition and Support for US Foreign Policy

Edited By:

Jack Covarrubias
University of Southern Mississippi, USA

and

Tom Lansford
University of Southern Mississippi, USA

ASHGATE

855833382

Published by
Ashgate Publishing Limited
Gower House
Croft Road
Aldershot
Hampshire GU11 3HR
England

Ashgate Publishing Company
Suite 420
101 Cherry Street
Burlington, VT 05401-4405
USA

Ashgate website: http://www.ashgate.com

British Library Cataloguing in Publication Data
Strategic interests in the Middle East: opposition or
  support for US foreign policy
  1. United States – Foreign relations– Middle East
  2. Middle East – Foreign relations – United States
  3. United States – Foreign relations – 1989– 4. Middle East
  – Foreign relations – 1979– 5. Europe – Foreign relations –
  Middle East 6. Middle East – Foreign relations – Europe
  7. Europe – Foreign relations – 1989– 8. Asia – Foreign
  relations – Middle East 9. Middle East – Foreign relations
  – Asia
  I. Covarrubias, Jack II. Lansford, Tom
  327.7'3'056

Library of Congress Cataloging-in-Publication Data
Strategic interests in the Middle East: opposition or support for US foreign policy /
edited by Jack Covarrubias and Tom Lansford.
      p. cm.
  Includes index.
  ISBN 978-0-7546-7033-9
  1. Middle East--Foreign relations--United States. 2. United States--Foreign
relations--Middle East. 3. United States--Foreign relations--2001---Public opinion.
4. World politics--21st century. I. Covarrubias, Jack. II. Lansford, Tom.

DS63.2.U5S77 2007
327.1273056--dc22

                                                                    2007009688

ISBN 978 0 7546 7033 9

Printed and bound in Great Britain by TJ International Ltd, Padstow, Cornwall.

Contents

List of Tables

Acknowledgements

The editors express their deep appreciation for Ms Kirstin Howgate of Ashgate for her patience and guidance in preparing this manuscript.

Tom Lansford would like to thank Denise von Herrmann for her support through the years at the University of Southern Mississippi. I would also like to thank my parents, Max and Ivy Lansford and brother and sister, David and Cynthia, and their respective families. As always, special thanks go to Mr James D. Buffett for assistance in manuscript preparation. Finally, my deepest love goes to my wife, Gina, and our daughters Ella and Kate, the inspiration for all that I do.

Jack Covarrubias would like to thank Ms Anna Rulska for her support and expertise in the completion of this work. In addition, he thanks Ms Cynthia Hartman and Ms Melodee Baines for their friendship over the course of this project. His love goes out to his wonderful daughter Savannah, his friends and family for their devotion, and finally, to Tracy for her patience.

List of Contributors

Tom Lansford is the Assistant Dean of the College of Arts and Letters, Interim Chair of the Department of Political Science, International Development and Affairs, and an Associate Professor of Political Science at the University of Southern Mississippi. Dr Lansford is a member of the governing board of the National Social Science Association, an associate editor for the journal White House Studies and an associate editor for Politics and Ethics Review. He has published articles in journals such as Defense Analysis, The Journal of Conflict Studies, European Security, International Studies, Security Dialogue and Strategic Studies. He is the author or co-author of a number of books, including most recently *The Lords of Foggy Bottom: The American Secretaries of State and the World They Shaped* (2001), *All for One: NATO, Terrorism and the United States* (2002), *A Bitter Harvest: US Foreign Policy and Afghanistan* (2003) and *Strategic Preemption: US Foreign Policy and the Second War in Iraq* (2004). He is also coeditor of several collections including *America's War on Terror* (2003), *George W. Bush: A Political and Ethical Assessment at Midterm* (2004), and *Transatlantic Security Dilemmas: Old Europe, New Europe and the US* (2005).

Jack Covarrubias is a Visiting Professor of Political Science at the University of Southern Mississippi. He is also a member of the governing board of the National Social Science Association. Over several years in the military and academia his research interests have ranged from security studies, American foreign policy and international development. He has published numerous works must recently including the co-authored book *To Protect and Defend: Homeland Security Policy* (2006) and the co-authored chapter "The Best Defense? Iraq and Beyond," in the edited volume *The Second Term of George W. Bush: Prospects and Perils* (2006).

Evan Campbell is a doctoral student at Old Dominion University. He holds an MA in history from the University of Massachusetts at Amherst and completed a Masters thesis at the University of Tübingen in Germany. His research interests include counter terrorism, Middle Eastern studies, and German foreign policy.

Jie Chen is the Louis I. Jaffe Professor of Political Science, Chair of the Department of Political Science, Old Dominion University. Dr Chen is the author of Popular Political Support *in Contemporary China* (Stanford: Stanford University Press, 2004) and has published numerous articles in scholarly journals, such as *Public Opinion Quarterly*, *Journal of Politics*, *Social Science Quarterly*, *Comparative Political Studies*, *Political Research Quarter*, *Modern China*, and *Asian Survey*.

Mira Duric is author of _The Strategic Defence Initiative: US Policy and the Soviet Union_ (2003), and "Russia and the 'Old' Europe versus 'New' Europe Debate: US Foreign Policy and the Iraq War 2003," in the edited collection, _Old Europe, New Europe and the US: Renegotiating Transatlantic Security in the Post 9/11 Era_ (2005). She has taught at the Universities of Nottingham and Leicester, England.

George Ehrhardt is an Assistant Professor of Political Science at Appalachian State University. He has published articles in journals such as _Japanese Journal of Political Science, Pacific Affairs_, and _Korean Journal of Defense Analysis_.

Daniel J. Graeber is a freelance author and political analyst working in Grand Rapids, Michigan. In 2005, he circulated a White Paper to government officials and academics regarding US policy towards Hamas. In 2006, he served as an adjunct Professor of Ethics at Grand Valley State University. He holds an MA in Diplomacy and International Conflict Management from Norwich University, where his focus was international relations theory and the role of non-state actors.

David Jackson is an Associate Professor of Political Science at the Bowling Green State University. His research and publications focus on the impact of culture on American politics and developments in Canadian politics. He also works extensively with organizations building the concept of civic culture in the Polish education system.

B.J. Jordan is a doctoral student associated with the University of Southern Mississippi's International Development Program. He specializes in Far Eastern and Middle Eastern security studies. He was selected political science student of the year at Southern Miss. in 2004 in conjunction with his paper "Prohibitions on the CIA: A Detriment to US Security." He is a retired Miami-Dade Sheriff's Department Sergeant and a six-year Navy Cryptographic Technician and Viet Nam veteran.

Jack Kalpakian is an Assistant Professor of Political Science at Al Akhawayn University in Infrane, Morocco. He has published several works including "America and Islam: The Blinding Effect of the Cold War" in the _International Journal of Politics and Ethics_(2002) and the book _Identity, Conflict and Cooperation in International River Systems_ (2004).

Daniel Kuthy is affiliated with Georgia State University where his research interests include security studies, democratization and French foreign policy. He is an editor for the journal _International Topics_.

Chunlong Lu is a recent Ph.D. of the Graduate Program in International Studies at Old Dominion University. His research interests include Chinese politics, middle class, political participation, and democratization. He has recently published articles in _China Perspectives,_ and _International Review of Modern Sociology_.

Robert J. Pauly, Jr is Assistant Professor of Political Science and Director of the International Policy and Development PhD. Program at The University of Southern Mississippi. His principal research interests are US foreign policy toward the states of Greater Middle East and the conduct of the Global War on Terrorism. His most recent books are *To Protect and Defend: US Homeland Security Policy*, with Jack Covarrubias and Tom Lansford (Ashgate, 2006) and *US Foreign Policy and the Persian Gulf: Safeguarding American Interests through Selective Multilateralism* (Ashgate, 2005).

Anna Rulska is a doctoral student at Old Dominion University. Her research and interests include politics of the European Union, with a focus on energy security, the relationship between the Old and New Europe, and transatlantic relations. She also serves as the Editor-in-Chief of *International Topics*, a peer-reviewed journal which publishes the works of graduate students in international relations.

Mark Sedgwick is an independent scholar whose publications focus on international security and development.

Vaughn P. Shannon is an Assistant Professor of political science at the University of Northern Iowa and Associate Director of UNI's Center for International Peace and Security Studies. He has published on Middle Eastern affairs for *Harvard International Review*, and his book, *Balancing Act: US Foreign Policy and the Arab-Israeli Conflict* (Ashgate, 2003). He has published widely in journals such as *International Organization*, *International Studies Quarterly*, *European Journal of International Relations* and *Foreign Policy Analysis*.

Eva Svobodová is a Concept Analyst with Science Applications International Corporation (SAIC), currently working as Political Analyst at NATO's Allied Command Transformation in Norfolk, Va. She is also a PhD Candidate in the Graduate Program in International Studies at Old Dominion University, Norfolk, Va. Ms Sigmon's areas of expertise include international security, transatlantic relations, European Union, NATO, Central and Eastern Europe, and Afghanistan.

Chris White is a doctoral candidate at Old Dominion University. He earned a Masters in International Studies from North Carolina State University and was a Fulbright teaching assistant in Salzburg, Austria. His research interests focus on German foreign policy, where he has traveled extensively, International Law and the European Union.

Steve A. Yetiv is a Professor of Political Science in the Graduate Program for International Studies at the Old Dominion University. His extensive publications include books and articles on American foreign policy in the Persian Gulf region and the politics of oil in the Middle East.

Chris Zambelis is a Policy Analyst with the Strategic Assessment Center of Hicks and Associates, Inc., a subsidiary of Science Applications International Corporation

(SAIC). He specializes in Middle East politics and international terrorism issues. He is a regular contributor to a number of publications and has studied and worked with international organizations in East Europe and the former Yugoslavia, the Middle East, and Washington, D.C. He is a graduate of New York University and holds an M.S. in Foreign Service from Georgetown University.

Preface

The discordant nature of the Middle East stems from many beginnings. A student of the subject could focus on any one of them and make a legitimate argument in favor of that particular era. For example, the rise of Islam and its clash with the Byzantines in the seventh century, or the eleventh century conquest by the Turks, or perhaps the many Christian Crusades that helped drive the region into competing blocks of power can all serve as markers that help explain the current state of this region however incomplete that argument would be. The Mongols who swept through the region, followed by the Ottoman Turks, just to give way to the Europeans with the end of the First World War left a memorable stamp as well. No one of these events can explain why the Middle East gradually fell behind the West. However, each case contributes to the puzzle called the Middle East. The end effect of this unique combination of history, politics, and circumstance created a region which over the centuries benefited from, and was equally challenged by, its existence at the crossroads of empire and conquest.

Two specific events serve as detrimental markers for the contemporary Middle East and set the stage for its modern importance. The discovery of oil in the Zagros Mountains of Persia (modern day Iran) in 1908 and the modern era of the combustion engine both precipitated the struggles of the twentieth century. The mechanization of the First World War heralded the rise of oil as both a strategic and economic commodity that could directly impact the fate of great powers. Consecutively, the discovery of oil throughout much of the Middle East in the first half of the century led to the deliberate need to access this valuable resource and thus weight to the political desire of Europe, and later the US, for influence in the region. Hence, by the end of the First World War, 20 percent of British oil needs were supplied through its Middle Eastern holdings. By the 1920s, through mandate of the European-led League of Nations, much of the region had been divided into largely British and French direct and indirect spheres of influence. The modern boundaries of the Middle East are a result of this period of time.

Parallel to discoveries of oil begun one of the most troublesome dynamics of the region—namely the complicated, and oftentimes bellicose, relationship between the Jewish and the Palestinian peoples. The modern roots of Zionism start in the late nineteenth century with the Dreyfus Affair and the writings of Theodor Herzl. While tensions over the fate of the Jewish population in Europe can be traced back a number of years before Herzl, it was his call for a Jewish state and the first Zionist Congress in Basel, Switzerland in 1897, which focused on Palestine as the location for the Israeli state. In the eve of the First World War, the areas now known as Israel and Palestine were by no means sovereign; rather, the Ottoman Empire played a role of an administrator of these territories. With roughly 100,000 persons of Jewish affiliation and some 500,000 Arabs in the region, it quickly became obvious to both sides that peaceful and harmonious existence side by side, as was Herzl's original vision, was not in the cards. As put by the future Prime Minister of Israel David ben Gurion in 1919: "No solution! There is a gulf and nothing can bridge it.... I do not know what Arab will agree that Palestine should belong to the Jews.... We, as a nation, want this country to be ours; the Arabs, as a nation, want this country to be theirs."[1]

As foresight to the divide, a 1905 book by Najib Azouri, a Christian Arab in Jerusalem, titled *Le Reveil de la Nation Arabe dans l'Asie Turque*, predicted that emerging Arab nationalism and the Jewish desire to create a Jewish state in Palestine would lead to open-ended conflict. "The fate of the world will depend on the final result of this struggle between two peoples representing two contrary principles."[2]

British intentions in the region to establish a Jewish homeland in Palestine, as spelled out in the Balfour Declaration of 1917, became reality with the British mandate over the region in the post-the First World War environment. Thus, the seeds of what would become Israel were planted, along with the mistrust of Arabs against European intentions.

US Interests

The foundations of American interests in the region lay purely along economic lines. In the post-First World War environment, the US returned to its isolationist policies which, in contrast to the British and French intentions, allowed for no "direct colonial interests" in the Middle East.[3] In essence, the entirety of Washington's interests in the region in the pre-Second World War era can be summed up along two distinct intersecting lines. First, the US was both the largest producer and consumer of oil; second, the nature of American capitalism provided incentive for US companies to explore new sources of this mineral wealth. The first avenues of American policy in the region came, therefore, through various corporations that desired to conduct business within the Middle East. US mainstays, such as Standard Oil and Mobile Oil Corporation, led the drive to bring the United States into the Middle East in the 1930s, particularly in British mandate areas such as Saudi Arabia and Kuwait. However, large discoveries in Texas and other areas of the US, coupled with depressed crude oil prices due to overproduction, took away incentive for American investment abroad.[4]

---

1   Morris, B. (1999), *Righteous Victims: A History of the Zionist-Arab Conflict, 1881–1999*, New York: Knopf.

2   As discussed in Mandel, N.J. (1976), *The Arabs and Zionism Before World War I*, Berkeley: University of California Press.

3   Vo Xuan Han (1994), *Oil, The Persian Gulf States, and the United States*, London: Praeger.

4   Ibid.

During the Second World War, US economic development in the Middle East had all but stalled. Allied investment and production did not fair much better.[5] The majority of allied supplies during the war came from the Americas, not the Middle East—a contested war zone. However, with some 85 percent of the allied war effort powered by American energy, there was a fear that supplies would dwindle. American strategists of the time understood the strategic importance of oil and the need to secure future reserves. Therefore, President Franklin Roosevelt declared in 1943 that "the defense of Saudi Arabia is vital to the defense of the United States."[6] Roosevelt later formalized the relationship between Riyadh and Washington by meeting with the Saudi king in 1945 marking him the first sitting President to visit the region.

A number of factors contribute to US policy toward the Middle East in the immediate post-Second World War era. The rapid reindustrialization of Europe and the economic growth of the United States in the post-war environment demanded an increased amount of energy—particularly at a time when the world was drastically converting to oil as its primary energy source. In the economics of development, it was cheaper to develop production in the Middle East than in much of the West. However, perhaps the most pressing issue was the strategic importance of the region in the growing Cold War confrontation against the Soviets. While the US and its European allies had a good deal of time to develop a relationship with the Middle East, the Soviet system, characterized by proximity and, perhaps, frustration with the West, was making inroads into Middle Eastern society.[7] Thus, the American answer to the supposed Soviet threat was often interpreted as support for less than democratic regimes and outright threats of armed intervention against Soviet incursions into the region. The main thrust of US policy regarding the Middle East, aside from Israel, during the Cold War can be summed up as keeping the Soviets out while preventing the region from sliding into instability.[8] Luckily, each side of the bipolar order understood the necessity of "keeping the Straits of Hormuz open" in order to prevent regional divides from going global.[9]

The post-Cold War policy of the United States in the Middle East displays many similarities to the Cold War strategy—namely, maintaining a western-centric stability in order to assure the free flow of energy from the region. Couched within this policy, and sometimes seemingly in contradiction, is the traditional support of the United

---

5   Longrigg, S.H. (1968), *Oil in the Middle East: Its Discovery and Development*, London: Oxford University Press.

6   Hart, P.T. (1999), *Saudi Arabia and the United States: Birth of a Security Partnership*, Bloomington: Indiana University Press.

7   Brock, R. (1952), *Blood, Oil & Sand*, New York: The World Publishing Company. The author provides an early, and delightful to read, account of the rising East–West confrontation in the Middle East.

8   The most important US policies informing on the Middle East during the Cold War are the Truman Doctrine, the Eisenhower Doctrine, the Nixon Doctrine, and finally the Carter Doctrine. These various policies were used to support Iran, Saudi Arabia, and other Middle Eastern states against both internal and external threats, the collapse of the pro-US regime in Iran and the Soviet invasion of Afghanistan not withstanding.

9   Farid, M. (ed.) (1981), *Oil and Security in the Arabian Gulf*, New York: St. Martin's Press, especially ch. 3, 4, and 5.

States for Israel—a stance which Washington has maintained since Israel's founding in 1948. The major US interventions in the region have been conducted mostly with these two factors in mind.[10] The first Gulf War against Iraq in 1990/91 started, at least partially, in order to prevent any one particular state within the region from becoming too powerful. The 2003 war against Iraq can be seen in a very similar light. With a marked increase in anti-US and anti-Western sentiments in the region, the rise of Iran as a potential nuclear power, and the example of the September 11, 2001 terrorist attacks, US strategists "rolled the dice" for a democratic Iraq, hoping for a positive outcome, instead of the potential bleak future prospects.

Complementarily, US efforts toward the Middle East peace process also focus on stability in the region. The United States has stood at the forefront of endeavors to find a peaceful solution to the conflict—a solution that would respect the right of Israel to exist, the need of Palestinians for autonomy and sovereignty, and appease Israel's regional neighbors. This position has often forced the US to take a stance in opposition to either side. It was President Carter's 1978 initiative that led to the Camp David Accords and a new era of Israeli-Arab relations. While efforts stagnated or worsened throughout the 1980s, shuttle diplomacy by Secretary of State James Baker in the aftermath of the first Gulf War led to mutual recognition between the PLO and Israel, and a new round of negotiations sponsored by the Clinton administration in the 1990s. While efforts toward Middle East peace once again slipped into violence with the outbreak of the Second Intifada in late 2000, renewed attempts by the Quartet, coupled with the US proposed 2002 Road Map offering a two state solution, and elections in Palestine upon the death of Yasser Arafat in 2005, may reinvigorate hope for achieving a lasting peace in the region.

An Overview of the Book

This project is not designed to be a reader in US foreign policy towards the Middle East. The above incomplete and brief overview sets the stage for an exploration of policies of the major actors involved in the region. Indeed, a vast number of other works analyze US interests in the Middle East in far more depth, and with far more expertise, than could ever be covered in a single introduction. The United States, arguably the most powerful nation in the Middle East and in the world, is undeniably linked to the region in many ways. Thus, each chapter of this book bases its fundamental argument on the need of actors to take into account the United States in their dealings with the region.

In each case, the authors were tasked with exploring the major policies of select actors towards the Middle East. Any such list of states is understandably incomplete. For example, the European Union was left out despite its vital role in the region. Because important members of the EU are indeed discussed, major EU policies are introduced indirectly.

---

10   Richman, S.L., "'Ancient History': US Conduct in the Middle East Since World War II and the Folly of Intervention," *CATO Policy Analysis 159* (August 16, 1991). Richman provides an interesting overview of the various US incursions in the Middle East from Iran in the 1940s until the first Gulf War.

The book is divided into four distinct sections. The first section covers the European region. The actors selected have played an important role in the Middle East for a number of decades as colonial powers, strategic partners, and warring states. The second section deals with the Far East and represents relative new-comers to Middle Eastern dynamics, as they strive for energy security and political influence. The third section introduces important states within the region that struggle for power, prestige and survival under the wings of foreign powers and interests. The final section covers select international organizations and their struggle for identity and legitimacy in what is still very much a state-centric world.

The words of Ray Brock aptly describe the fundamental approach and goals of this project:

> The immense mosaic of the mighty Middle East, stained deep with the blood of centuries of warring peoples and crosshatched with endless intrigue, resembles nothing so much as a baffling picture puzzle, with some mischievous malefactor constantly stealing the pieces.[11]

These words hold true today as much as they did some 50 odd years ago. Today the 'malefactor(s)' have multiplied as globalization has allowed the hands of many more to make their interests known. The Middle East continues to struggle with its own internal dissonance and the desire of many external actors to shape the fate of the region. Hopefully, this book will provide some light into how these varied interests and complicated puzzle pieces are interconnected. Once again the Middle East finds itself puzzling together new beginnings.

Jack Covarrubias

---

11   Brock, R. 206.

SECTION I
Europe and the US in the Middle East

Chapter 1

Britain and the Middle East: In Pursuit of Eternal Interests

Mark Sedgwick

"The national interest is clearly defined by the government"

—Sir Steven Wall, ca 2005

"We have no eternal allies, and we have no perpetual enemies. Our interests are eternal and perpetual, and those interests it is our duty to follow."

—Lord Palmerston, ca 1848

Two broad interests have dominated Britain's approach to the Middle East from the colonial era to the current day, and most likely they will continue to do so for decades to come: the control of oil and the desire for regional stability. However, cursory research into the contours of the United Kingdom's foreign policy towards the region reveals a variety of other "interests" that either encourage, temper, or conflict with the two time-honored, overarching goals concerning oil and stability. If ensuring the free flow of oil and keeping regional instability to a minimum are Britain's primary interests in the Middle East, where do other "interests"—such as generating political and economic reform in the region—fit into the grand scheme of UK foreign policy?

Guided by the premise that both exogenous and endogenous factors influence the definition of interests as defined here, the goal of this chapter is to look both *outside* and *inside* the "black box" of the state in order to examine what factors shape UK interests in the Middle East. First, however, understanding which actors make British foreign policy and what forces are at play is the goal of the next section.

The Architects of British Policy

Both formal and informal factors have animated the institutional actors whose combined activities have produced British foreign policy. Such formal factors have included the bureaucratic structure, institutional mindset, and leadership of the Foreign and Commonwealth Office (FCO), other pertinent ministries (i.e., Treasury, Ministry of Defence, Board of Trade, and various intelligence services), the Prime Minister's office, and the Cabinet. Parliaments have put their mark on foreign policy formation as well. John Young has also pointed to particular values prevalent in

British policy making circles that stress defense of liberal democracy, the rights of individuals, and property rights. Mingled with these altruistic notions are those that are perhaps more self-serving, for instance, the drive for prestige on the world stage (not unlike the post-colonial French fixation on *rank* and *grandeur*) and belief in the efficacy of British pragmatism.[1]

Many a pundit and quite a few academics have posed the rhetorical question: Who makes Britain's foreign policy? Despite John Young's depiction of a host of critical actors, the short answer to this question is that today the Office of the Prime Minister has usurped the job of foreign policymaking, with the Foreign Office and Parliament trailing behind. Critics of the Blair Government have even accused the Prime Minister of introducing presidentialism to British politics, whereby 10 Downing Street makes major policy decisions with little oversight from the legislative body, and creates a serious point of friction between Parliament and the Prime Minister.[2] Likewise, observers have noted that even in the relationship between the Cabinet and the Prime Minister's office, department heads—such as the Foreign Secretary— tend to protect their departmental independence while the PM and his staff strive to centralize the making of foreign policy in a way that maximizes executive autonomy. The resulting contest between various parts of Government leads to, what Paul Williams has called, "multiple foreign policies," where the government uses varying combinations of actors, institutions, and external leverage devices while pursuing several—sometimes contradictory—policy paths simultaneously.[3]

Traditional British Interests

From the Colonial Era through the end of the Second World War, the UK favored a balance of global power in order to achieve the goal of international stability. In the minds of British statesmen, stability made it easier to protect the homeland and the Commonwealth, as well as to ensure continued economic prosperity. The use of British military and commercial power was understood as appropriate to protect Britain's global "prestige, markets, strategic outposts, and lines of communication."[4] Gaynor Johnson has pointed out that the UK Foreign and Commonwealth Office (FCO) was the most consistent advocate of balance of power politics and the strategy of limited involvement, the preferred means by which to ensure Britain's vested interests in the period leading up to the Second World War.[5]

---

1   Young, J.W. (1997), *Britain and the World in the 20th Century*, London: Arnold Publishing, 1–4.

2   Spyer, J. (2004), "An Analytical and Historical Overview of British Policy Toward Israel," *Middle East Review of International Affairs* 8/2, 4.

3   Williams, P. (2004), "Who's Making UK Foreign Policy?" *International Affairs* 80/5, 912.

4   Goldstein, E. and McKercher, B.J.C. (2003), "Power and Stability in British Foreign Policy, 1865–1965", *Diplomacy and Statecraft* 14/2, 1.

5   Johnson, G. (2004), "Introduction: The Foreign Office and British Diplomacy in the Twentieth Century," *Contemporary British History* 18/3, 1–12.

It is possible to compile a broad list of UK foreign policy goals for the period immediately following the end of the Second World War that is equally applicable to the present day. One goal was to stimulate economic growth through protection and expansion of trade. Another set of goals was to secure global interests, protect the near abroad, and cultivate strategic alliances. A final goal was to manage integration in an increasingly integrated world. This refers to cultivation of—and dedication to—a rules-based international order built upon law, institutions, and other fora that demand increasing levels of cooperation between states. Under this heading falls Britain's membership in, for instance, the European Union and NATO. Based on the imperatives generated by these overarching foreign policy goals, the UK found the promotion of peace and stability—rooted in non-interventionist beliefs—a public good that not only appealed to an international audience, but also served narrow British interests as well.[6] Before delving into a discussion of current British interests in the Middle East, however, it is helpful to become acquainted with the history of the UK's interests there.

Britain's Middle Eastern Interests: an Historical Overview

After the First World War, British statesmen favored territorial expansion in order to provide greater security for the Empire. The downside of expansion was an increase in both commitments and potential problems—the experience in the Middle East highlighted this caveat. Even in the 1920s, British officials were concerned that their administration in the region could cause an Islamic counter-revolution capable of spreading all the way to Muslim populations in British India (the Punjab). Decades later, Churchill saw that the Middle East was vital to securing Britain's war aims, and would become increasingly important to Britain after the Second World War for both strategic and economic reasons. The British decision to grant independence to India in 1947—a major step on the road to decolonization—had the ironic effect of causing Britain to perceive the Middle East as more important to the last vestiges of empire than ever. Its military bases in the region allowed it to simultaneously project British power and thwart Soviet expansion. Part of Britain's security plan for the region included guarantees to Gulf States such as Oman, Kuwait, and Bahrain, although Egypt, home to the largest collection of British military assets outside of Europe, continued to be the center of Britain's focus.[7] After the Second World War, British interests in the Middle East became increasingly intertwined with American interests.

In the immediate post-war era, British policymakers placed great emphasis on the Middle East since it appeared the region was the last piece of the old empire where British influence remained relatively strong. Despite the philosophical divisions between the two countries caused by the UK's reluctance to give up the remnants of colonialism—especially the UK's self-fabricated favored trading status in the region—Britain and the US produced joint statements that indicated the

---

6   Young, 3–4.

7   Ibid.

"the objectives of the two countries [in the Middle East] were identical."[8] These objectives took into account British interests from the past—unfettered access to the Suez Canal; the fundamental nature of oil financially, strategically, politically, and militarily; and protection of commercial interests in banking, insurance, and mining—as well as new goals, such as the deterrence of communism. To ensure their common interests and promote regional prosperity, both states sought to maintain regional stability. Meanwhile, the rising threat of communist expansion—assessed with greater apprehension in Washington than in London—made oil more important to foreign policy strategists than ever. In addition to making sure their access to Middle Eastern oil was guaranteed, US and British officials wanted to deny the Soviet Union access to it.[9]

Strategic cooperation between Her Majesty's Government and British oil companies was an ingredient of UK foreign policy as well, and nowhere was this more evident than in Iran. Britain refused to accept its loss of control over the Anglo-Iranian Oil Company (AIOC) after Iranian Prime Minister Mohammed Mossadegh nationalized that entity in 1952. In the early days of the Eisenhower administration, the British appealed to the new president to help topple Mossadegh because of the Iranian leader's supposed communist sympathies. Examining the result of Operation Ajax, the covert coup staged by the British and Americans that brought down Mossadegh's Government, one finds a sterling example of the US ascending the ladder of Middle Eastern hegemonic pre-eminence while Britain was descending. On the one hand, the coup appeared to produce an outcome in line with Britain's desires, since Mossadegh had been eliminated and the Westward-leaning Shah was returned to power. On the other hand, US oil companies ended up winning major concessions when the Shah allowed new oil contract negotiations. The end result of the joint intervention was that the UK experienced a net loss of access to Iranian oil.[10]

A general consensus among historians is that the Suez Crisis, which occurred later in the Eisenhower era, taught Britain that it could not afford to affront directly US preferences in the region, and that its post-colonial aspirations of exercising significant power in the Middle East would not be realized.[11] However, the US relied on at least partial British management of the region up to—and even after—the Labor government started withdrawal of its military from the area in 1968.[12] Even though the British willingly chose to reduce their obligations in the Middle East, they still had interests in the region that necessitated ongoing concern and management. Naturally, Britain's leaders wanted to retain as much influence in the region as possible in

---

8   Marsh, S. (2003), *Anglo-American Relations and Cold War Oil*, London: Palgrave, 22.

9   Marsh, 22–27.

10   Richman, S.L., "'Ancient History': US Conduct in the Middle East Since World War II and the Folly of Intervention," *Cato Policy Analysis 19*, available at http://www.cato.org/pubs/pas/pa-159.html.

11   Gordon, P.H. (2005), "Trading Places: America and Europe in the Middle East," *Survival* 47/2, 87–99, especially 95–6.

12   Peterson, T.T., "Richard Nixon Confronts the Persian Gulf, 1969–1972", available at http://www.h-net.org/~diplo/reports/SHAFR2004/Petersen.pdf#search=%22British-Iranian%20%22arms%20sales%22%20history%22.

order to protect those interests. Selling arms to and keeping good relations with the smaller Gulf States helped buy influence, as did arms sales to the Shah's Iran and the Saudis.[13] Britain was cooperative with US policy toward Saudi Arabia and Iran and the elevation of these two countries to the status of twin pillars with which Western states could comfortably ally.[14] The "twin pillar" policy came to a crashing halt, however, after the Iranian Revolution. When the Islamic Republic went to war against Iraq, the UK and the US aided the regime in Baghdad in order to dash Iranian hegemonic aspirations.[15] Spurning Tehran earned Britain the status of Iranian state enemy number three, just behind the US and Israel. Except for one brief interval, from 1980 until 1998, Britain had no diplomatic relations with Iran. However, starting in 1998 UK diplomacy shifted into a mode of "constructive engagement" with Iranian officials that stressed cultural exchanges and commercial potentialities. Washington, diplomatically *persona non grata* in Tehran from 1979, showed little enthusiasm for British attempts to restart diplomacy with Iran.[16] It is possible that without the British quasi-rapprochement with the Iranian regime, Washington would have no means of sending "confidence building" signals to Tehran, a capability that is especially important as the US seeks to curb Iran's nuclear weapons ambitions diplomatically.

In the Saudi kingdom, Britain maintained its influence and complemented US policies by helping to turn petrodollars into British-made munitions. For instance, the al-Yamana arms sale represented the largest single defense contract in UK history. Traditional British interests in the Gulf were consistent with its goals elsewhere in the Middle East: containing communism (Yemen was a concern), keeping oil supplies secure, nurturing and exploiting export markets, and keeping ocean lanes open. By choosing not to support Israel in 1967, Britain earned bonus points in Riyadh, a status that won the UK a spot on the Saudi "most favored" list when other Western nations were cut off from purchasing Saudi oil in the late 1960s and early 1970s.[17] It is interesting to note that when Iraq attempted to annex Kuwait in 1990, King Fahd directly requested help from the UK's military the day *after* he accepted American military assistance.

---

13   Peterson, 1–4.

14   O'Sullivan, C., "Observations on US Strategies in the Persian Gulf Region, 1941–2005: From the Atlantic Charter, the Twin Pillars and Dual Containment, to the 'Axis of Evil' and Beyond," *Columbia International Affairs Online*, available at http://www.ciaonet.org/wps/suc02.

15   Hubbel, S. (1998), "The Containment Myth: US Middle East Policy in Theory and Practice," *Middle East Report 208*, available at http://www.merip.org/mer/mer208/hubbell.htm.

16   Rundle, C. (2002), "Reflections on the Iranian Revolution and Iranian–British Relations," *Durham Middle East Paper* 68, (March), available at http://eprints.dur.ac.uk/archive/00000148/01/68DMEP.pdf.

17   Nonneman, G. (2001), "Saudi–European Relations 1902–2001: A Pragmatic Quest for Relative Autonomy," *International Affairs* 77/3, 631–59.

British Interests in the Twenty-first Century

After the Cold War, the UK found a measure of freedom to express and pursue interests in the Middle East that differed from America's. Not since the early post-Second World War days had Britain exercised as much independence from the playbook written in Washington. The fact that the UK engaged with Iran and supported the Palestinian Authority (PA) project provide two examples that the end of bipolarity and the demise of a common threat allowed states to focus their sights on previously unattainable goals.[18] During this transitional period, Britain gravitated toward the "third way" domestically and toward greater acceptance of European views on external issues. One example of the latter was the increasing rhetorical emphasis put on multilateral relationships over bilateral ones. However, assessing the Government's goals as put forth by the Foreign Office in early 2006, one sees that the bilateral relationship with the US is still a cornerstone of British foreign policy. At the time of war against terror, the government has outlined its most vital interests. The first item on the list was global security, particularly the threat posed by terrorism and proliferation of WMDs. Next came what EU elites refer to as "human security," the dangers presented by international crime. Third was support for multilateralism, followed by support for the EU and its institutions. The fifth goal cited was energy security, which was linked to open trade. Values-based interests—such as advocacy of human rights, democracy, and good governance— were next on the list, with migration control, support for Britons living abroad, and security for the Overseas Territories closing out the listing. In regards to the Middle East, the government has stated its desire to "build stronger relationships with the Muslim world."[19] However, given that the government has placed top priority on its "partnership" with America, it may be difficult to make credible headway in those foreign capitals where minarets rule the skyline.

Britain shares the concerns of its EU partners regarding post-war Iraq due to general fears about security and the possibility of widespread instability. However, Britain's economic interests were not as great as the other EU states, which combined provided over 55 percent of Iraq's pre-war imports. Long before George W. Bush and Tony Blair came to lead their respective countries, Britain supported the US against the regime of Saddam Hussein in the first Gulf War. Rynhold has stated his belief that Britain was primarily motivated in 1991 by a desire to maintain stability and support rules-based order, interests that seemingly were inviolable until 2003.[20] Since then, British goals have reflected a desire to return to stability by promoting democracy in the region. In late 2005, then Foreign Minister Jack Straw opined

---

18   This is the crux of William Wallace's argument when he assessed what the end of the Soviet Union meant for Britain. See Wallace, W. (1992), "British Foreign Policy after the Cold War," *International Affairs* 68/3, 423–42.

19   UK Foreign and Commonwealth Office (2006), *Active Diplomacy for a Changing World: The UK's International Priorities*, (March 28), available at http://www.fco.gov.uk/Files/kfile/fullintpriorities2006.pdf.

20   Rynhold, J. (2005), "Britain and the Middle East" in *BESA Perspectives*, Vol. 11, November 7, The Begin-Sadat Center for Strategic Studies, available at http://www.biu.ac.il/Besa/perspectives11.html, 22.

that the government's support for democracy was "a process which is greatly in the interests of the Middle East, of the UK, and of the whole international community."[21] However, Blair's goal of being a bridge between Washington and Brussels has lost its vitality; of far more concern at 10 Downing Street is the ability to honor the commitment Britain implicitly has made to the cause of political reform in Iraq. Though a significant percentage of the British electorate is uncomfortable with the country's participation in the war, they nonetheless support America's leadership in reconstructing Iraq by a margin of almost four-to-one. That margin is a startling reversal of overall EU survey results indicating a three-to-one rejection of US reconstruction leadership.[22]

In the case of Iran, Britain has acted—and will continue to act—in cohesion with its major EU partners, France and Germany, in seeking a diplomatic solution to the Iranian regime's apparent desire to produce nuclear weapons. Proponents of this "trilateral" effort have pointed out that in addition to contributing to a solution, the "EU3" are actually acting together, doing their part in the name of Europe, and have the potential to relieve Washington from the burden of leadership. In addition, because the three nations—not the EU—are conducting negotiations with Iran, they have the latitude to downplay issues—such as human rights—that some EU states would insist upon elevating to prominent status.[23]

As of fall 2006, neither the EU3, nor the EU3 with heavy behind-the-scenes US involvement, has been able to bring Tehran to heel. In fact, France clouded the diplomatic waters by declaring that Iran would not have to give up uranium enrichment prior to negotiations that would be the last step before sanctions.[24] The UK's political leaders and strategists now look at the Iranian situation as far more important to the region—in other words, shows the greatest potential for widespread destabilization—than the Israeli–Palestinian conflict.[25]

The Contours of the Anglo-American "Special Relationship"

Despite Wallace's insistence that the special relationship between the US and UK is dead, it is useful to review what this particular bilateral relationship has meant to

---

21   *Foreign Secretary Straw's Speech to the Fabian Society, London* (March 10, 2005), available at http://www.fco.gov.uk/servlet/Front?pagename=OpenMarket/Xcelerate/ShowPa ge&c=Page&cid=1007029391647&a=KArticle&aid=1109172362793%20&year=2005&mo nth=2005-03-01&date=2005-03-10.

22   de Vasconcelos, A. (2005), "The EU and Iraq," in Walter Posch, (ed.), *Looking Into Iraq*, Institute for Security Studies.

23   Drozdiak, W., Kemp, G., Leverett, F.L., Makins, C.J., and Stokes, B., (eds), "Partners in Frustration: Europe, the United States and the Broader Middle East," *The Atlantic Council*, November 1, 2004, available at http://www.acus.org/docs/0409-Partners_Frustration_Europe_ United_States_Broader_Middle_East.pdf, 10.

24   Arnold, M. and Dombey, D., "Chirac Calls for UN to Scale Down Iran Sanctions," *Financial Times*, September 18, 2006, available at http://us.ft.com/ftgateway/superpage. ft?news_id=fto091820060837157545.

25   Rynhold, 24.

Britain, and the ingredients that have given it special character. To begin, US and UK foreign policy has been remarkably congruent in the post-Second World War era. John Calabrese has argued that a combination of belief and substance animates the "special relationship" the two states have enjoyed. An example of congruent belief is the shared notion of responsibility for international order. Substantively, the US and the UK both promote consultative and cooperative mechanisms such as those found in NATO.[26] In these, and a host of other, ways, policy congruence is best understood as the result of each state's desire to see its own goals met. Thus, the calculus of congruence can be expressed as follows: for the UK, support for US policy allows Britain to use America as a "power multiplier," exponentially strengthening Britain's stand-alone capabilities; for the US, British support for American policies gives those policies a mark of legitimacy, and provides Washington access to British soft power assets.[27] One should note that this equation is unequal. Many analysts have pointed out that the foreign policy component of the US–UK special relationship has resembled "an essentially lop-sided partnership."[28]

Broadly understood, the UK desires two outcomes as a result of its investment in the special relationship. First, London wants continuous Washington dedication to America's role as world leader. Second, the UK wants to exert its influence over how that role is played. Hence, the relationship is based upon interests—many of them shared, but ultimately, all of them based on national gain.[29] By generally supporting US foreign policy, as well as formulating its own set of policies that stay close to those of its American ally, Britain continuously seeks to push the US into exerting global leadership in issue areas that directly complement British goals. While debate rages regarding the efficacy of London's attempts to influence Washington, it does appear that British policy makers still hold fast to Harold Macmillan's belief that Britain can "act as Greece to America's Rome, steering 'new world' power with 'old world' wisdom."[30]

The "Special Relationship" vis-à-vis the Middle East

According to Calabrese, both the US and the UK have worked jointly since the end of the Second World War to promote security and stability in the Middle East, and

---

26   Calabrese, J. (2001), "The United States, Great Britain and the Middle East: How Special the Relationship?" *Mediterranean Quarterly* 12/3, 57–84.

27   For a discussion of how lesser states use larger states or other political entities (i.e., the EU) to magnify their power–projection capability, see Treacher, A. (2001), "Europe as a Power Multiplier of French Security Policy: Strategic Consistency, Tactical Adaptation," *European Security* 10/1, 22–44.

28   Stevens, P. (January 2006), "The Special Relationship and Foreign Policy: Panel Chairman's Report," in *US–UK Relations at the Start of the 21st Century*, McCausland, J.D. and Douglas, T.S. (eds) (Strategic Studies Institute), 135–144, available at https://www.strategicstudiesinstitute.army.mil/pdffiles/PUB633.pdf.

29   Of course, in this instance *gain* could be measured—as realists do—in terms of relative military power, or it could be measured by realization of an international consensus on human rights, made stronger by the weight of serious US commitment.

30   Stevens, 138.

despite incidences such as Suez Canal crisis, "British–American differences over the [region] were little more than distractions and irritants."[31] Having looked at specific cases since the end of the Cold War, Calabrese has seen a high degree of coordination, cooperation, and policy convergence. In the case of Iran, however, convergence appeared to be more the exception than the rule during the 1990s. After the end of the first Gulf War, Britain hewed closely to the European Union preference for critical dialogue and direct engagement with Tehran. Nonetheless, it did not invest all its diplomatic capital in this approach, and instead left "wiggle room" between voices in Brussels that called for aggressive engagement on a multitude of fronts (diplomatic, economic, cultural, and so on) and those in Washington that advocated continued isolation of the Iranian regime. Calabrese argued that London's ability to force a moderate implementation of the Iran–Libya Sanctions Act (ILSA) was an example of Britain's success in playing out its self-appointed role as a bridge between America and Europe.

Convergence does not reside only within the realm of interstate policymaking, as the recent case of British Petroleum's activities in Iran seems to indicate. In early 2003, BP admitted that it was becoming "a major crude oil and oil products client of Iran,"[32] by participating in joint ventures with the National Iranian Oil Company and other Iranian oil firms. BP's future plans for investment in Iran's liquefied natural gas sector—an area ripe for rigorous exploitation—had the goal of turning that company into a significant player in the Iranian energy industry.[33] In early 2005, BP changed course dramatically, however, deciding not to enter into contracts with Iranian state-controlled oil and gas entities. Signaling the fact that US foreign policy preferences conditioned this change, BP's CEO Lord Browne of Madingley explained, "To do business with Iran ... would be offensive to the United States" and that "[BP is] very heavily influenced by [its] American position."[34] What Lord Browne left unsaid is that the Ilsa was in force in February 2005 and is still in force.[35] Considering no company had ever been sanctioned under this law, it is hard to imagine BP felt it would be the first to draw a fine. It is more likely that some aspect of the special relationship was at play, specifically, the part that suggests British interests are best served by supporting American foreign policy preferences.

Policy coordination between London and Washington was also evident during the immediate post-Cold War years as a result of the challenges posed by Iraq. Although President Bill Clinton and Prime Minister John Major held significantly divergent policy preferences in many issues areas, on Iraq their thinking dovetailed. Both men

---

31   Calabrese, 65.

32   Peimani, H. (2003), "BP Marches Back into Iran," *Asia Times Online,* February 27, available at www.atimes.com/atimes/Middle_East/EB27Ak06.html.

33   Ibid.

34   Boxell, J. and Morrison, K. (2005), "BP to Eschew Deals with Iran," *Financial Times*, February 2, 2.

35   The original bill, passed in 1996, was due to be revised for a second time in August 2006. However, competing bills have delayed a final vote and a stopgap bill extended coverage until late September 2006. See Katzman, K. (2006), "The Iran-Libya Sanctions Act," *CRS Report for Congress*, August 8, available at http://fpc.state.gov/documents/organization/71856.pdf.

believed in the use of force as a primary tool against Saddam Hussein's regime, and both believed that the sanction regime put into place in 1991 needed continuous support. Calabrese has argued that Britain's military and diplomatic backing for sanctions imposed on Baghdad lent international credibility to US goals. The costs Britain incurred for support of America's foreign policy toward Iraq in the 1990s were significant: both Russia and many of Britain's EU partners were not keen on sanctioning an important source of energy and a burgeoning trade market. However, if one accepts the logic proposed by Calabrese, despite the apparent imbalance of the Anglo-American relationship vis-à-vis Iraq in the 1990s, Britain was compelled to play this part in order to keep the US engaged with the Iraqi question.

The UK–EU Relationship and European Policy Preferences for the Middle East

Britain's relationship to the EU is on par with its relationship to the US in many respects, although significant disparities emerge upon examination. For instance, Britain does not look to Europe for security guarantees. France is the only other European power with a serious military capability, but it cannot provide what Britain needs in terms of intelligence and muscle that would allow the UK to project force with any degree of efficacy. Thus, the UK–US relationship towers above the one between the UK and the EU in the area of security and defense. However, Britain is a member of the Union, with both rights and responsibilities that come with membership. Although the UK has formal commitments to NATO, Britain shares an *acquis* with its EU partners that legally binds it to the Union. No such conventions exist between the UK and the United States. Obviously, there are a host of other differences in the two alliances—mostly concerned with formal versus informal structures—that are not germane to this discussion. Paul Williams made a significant argument in 2002 maintaining that British policymaking has become "Europeanized" to a remarkable degree, in content, mechanics, and ideological underpinning.[36] While Williams would no doubt admit the Iraq War has damaged his thesis somewhat, when one investigates the extent of British engagement with EU policies—especially those concerning the Middle East—it is obvious that British officials give due diligence to policy ideas prevalent on the Continent.

In the 1990s, foreign policy analysts pointed out that although American and European foreign policy objectives in the Middle East appeared to go hand in hand, the US and Europe differed over the preferred means to reach those goals. Geographic proximity had something to do with these differences in approach. From a security standpoint, Europe's closeness to the Middle East has made it more sensitive to the region's relative stability or instability. In addition, European-Middle Eastern trade has greater potential than that between American and Middle Eastern states. This combination of interests has conditioned European diplomats—with

---

36   Williams, P., *The Europeanization of British Foreign Policy and the Crisis in Zimbabwe*, Draft Paper for Workshop at the London School of Economics, available at http://www.lse.ac.uk/Depts/intrel/pdfs/EFPUEuropeanizationofBritForPol.pdf#search=%22The%20Europeanization%20of%20British%20Foreign%20Policy%20and%20the%20Crisis%20in%20Zimbabwe%22.

British officials providing no exception—to keep lines of communication open to their Middle Eastern neighbors. However, Britain has been the most likely of all its fellow member states to defer to American mediation in regional conflicts, including the Middle Eastern Peace Process.[37]

Oil Security Issues and the British Response

Facing a world in which oil was being correctly perceived as the future lifeblood of both commerce and international security, Winston Churchill advised "safety and certainty in oil lie in variety and variety alone."[38] Long after Churchill left the political stage and demand for energy reached epic levels, national leaders no longer had the luxury of relying on the type of diversification scheme the British statesman had envisioned. Reflecting the increasingly important dynamic between energy sources and traditional statecraft, one international relations scholar has noted, "[o]il politics is no longer just an industrial matter or a regional matter, but a worldwide security matter. Oil politics is at the core of world politics."[39] Another observer, giving due recognition to the geographic and political nexus of energy suppliers and those making the most demands, has written, '[i]f the chief natural resource of the Middle East were bananas, the region would not have attracted the attention of ... policy makers as it has for decades.'[40] Finally, the following concise statement put a fine point on the energy security concerns facing the world's most voracious consumers:

> Most of the world's exportable surplus of oil actually lies in the gargantuan reservoirs of two countries, Saudi Arabia and Iraq. Not China, nor the United States, nor Japan, nor Britain, nor any other knowledgeable country dependent upon that supply could tolerate a hostile, unreliable government in control of those fields.[41]

With this declaration, Charles Doran appears to have laid down a gauntlet to the leaders of the world's largest economies, placing accountability for the management of Saudi and Iraqi oil in their hands.

In general, the UK is concerned about oil—and, increasingly, natural gas—for two reasons. First, the Government must ensure UK access to oil for domestic consumption. Second, guaranteeing international access to energy supplies is necessary in order to facilitate the growth—or at a minimum, stability—of the world economy. These two concerns broadly compose the UK's conception of *energy security*. The Labour Government has addressed the salience of energy

---

37 Stein, K.W. (1997), "Imperfect Alliances: Will Europe and America Ever Agree?" *Middle East Quarterly* 4/1, available at http://www.meforum.org/article/339.

38 Winston Churchill quoted in Yergin, D. (2006), "Ensuring Energy Security," *Foreign Affairs* 85/2, 69–82.

39 Doran, C. (2005), "Oil Politics is World Politics," *Nitze* School of Advanced International Studies, Johns Hopkins University, available at http://www.sais-jhu.edu/pubaffairs/publications/saisphere/winter05/doran.html.

40 Richman.

41 Doran.

security as part of its overall energy strategy. In agreement with preceding British administrations, the Blair government has noted its belief that "security of supply requires that [the UK] have good access to available fuel supplies."[42] Since Britain's North Sea oil and gas fields are in decline, future supplies increasingly will come from the international marketplace.[43]

The fact that the world's largest gas and oil reserves are in the Middle East, Russia, Central Asia, and Africa; that OPEC's share of exports to the UK will be around 50 percent come 2030; and that world demand will continue to rise in the coming decades—thereby increasing competition among the world's oil and gas consumers—leads the Government to speculate ambiguously that future international energy transactions will promote "increased political intervention."[44]

British Energy Security Strategy and Iraq

Aside from market issues, the UK has been faced with constraints posed by international conflict and regional instability. In the Middle East, of course, the single biggest issue British leadership faced was in Iraq. Critics of Anglo-American intervention have argued that bald-faced pragmatism prompted the invasion, that the US and UK instigated a "war for oil." At least one analyst has noted that if cost-benefit analysis concerning potential gains from Iraqi oil were basis for the decision to go to war, no troops would ever have been committed to combat.[45] Most experts agree that Iraq's proven oil reserves are fourth in the world behind Saudi Arabia, Canada, and Iran.[46] However, even the most optimistic post-conflict scenarios indicate that returning Iraqi oil to the world market will provide only a miniscule increase in relation to current world demand.

A host of factors led to war in Iraq. To re-iterate, the primary rationale driving the US and its partners concerned the Iraqi regime's possession, intent to produce, or intent to proliferate weapons of mass destruction that would further destabilize the region and threaten global expectations for stability and peace. For over a dozen years, Iraq had been singled out by the world community as a potential proliferator, and after 9/11, as a nation that sponsored or otherwise condoned terrorism. Some

---

42   "The Energy Challenge", (July 11, 2006) HM Government Publication, available at http://www.dti.gov.uk/files/file32001.pdf, 18.

43   This report makes the distinction that gas does not have a global market comparable to oil, since gas is usually delivered to regional markets via pipelines. Meanwhile, the government estimates that though the UK only imports about 10 percent of its current gas needs, by 2020 that share could increase to 90 percent. Obviously, concerns about gas supplies are as vital as those regarding oil, but the discussion in complex. Regarding oil, the primary goals are to reduce consumption, maintain current production, encourage new development, and keep the market as open and predictable as possible. Regarding gas, the goals are to reduce consumption, encourage delivery and storage infrastructure (the building of more pipelines and LNG holding facilities), and keeping regional markets open.

44   "The Energy Challenge," 19.

45   Hepburn, D.F. (2003), "Is it a War for Oil?" *Middle East Policy* 10/1, 29–34.

46   "Rank Order: Oil: Proven Reserves," *CIA World Factbook*, available at https//www.cia.gov/cia/publications/factbook/rankorder/2178rank.html.pdf.

leaders stressed humanitarian reasons as well, correctly noting the regime of Saddam Hussein was an exceptionally brutal transgressor of fundamental human rights. Though these goals were of paramount importance in arguments advocating military intervention, strategic goals also must have entered the calculus of key decision-making units.

Certainly, one such strategic and time-honored concern was energy security, though political leaders are loath to admit this fact. It is likely that the US and UK were not calculating short- or mid-term returns from increased Iraqi oil production. Rather than securing Iraqi oil for their own exploitation, per se, their overarching goal may have been to ensure that Iraqi oil would become part of increased global supply. In this way, one could argue that as far as oil was concerned the coalition's actions were aimed at perpetuating the rules-based norms of international trade—something that coalition members like the UK could readily condone. Simon Bromley has made the argument that when it fashions policy to ensure free flow of energy supplies, the US acts not only out of self-interest, but also out of the desire to "create the general pre-conditions for a world oil market."[47] This study extends this preference to the UK as well. Britain does not bear the majority of costs for shaping the energy trading system, but neither does it get its preferences fulfilled to its exact liking. Partnering with the US, however, allows the UK to realize its overarching goal of encouraging global free trade. From a realist perspective, China should also welcome these Anglo-American efforts.

The Special Case of Israel-Palestine and the Peace Process

The formulation of British interests in regard to Israel and the "Palestinian question" may be considered a special case when one compares it to the UK's goals in the broader Middle East. Not overlooking the region's possession of vast oil reserves, the ongoing conflict between Israel and its Arab neighbors is the seminal element conditioning political behavior in the region. Compared to other Western states, Britain holds a truly unique position vis-à-vis Israel: having both directly and indirectly facilitated the creation of the state, at many points since Israel's creation—and for the sake of British interests—the UK has appeared to reject the state it helped to create.

A Tale of Two Orientations

In actuality, Britain has never "rejected" Israel. Rather, shifting interest calculations have caused variations in Britain's conduct toward the Jewish state. Over time, divergent voices in British foreign policymaking institutions have tended to consolidate around discernable pro-Arab or pro-Israeli centers of gravity. According to recent analysis, the pro-Arab viewpoint has been most prevalent in decision-making units favoring a *diplomatic orientation* toward foreign policy. Jonathan

---

47   Bromley, S. (2005), "The United States and the Control of World Oil," *Government and Opposition* 40/2, 225–55, especially 254.

Rynhold defines this orientation as one that values good relations with existing power structures (or those about to assume power), avoids confrontations, shuns overly close association with American policies in the region, views Israel as the region's pre-eminent "irritant," and hews close to the dominant EU perspective on the subject. It is not surprising that this approach predominates at the Foreign and Commonwealth Office, home to the UK's diplomatic corps.[48] In contrast to the diplomatic orientation, the *strategic orientation* finds its greatest expression in the Prime Minister's Office. The strategic school tends to divide regimes into categories (differentiating between those that are moderate and those that are hostile), focus on threats (military, economic, and ideological) emanating from these regimes, look approvingly upon American policies in the region, and show appreciation for Israel as an important democratic ally in the Middle East.

British–Israeli History: Ins and Outs

Having examined the dichotomous orientations toward Israel-Palestine in the UK, it is instructive to look at Britain's relationship to the forces and factors angling for control of Palestine since the end of the Second World War in order to ascertain the UK's interests there today. Of course, Britain's historic connection to the region predates 1945. The British government signalled its commitment to the establishment of a Jewish homeland in 1917 with the so-called Balfour Declaration, and while Palestine was under British Mandate, Diaspora Jews moved to the region in significant numbers.[49]

By the 1930s, British strategists became concerned with the prospect that Arab populations could gravitate toward the *Axis* Powers. Thus, in the run up to war against Nazi Germany, the fate of Jewish settlers, with Zionist preferences, was of minimal interest to London. When after the war Britain decided to exit Palestine and delegate the management of growing Jewish–Arab territorial contestation to the nascent UN, British relations with the Zionists were severely strained. War between proto-Israeli forces and the Arabs in 1948–49 further weakened ties binding the emerging Israeli state to Britain, with policymakers in London signaling their preference to support the Arab status quo in the Middle East by playing a key role in the formation of the Arab League. In 1949, Foreign Secretary Ernest Bevin equated support for Arab regimes with a fundamental British interest when he opined, "It would be too high a price to pay for the friendship of Israel to jeopardize, by estranging the Arabs, either the base in Egypt or Middle Eastern oil."[50]

By 1956, however, strategists at Whitehall came to see Arab nationalism as a threat to British interests in the region—particularly, access to oil, regional stability, and commercial investments. This threat recognition caused a change in thinking about Israel's role in the region. By supporting and strengthening Israel, British

---

48   Rynhold.

49   Youngs, T. (2005), *The Middle East Peace Process: Prospects after the Palestinian Presidential Elections*, International Affairs and Defence Section, House of Commons Library, March 29.

50   Bevin quoted in Spyer, 8.

policymakers hoped to stem the tide of pan-Arab nationalism linked with the perceived growth of Soviet influence in the Middle East. Using this logic, Britain was able to enlist Israeli support in what became a foreign policy debacle for the former colonial power: the Suez Crisis. Though the trilateral (British/French/Israeli) attempt to take the canal back from Egyptian control ended in failure when US diplomatic pressure brought it to a halt, until 1967 Britain viewed support for the Jewish state as a means to ensure stability and avoid regional conflict. Thus, London was considering its own goals when it facilitated transfers of British arms to Tel Aviv beginning in 1960. As one British statesman noted:

> We do not give the Israelis arms because they are pro-Western or because we admire their achievement. We give them arms because our interests in the Middle East are to keep peace and quiet, and to prevent war. Anything which makes war more likely is against the interests of the Western powers.[51]

Of course, one must place this operating logic in the context of the Cold War, a time when the ultimate threat to Britain sprang from Soviet Russia and broader communist ideology.

By 1967, however, London was forced to change course when it appeared it would have to take sides in an impending conflict spawned by the closure of the Straits of Tiran to Israeli shipping. Of course, by not responding to such an affront, Britain risked the weakening of international norms concerning free trade—that being *another* longstanding British interest. According to Jonathan Spyer, Britain's policymakers at the time were more afraid of the harm "open identification with Israel might do to British political and economic interests in the region."[52] Spyer has written that the diplomatic pattern one finds in the run up to the 1967 Arab–Israeli War exemplifies enduring British–Israeli relations. He has also noted that pragmatism guided British policymakers in their relations with Israel and its Arab neighbors. Hence, the decision to keep an open connection to Yasser Arafat during the early years of the Popular Front for the Liberation of Palestine (which later became the PLO) was based on the belief that at some point in the future British strategists and diplomats would have to deal with him in a meaningful way.

Another consistent British concern vis-à-vis Israeli policy was oil access, an interest put in jeopardy by the Arab-imposed oil embargo against the West in reaction to the second Arab–Israeli War in 1973. Since the late 1970s British policy toward Israel has been in close alignment with the European Union-led consensus predicated upon the belief that conflicts are universally amenable to negotiated solutions.[53] When Britain supported the EU's 1980 Venice Declaration calling for a joint PLO–Israeli diplomatic approach to solve the Middle Eastern impasse—a move consistent with its decades-old goal of upholding its honest broker status in Arab capitals—Washington policymakers criticized their British ally. However, with the pan-Arab threat seemingly in the past, Britain may have found it easier to pursue an interest-based policy track that diverged from American preferences. After all,

---

51   This quote is attributed to an unnamed British Ambassador to Israel by Spyer, 10.
52   Ibid., p. 11.
53   Ibid., p. 15.

in the Thatcher era trade relationships between the UK and several Arab states in the Middle East blossomed—especially when one considers the importance of arms sales to Saudi Arabia (over $40 billion from the al-Yamama deals alone). From a realist point of view, Britain was following a prudent course relative to its state-defined interests.

When the communist threat to Western interests in the Middle East ended with the fall of Soviet regional hegemony, British leaders were able to formulate policy toward Israel that again differed from their counterparts in Washington. For instance, Conservative Prime Minister John Major traveled to the PA to meet with Chairman Arafat, and also lent the UK's financial support to the project of building up the proto-Palestinian state.[54] At the same time, however, bilateral trade between the UK and Israel grew dramatically, to the point that in 2000 Israel became the UK's number one Middle Eastern trade partner (a position it has since relinquished). A significant component of increased trade was in the defense sector. For instance, Israel Aircraft Industries cracked what traditionally had been a closed British arms market when it sold combat training systems to the Royal Air Force.[55] Not forsaking its trade and investment relationships with Arab states in the Middle East, in the immediate post-Cold War era Britain had to carefully manage its relationship with Israel since commercial ties were not the UK's only significant interest there—defensive and security interests were in play as well.

Britain and the Middle East Peace Process

The UK has always preferred that the US lead the Middle East Peace Process (MEPP). Though other EU members have sought active roles in fashioning a Brussels-based approach to the MEPP—most notably France—Britain has embraced the EU's rhetorical stance while simultaneously hoping to leverage the Union's diplomatic assets in support of Washington's consistent engagement. As in so many other issue areas, London has sought to find a balance between American and European preferences.

British efforts to keep the US focused on resolution of the peace process promised some measure of success, first under the auspices of the Oslo Accords, later with the passage of UNSC Resolution 1397 (the first official Council endorsement of an independent Palestinian state), and most recently with the introduction of the Quartet's Roadmap to Israeli–Palestinian Peace.[56] However, violence in the region between Israel and various Palestinian militias in PA territory, the Syrian Army in the Golan, and Hezbollah militants in southern Lebanon—as well as the destabilizing

---

54   The Foreign Office has reported that in the years 2001–2005 it spent almost £150 million to finance its *Palestinian Programme*. See "UK Financial Support to the Palestinian Authority," UK Foreign and Commonwealth Office, available at http://www.fco.gov.uk/servlet/Front?pagename=OpenMarket/Xcelerate/ShowPage&c=Page&cid=1115140443221.

55   Spyer, 17.

56   The *Quartet* is composed of representatives from the US, Russia, the EU, and the UN, all tasked with bringing international pressure to bear on the parties responsible for final settlement of the peace process.

effect of Palestinian suicide bombers during the second *intifada*—presented obstacles to a diplomatic solution regardless of American engagement. Still, London saw promising potential in Israeli Prime Minister Sharon's plan to disengage—albeit unilaterally—from Gaza, a move ostensibly hastened by concerns in Tel Aviv about the costs of occupation. The Blair Government gave the plan verbal support, indicating the belief that *any* disengagement would "be a real opportunity for progress" along the Roadmap.[57] It is important to note that although the UK sought a primary role for America in the MEPP, London felt free to express its own concerns about Israeli policies in a way that challenged Washington's official pronouncements. For instance, the FCO consistently aired its view that Israeli settlement activity in the occupied territories (Gaza and the West Bank) was in violation of international law, as was the Israeli barrier wall then under construction. According to the Foreign Office, the bottom line was that "Israel must withdraw from Palestinian areas on a permanent basis." Again, these British preferences aligned more closely with EU rhetoric than the rhetoric emanating from Washington.

The death of Yasser Arafat spawned guarded optimism that a negotiated settlement between Israel and the Palestinian Authority could bring the Middle East Peace Process to an appropriate conclusion. The January 2005 election of Mahmoud Abbas as president of the PA also fueled high expectations at both Whitehall and 10 Downing Street, although concerns still existed regarding Abbas' ability to consolidate his authority and quell irredentist militias operating outside PA control.

Despite—or perhaps, because of—pessimism related to Abbas' efficacy as a peace broker, the UK hosted a conclave of high-ranking Palestinian officials in London during late winter 2005. At the meeting, the British hosts stressed the need to renew institutions that Fatah had controlled since the PA was formed. It was also in London that the Palestinians announced new legislative elections intended to expand the mandate of the Authority, as well as to increase participation and, hence, bolster the PA's legitimacy as a practitioner of "good governance." Later that year, Abbas told the audience at the 10th Anniversary European-Mediterranean Summit meeting that took place during Britain's EU presidency: We in the Palestinian National Authority are committed to … holding the parliamentary elections on time … to building democratic institutions, and to enhancing the rule of law.[58]

Of course, these Palestinian aspirations closely dovetailed with British means-levels interests regarding successful exportation and adoption of values deemed necessary to ensure stability. Irony reared its head when the January 2006 Palestinian legislative elections delivered a majority for Hamas, the political/military faction simultaneously responsible for fueling the second *intifada* and building a social and political network of sufficient legitimacy to democratically defeat the corrupt Fatah party. With this outcome, the British means-levels interest of inculcating democracy in the Middle East came in direct conflict with its ends-level interest of ensuring stability via resolution of the peace process. Hamas had traditionally rejected all talk

---

57   Youngs, "The Middle East Peace Process," 44.
58   "President Abbas Addressing EuroMed Summit," *Palestine News Agency*, November 28, 2005, available at http://english.wafa.ps/body.asp?id=4730.

of a two-state solution ('an independent Palestine alongside a secure Israel'[59] located at the terminus of the Roadmap), and according to many commentators its primary raison d'etre has been to eliminate the Israeli state and reclaim Palestinian territory annexed by the UN and subsequently occupied by Israel since 1948.[60]

Most Western states reacted to the Hamas victory by reminding Palestine's new leaders that violence and democracy were incompatible. The leadership of Hamas must choose, Tony Blair said, "between a path of democracy or a path of violence."[61] In a move that appeared to guarantee continued *instability* in the region, Britain supported the Quartet's dictate to Hamas that it renounce violence against Israel or risk losing Western monetary support. When Hamas failed to comply, the Palestinian Authority stopped receiving euros, dollars, and pounds that before the election amounted to over $1 billion per year and almost entirely constituted the Authority's annual budget. The UK alone had been contributing £33 million per annum directly to the Palestinian Authority, and another £49 million a year via the EU.[62] In April 2006, Britain's International Development Secretary Hilary Benn told Parliament, 'Without progress against the Quartet's conditions, the UK Government cannot provide direct financial aid to the Palestinian cabinet or its ministries."[63]

Eventually, in July 2006, the EU sent $130 million to Fatah to help meet basic needs in what had become a dire situation; however, not only was the EU's goal to reduce suffering, but also—and perhaps even primarily—to support President Abbas. The irony in this situation was that both the US and the EU found themselves on the same side, as prior to the election Brussels sought to engage Hamas while Washington tried to isolate it. However, as long as the elected government was dead in the water, the military wing of Hamas was bound to exercise its only option: more aggression against Israel.

The increase of Kassam rocket attacks emanating from Gaza, as well as the kidnapping of an Israeli soldier in June 2006, precipitated greater instability in the region, especially when Hezbollah in Lebanon chose the occasion to instigate its own military confrontation with Israel. It would appear, then, that British actions in this instance were inconsistent with the country's avowed interest in stability. Tony Blair's embrace of transformational Middle Eastern foreign policy makes it unlikely that Britain has demoted the goal of stability in the face of the MEPP or any other Middle Eastern variable. The UK still honors the potential US role for

---

59   Youngs, T. (2006), *The Palestinian Parliamentary Election and the Rise of Hamas*, International Affairs and Defence Section, House of Commons Library, March 15.

60   Ibid.

61   Henderson, S. (2006), "European Policy Options toward a Hamas-Led Palestinian Authority," in Satloff, R. (ed.), *Hamas Triumphant: Implications for Security, Politics, Economy, and Strategy*, Policy Focus #53, The Washington Institute for Near East Policy, 54.

62   *Countries and Regions: Middle East Peace Process: Frequently Asked Questions: Palestinian Issues*, UK Foreign and Commonwealth Office, available at http://www.fco.gov. uk/servlet/Front?pagename=OpenMarket/Xcelerate/ShowPage&c=Page&cid=1115148832 197; Also, Pan, E., "Hamas and the Shrinking PA Budget," Council on Foreign Relations, available at http://www.cfr.org/publication/10499/.

63   Hansard (April 18, 2006), *Column*, 529W.

peacemaking in the region—even though by the Fall of 2006 prospects for peace were not good—and Tony Blair's Government was forced to accept the American decision not to push Israel too hard for a ceasefire in light of fighting in Lebanon between Hezbollah and the Israeli military in July 2006. Thus, the UK's preference set *appears* little changed. Perhaps a look at the UK's response to global Islamic terrorism and the proliferation of weapons of mass destruction can shed more light on British interests in the Middle East.

The British Perspective on Weapons of Mass Destruction and Terrorism

London's willingness to commit to military campaigns in Afghanistan and Iraq attests to Britain's strategic concern with both Islamic terrorism and the proliferation of WMDs. The same concern has stirred the UK to help lead intensive negotiations with Iran over Tehran's likely nuclear weapons ambitions. In its 2004–05 session, Parliament reiterated its support for the UN Counter-Terrorism Committee and the passage of UN Security Council Resolution 1540. That resolution calls on all states to criminalize the proliferation of WMDs, to clamp down on the export of potentially lethal material components and technologies, and to make sure "sensitive materials" stay inside their borders.[64] In the Foreign Office's response to the House report, Secretary Straw declared that UNSCR 1540 was not meant to supersede or supplant existing multilateral anti-proliferation regimes such as the NPT. Instead, the resolution was meant to complement existing proliferation safeguards.[65]

Iran has concerned both the Foreign Office and members of the Foreign Affairs Committee for some time, primarily due to its WMD threat. In testimony before Parliament in early 2006, Secretary Straw noted that out of four potential nuclear states on the 1990 horizon—Israel, Iran, Iraq and Libya—the programs of the latter two had been eliminated from concern thanks to Anglo-American efforts. Straw also declared that Iranian desires to develop a nuclear arsenal would cause other large Middle Eastern states to quickly obtain that capacity as well. In terms of the menace to regional stability posed by nuclear weapons, the Secretary reminded the Committee that the region's other nuclear power, Israel, has not threatened to wipe Iran off the map, whereas Iran has threatened Israel with that fate. Straw re-iterated that the British Government's preferred method for applying pressure on the regime in Tehran was the United Nations Security Council (UNSC) and the International Atomic Energy Agency (IAEA). Straw also displayed confidence that the US was as committed to finding a diplomatic solution to the stand off with Iran, as was the UK and its EU partners. He went so far as to say that he acted as an intermediary between Washington and Tehran by communicating "confidence building measures" that the US was willing to extend to the Iranian leadership. In this case, it appears that the Blair notion of "bridge building" may end up working better *outside* the European

---

64   "Sixth Report of Session (2004–05): Foreign Policy Aspects of the War against Terror," House of Commons Foreign Affairs Committee (March 22, 2005).

65   "Response of Secretary of State for Foreign and Commonwealth Affairs," UK Foreign and Commonwealth Office (June 2005).

venue, or even that London has been successful in moderating US preferences in the Middle East, substituting multilateral diplomacy for unilateral force projection.[66]

The Threat of Terrorism

In a report issued by the House of Commons Foreign Affairs Committee in 2005, Iran and Syria were singled out as states that show little effort in curtailing terrorist activity in both *Iraq and Israel/Palestine*. The EU's paltry effort to put effective anti-terrorism measures into place also drew the ire of Committee members.[67] In oral testimony given to the same Committee later in the year, Straw redefined the government's perspective of the terrorist threat facing Britain as the difference between upholding good and eradicating evil.[68] However, when addressing audiences in the Muslim world, representatives of the Foreign Office have eliminated good vs. evil rhetoric from their speeches, preferring to speak of terrorists who act in the name of Islam as fanatics who possess a "distorted vision of Islam."[69]

The FCO's Kim Howells has stated that extinguishing the violence spawned by terrorism—ostensibly the definitive goal of the UK's approach to counter terrorism— could have a profound effect on international stability. The stability of the Middle East is certainly of paramount interest to the UK, as the discussion of energy security bears out quite graphically. However, terrorism emanating from the Middle East has threatened Britain's internal security, just as 9/11 threatened the internal security of the US. In both nations, stability as an overarching interest has received strong competition from the goal for which every state ultimately strives—survival. The fact that survival has—at least to some extent—supplanted stability as the overarching goal sought by both Tony Blair and George W. Bush became obvious as soon as those leaders committed their nation's resources to intervention in Iraq. Certainly, even the most optimistic strategists in Washington and London understood that under the best of circumstances, sending 200,000 troops into Iraq to disarm and unseat the ruling regime would cause regional instability—if only in terms of cross-border migration, let alone its potential to ratchet up anti-Western sentiment and produce more jihadists in the region. Perhaps instability was recast as a virtue, not a vice: Iraqi instability would put pressure on Iran and Syria. The argument against fomenting instability in Iraq, however, would have been the potential deleterious effect upon NATO member and EU aspirant Turkey.

---

66   "Oral Evidence given by Rt Hon Jack Straw, a Member of the House, Secretary of State for Foreign & Commonwealth Affairs, and Dr David Landsman OBE, Head of Counter-Proliferation Department, Foreign & Commonwealth Office," House of Commons Committee on Foreign Affairs (February 8, 2006).

67   "Sixth Report of Session (2004–05)."

68   Testimony of Jack Straw, David Richmond, and Dr Peter Gooderham to the Foreign Affairs Committee, October 24, 2005.

69   "Counter Terrorism: The UK Approach," Speech by Kim Howells, Kuala Lumpur, Malaysia (July 22, 2005).

The Role of Religion in Shaping British Interests

Despite the potential pitfalls inherent in assessing what effect religious identity has on determining UK foreign policy or interests, examining the intersection of British foreign policy and religion does reveal a few topics worthy of consideration. One topic is the potential effect upon British interests by the rise of political activity that is decidedly "Muslim" in orientation. Why would the extent of Muslim participation in politics or policy formation be of serious academic interest when the country under examination has an overwhelming legacy of Judeo-Christian thought and practice, and where identity with Christianity is the rule for over 70 percent of its citizens? In other words, why single out Muslim identity as a potential variable in a nation primarily composed of self-identified Christians? A plausible answer is two-fold: first, Huntington's thesis regarding a clash of civilizations cannot be discounted, and the fact that some interpretations of Islam stress the incompatibility of Western democratic polities with Koranic exhortations indicates the existence of some degree of cultural collision; second, the rise of Islamic-based political advocacy in Britain is noteworthy both for its aims and its growing visibility in British politics. As one analyst has noted, "establishing international links and affecting international issues are ... some of Muslim organizations' explicit aims and interests."[70]

The Reach of Islam in Britain

Muslims in Britain number approximately 1.8 million, or roughly 2.9 percent of the British population. Robert Pauly has noted the most prevalent characteristic of British Muslims is their diversity. A host of variables such as ethnicity, nationality, economic status, level of commitment (religiosity), and age render a heterogeneous Muslim community in Britain that makes references to "Muslim opinion" or "Muslim voting habits" problematic.[71] However, British Muslims often refer to a homogenous Muslim community in making their appeals to the rest of Britain's cultural divisions, as well as to the Government. This is especially true for groups of Muslims who have formed social and political advocacy groups such as the Muslim Association of Britain (MAB) and the Muslim Public Affairs Committee (MPAC). That literally hundreds of organizations purporting to advance Muslim preferences exist in the UK reflects the diversity of Islam in Britain. However, groups such as the Mab and MPAC attempt to speak for a unified British-Muslim voice that transcends differing interpretations of Islam—especially differences based upon the embrace or rejection of modernity. The extent to which these groups have been successful in their endeavor is a topic beyond the scope of this examination. Nonetheless, from an intuitive standpoint one surmises that Muslim voices *are* making themselves heard based on the sensitivity to Muslim concerns emanating from governmental

---

70   Radcliffe, L. (2004), "A Muslim Lobby at Whitehall? Examining the Role of the Muslim Minority in British Foreign Policy Making," *Islam and Christian-Muslim Relations* 15/3, 368.

71   Pauly, R.J. (2004), *Islam in Europe: Integration or Marginalization?* Aldershot, UK: Ashgate Publishing Limited.

and public safety institutions across Britain. Perhaps heterogeneity is less damaging to the promotion of Muslim preferences—at least domestic ones—than some commentators have speculated, especially if those receiving the Muslim message are not attuned to the diversity in Britain's Islamic community.

Islam has become a seminal force in shaping the identity of young Muslims raised in the West—especially Western Europe. In Britain the revised identity of second- and third-generation immigrants from "Asian" to "Muslim" has come about in conjunction with growing distrust of established Muslim leaders who are considered part of a Government-dictated status quo. Commentators from within the Muslim community have suggested that younger Muslims, feeling underrepresented politically, can come under the influence of imams "from deeply entrenched patriarchal traditions"[72] who stress the interconnectedness of global Islam and urge local action to counter perceived injustices suffered by their coreligionists in Palestine, Chechnya, Kashmir, and elsewhere. Such injustices are directly linked to US and British foreign policy, which is also increasingly perceived as the genesis of strident Western bias against Islam, increased military conflicts (in the war against terrorism), and domestic security measures that unfairly target Muslims living in the West.[73] On the one hand, mobilization of a new generation of British Muslims for the purpose of expressing political opposition seems perfectly compatible with representative democracy. On the other hand, concerns emanating from both non-Muslim British citizens and some government officials have centered upon the extent to which such opposing views will be displayed outside of political channels—in other words, through homegrown terrorist activity like the London transit bombings on July 7, 2005, the attempted attack of the same target a few weeks later, and the thwarted airliner attack of August 2006. In addition to this existential domestic terrorist threat directly linked to forms of Islam preached and practiced in Britain, Muslim groups with no intention of using the UK's political framework to create change, such as *Hizb al-Tahrir*, continue to call for the imposition of *khilafa* (Islamic rule) throughout the world—including, of course, in Britain. For such groups entering the secular political process is *haram* (forbidden).[74]

Conclusion

This examination has revealed that British interests in the Middle East have remained fairly consistent over the last half-century. Energy security still exercises significant influence over those who are in charge of protecting Britain's core interests, as does the demand of facilitating commercial trade. However, a significant change in the means by which those interests are obtained is now occurring, hastened by threats to security emanating from the region. In response to global Islamic terrorism and the fear of both regional and worldwide instability that it is capable of producing, Tony Blair's Government has endorsed the seemingly incongruous concept of

---

72   Sardar, Z. (2006), "Can British Islam Change?," *New Statesman*, July 3.

73   Ibid.

74   Hussain, D. (2004), "Muslim Political Participation in Britain and the Europeani-zation of the FIQH," *Die Welt des Islams* 44/3, 387.

transformational foreign policy that seeks as its long-term goal political and social reform in the greater Middle East—even at the expense of short-term instability.

Questions remain concerning the scope and pace of regional transformation. Here, as in many other issue areas, the UK finds itself somewhere between EU and US preferences. While the EU currently prefers an organic and unhurried pace for Middle East reform—even to the point that it is willing to halt expansion of the Union—the US seeks quick results, especially where security concerns are the most pressing. By taking on a major role in the Iraq War, Britain signaled that its position tilts toward faster transformation. However, as the case of Britain's relationship to Saudi Arabia has shown, the reform impetus seems to be selectively applied. Though many in the EU—Britons among them—believe Saudi Arabia represents a serious future threat to regional—and even world—security, Britain does not pursue a policy of accelerated reform in Riyadh. It would also appear the Saudis understand that the Western states have no great desire to push them toward rapid reform.

This investigation has also revealed that domestic politics, religious ideology, and concern for human rights have minimal influence on the ultimate arbitration of Britain's national interests. However, where they *do* have influence is in the difficult to decipher area between rhetorical argumentation and measurable behavior, between impassioned debates in Parliament regarding its ally's treatment of terrorist detainees, and decisions made at 10 Downing Street to moderate the expression of such concerns while continuing a joint military mission. It is actual British behavior—not rhetoric—that tells the observer volumes about the nation's intent to pursue its eternal interests tied to security, trade, and prosperity—even when those interests are promoted as representing globally beneficial goals. Perhaps as interests become increasingly contested in the future, a communitarian ethos will come into prominence, and strains of British thought already trumpeting the notion that British power and influence can only be used for 'good' will hold sway. Certainly, such a shift would also have to coincide with a particularly secure interval when the types of threats experienced today are much less prevalent, or nonexistent. Although the thought of such a world is appealing, one sees no sign of its approach on the horizon.

Chapter 2

Old Interests, New Purpose: French Foreign Policy in the Middle East[1]

Daniel W. Kuthy

In the 1960s, many US policy makers perceived French President Charles de Gaulle's foreign policy, which sought to position France as a third force, independent of the United States and the Soviet Union, as a source of frustration. His pursuit of "grandeur," "rank," independence, and maneuverability, followed by subsequent French presidents, often led to friction between France and the United States. This proved to be particularly true with regard to issues and policies concerning the Middle East.[2] Although the French role in the Middle East may not be as extensive as it once was, France remains an influential power in the region.

The role of "Gaullism" remains critical to understanding French foreign policy towards the Middle East. France's relationship with the United States carries significance in this context as well because the United States was, and remains, the dominant outside power in the region. For de Gaulle, the primary goals of France's foreign policy included safeguarding its independence and maneuverability, protecting its economy, providing a greater sense of national identity domestically, and reinforcing the new institutional structures of the 1958 Constitution. In short, he sought an independent French foreign policy to improve France's position in the world.[3]

After the Suez Crisis of 1956, de Gaulle saw the necessity for a change in France's Middle East policy.[4] When he returned to power as the first president of the Fifth Republic, he recognized that France's continued occupation of Algeria would undermine any efforts to play an important role on the world stage. The end of the Algerian War and the signing of the 1962 Evian Accords opened the door to improvements in Franco-Arab relations. While de Gaulle supported the existence

1   I would like to thank Dr Pia C. Wood at Wake Forest University for her ideas and recommendations that were critical to the shape and content of this chapter.

2   For the purpose of this chapter, the term "Middle East" is being used broadly to encompass North Africa.

3   Cerny, P.G. (1986), *Une Politique de Grandeur*, Cambridge: Cambridge University Press, 145.

4   Brown, C.L. and Gordon, M.S. (1996), *Franco–Arab Encounters: Studies in Memory of David C. Gordon*, Beirut: American University of Beirut, 11.

of the State of Israel, he also believed that it was important for France to maintain good relations with the Arab world. De Gaulle's shift in policy away from Israel and toward the Arab countries in 1967 was, in large part, due to his recognition of the limits of French power at the time. De Gaulle's *politique arabe* was aimed at amplifying French influence in the region.[5]

According to Rémy Leveau, the development of France's Arab policy has always been dominated by three factors: a cultural project to modernize the Arab world; short-term concerns over domestic policy; and international political rivalries.[6] The increased focus of the French Government on the promotion of *la Francophonie*, its large domestic Arab population, concerns over terrorism in France, and a quasi-rivalry with the United States, have shaped the formulation of France's Middle East policy.[7]

In addition to foreign policy concerns, "Gaullism" also focused on domestic issues. De Gaulle was determined to build a strong sense of nationalism within France in order to avoid civil war and internal strife that had threatened to tear the country apart in the years following the Second World War.[8] By establishing a strong and independent foreign policy for France, de Gaulle attempted to give a source of pride and unity for the French people. Domestic issues are still important in the formulation of French foreign policy today, particularly vis-à-vis the Middle East and North Africa.

The concepts of Gaullism are alive and well in the present foreign policy of France in the Middle East. This chapter argues that two of de Gaulle's aims remain important for the foreign policy of the Chirac government: to give the country a greater, more cohesive sense of national identity and unity through its foreign policy; and to increase the standing of France in the international community. The French Government's desire to maintain stability in the region complements these two goals.

This chapter focuses on French foreign policy in four regions/issue areas in the Middle East: the Maghreb; Lebanon and Syria; the Iraq War; and the Israeli–Palestinian dispute. The interaction between France and the Middle East is important to examine, because while France may not act as the decisive voice on most Middle East issues today, it still exercises an influent role in the region. Moreover, this region holds special importance for France, both internationally and domestically.

---

5   Ibid., p. 12.

6   Leveau, R. (2001), "France's Arab Policy," *Diplomacy in the Middle East: The International Relations of Regional and Outside Powers*, New York: I.B. Tauris, 4.

7   *La Francophonie*, officially known as the International Organization of Francophones (OIF), is an organization of states and some sub-state (non-state) entities. It is funded by the French Government and works primarily to promote French language and culture around the world; available at www.francophonie.org.

8   Leveau, 9.

French Foreign Policy in Middle East: A Perspective on *Politique Arabe*

This section provides a general outline of French policy towards the Middle East today. In a May 2004 survey in six Arab countries, President Jacques Chirac was found to be the second most admired world leader (outside of participants' own country), only behind the late Egyptian leader, Gamel Abdel Nasser.[9] In a speech at the University of Cairo on April 8, 1996, Chirac explained France's Arab policy as being based on four primary principles: 1) Equal dialogue and partnerships; 2) Dedication to the right of peoples to freedom and self-determination; 3) Support for Arab countries' aspirations towards solidarity, as well as French support for the Arab League and regional groups of the Maghreb and Machrek; 4) Support for the aspirations of the Arab world for openness and peace, to combat extremism and the fanaticism of forces of hatred in the world.[10] In this speech, Chirac claimed that he did not just speak for France, but for the European Union as a partner of the Arab world also.[11] Chirac, therefore, attempted to position France not simply as a leader for the Arab nations, but of the EU as well.

France has sought to present itself as a leader of the Developing World, particularly in the Middle East and Africa. This in turn works to increase the stature of France in the international community. According to Pierre Hunt, Chirac's *politique arabe* is not a pro-Arab policy per se, but it is more founded on long-term objectives of security and development.[12] In this policy, France often has sought to engage states and groups that are seen as dangerous by both Washington and some of its allies within Europe. For example, the French Government has resisted pressure to label Hezbollah a terrorist group, upsetting many of its allies, and in 2002, invited the Hezbollah Secretary-General to the Francophone summit in Beirut.[13] However, this quest for support among more radical elements of Arab society is not as unconditional as some would claim. For example, while France's approach to Hamas may have been somewhat ambiguous in the past, in a July 2005 interview with *Haaretz*, President Chirac stated that, "Hamas is a terrorist organization that cannot be an interlocutor of the international community so long as it does not renounce violence and does not recognize Israel's right to exist. This is the unambiguous position of the EU and it will not change."[14] These trends in French foreign policy display a preference of

---

9   Telhami, S. (2004), "Arab Attitudes Towards Political and Social Issues, Foreign Policy, and the Media," Anwar Sadat Chair for Peace and Development, University of Maryland, and Zogby International, available at http://www.bsos.umd.edu/SADAT/pub/Arab %20Attitudes%20Towards%20Political%20and%20Social%20Issues, %20Foreign%20Polic y%20and%20the%20Media.htm.

10   Boniface, P. and Billion, D. (2004), *Les Défis du Monde Arabe*, Institut de Relations Internationales et Stratégiques, Paris: Presses Universitaires de France, 229–30.

11   Ibid.

12   Youssef, A. (2003), *L'Orient de Jacques Chirac: La Politique Arabe de la France*, Monaco: Éditions du Rocher, 135.

13   Guitta, O. (2005), "The Chirac Doctrine," *Middle East Quarterly* 12/4, 52.

14   Makovsky, D. and Young, E. (2005), "Toward a Quartet Position on Hamas: European Rules on Banning Political Parties," *The Washington Institute on Near East Peace Policy*, available at http://www.washingtoninstitute.org/templateC05.php?CID=2369.

the French Government towards engagement, rather than containment, of some of the more difficult countries or actors in the region. Engagement is a common aspect of French foreign policy, whether the party is Iran, Iraq, Hezbollah, or Hamas, and it is one of the major differences and points of contention between French and US foreign policy.

France seeks to promote good relations with states in the Middle East as a way of increasing its standing in the region and in the larger international community. These relationships are important for France economically, but they also serve a vital role in a soft power campaign that attempts to increase France's influence in the world and to make it less of a target for terrorist attacks.[15] The International Organization of Francophones (OIF) provides one example of the French Government's soft power approach to foreign policy. Through its bilateral actions, and through the OIF, France has sought to establish a political bloc with itself at the head.

Although the OIF is primarily a cultural organization, its power extends beyond this realm. Within its bounds, France spends over $300 million per year to promote French language and culture worldwide with the expectation that this will help to improve its soft power capacity. The organization also offers a forum for political cooperation among francophone countries, with France placed at the head. Out of the 50 states and governments that are a part of the organization, 15 are Muslim, and seven are members of the Arab League.[16] The Chirac administration has increased France's involvement and spending on the OIF, and it has sought to increase the involvement of Arab countries in the *Francophonie*. France also works with the Arab League in order to promote its interests and to increase its influence. It offers itself as a voice to these nations in international affairs and, in turn, to gain influence among them.

Like many outside powers in the region, France takes a pragmatic approach in pursuing its foreign policy goals in the Middle East, often supporting anti-democratic governments with negative human rights records. France interacts with its allies within the European Union (EU) on foreign policy, but it is not limited by this. It uses the EU to amplify its influence in the Middle East and, in turn, it uses the influence that it gains in the Middle East to enhance its standing within the European Union and in the world international community in general. As in its general foreign policy, France reserves the right to operate independently and takes an active role.

Economic and cultural ties are also important components to France's relations with the Arab world, especially with former colonies.[17] The economic relations of France with Middle Eastern nations are of great importance, but this aspect of the relationship is not simply a separate goal. It is also used as a tool by France in

---

15   Soft power is defined by Joseph Nye as the ability to get others to want what you want. It involves an attractiveness of cultural and/or political ideas of a society. While this is generally used in reference to the United States, it is by no means a term that applies explicitly to the US See Nye, Jr, J. (2004), *Soft Power: The Means to Success in World Politics*, New York: Public Affairs.

16   *Agence Internationale de la Francophonie*, available at http://agence.francophonie. org/agence/membres.cfm.

17   Schäfer, I. and Schmid, O. (2005), "L'Allegmagne, la France, et le conflit israelí-palestinien," *Politique Étrangère* 70/2, 418.

seeking to strengthen its relationships with these countries in a more general sense. This helps to establish a solid political relationship with strong societal and cultural links, as well as economic.

France seeks to play an important role in the Middle East, and feels justified in doing so, in part because it has close cultural ties to many of the countries in the region, whether through colonization, immigration, or linguistic evangelization. In addition, its proximity to the Middle East, especially North Africa, makes France intensely feel the effects of disturbances in the region, whether they are international issues such as trade and peace, or domestically pressing concerns such as immigration and terrorism. More than any other outside power, for France the lines between the domestic and the international become blurred when it comes to dealing with the Middle East, especially North Africa.

Maghreb and Mediterranean Policy

France has a long and deeply involved colonial history in the Maghreb (Libya, Algeria, Tunisia, Morocco, and Mauritania).[18] In its policy towards the Maghreb countries, France seeks primarily to ensure stability and good relations and to maintain its standing in the region, so that it can wield greater influence on the international stage. France once held colonies or protectorates in many of these countries. With close and strong economic ties between France and the countries of the Maghreb, France today acts as the largest trading partner of Algeria, Morocco, and Tunisia.[19]

The Mediterranean Sea, once considered the center rather than a boundary of the French Colonial Empire, in the past decade has increasingly come to be viewed as such, often compared to the way that the United States views the Rio Grande River as its border with Mexico. North African immigration to France makes French Maghreb policy not only a matter of foreign policy, but a domestic political issue as well.[20]

According to a 2000 estimate in a report by the French High Council on Integration, Muslims, primarily from North Africa, account for more than 8 percent of the French population nationally, but their numbers are increasing at a rate of 3.7 percent annually and are not dispersed evenly across the country.[21] This compares to an estimated annual growth rate in the population overall of 0.37 percent.[22] The growth rate among the Muslim community is about ten times that of society as a whole and accounts for nearly all of the population growth in France. Given the statistics above, some demographers estimate that Muslims will make up 25 percent

---

18   France invaded Algeria in 1830 and conquered it over the next 17 years. It established a protectorate in Tunisia in 1881, and one in Morocco in 1911.

19   Émié, B. (2004), "L'action déterminée de la France dans le monde arabe et méditerranéan," *Les Défis de Monde Arabe*, Institut de Relations Internationales et Stratégiques, Paris: Presses Universitaires de France, 244.

20   Brown and Gordon, 12–3.

21   Pauly, 38.

22   "France," *CIA World Factbook*, available at https://www.cia.gov/cia/publications/factbook/index.html.

of the French population by the year 2030.[23] As this population, with ties to its homeland or land of heritage, grows, the potential pressure on France relative to issues in North Africa will likely increase.

France works to support stability in the region through cultivation of close cultural, political, and economic ties with these countries and their societies. This is in part because French policy makers fear the potential of Islamists taking over the government of a country, or gaining significant power. In addition, due to France's proximity to the region, a civil war in the Maghreb would likely trigger a large flow of refugees to France, as happened in the last Algerian Civil War. Such a conflict not only would strain the economy and exacerbate difficulties that France currently has with integrating its Muslim communities, but also it could spread to France in the form of terrorist attacks, as occurred during the Algerian Civil War in the 1990s.

Under *la politique mediterraneene* in the early 1990s, the French Government emphasized the importance of formulating its foreign policy towards Mediterranean countries within a multilateral framework. Under this policy, France was influential in drafting and convincing other nations to sign the Barcelona Declaration between the EU and 12 Mediterranean countries in November of 1995,[24] which provided a foundation for the Euro-Mediterranean Partnership. Today, the Partnership includes the 25 EU members and 10 Mediterranean partners (Algeria, Egypt, Israel, Jordan, Lebanon, Morocco, Palestinian Authority, Syria, Tunisia and Turkey). Libya has held observer status since 1999. The Euro-Mediterranean Partnership has three main goals under the Barcelona Process:

1. The definition of a common area of peace and stability through the reinforcement of political and security dialogue (Political and Security Chapter).

2. The construction of a zone of shared prosperity through an economic and financial partnership and the gradual establishment of a free-trade area.

3. The rapprochement between peoples through a social, cultural and human partnership aimed at encouraging understanding between cultures and exchanges between civil societies.[25]

Since 2004, these Mediterranean partners have been included in the European Neighborhood Policy.[26] At the November 2005 meeting of the Euro–Mediterranean Partnership (EMP), the EU and its Mediterranean partners could not agree on how to proceed within the guidelines of the Barcelona Process. As a result, the parties produced only a general statement that they would work together to combat terrorism. The Barcelona process has improved trade liberalization and boosted trade amongst EMP states. In addition, macroeconomic stability has improved in the region.

---

23   Guitta (2005), 43.

24   Wood, P.C. (2002), "French Foreign Policy and Tunisia: Do Human Rights Matter?" *Middle East Policy* 9/2, 93–5.

25   *Overview: Euro-Mediterranean Partnership/Barcelona Process*, European Union—External Relations, November 27, 2005, available at http://europa.eu.int/comm/external_relations/euromed.

26   Ibid.

However, the EMP has not been successful in one of its primary goals of closing the inequality gap between Europe and the rest of the southern Mediterranean.[27]

In December 2003 in Tunis, France worked to organize a summit, "cinq + cinq" to discuss economic and other issues in the Mediterranean region. This summit included five countries on each side of the Mediterranean with the hope that they could use this forum to come to an agreement on certain key issues. The participating countries were: France, Spain, Portugal, Italy, and Malta from Europe, and the five UMA (Arab Maghreb Union) members (Tunisia, Algeria, Morocco, Libya, and Mauritania). France hoped that this meeting would help to promote cooperation among these Mediterranean countries in solving problems of concern. Furthermore, a part of France's wider effort was to promote free trade across the entire Mediterranean.[28] In addition to this, in June 2006 the same set of countries signed the "5 + 5 défense," which aims at achieving cooperation in security on issues including immigration, drug smuggling, and terrorism.[29]

The French Government historically has overlooked human rights issues in favor of stability in these countries, even in the face of domestic pressure from the Maghreb immigrant population within France. The French press at times has denounced the closeness of French relations with regimes that are seen as authoritarian, such as President ben Ali in Tunisia and Morocco under former King Hassan II.[30] This domestic pressure at times has influenced government to change its policies.

Algeria holds a particularly important place in French foreign policy because over two million people either from Algeria or of Algerian descent live in France today.[31] Given this fact, coupled with concerns over terrorism, France's Algerian policy encompasses not only matters of foreign policy, but domestic issues as well. With the outbreak of the Algerian Civil War and later terrorist acts on French soil in the early 1990s, Charles Pasqua, Minister of the Interior, rather than Foreign Minister Alain Juppé, took the lead in relations with Algeria.[32] As one of France's largest trading partners, in 2004 Algeria provided France with approximately 88 percent of its liquefied natural gas (LNG) needs.[33] The secret services of France and Algeria cooperate very closely on questions of international terrorism.[34] Under Chirac, the relationship between the two countries has become especially close. His visit to Algeria in March of 2003 was part of an effort to build a special partnership between

---

27   Nsouli, S.M. (2006), *The Euro-Mediterranean Partnership Ten Years On: Reassessing Readiness and Prospects*, International Monetary Fund, June 23, available at http://www.imf.org/external/np/speeches/2006/062306.htm.

28   Émié, 245.

29   *Tunisie*, French Ministry for Foreign Affairs, available at http://www.diplomatie. gouv.fr/fr/pays-zones-geo_833/tunisie_411/index.html.

30   Dalloz, J. (2002), *La France et le monde depuis 1945*, Paris: Armand Colin, 223.

31   Shurkin, M.R. (2003), "Chirac in Algeria," *US–France Analysis Series*, The Brookings Institution, 1, available at http://www.brookings.edu/fp/cusf/analysis/shurkin.htm.

32   Tlemçani, R. (1997), "Islam in France: The French Have Themselves to Blame," *Middle East Quarterly* 4/1, available at http://www.meforum.org/article/338.

33   *World LNG Imports by Origin, 2004*, United States Department of Energy, available at http://www.eia.doe.gov/emeu/international/LNGimp2004.html. Accessed 08/28/2006.

34   Dalloz, 201.

France and Algeria. The Algiers Declaration, signed both by President Chirac and President Bouteflika, spoke of recasting the relationship between the two countries and building privileged ties. The declaration included, among other things, a promise to increase cultural and intellectual exchanges between the two countries.[35]

Especially under Chirac's presidency, France has worked to build special relationships with Tunisia and Morocco in order to increase French influence and promote economic and regional stability. In October 2003, President Chirac visited Morocco for the first time since Mohammed VI assumed the throne in 1999. During the visit, the president reaffirmed the strategic partnership between France and Morocco,[36] and he expressed support for the efforts of Mohammed VI to introduce liberal economic, social, and political reforms. Fifty years after Morocco regained its independence from France, the two countries have reconciled and enjoy close relations, which extend to the realms of economic, cultural, security, and political issues. Most of the top governmental and professional classes in Morocco and Tunisia relate to their counterparts in France through academic exchanges, professional and governmental conferences, and French schools in the two countries.

The Maghreb is the area in the Middle East where France exercises the greatest degree of influence. France serves as a vital link between the European Union and southern Mediterranean, including the Maghreb. It has led the way in promoting an increased European role in the region, while maintaining independent relations with these countries. Although France has been helpful in providing stability in the region, some would argue that it must encourage, and press regimes in the region if necessary, to make democratic and economic reforms at a greater rate.[37] In the absence of such reforms, there exists danger of revolution and the possibility that the people of the Maghreb will see France as backing repressive governments. On the other hand, if France pushes for reforms too hard, it may alienate the governments of the North African countries, or lead to radical Islamic governments in some countries by popular election (demonstrated by the vote in the Algerian elections of 1991). Since the 1970s, Chevenement argued that French foreign policy must support secular leaders' efforts to combat religious revivalism in the Maghreb and in the Middle East—not as an end in of itself, but as a bulwark against the influence of Islamist groups within the French population.[38] This logic still informs French foreign policy in the region today.[39] In addition, French foreign policy tends to emphasize economic development over political reform.

---

35   Shurkin, 3–4.

36   "Maroc," Ministère des Affaires Etrangeres, available at http://www.diplomatie. gouv.fr/fr/pays-zones-geo_833/maroc_410/index.html.

37   Abderrahim, K. (2004), "La France et le monde arabe: entre rêves et réalités," *La revue internationale et strategique* 53, 94.

38   Chevenement has made this argument from the 1970s until the present day. He was in favor of supporting Saddam Hussein, Bouteflika and Chadli in Algeria, as well as other secular autocrats in North Africa and the Middle East. He saw these regimes as crucial to containing violent Islamic extremist groups.

39   Styan, D. (2006), *France & Iraq: Oil, Arms, and French Foreign Policy Making in the Middle East*, New York: I.B. Taurus, 198–9.

Lebanon and Syria

French foreign policy towards Lebanon and Syria has proved difficult in recent years, as France has tried to pursue its general goals of "grandeur" and stability under rapidly changing conditions. As was agreed in the Sykes-Picot Treaty of 1916, France formed a protectorate in the area known as the Levant (Syria and Lebanon).[40] The French mandate in Syria officially ended with the withdrawal of the last French troops from the country in April 1946, and from Lebanon in December of the same year.[41] In the late 1970s, Lebanon became an area of focus in French foreign policy in the Middle East due to Lebanese Civil War, and it has remained important since then.[42]

France has worked hard to build more friendly relations with Syria since the early 1990s, which helped to repair France's image in the Middle East.[43] France became an important partner with the Syrian Government in developing its economy in the 1990s, supporting closer Syrian-European ties, and promoting a more positive image for Syria in the world. In 2004, France changed course in its approach to Syria because of its meddling in Lebanese politics and Bashar Assad's (the president of Syria) refusal to accept French recommendations for reform. It worked to isolate the Syrian regime, and it demanded that Syria withdraw its troops from Lebanon and stop interfering in internal Lebanese politics.[44] Syrian troops moved into Lebanon in June 1976 at the request from the Maronite-dominated Government of Lebanon. Even with the end of the Lebanese Civil War and the Ta'if Accords that reformed the Lebanese constitution, the approximately 15,000 Syrian troops did not leave Lebanon.[45]

In 2004, France focused international attention on Lebanon at a time when the United States was preoccupied in Iraq. The French brought focus to what it perceived as a Syrian attempt to rewrite the Lebanese Constitution[46] and to impose an extension of *Emile* Lahoud's presidency. Chirac called, publicly and explicitly, for Syria not

---

40   The Sykes-Picot treaty was signed between Great Britain and France. The two states agreed to divide the holdings of the Ottoman Empire in the Arab world between themselves in the form of protectorates following the First World War.

41.   See Zisser, E. (2004), "France and Syria: From Enemy to Friend," *France and the Middle East: Past, Present, and Future*, Jerusalem: The Hebrew University Magnes Press.

42   As a member of the multinational UN forces in Lebanon, France sent 800 troops to the country, and it lost 56 soldiers in the October 1983 suicide attack on the US Marine barracks that killed 241 American soldiers.

43   Syrians, and many Arabs, resented France's invasion of their country in order to impose a French protectorate over the country following the First World War. To further improve France's image in the Arab world, the French Government needed to make amends.

44   Cohen, R., "Globalist: A blood bond brings two allies together," *International Herald Tribune* (March 12, 2005), available at http://iht.nytimes.com/protected/articles/2005/03/11/news/globalist.ph.

45   Pan, E., *Middle East: Syria and Lebanon*, Council on Foreign Relations, February 18, available at: http://www.cfr.org/publication/7851/middle_east.html#1.

46   Ignatius, D. (2005), "The New Dynamics in Syria and Lebanon," *A Briefing by the Saban Center for Middle East Policy at the Brookings Institute*, June 22, available at www.brookings.edu/events/20050622.htm.

to interfere in the Lebanese presidential election. This demand from the French was completely ignored by the Syrians and Lahoud's presidency was artificially extended.[47] Shortly after Prime Minister Rafik Hariri, an outspoken opponent of Syria's presence in Lebanon, resigned in protest, he was assassinated in a plot that a UN investigation later tied to Syrian intelligence. After Hariri's assassination on February 14, 2005, France worked closely with the US in demanding the withdrawal of foreign troops from Lebanon. Under intense international pressure and without French support, Syria found itself woefully short on allies, which helped to force it to withdraw its troops from Lebanon. The French Government, and Chirac in particular, was deeply disappointed by Syria. France had staked a lot on the idea that Bashar Asad, President of Syria, was a reformer. At the funeral of his father, Hafez Al-Asad in 2000, Chirac was one of few Western leaders in attendance. Chirac told Bashar, "I extended the hand of friendship to your father, and I extend it to you today."[48] In order to assist, France sent a team of high-level experts to assess the Syrian bureaucracy and provide advice for reforms. This group made strong, but quiet recommendations for real reforms in the country, and France offered to aid Syria in making these reforms, but the Asad government did nothing. This angered the French Government, and led to a setback in its relationship with Syria.[49]

The Syrian rejection was troubling for the Chirac government, because it showed that France lacked any real influence in Syria. French moves to isolate Syria internationally show the Paris government's acknowledgment of its loss of influence there. These efforts to isolate Syria included France's co-sponsorship with the US of United Nations Security Council Resolution 1559, which was passed on September 2, 2004 and called for foreign forces to withdraw from Lebanon and for the respect of Lebanon's sovereignty. France played an important role in garnering international support for this resolution, especially in the Arab world. While perhaps France could not have passed such a resolution without US support, the reverse is undoubtedly true as well.

French actions with regard to Lebanon helped significantly in 2005 when much of the international community came together to pressure Syria to remove its troops from Lebanon in the wake of Hariri's assassination. The pressure that France applied on Syria was a bold move in its Middle East policy, one which could have potentially hurt its image in the region as a friend of the Arab world. French actions helped in an attempt to portray itself as a force for justice and a voice for weaker nations in the world. Unfortunately, however, these actions leave France today with less influence over Syria than it previously had.

France has worked to promote a "soft landing" for Hezbollah, helping the organization to make a fuller transition into the political world, and to accept the role

---

47   Abdulhamid, A. (2004), "Will the Syrian Regime Take on the World?," *The Daily Star*, September 3, available at http://www.brook.edu/views/op-ed/fellows/abdulhamid 20040903.htm.

48   Little, A. (2004), *France and Syria: A Tangled History*, BBC News, September 7, available at http://news.bbc.co.uk/2/hi/middle_east/3635650.stm.

49   Ignatius.

that it plays in Lebanon.[50] Nasrallah (the leader of Hezbollah) was invited to attend the 2002 *Francophonie* summit in Beirut. When Prime Minister Lionel Jospin, in 2000, labeled Hezbollah a terrorist organization, Jacques Chirac strongly reprimanded him. Although France has called for Hezbollah to disarm, Paris officially refers to the organization as a social group.[51] Gerard Araud, French Ambassador to Israel stated in September of 2005 that France would like to give Hezbollah "a share in the democratic process and to understand that in this democratic process there's no place for weapons and for terrorism."[52] Prior to this summer's fighting between Hezbollah and Israel, the United States had taken some tentative steps in following French lead in engaging Hezbollah. France played a crucial role in securing the Syrian withdrawal from Lebanon, and its attention is important to ensure that Lebanon truly regains its independence and does not fall into chaos and civil war once more.

Like most of the international community, France initially showed understanding of Israel's retaliation against Hezbollah in July of 2006. However, as more Lebanese felt the effects of the Israeli attacks, France, like many other countries, urged a cessation of hostilities. Jean-Marc de la Sablière, the French representative to the UN Security Council, played a crucial role in crafting a resolution that was essential in bringing a halt to the hostilities, and which included strengthening the United Nations force in Southern Lebanon. Although it eventually agreed to lead the strengthened UNIFIL mission, France was not enthusiastic about accepting the leadership role, which included the deployment of an additional 1,500 French troops to Southern Lebanon. France's troop commitment was of vital importance in drafting and passing United Nations Security Council Resolution 1701, which calls for a cessation of hostilities between Israel and Hezbollah, the creation of a buffer zone through the use of international peacekeepers, and aims at assisting Lebanon in efforts to reaffirm sovereignty throughout its territory.[53]

Iraq War

The dispute between the United States and France over the 2003 invasion of Iraq traces its roots to the September 11, 2001 terrorist attacks and the different reactions that the two countries had to them. The Bush administration considered the attacks as drawing the United States into a war against terrorism. France, on the other hand, viewed the attacks as a grave crisis that needed to be dealt with seriously, even with military force, but as opposed to Washington, Paris did not see this as the beginning of a long war on terror. The French Government and people offered tremendous

50   Ajami, F. (2005), "The Autumn of Autocrats," *Foreign Affairs* 84/3, available at http://www.foreignaffairs.org/20050501faessay84304/fouad-ajami/the-autumn-of-the-auto crats.html.

51   Guitta, O. (2005), *France and Hizbullah: The End of the Affair*, The Brookings Institution US–Europe Series 2/4, available at http://www.brookings.edu/fp/cuse/analysis/ guitta20051103.htm.

52   Ibid., p. 4.

53   United Nations Security Council, 5511th Meeting (Night), August 11, 2006, available at http://www.un.org/News/Press/docs/2006/sc8808.doc.htm.

support to the United States in this difficult time, but they did not fully understand the extent to which these attacks would change the way that the United States viewed the world and dealt with its foreign affairs. France supported the use of military force in Afghanistan, but it saw Operation Enduring Freedom as the response to the 9/11 attacks, rather than the first step in a response. For the American Government, and for many American people, overthrowing the Taliban regime was not sufficient in what they saw as a new security normalcy, one in which the Bush administration believed that the United States must aggressively, even with preemptive action, assure America's national security interests. For France, the response to 9/11 was to attack al-Qaeda and its Taliban hosts, whereas the United States now fought a new feeling of insecurity. This resulted in an absolute disagreement between the French and American governments when the Bush administration decided to take action against Iraq. The lack of understanding between the two sides made it difficult for the United States to delay the war or for France to step aside. Once the disagreement had become so open and captured public opinion in France against the war, the Chirac government could not back down from its stance against the war or compromise without suffering a major loss of face.

In early 2003, when the issue of war in Iraq was being discussed in the United Nations Security Council, Dominique de Villepin, then Foreign Minister of France, claimed that more time should be given for the inspections in Iraq. He said that the inspections showed great promise, not only for discovering whether or not Iraq still possessed weapons of mass destruction, but that the Iraqi inspections regime could potentially be used as a model for a permanent disarmament body in the United Nations.[54] De Villepin claimed that the French Government opposed the war primarily because it lacked international legitimacy and was a violation of state sovereignty. In addition, the French Government asserted that the war would only exacerbate the problems with terrorism and threaten regional stability, which should be the overriding goal.[55] When the war seemed inevitable, de Villepin argued that in the reconstruction and peace efforts, action should be based on two principles: the respect for the unity and territorial integrity of Iraq, and the preservation of its sovereignty.[56] In a speech on April 11, 2003 in Moscow, Chirac said that only the United Nations would be able to confer legitimacy on the new Iraqi Government and give it the necessary moral authority to be respected in the eyes of the nations of the world.[57]

The French Government was worried that the United States was not adequately prepared for the post-war situation in Iraq.[58] Mainly, the French Government did not feel the same sense of urgency as the American Government to act in Iraq. While

---

54   de Villepin, D. (2004), *Toward a New World*, Hoboken: Melville House Publishing, 81.

55   Ibid., pp. 81–83.

56   Ibid., p. 83.

57   Michaud, Y. (2004), *Chirac dans le Texte: La Parole et L'impuissance*, Paris: Stock, 111.

58   Hoffman, S. (2004), in forward to the book: de Villepin, *Toward a New World*, xxix–xxvi.

the Bush administration viewed Iraq as an imminent threat to its security, France did not share the same perception, and it did not feel the same vulnerability to terrorism or urgency to act in order to combat this threat. France today sees terrorism as a police and intelligence matter, rather than an issue requiring international military action. The French, furthermore, do not foster the same zeal to spread democracy as do Americans. This idealistic notion of foreign policy is rather alien in the French political discourse, which either caused skepticism that the spread of democracy was the real reason, and/or made many in France nervous about what the implications of such a course of action would bring.

Chirac's opposition to the US war in Iraq led to a tremendous increase in his popularity in the Arab world, which became an essential part of French foreign policy in the Middle East, and especially in the Maghreb region.[59] The French opposition to the war was not a separate issue, but it was a larger part of France's relations with the Arab world in general. France seeks to present itself as a Western power that understands the Arab world in order to enhance its influence in the region. By opposing the war in Iraq, unpopular in most of the Middle East, France was effective in portraying itself as a friend to the Arab world.

Many in France were concerned that the war could potentially increase the risk of terrorism, which threatened France in part due to its proximity to the Middle East, as well as it large Arab population and past problems with terrorism. Past civil war in Algeria has found its way to France in the form of terrorism. As the March 11, 2003 attacks in Madrid demonstrated, support for the war in Iraq can contribute to terrorist attacks at home. Approximately 55 percent of French people surveyed in 2004 believed that the Iraq War hurt the fight against terrorism, in contrast to only 33 percent who thought that it helped.[60] France's opposition to the war has worked as a mechanism to increase both its standing in the international community, and domestically to aid Chirac's Conservative Party at home. By his posture opposing the United States, Chirac was able to play on anti-Bush sentiment to increase his own popularity. If the United States went to war in Iraq without UN approval, this also could potentially weaken the credibility of the United Nations, especially of the Security Council—one arena in which France can continue to claim world power status based on its permanent membership in the UN Security Council. To see the legitimacy of this institution weakened could indirectly dilute French power.

The French population strongly opposed the war in Iraq. According to a Pew Center poll from March of 2004, 88 percent of French people believe that the Iraq War was wrong, similar to the 83 percent who thought the same in May of 2003.[61] Certainly, strong popular opinion provides a reasonable pressure for action in a democratically elected government. Opposition to the war also appealed to the large

---

59   Abderrahim, 93.

60   *A Year After the War in Iraq*, survey conducted by the Pew Research Center for the People & the Press (March 16, 2004), available at http://people-press.org/reports/print. php3?PageID=796.

61   Ibid.

Muslim minority within France.[62] There was a strong concern among many in the French Government, that the war in Iraq could potentially destabilize the region, especially in the event of a civil war or a weak Iraqi state. In addition, de Villepin was worried that a US invasion of Iraq might feed hatred of the West in the Islamic world and push towards a clash of cultures.[63]

France, as Iraq's largest trading partner in 2002, enjoyed strong economic ties with Baghdad. While certainly significant to Iraq, this economic exchange accounted for only about 0.2–0.3 percent of French international trade.[64] Furthermore, if French trading relationships played an important role in the decision to oppose the war in Iraq, one should also consider the level of French trade with the United States and its coalition partners. In 2004, for example, France ran a trade surplus with the United States that exceeded six billion dollars.[65] Were trade as large a factor in this decision as some argued, certainly the French Government would have been worried about the economic impact its vocal opposition to the war might have had in its relationship with the US. In fact, some French companies and industries suffered a significant drop in their exports to the United States in the time since the dispute over the Iraq War, due in part to anti-French sentiment.

Although trade with Iraq prior to the war was not a large part of the French economy, French companies had agreed to large oil contracts with Iraq that would have been signed in the event that the UN sanctions were lifted. With a new regime, these contracts would most likely not come to fruition. The potential for French companies to lose these contracts is certainly not insignificant, but it does not seem to be enough reason for France to have so publicly opposed the United States and to have risked harming relations with some of its most important allies and trading partners. If economic concerns were France's only reason for opposing the war, they most likely could have been worked out in reconstruction contracts. Economic motivations in the French decision to oppose the war were most likely relatively small.

In the post-war period, France has moved to work more closely with the United States in the Middle East. France has gradually come to lend some support towards the stabilization process in Iraq through a limited role for NATO in training of Iraqi security forces and it has expressed willingness to assist in efforts to reduce Iraq's foreign debts. Although France was not in favor of the war, it sees the need to bring

---

62   Estimates of the Muslim population in France range widely from 4.8 million to over 7 million. This means that approximately 7–12 percent of French people claim themselves as Muslim. This number is difficult to accurately determine, because Islam has no hierarchic structure that keeps uniform, official records of initiation into the religion, such as those kept for baptisms.

63   Hoffman, xxix–xxv.

64   Vaisse, J. (2003), "Making Sense of French Foreign Policy," *In the National Interest*, July 2, available at http://www.inthenationalinterest.com/Articles/Vol2Issue26/Vol2Issue26Vaisse.html.

65   *CIA World Factbook*, available at https://www.cia.gov/cia/publications/factbook/index.html.

stability to Iraq.[66] Unfortunately, for France, however, it has less room to maneuver relative to its relationship with the new Iraqi Government than it had previously. The war in Iraq was unfavorable to France because it left the French Government less flexibility in its actions, primarily because the current Iraqi Government is beholden to the United States on many issues. In addition, the war has, at least for now, made the region less stable. It has not reduced terrorism, and it certainly has contributed to increased tension between the West and the Islamic world.

Israeli–Palestinian Dispute

The French stance relative to the Israeli–Palestinian dispute plays a crucial role in the two central aims of Gaullism, both internationally and domestically. France initially supported the Israeli state. It recognized Israel early, on May 11, 1949, and quickly became the largest supplier of arms to the young state. The Six Day War of October 1967 marked an important turning point in French-Israeli relations. Until then, there had been a tacit alliance between France and Israel, but de Gaulle strongly condemned the Israeli preemptive attack, in order to improve Arab-French relations.[67] France declared an arms embargo on all combatant countries in the region, but since it had no contracts with any of the combatant Arab countries, this only affected Israel. As a result, Israel turned to the United States for arms sales, forming the special relationship between these two countries that exists today. While this was unfortunate for French influence, de Gaulle believed that such a shift was necessary in order for France to increase its influence with the Arab world and in the wider international community.

De Gaulle's greater emphasis on Franco-Arab relations continued with the change of administrations and parties in power. France recognized early the Palestinian Liberation Organization (PLO) and the right of Palestinians to create a second state. It was important in pushing for the Western European Union to agree to the Venice Declaration with the PLO. This declaration was made on June 13, 1980 and called for Israel to respect UN resolutions 242 and 338.[68] France's participation in the Persian Gulf War significantly damaged its reputation in the Arab world, because many people in the region resented the interference of the United States and its allies, as well as the presence of foreign, non-Muslim troops in Saudi Arabia, which contains the holy cities of Mecca and Medina. In the early 1990s, French officials replaced

---

66   de Villepin, D. (2003), "Reconstruction of Iraq," originally published in *Le Monde*, September 12, available at http://www.ambafrance-us.org/news/statmnts/2003/villepin_iraq091203.as.

67   Bozo, F. (1997), *La Politique étrangère de la France depuis 1945*, Paris: Éditions la Découverte, 53.

68   *Venice Declaration*, available at http://www.knesset.gov.il/process/docs/venice_eng.htm. UN Security Council Resolutions 242 and 338 called for cessation of hostilities between Israel and the Arab parties, and for Israel to withdraw from the lands that it occupied in the October, 1967 (Six Day) War, These territories included the Gaza Strip, the West Bank, the Sinai Peninsula, and the Golan Heights.

the phrase *politique arabe* with *politique mediterraneene* as part of a campaign to restore France's good name in the Arab world.[69]

Concerning the Israeli–Palestinian dispute today, France fully supports a two state solution, such as that outlined in the Roadmap for Peace initiative that was proposed by the Bush administration in 2002. While it supported the Israeli pull out from the Gaza Strip, French officials have insisted that this must be a part of the larger framework for a negotiated two-state settlement between Israel and the Palestinians. France, along with the EU in general, has given significant funding to the Palestinian Authority for development in the occupied territories. It sees itself as a vital partner in the future of the peace process.

Chirac, in his comments on the occasion of Yasser Arafat's death, said that, "France, like its partners in the European Union, will maintain, firmly and with conviction, its commitment to two states ... living side by side in peace and security ... France, of course, will continue to tirelessly act for peace and security in the Middle East and will do so with respect for the rights of the Palestinian and Israeli people.'[70] In these comments, Chirac still speaks of France in alliance with other EU powers to bring peace and security in the Arab-Israeli conflict. This statement also shows Chirac as making it known that France is not merely contained within the European Union and its efforts. In comparison, German Chancellor Schröder, British Prime Minister Blair, and Irish Prime Minister Ahern, all simply mentioned Arafat's struggle for Palestinian statehood and regretted that he did not live to see it.[71] They made no mention of the shared grief of their people with the Palestinians, as President Chirac did, nor did they give Arafat the same level of praise.[72] In addition, Yasser Arafat was flown to Paris in order to receive medical attention, and he eventually died there. The comments and actions by Chirac fit well within the tenets of Gaullism, leaving France room to maneuver and maintain a separate foreign policy.

In his presidency, Chirac has additionally sought warmer relations with Israel, and has also attempted to improve France's standing in the eyes of both Israel and the Palestinians, perhaps in an effort to place France in a position to play a role in negotiating a solution. This has included acknowledging, for the first time, France's responsibility for war crimes by the Vichy government towards French Jews, and a public anti-Semitism campaign in France.[73] In the last several years, France and Israel have exchanged several visits by high-ranking officials, including a state visit by Ariel Sharon to Paris in July of 2005.[74] In a 2005 interview with the Israeli daily

---

69   Wood, 92–3.

70   "Arafat's Death: Global reaction in quotes," *BBC News World Edition* (November 11, 2004), available at http://news.bbc.co.uk/2/hi/middle_east/4001697.stm.

71   Ibid.

72   "Leaders mark Arafat's passing," *CNN* (November 11, 2004), available at http://www.cnn.com/2004/WORLD/meast/11/11/arafat.reaction.

73   Primor, A. (2005), "Yes, this friend is in need," *Haaretz*, November 23, available at http://www.haaretz.com/hasen/pages/ShArtDisengagement.jhtml?itemNo=603331.

74   "Relations Politiques: La France et Israel," Ministere des Affaires Etrangeres, available at http://www.diplomatie.gouv.fr/fr/pays-zones-geo_833/israel-territoires-palestin iens_413/france-israel_1160/relations-politiques_4636/index.html, accessed October 15, 2006.

Haaretz, President Chirac was sensitive to a reference to France's "pro-Arab policy." When asked about the effectiveness of this policy, he responded that, "Sir, there is no such thing here as a pro-Arab policy at Israel's expense. We have always had a policy that was friendly at one and the same time both to Israel and to the Arab countries. One has never come at the expense of the other."[75] While there may be a desire by the French administration to improve relations with Israel, it may prove difficult to overcome the perception of France's foreign policy as pro-Arab. The principle of "land for security" holds an important place in Chirac's position towards the Israeli–Palestinian dispute, as the French Government is dedicated to the creation of a separate, viable, and independent Palestinian state.

While previous French presidents kept alive the *politique arabe* of Charles de Gaulle, President Chirac has been very active in promoting close relations with the Middle East and North Africa in political, cultural, and security areas. His administration has actually gone far beyond even the policies of de Gaulle towards the Arab world. While the French Government insists that positive relations with Israel are important, it also continues to strongly support the Palestinian Authority and the Palestinian cause in general. Chirac still believes that France can be important to brokering a final peace deal between Israel and the Palestinians, as well as its Arab neighbors who have not made peace with Israel. France has maintained favor with the Palestinians, and it has made attempts to improve relations with Israel. However, Paris does not have the power or influence to bring the two sides to the peace table, or the leverage to pressure the two parties when necessary. France cannot help the two parties to negotiate a peace settlement alone, but it can play an integral role in this process.

The French Government, like its allies in Europe and the United States, insists that if Hamas is to be a partner in negotiating a peaceful, two-state settlement, it must first renounce terrorism and recognize Israel's right to exist.[76] Since the victory of Hamas in the Palestinian elections of 2006, France has shown no real signs of backing down from this stance. In spite of this policy, Chirac has actively called for international aid to continue to the Palestinian people, including the payment of salaries of Palestinian officials. This shows France's attempt to demonstrate that it is not anti-Palestinian, even though it is currently at odds with the new Hamas government. Although France and the European Union have not fully resumed aid to the Palestinian Authority, they have worked in other ways to continue some aid to the Palestinian people. They have set up a mechanism that attempts to provide basic services to the people in the Gaza Strip, such as healthcare and water, are reaching between 30 percent and 40 percent of people in the territory in one form or another. In addition, half of the government workers are receiving an allowance provided by this aid project.[77] While it is not directly involved, France is supportive of the efforts

---

75   Primor.

76   Statement Made by the Foreign Ministry's Spokesperson, Paris, February 14, 2006, available at http://www.ambafrance-us.org/news/standpoint/stand161.asp, accessed September 29, 2006.

77   Daily Press Briefing by the Ministry of Foreign Affairs Spokesperson, Embassy of France in the United States (October 6, 2006), available at http://www.ambafrance-us.org/news/briefing/us061006.asp#1.

by Qatar to help negotiate a unity government between Palestinian President Abbas and Prime Minister Haniyeh.

Conclusion

Charles de Gaulle famously stated: "France has no friends, only interests." This element of pragmatism is important to understanding French foreign policy today. Not built to be antagonistic towards US interests, French foreign policy seeks to promote the national interests of France. In the Middle East today, Paris attempts to ensure stability; promote a more cohesive sense of national identity at home; and improve France's standing, in the Middle East, within the European Union, and in the world in general. The efforts to extend French influence take many forms: political, economic, and cultural.

Politically, France attempts to encourage countries within the region to follow its leadership in issues on the world stage, thus broadening French international influence. Economically, Paris has steadily increased its involvement in the Middle East over the past 40 years. Today, the region is vital to French foreign trade, and the economic relationship between the Middle East and France affects the extension of French influence in the area. Arms sales, economic on one hand, also include a political component to the decision making process which carries far more significance than general economic connections. France administers extensive programs throughout the Middle East that promote French language and culture, which although expensive, are deemed worthwhile in the long term by the Chirac Government. These programs bolster France's influence, in a subtle way, as part of a soft power campaign, helping to create a politically, socially, and culturally sympathetic bloc.

While France holds notably less weight in the Middle East than the United States, it remains a force in the region. Paris acts as the second most prominent outside power in the Middle East today. In addition, France possesses the ability to influence some countries and societies that lay outside of the US reach—in part because of French policies of engagement versus containment. While the United States holds more sway with most governments in the Middle East, France enjoys far greater popularity among the people, granting it a certain degree of soft power that currently eludes the United States in the region.

At this point, the French find itself at a crossroads in foreign policy towards the Middle East. The *politique arabe* implemented by de Gaulle almost 40 years ago has provided mixed results for France. While Paris has gained a degree of influence in some Arab states, and has remained an important voice in Middle East issues, the policy has not yielded the increase in stature of France internationally for which de Gaulle had hoped. French standing in the Maghreb is still strong—much stronger than when de Gaulle began his *politique arabe*. However, French efforts to increase influence in the Levant and the rest of the Arab world have not achieved the same degree of success, and the future role of France in the region is uncertain today.

While French policies and interests sometimes conflict with those of the United States, the two countries can be far more effective in cooperation. The recent case of

Lebanon, where both countries worked together effectively to demand and obtain a withdrawal of Syrian troops and to stop the fighting between Israel and Hezbollah, provides a clear and successful example. The Israeli–Palestinian dispute also offers a potential opportunity for cooperation. French foreign policy in general, and in the Middle East in particular, is not simply contrary or anti-American in nature. Rather, France pursues different, independent goals relative to those of the United States, and while these may be conflicting at times, French foreign policy should not be viewed as inherently hostile towards US interests.

Chapter 3

Germany and the Middle East: The Construction of Moral Interests

Jack Covarrubias and Chris White

For most of Germany's post-Second World War history, the idea of a foreign policy towards the Middle East conjured up images of a renewed bid for European domination and world conquest. As a result of this continued wariness towards the German state, the strange fungibility of international politics coupled with the abhorrence of the possibility of German troops in conflict against an Israeli state made it all but impossible for Germany to have a Middle East policy outside of the context of its normative institutional obligations. Berlin's policy towards the Middle East was, therefore, generally geared towards specific actors within the community and could not be accurately labeled as a broad, regional foreign policy. For example, Germany accepted obligations with regards to Israel, developed specific interests with various regional actors, and later supported the concept of Palestinian statehood—goals seemingly at odds for a general foreign policy orientation towards the Middle East. However, developing a coherent policy towards the Middle East has been an enormous challenge for the entire international community - particularly because the continuing Israeli–Palestinian conflict remains one of the primary sources of turmoil in the region and shows no signs of lessening in the near future.

Germany, like the vast majority of states external to the region, has no specific policy of its own towards the Middle East. Instead, it has treated its polices as secondary to a general European approach to Middle Eastern affairs, with the understanding that Germany plays an important part in formulating that policy. As the largest and most economically robust state in the European Union, it is near impossible to speak of a policy that does not involve significant German influence. However, because of the supranational inclination of Europe and the broad divisions concerning the Middle East in general and Israel specifically, Germany has continued to place its historic obligations before its institutional concerning the region. The shadow of Hitler and the atrocities of the Second World War still affect German society and its politics. Consequently, Israel is the most salient factor in Berlin's approach to the Middle East. German policies are geared around a civilian power approach to world politics first and foremost which includes an unquestioned support of Israel's right to exist.

Since reunification in 1990, Germany is more willing to actively promote its foreign policy interests abroad as it accepts an interpretation of its international obligations that demands a more proactive approach. Germany is more willing to question the motivations of its major partners when they conflict with its own ideas of international morality. The 2003 debate over the war in Iraq resulted in a major split among EU member states regarding the military intervention against the Hussein regime. When it became readily apparent that Germany, France, and other important US allies opposed intervention, former Defense Secretary Rumsfeld argued that these dissenting states represented "Old Europe" and were not representative of the entire EU. Furthermore, Germany is more willing to question Israeli operations in Lebanon and the Palestinian territories and it has taken a leadership role in the debate over Iranian nuclear development. Germany may lose its voice as a mediator within the Middle East by pursuing a more active foreign policy in the region. As actors take issue with German motivations and political opinions, Germany may finally have to choose sides—something it has been highly reticent to do since the end of the Second World War.

Taking Stock

With the end of the Cold War and the unification of Germany, the state is gradually losing its inhibitions against acting independently in a regional and global context. German reunification coincided with the collapse of the Soviet Union forcing Berlin to develop a new foreign policy outside the framework of the Cold War. The success of the state as an economic power within Europe and the world in general, coupled with its view of world politics, or *Weltanschauung,* geared around the primacy of international norms and regulation, is creating a new impetus for Germany to have a revolutionary mission that includes the staunch promotion of human rights and international morality.[1] With respect to its Kantian view of the world as a state of war in need of the civilizing power of international governance and a deep acceptance of individual human rights, Germany struggles with the idea that such a world must be *established* often in the context of individual state action.[2] Thus, the basic dilemma in the current German foreign policy is the classic duality framed by Kant over 200 years ago: the relationship between politically motivated behavior and the desire to behave as a moral actor.

This duality has created a state that has often been unwilling to act independently in fear of the reputation costs it may incur for acting unilaterally. Germany, like the other European NATO member states, managed to prosper under the cloak of American security for decades without having to commit significant resources. The parsimonious solution to any German foreign policy issue must be framed in a two-fold construct. First, under what type of leadership is Germany's position going to be grounded? Second, how does this position square with its current legacy as a pacifist power and with its historical failures as a hostile state responsible for some of the most horrid atrocities in the twentieth century?[3] In the context of the bipolar system

---

1   Karp, R. (2005/06), "The New German Foreign Policy Consensus," *The Washington Quarterly* 29/1, 61–82.

2   Kant, I. (1795), *Towards Perpetual Peace*, available at http://www.constitution.org/kant/perpeace.htm.

3   This is an offshoot of the debate that was brought up with German unification. The question was, and perhaps still persists in some form, is how does unification affect

and in the immediate post Cold War unipolar system, this position was perfectly acceptable and proved to be extremely advantageous for the German state. American leadership during the Cold War was not worth questioning when framed against the larger choice between democracy and communism. Moreover, the unequal partnership that developed in the Cold War years allowed the German economy to blossom without the massive military expenditures that the US incurred. Embracing a Europe obsessed with a post-modern role in the world order was easy in a system seemingly destined to forge into "the end of history."[4]

Once it became apparent that peace and tranquility were not going to be the hallmarks of the new world order, Germany's position as a civilian *power* became increasingly untenable. The failure to embrace the "hour of Europe" as it was so notoriously put by Jacques Poos, foreign minister of Luxembourg during the beginning of the Balkans crisis, was a wakeup call for Europe in general and Germany in particular.[5] That failure became more apparent with each crisis in the 1990s in such places as Rwanda and in the Middle East, where there was no effective European response largely due to political reasons but also because of inadequate capabilities.[6] The European Union has tended to provide financial support instead of committing troops, which allows it to be involved in international responses, but not face the dilemma of actual military engagement.

Tied to this foreign policy evolution is the rise of Germany in the world community. With the end of the Cold War nearing, the two Germanys no longer had to reside as half powers dependent upon their Cold War benefactors. Reunification facilitated a further change in foreign policy where for the first time in decades a whole state, independent of foreign control, was allowed to act with respect to its own interests. However, this new German state did not resemble any other state in how it embraced newfound independence. Instead, it chose to tread softly and well within the boundaries of the institutions that had guided it so successfully in the post-war years, particularly concerning its role as a member state within the European Union and its ties to NATO.

Germany's unique history and size meant that it could have a leadership role within both organizations, although extenuating circumstances meant that Germany would take many years before embracing its proper position as a European leader. In terms of NATO, its historical reluctance to deploy forces abroad, and the pains that it went through to assure its European allies of its good intentions, meant that it would not strike an independent path. Thus, with the Persian Gulf War it willingly accepted a great deal of the financial burden without demanding a voice in the actual decision

---

German foreign policy? And would Germany still work within the institutional constraints it was bound by during the Cold War? For an example of this discussion and a look at Germany as a civilian power see Tewes, H. (2002), *Germany, Civilian Power and the New Europe: Enlarging NATO and the European Union*, New York: Palgrave.

4   Fukuyama, F. (1992), *The End of History and the Last Man*, New York: Avon Books.

5   Smith, D. (2002), "Europe's Peacebuilding Hour? Past Failures, Future Challenges," *Journal of International Affairs* 55/2, 441–60.

6   Haass, R.N. (1997), *The Reluctant Sheriff: The United States after the Cold War*, Council on Foreign Relations, 1997.

making process. In terms of the EU, it continued to allow the other traditional European leaders, France and the UK, to control the speed of integration, although with time it has embraced its leadership role more readily. As the largest European nation with a population 20 million greater than the next second most populous state, France, it is only natural for Germany to assume a central role in EU and world affairs.[7] In addition, it typically spelled out its own foreign policy in support of a European position and with consideration of its relationship with the United States.

Jackson Janes, Executive Director of the American Institute for Contemporary German Studies at the Johns Hopkins University, expertly describes the implications of German foreign policy:

> Germany's weight is not nearly as heavy as that of the United States, nor is that of the European Union. But the importance of Germany's decisions and actions, on its own or as a part of the EU, is significant for not only its own interests, but also those of many other parts of the world. The path which Germany chooses within Europe has and will determine in no small measure the choices Europe will have as it shapes its future.[8]

While the US may be the only global hegemon, in all reality Germany is the major player on the European continent and the real driving force behind the continued economic prosperity of the EU. Germany will account for approximately 20 percent of the total EU budget in 2007 with a contribution of over 23 billion euros, which is 1 percent of its gross national income.[9]

After reunification, and continuing to this day, Germany is one of the top three states within Europe, and among the top states in the world, in the traditional view of what defines power. At around $2.5 trillion dollars a year, Germany has the largest economy in Europe and the fifth largest in the world.[10] However, its global reach as far as world trade remains unsurpassed in terms of total exports. This is particularly striking in that Germany is the world's largest exporter, with 72 percent of its exports remaining in Europe.[11] Furthermore, Germany has the second largest import level behind the United States. These figures account for Germany's thirsty energy habits with some 70 percent of total energy requirements met through imports as of 2004.[12] The German military budget for 2005 was the ninth largest in the world at close to $32.7 billion dollars (2003 purchasing power parity), although Germany's

---

7   US Census Bureau International Programs Center, "Rank Countries by Population," Available at http://www.census.gov/ipc/www/idbrank.html.

8   Janes, J., "German Foreign Policy: Between Continuity and Constraints," *AICGS Advisor* (October 07, 2005).

9   *EU Financing of the General Budget*, available at http://eur-lex.europa.eu/budget/data/PEL12007_VOL1/EN/nmc-grseq42960935830-3/index.html.

10   "Germany," *CIA World Fact Book*, available at https://www.cia.gov/cia/publications/factbook/geos/gm.html.

11   Hiscock, G. (2005), *Germany Still the Export Achiever*, CNN (December 6), available at http://www.cnn.com/2005/BUSINESS/11/23/wto.germany.role/index.html?eref=sitesearch.

12   Dohmen, F. et al. (2006), "Germany's Energy 'Wake-Up Call'," Eurostat, *Spiegel Online International* (January 10), available at http://www.spiegel.de/international/0,1518,394403,00.html.

military expenditure is 1.5 percent of GDP compared to 3.7 percent for the US.[13] Perhaps more telling of its global reach is the fact that Germany was the fourth largest conventional arms supplier in the world in 2005.[14] While the majority of its military muscle is geared toward territorial defense, in recent years it has been more willing to engage in collective military responses to international crises, opting for a more active than passive role. As of 2006, Germany has over 9,000 troops deployed abroad, supporting NATO and UN operations in locations such as Afghanistan, Kosovo, and the Lebanese coast.[15]

The German role in the world largely rests upon its reputation as a civilian power, with the state visibly embracing a different formulation of what it means to be powerful.[16] To paraphrase the words of Hanns Maull, Germany has accepted a complex interdependent world characterized by: a) the necessity of cooperation in the pursuit of interests; b) the focus on soft power instruments with hard power used only as a last resort to guarantee the security of other means of interaction; and c) the acceptance of multilateral institutions as the legitimate means of dealing with international issues. In a more recent article, Maull spells out how these particular trends have influenced German foreign policy after reunification.[17] Under the guise of "never again," Germany has accepted a policy of deeper integration, the protection of human rights and international peace. Tied to this policy is an aversion to the use of force, which is understandable in light of Germany's colossal historical problems. The institutionalization of the policy of "never again" is complemented by additional concept of "never alone." Thus, when the use of military power or international pressure is exerted, typically as a last resort, it is done through a multilateral framework. The Germans also tend to stress "Politics, not force" which appeals to their pacifist tendencies. As a result of these policies, it is expected that Germany would attempt to solve its international problems through negotiation. Last, but perhaps not least, the Germans tend to embrace the "norms define interests" school of foreign policy. Germany accepts the universality of Western values and culture and has become increasingly more willing to export these values into the world, and Germany is now one of the staunchest supporters of human rights.

It is a combination of all these unique characteristics that helps identify Germany's policy in the Middle East and provides a framework concerning its interests in the region. As a nation-state, it has defined itself in terms of the national shame felt because of the legacy of two world wars and the horrors of the Holocaust. From the

---

13   Stockholm International Peace Research Institute (SIPRI) (2007), "The Fifteen Major Spenders in 2005," available at http://www.sipri.org/contents/milap/milex/mex_trends. html; "German Global Clout Grows as Berlin Heads EU, G8," *Deutsche Welle* (January 2), available at http://www.dw-world.de/dw/article/0,2144,2292260,00.html.

14   *SIPRI Arms Transfers Database*, available at http://www.sipri.org/contents/ armstrad/access.html#twenty.

15   "Germany Starts Rethinking its Foreign Deployments," *Deutsche Welle* (October 31, 2006), available at http://www.dw-world.de/dw/article/0,2144,2221383,00.html.

16   Maull, H.W. (1990/91), "Germany and Japan: The New Civilian Powers," *Foreign Affairs* 69/55, 91–106.

17   Maull (2000), "Germany and the Use of Force: Still a 'Civilian Power'?" *Survival* 42/2, 56–80.

ashes of a failed nationalist policy of conquest, it has become a symbol of morality in both action and deed. Germany has also strived to develop strong friendships within the leading democratic nations of the world. However, it looks upon its international interests with a firm grasp on its role as a "civilizing" power. Thus, it defines its role as "a good partner in the future, critical when necessary, but always reliable."[18] Therefore, German policy towards the Middle East has not progressed much beyond its original foundations within the EU and with the US. However, its relatively new role as a leader, instead of a follower, has increasingly forced Germany to take a more active position in formulating policies and sometimes disagreeing with its traditional partners. In some respects, the German goal of being both dependable and predictable to its partners of choice has created a more responsible power in the world more willing to engage in Middle Eastern affairs.[19]

German Interests

The emergence of Germany as a major world power has created new national interests with regards to Middle East. Its relationship with Israel, combined with a growing concern over such issues as Iranian nuclearization and a desire to remain a prosperous, stable European neighbor with broad access to Middle Eastern markets, has thus far meshed well with general European and US interests. It is expected that the nature of these interests will continue to broaden as Germany takes a more active role in developing a general policy towards the Middle East.

Economic

Economic interests have the least saliency as a driver of German foreign policy of all issue areas involved with Germany and the Middle East. The Middle East has never played a substantial role in the German economy accounting for only around 3 percent of total German trade in the 1990s.[20] This trend continues to this day, with German exports into the region accounting for approximately 3.2 percent of all German exports and imports accounting for about 2 percent of total imports in 2005.[21] However, many nations within the region list Germany as one of their most important trade partners. In the states comprising the Arab League, Israel and

---

18   Steinmeier, F.-W., "Foreign Minister Steinmeier's Message to US Congress in the Atlantic Times," *The Atlantic Times* (July 27, 2006) (Special Issue).

19   Brunstetter, S. (2005), "A Changing View of Responsibility? German Security Policy in the Post-9/11 World," in Tom Lansford and Blagovest Tashev (eds), *Old Europe, New Europe and the US*, Aldershot: Ashgate Publishing.

20   Perthes, V. (2002), "German Economic Interests and Economic Co-Operation with the MENA Countries," in Volker Perthes, (ed.), *Germany and the Middle East: Interests and Options*, Berlin: Heinrich-Böll-Stiftung; Stiftung Wissenschaft und Politik.

21   Federal Statistical Office of Germany (2006), *Ranking of Germany's Trading Partners in Foreign Trade* (December 9), available at http://www.destatis.de/themen/e/thm_aussen.htm. To keep in context with Perthes above, these numbers represent the Arab League, Israel and Iran for 2005.

Iran, 14 of the 24 count Germany in their top five import partners, while six count Germany in their top five for exports. One of the most significant states in the region is Iran, which counts Germany as its number one source for imports at 13.8 percent, obviously making German involvement with the nuclear issue in Iran somewhat unusual. Libya counts Germany as its second most important trading partner for both imports and exports at 10.4 and 15.2 percent respectively. Jordan, Lebanon, Syria and Israel all count Germany as a major trade partner as well ranging from 4.1 percent to 8.3 percent of total trade. These trends compare to EU trade with the Middle East, perhaps highlighting the important role that Germany plays within the EU economy as well.

Thus, it is apparent that Germany does have the potential to exert some influence on the region using its economic power. However, it has been pointed out that despite substantial foreign aid into the region and substantial economic reliance, at least on the behalf of Middle Eastern nations, Germany tends to keep its political relationship separate from economic relations.[22] This holds true within the context of the Middle East with the possible exceptions of Israel and Palestine. Germany was one of the main donors for Israel up until around 1995 and subsequently became the top donor state for the Palestinian territories once it became politically viable to do so. It should be noted, however, that the Middle Eastern market is expected to grow substantially over the next several decades. With a growth rate of nearly 2.4 percent, the Middle East is expected to double in population in the next 30 years, which is the complete opposite of the European continent that continues to experience stagnated or declining population growth. While the tremendous population growth in the Middle East represents a great deal of potential for economic growth, it also represents a growing security risk. Middle Eastern states are overwhelmingly poor and politically unstable and are ill equipped to handle a booming population. As Europe's neighbor, the potential spill over from unrest in the Middle East could dramatically affect European domestic and political life.

Israel

Germany has struggled to walk a fine line between its "special relationship" with Israel and its broadening interests in the greater Middle East. Thus, even as it has grown toward a more aggressive, interest-driven foreign policy commensurate with its emerging position as a world leader as opposed to merely being a leading EU member state, this conflict of interests with regards to the Middle East have placed it in an uncomfortable position. The German-Israeli relationship has been traditionally strong and robust across the spectrum largely based on the historical legacy of Germany's "final solution" perpetrated against the Jewish people during the Second World War. Furthermore, both states share a great deal of Western values which has facilitated a tradition of cordial relations beginning at least since the opening of

---

22   Perthes.

full diplomatic relations between the two states in 1965 and their mutual interest in staving off the Soviet threat during the Cold War.[23]

Germany has fostered deeper ties with Israel in recent decades and a vibrant bilateral relationship developed that more than one German leader has claimed as a fundamental pillar of Berlin's foreign policy. Thus, not only has the German relationship with Israel been formed through accepting responsibility of past wrongs, it has thrived because of intense cultural, economic and political ties across all levels of German and Israeli society.

One of the fundamental aspects of German foreign policy towards the Middle East in general is the security of Israel as an independent state and the promotion of Israel's right to exist both regionally and internationally.[24] Every German Chancellor has reaffirmed this special status and the right of Israel to exist as an independent state, which is completely rational in light of Germany's historical circumstances. While the debate as to how peace can be achieved in the Middle East has shifted, the status of Israel is beyond question for Germany. German Chancellor Merkel, speaking before the American-Jewish Committee in 2006 expressed this sentiment: "Israel's right to exist must never be called into question.... The sine qua non for lasting peace is the unequivocal recognition of Israel's right to exist, the rejection of violence and compliance with all existing obligations."[25]

It is this unequal and mostly unquestioned (at least officially) relationship that has often prevented Germany from speaking against Israeli actions within the Middle East.[26] Germany does not want to jeopardize its global civilian power reputation through attacking Israeli policies. The United States has faced a similar conundrum, although the relevant factors are quite different. Germany is largely a passive power and has consistently held its tongue over Israeli military operations within Lebanon and Palestinian territories despite almost universal EU condemnation. The German hesitancy towards opposing Israel is not shared by the other EU member states that do not feel the same historical obligations.

However, Germany has constantly weighed its obligations to Israel against broader interests within the overall political milieu of the Middle East. Its status as a net energy importer demands that it pays close attention to world oil markets that are often greatly influenced by turmoil in the Middle East. As one of the world's largest economies, Germany remains interdependent with the Middle East and other volatile regions. Germany's biggest energy suppliers are Russia, Saudi Arabia, Iran,

---

23   The relationship extends before this point. However, the debate over reparations for German holocaust victims was more to assuage German guilt, normalize the German state for the Europeans, and to gain foreign aid for Israel than to develop friendly ties between the two states.

24   Kaim, M. and Lembcke, O., "Berlin Instead of Camp David: German Middle East Initiatives in the Light of Transatlantic Complementarity," *British Foreign Policy Resource Center*, available at http://www.bris.ac.uk/Depts/GRC/FP/kaim.htm.

25   Chancellor Angela Merkel at the 100th Anniversary Celebration of American Jewish Committee, Washington, DC, May 4, 2006.

26   Pallade, Y. (2005), *Germany and Israel in the 1990s and Beyond: Still a "Special Relationship"?* Frankfurt: Peter Lang GmbH.

Nigeria, Angola, Sudan, Chad, and Venezuela.[27] These are all states characterized by extreme instability and are often problematic to the international community.

The openness of internal borders and the proximity of Europe to the Middle East threaten potential issues with refugees, immigration and terrorism.[28] These issues have placed Germany in a position where it has to weigh its special status with Israel against its role as a state with interests within the Muslim world. The conflict between the two positions has often meant that Germany would lay back and support US efforts within the region while focusing on "targeted economic assistance, by opening up regional markets, and being involved in infrastructural measures."[29] This is a role that Germany excels at and one that Israel supports.

Further, Germany traditionally supports Israel within the EU and within the UN, which has resulted in a number of contentious situations against the other major continental power, France. Both sides have repeatedly faced off against each other, preventing a common EU position extending beyond a general call for peace in the region. However, with the unfortunate destruction of many aid projects funded by German financing and efforts, the continuing humanitarian crisis in the Palestinian territory has resulted in an increased willingness to seriously question Israeli military actions. In 2002, for example, Germany thwarted efforts within the EU to impose severe sanctions on Israel but willingly imposed arms sanctions. That same year a consensus amongst the Quartet on the Middle East (the EU, US, UN and Russia) for a two state solution, which signaled at least the possibility for real peace negotiations, coincided with a paper written by former German Foreign Minister Joschka Fischer supporting the use of German troops within the Middle East conflict as part of a multilateral force and suggesting that Israel was incapable of solving this issue on its own. These events seemed to highlight international agreement and a stronger and more independent German role.[30] Although these efforts seemingly did not achieve the desired objective, by the 2006 crisis in Lebanon, Germany was actively participating both militarily and diplomatically in seeking an end to the conflict.[31]

It is important to note that Germany has only accepted a maritime mission in Lebanon, thereby preserving its status as a mediator of choice. In this manner, Berlin has assuaged its international obligations, while performing a service that practically

27   Dehmer, D. (2007), "Where Does Germany Import its Oil From?," *Der Tagesspiegel*, January 10, available at http://www.theberlinpaper.com/home/43569.html.

28   Archick, K. (2005), "European Views and Polices Toward the Middle East" in *CRS Report RL31956*, March 9.

29   Schröder, G. (1998), "Because we Trust in Germany's Vitality," Policy Statement by Chancellor Schröder before the German Bundestag on November 10.

30   See "Policy Statement delivered by Federal Chancellor Gerhard Schröder on the Situation in the Middle East" and "The Situation in the Middle East—Speech by Federal Minister Fischer to the German Bundestag" both dated April 25, 2002.

31   See "Speech by Foreign Minister Steinmeier in the German Bundestag on the participation of German forces in the UNIFIL mission in Lebanon" dated September 19, 2006.

guarantees it will not face off against its Arab partners.[32] This policy has also allowed Germany to bypass the possible dilemma of deploying forces that might engage the Israel Defense Forces (IDF).[33] While the mission may be questionable in its design, the implications for Germany and its path toward a more active foreign policy are significant for its continued development as a reinvented world power.

Germany has seemingly shifted from unquestioned support of Israeli policies to doing what it believes is best for the Jewish state. It remains unclear if this is a permanent shift in the relationship between Israel and Germany, but it nevertheless shows a willingness on the part of Germany to change policy when necessary. Participating in multilateral peace keeping missions brings the civilian power attributes of Germany more in line with its humanitarian national interests and bolsters its reputation as a power committed to norms of human rights and international morality. However, the potential for accidental armed hostility between Israel and Germany became all too clear in October 2006 when Israeli F-16s flew dangerously close to a German warship.[34] The question of German commitment to its multilateral obligations remains unresolved, particularly when highlighted against the potential of German troops facing off against the IDF. Israel currently supports German participation in the UN mandated operation as it serves Israeli interests to have multilateral forces as a barrier between itself and Hezbollah.[35] If the situation changes, Germany may have to make a choice between its historical obligations to Israel and its desired role as a neutral player committed to the realization of peace between the two sides.[36]

The Palestinian Question

Juxtaposed against Germany's support for Israel has been a strong acceptance of the right of Palestinian self determination.[37] While seemingly at odds with Germany's relationship with Israel, the German position, and concurrently the EU position, on the subject is that a viable Palestinian state is conducive, and even essential, to lasting peace and prosperity for both Israelis and Palestinians.[38] A combination of three salient factors including Germany's core value of support for human rights issues, a great deal of sympathy within Europe and within the German domestic

---

32	Heumann, P. (2006), "No One Will Be Able to Stop Hezbollah," *Spiegel Online* (November 2).

33	Mulvey, S. (2006), "Lebanon Question Challenges Germany," *BBC News* (July 26).

34	"Germany, Israel Confirm Naval Vessel-Planes Incident," *Deutsche Presse-Agentur* (October 25, 2006).

35	Boyes, R and Beeston, R. (2006), "German Troops May Face Jews—as Part of Mission for Peace," *The Times*. August 16.

36	Gröhe, H., Moosbauer, C., Perthes, V. and Sterzing, C., "Evenhanded, Not Neutral: Points of Reference for a German Middle East Policy," in Perthes.

37	"Venice Declaration on the Middle East," European Community, June 12–13, 1980.

38	"Presidential Conclusions," *Berlin European Council of the European Union*, March 24–25, 1999.

population for the plight of the Palestinians, and a general abhorrence for the use of force has allowed the state to become a trusted mediator within the Muslim world and for Israel.[39]

Prior to the 1991 Madrid Conference and the 1993 Oslo Accords, Germany had little to no official contact with the Palestine Authority out of respect for its special relationship with Israel.[40] However, once both Israel and Palestine called for a deepening in German involvement, it accepted the call and quickly became the role model for economic support. Germany continued to allow the US and the UN to "play the role of patron to the peace process" and attempted to remain on the sidelines as much as possible.[41] The EU, with Germany taking a lead role, began to exert pressure on PLO leader Yasser Arafat in 1999 to take a more moderate approach to its dealings with Israel. Foreign Minister Fischer was instrumental in these mediation efforts. With the failure of President Clinton's Camp David talks in 2000 and the subsequent al-Aqsa Intifada, the wave of violence that occurred in the aftermath of the failure at Camp David, it became apparent that Germany and the EU would have to play an even more active role in the peace process. This is the environment in which Germany accepted its stronger leadership role as a stabilizing force in the region.[42]

With the death of Arafat in 2004 and the holding of democratic elections in Palestinian territories, there is a growing feeling that a solution may actually be possible.[43] A new window may have opened in the Israeli–Palestinian conflict. However, 2006 has proven to be one of the deadliest years of the Second Intifada with 683 lives lost, mostly by the Palestinians.[44] The growing unease with a Palestinian elected body headed by Hamas, the Palestinian Sunni Islamist organization that refuses to recognize Israel's right to exist, and the continued frustration over the failure of the Oslo Accords by both sides means that, while possible, a solution in the near future may simply be wishful thinking.

While Germany, the EU and the US still embrace the Quartet as the arbiter of choice for the conflict, there is reason to believe that this may not be an acceptable and effective formulation. The EU has not maintained a consistent foreign policy towards the Middle East nor is it trusted by Israel. The United States is tied down

---

39   In line with this sentiment, an unpublished October 2003 EU poll listed Israel as the greatest threat to international peace assumingly because of the way it was handling the Palestinian question. Peter Beaumont, "Israel Outraged as EU Poll Names it a Threat to Peace," *The Observer*, November 2, 2003.

40   Pallade, Y. (2005), *Germany and Israel in the 1990s and Beyond: Still a "Special Relationship"?* Frankfurt: Peter Lang GmbH.

41   Schröder.

42   In 2002, the year of the Idea Paper, 385 Israel and Palestinians were killed. Over the course of 2000–2006, B'Tselem counts 5,063 total deaths; B'Tselem Press Release, available at http://www.btselem.org/English/Statistics/Index.asp.

43   Hubel, H. (2006), "The Israeli-Palestinian Conflict in the EU–US Relationship," German and American Perspectives on Israel, Palestine, and the Middle East Conflict, American Institute for Contemporary German Studies.

44   *B'Tselem Press Release* (December 28, 2006), available at http://www.btselem.org/english/Press_Releases/20061228.asp.

with its own Middle East issues in Iraq and is not trusted by the Palestinians. Germany is viewed as a mediator by both sides but seems unwilling to work outside of the confines of its institutional partners. This situation may change with German EU presidency in the first half of 2007.[45] It is expected that Germany will use this opportunity to renew the peace process and revitalize the Quartet.[46]

Iranian Threats to Israel

While Germany views a solution to the Israel-Palestinian issue as the cornerstone for solving the Middle East dilemma, it is the continuing confrontation with Iran over its nuclear ambitions that may pose the biggest threat to European peace and stability, and to Germany's desire to maintain an open dialogue with all of its Middle Eastern partners. Even though its position concerning Iraq has improved its reputation within the region, it finds itself having to choose between Israel and an Iranian regime apparently bent on Israel's destruction. The choice may appear to be straightforward, as Germany has traditionally supported Israel. However, the policy decisions available to Germany leave little room to maneuver from a diplomatic standpoint. This is not a position that Germany has readily accepted or finds completely agreeable.

Germany has consistently used "constructive engagement" as its major foreign policy tool.[47] Germany has actively accepted the idea that Iran could be moderated through a policy of small trust building steps instead of embarking on a policy of condemnation and avoidance like the US had tended to pursue. To this effort, Germany was the first Western nation to send its foreign minister to Iran for a state visit in 1984. After the end of the 1980–1988 Iran–Iraq War, Germany quickly became Iran's largest trade partner and adamantly discouraged the US approach of diplomatic isolation. In the past, Germany has found sanctions against the Iranian regime to be counterproductive to the overall goal of promoting democratization and encouraging state normalization.

The recent upsurge in anti-Semitic rhetoric by Iranian President Ahmadinejad, coupled with the fear of nuclear proliferation in the region, has forced Germany to question its policy of choice with Iran. Current diplomatic efforts have been extremely ineffective and Iran refuses to cease its nuclear program. After all, it is difficult to interpret "Israel must be wiped off the map" in any other way than the obvious.[48] Germany has developed a policy under the assumption that Iran is a rational state actor, which may be a grave mistake as long as the Ahmadinejad regime is in power. Coupled with the history of Iranian deception concerning its

---

45   *Germany 2007—Presidency of the European Union*, available at http://www. eu2007.de/en.

46   "Germany at EU Helm Seeks to Revive Mid-east Quartet," *Deutsche Welle* (December 28, 2006), available at http://www.dw-world.de/dw/article/0,2144,2292736,00. html.

47   Gerschoffer, M.A. (1998), *Germany's Iran Policy: Beyond "Critical Dialogue*," Monterey, CA: Naval Post Graduate School.

48   "Ahmadinejad: Wipe Israel Off Map," *Aljazeera* (October 28, 2005), available at http://english.aljazeera.net/news/archive/archive?ArchiveId=15816.

nuclear ambitions, fear amongst the Western powers of a renewed revolutionary Iranian spirit is well warranted.[49]

Germany has once again accepted its role within the confines of a multilateral framework, the EU3, a collective negotiating strategy designed as an alternative to US engagement with Iran. Germany, France, and Great Britain have taken the lead in negotiating a settlement with Iran through diplomatic efforts. Germany has accepted that sanctions may be a necessary tool, although it has completely discounted any possibility of force.[50] UN Security Council Resolution 1737, passed in late December 2006, was a mild version of a draft proposal endorsed by the EU3 some two months earlier. Despite its watered down form, the resolution should be recognized as a continuation of a German policy trend focusing on what is essentially continuous warnings coupled with a demand for negotiation. However, the shift into accepting sanctions against the regime is an unusually bold step for a Germany that has been reticent in imposing any restrictions on Iran. It can be assumed that Germany will embrace even harder measures if the threat from Iran continues to grow unchecked. The Iranian nuclear issue has persisted for some time, most likely because Iran believes it can negotiate from a position of strength with the US bogged down in Iraq and the EU unwilling to impose real sanctions.

It is striking that Germany seemingly has to choose amongst several bad options. Allowing a nuclear Iran may lead to increased tensions within the region and the possibility of another war over Israel. Escalation of German denial of Iran's nuclear "rights" may deepen the wedge between the West and the Middle East without the benefit of Germany as a mediator. If Berlin does nothing, it will have shown the inadequacies of its policy methods. An effective solution to the Iranian nuclear issue must involve the EU, US, and the other Middle Eastern states. If Iran is able to eventually construct a nuclear weapon, it can only serve to weaken peace and security efforts in the region.

United States

The US–German relationship has been one of lasting continuity and prosperity since the end of the Second World War. Both states have remained staunch political allies and each considers the other as one of their most important trading partners. The recent war in Iraq has strained US-German relations, although Chancellor Merkel has repeatedly stated that she wishes to rejuvenate the partnership and reverse the negative trend that has developed over the past few years.[51] Although Germany will undoubtedly continue to encounter decisions that may require a foreign policy divergent from US interests, more often than not it will be advantageous for the

---

49   "E3/EU Statement on the Iran Nuclear Issue, Berlin," German Embassy, Washington, DC. January 12, 2006.

50   "Germany Rejects Iran Military Options," *Reuters* (August 14, 2005), available at http://www.abc.net.au/news/newsitems/200508/s1437072.htm.

51   Knowlton, B. (2007), "Merkel presses Bush on Mideast and Trade," *International Herald Tribune* (January 4), available at http://www.iht.com/articles/2007/01/05/europe/web.0105merkel.php.

two states to maintain cooperative policies as global leaders in the international community.

While Germany has typically maintained a passive foreign policy, such as disagreeing with the war in Iraq, it has been united with the US in opposition to Iranian nuclear ambitions. Chancellor Merkel stated in January of 2006 that Germany "will certainly not be intimidated by a country such as Iran."[52] Merkel understands that a nuclearized Iran is dangerous not only for the US, but also for Europe, regardless of economic considerations. While Berlin maintains a general abhorrence to the use of force, there is a strong possibility that it would get on board with military intervention in Iran if diplomatic efforts by the Quartet continue to stall. Radical Islam is spreading in a number of major European cities, much to the dismay of Germany and the EU, and combating global terrorism is a chief concern on both sides of the Atlantic.

The US has more successfully integrated its Muslim population into mainstream society compared to Europe, where minority groups are often marginalized, with the riots in France in late 2005 serving as one of the more recent expressions of the outrage felt in many communities. Moreover, the Madrid bombings showed Europeans that Americans were not the only Westerners subject to al-Qaeda hostility. German investigators have worked closely with the US on anti-terrorism efforts, as Hamburg proved to be one of Europe's "Islamist hotbeds" and was an operations center for some of the 9/11 hijackers.[53] The growing anti-American sentiment in Europe, and among its Muslim communities in particular, makes it increasingly difficult for Germany and other states to maintain close relations with Israel without upsetting Middle Eastern diaspora communities. Again, it may prove to be extremely difficult for Germany to continue its evenhanded approach towards the Middle East. Continued US-German political and economic cooperation on foreign policy concerns is advantageous for both states in their relations with the Middle East.

Conclusion

Germany has proven reluctant to venture too far outside of its civilian power trappings particularly when it comes to the Middle East. There are signs that this may be changing. Its recent deployment to Lebanon, its willingness to impose sanctions on Iran, and its readiness to question its traditional partners of choice seem to reflect an emerging foreign policy independent of general EU and US interests. If this means a defining policy towards the Middle East remains to be seen. As of 2006, Germany has successfully negotiated past the need to openly renege on its commitments to any particular side, although maintaining an evenhanded approach may become increasingly difficult. With its engagement in Lebanon, Berlin has appeased both the Lebanese and Israel while thus far risking little of its pacifist reputation. With the

---

52   Amanpour, C. and Burns, C. (2006), "Bush, Merkel united on Iran's nuclear threat," *CNN World Online*, January 13, available at http://www.cnn.com/2006/WORLD/meast/01/13/iran.nuclear/index.html.

53   "The Hamburg Connection," *BBC News* (August 19, 2005), available at http://news.bbc.co.uk/1/hi/world/europe/2349195.stm.

debate over the Palestinian territories, it has continued an approach of multilateral engagement that respects the right to exist for both parties. With the debate over Iran, it has proven more willing to accept sanctions but has not yet had to commit to drastically altering its pre-existing stance.

In all of these cases, Germany could face what amounts to an ultimatum against its status as a moral power in the world. Does it continue to side with Israel? Or does it take a position more concerned with overall regional demands? With German forces in the region, Lebanon could easily turn into a checkmate in which Germany will either have to engage the IDF or not. The choice is easier regarding Iran because of the heated rhetoric of the Iranian leadership. However, Germany's alignment with the West in general on this issue ultimately may change the perceptions of Middle Eastern states away from Germany as a mediator power. In each case, Germany may have to choose over competing moral obligations. Moreover, pursuing a foreign policy completely at odds with the EU and US may be overly ambitious at this juncture.

Germany has therefore opted to couch its policies in the international organizations with which it so readily defines itself. Thus, current German foreign policy decisions tend to have the cover of international legitimacy. In a world in which morality is often defined by majority opinion, it is easy to go against a United States that is seemingly clearly in the minority. Former Chancellor Schröder even used German opposition to the US invasion of Iraq as a primary theme in his 2002 reelection campaign. It is becoming easier to question Israel when the international community seems to agree on what an effective solution would look like, yet the violence continues. However, what appears to be an easy choice with Iran could ultimately lead to a future that all parties fear. Once Iran has successfully developed a nuclear weapon, diplomatic efforts would become all but irrelevant. The German phoenix is not hatching into a world in which its choices are easy, although it is not alone and will continue to enjoy broad support from the EU and its partners abroad.

In sum, even as Germany seems to be coming into its own on the international front, the Middle East may be its ultimate undoing. It would be tragic to see Germany become a new "Reluctant Sheriff" in a world in which sheriffs are no longer popular.[54] However, it may not have a choice in the matter. Germany's obligations to Israel and to its own interests of morality, prosperity, peace and stability require it to actively participate in international efforts toward any solution that would allow those goals to come to fruition.

---

54   Haass.

Chapter 4

US–Russian Competition in the Middle East: Convergences and Divergences in Foreign Security Policy

Mira Duric and Tom Lansford

Introduction

Any examination of Russo–American interaction in the Middle East must be assessed within the context of past American–Soviet and contemporary competition in the region between the two powers. Alliances and patterns of cooperation created in the Middle East during the Cold War continued to influence relations between the former superpowers in the post-bipolar era. The dramatic shifts in international diplomacy following the break up of the Soviet Union, and the post-September 11, 2001 global system, including the rise of Islamic fundamentalism and the US-led global war on terror, have mainly reinforced the existing foreign and security policies of both states toward the region.

The end of the Cold War and the 1991 Persian Gulf War inaugurated a period in which security competition between the two nations decreased, only to be replaced by increasing economic rivalry between Moscow and Washington. Meanwhile, divergences over the US dual containment policy toward Iran and Iraq reduced regional security cooperation in the 1990s, a trend that accelerated with the 2002 US-led invasion of Iraq. President Vladimir Putin endeavored to utilize the insurgency in Iraq and the broader dissatisfaction with US policy among Arab to enhance Russia's influence in the Middle East. Concurrently, Moscow has also attempted to enhance its economic and security ties with traditional US allies Israel and Turkey. Russia's renewed drive for influence in the Middle East is a facet of the country's effort to regain its former global role and promises to reintensify its twentieth century rivalry with the United States.

The Historic Legacy

Since the Second World War, the Middle East has been an area where the proxy conflict between Washington and Moscow was manifested through the pursuit of regional allies. US policy was based on the support of key strategic partners, Turkey, Iran and Israel. Meanwhile, post-Second World War Soviet policy was expansionistic for two reasons. First, Moscow sought to protect its southern borders by installing pro-

Soviet regimes along its periphery. Second, successive Soviet leaders believed they could exploit growing anti-colonialism among the Arab populations to undermine the Western powers, particularly Great Britain.[1] The result was that the Middle East remained a "key" area of interest for Soviet policy throughout the Cold War.[2] The initial efforts to gain influence in the region were rebuffed through the practical and potential implications of the 1947 Truman Doctrine (including military aid to Iran and Turkey) and the 1957 Eisenhower Doctrine.[3] In the aftermath of the Suez Crisis, Soviet policy increasingly embraced Arab nationalism in an effort to establish an alternative pole to the pro-Israeli stance of successive US administrations. The regime of Nikita Khrushchev reduced its ideological efforts and instead adopted an increasing anti-Israeli stance on regional issues. The divergence between the two superpowers was highlighted during the Six Day War (June 5–10, 1967), in which the US supported Israel while the Soviets were pro-Arab. By the late 1960s, the Soviets had 2,000 military advisers in the area, mainly in Iraq, and provided more than $1 billion in military aid to various states as inducements for closer cooperation.

The US and Soviet Union supported different sides in the frequent clashes between Egypt and Israel, following Tel Aviv's victory in the Six Day War. On the Jewish festival of Yom Kippur in 1973, Egypt and Syria launched a surprise attack on Israeli forces. Predictably, Washington supported Israel, while the Soviets backed the attacking Arab states.[4] During the 1979 Iranian Revolution, the USSR supported the overthrow of the Shah. Soviet leaders then watched the subsequent hostage crisis in Tehran with bemusement. The inability of the Carter administration to resolve the incident was perceived as proof on the impotence of the United States and contributed to the Soviet decision to invade Afghanistan. However relations with Tehran deteriorated rapidly, and, by 1983, the Iranian Communist Party had been banned and its leadership arrested. Meanwhile, the Carter administration attempted to convince moderate Arab states that the Soviets were the main threat to regional stability, even as Islamic radicals increasingly embraced a holy war against modernity (which included the United States).[5] The Soviet invasion of Afghanistan undermined Moscow's standing in the region and drew thousands of Muslim fighters

---

1   Lesperance, W. and Lansford, T. (1999), *Untying the Gordian Knot: Great Power Policies in the Persian Gulf*, Needham Heights, MA: Pearson, 20.

2   Smith, M.A. (2000), "Russia and the Far Abroad," *Conflict Studies Research Centre* (December 21), available at http://www.da.mod.uk/CSRC/documents/Russian/ F72#search=%22Russo-US%20competition%20in%20the%20middle%20east%22.

3   The Truman Doctrine provided economic and military aid for states in the region fighting communist insurgencies. For a detailed examination on the implications of the Truman Doctrine, see McGhee, G.C. (1990), The *US–Turkish–NATO Middle East Connection: How the Truman Doctrine Contained the Soviets in the Middle East*, New York: St. Martin's. The Eisenhower Doctrine was designed to contain both Soviet influence and the spread of Arab nationalism; see Yaqub, S. (2004), *Containing Arab Nationalism: The Eisenhower Doctrine and the Middle East*, Chapel Hill: University of North Carolina Press.

4   Young, J.W. (1993), *The Longman Companion to the Cold War And Detente 1941–91*, London: Longman, 130–1, 135–6.

5   Farber, D. (2006), *Taken Hostage: The Iran Hostage Crisis and America's First Encounter with Radical Islam*, Princeton: Princeton University Press, 5–6.

to South Asia to combat the occupation. Iraq became the only state with substantial security cooperation with Moscow. Nonetheless, Moscow continued to challenge American primacy in the region and opposed the US-led Western intervention in Lebanon (1982–84), and the US air strike on Libya (April 1986).

Through the 1980s, Soviet security policy in the Middle East was expressed mainly through arms sales which served to provide badly needed foreign currency to Moscow and buy goodwill among the Arab capitals. Even nominally pro-Western states such as Kuwait purchased Soviet weaponry. By 1988, Moscow had established military, commercial and/or diplomatic relations with all states in the region. However, Soviet arms sales and weapons transfers also produced a backlash among some states that objected to Moscow's arming of their neighbors and rivals.[6] The Soviets were able to become the region's main supplier of weapons as a result of restrictions on US sales and broader policy constraints on arms sales in the Middle East in an effort to prevent arms races in the area.[7] Thus, even as governments in the region condemned the continuing Soviet occupation of Afghanistan, and provided both tacit and overt support for the anti-Soviet mujahideen, various Middle East states continued to purchase arms from Moscow. The Soviets were criticized by some Arab leaders for destabilizing the region through arms transfers.[8]

In 1989, a state visit to the Soviet Union by Iranian Parliamentary Speaker (and future President) Ali Akbar Hashemi-Rafsanjani marked a turning point in relations between Tehran and Moscow. Rafsanjani's foray was reciprocated by Soviet Foreign Minister Eduard Shevardnadze who initiated a series of new diplomatic and military initiatives, including an agreement in principle for cooperation on the development of nuclear technology.

The Post-Cold War Era

The end of the Cold War ushered in a brief period of cooperation between Moscow and Washington. Both powers supported Iraq in the Iran–Iraq War in order to contain Iran. Both nations also condemned Iraq's invasion of Kuwait in August 1990. Following intense diplomatic efforts by the administration of George H. W. Bush, the regime of Mikhail Gorbachev lent its support to the US-brokered coalition against Saddam Hussein during the 1991 Persian Gulf War after Soviet efforts to mediate the conflict failed. The Soviet Union voted in favor of UN Security Council Resolution 678 which authorized the use of force against Iraq (China abstained, while Cuba and Yemen voted against the measure). However, the liberation of Kuwait marked the high point of US-Russian cooperation in the region.

After the war, there was renewed competition between the two former Cold War adversaries in arms sales. The military success of the American-led coalition during

---

6   Yetiv, S. and Lansford, T. (1998), "The Third World in the 1990s: Global Interaction in Southwest Asia in an Increasingly Interconnected World," *The Journal of Conflict Studies*, 28/1, 74.

7   Ibid.

8   See, for instance, Saivetz, C.R. (1989), *The Soviet Union and the Gulf in the 1980s*, Boulder: Westview Press.

the liberation of Kuwait encouraged countries to increasingly seek US weapons and security guarantees. By 1992, the US dominated the region's weapons sales, accounting for almost 50 percent of total sales through the 1990s.[9] Moscow lost its main customer in Iraq, but was able to renew arms sales to Iran, including a $10 billion deal to supply aircraft, main battle tanks, and surface-to-air missiles.[10] Henceforth, Iran became Russia's main arms market as the tensions between the two states diminished. In addition to access to Tehran's lucrative arms market, Russia was able to gain tacit Iranian consent for its campaign against Islamic rebel in Chechnya. Tehran declined requests from the Chechen separatists for arms or monetary support and refused to criticize Russia's efforts to suppress the insurgency. Iran even offered repeatedly to mediate the crisis, offers that were rebuffed by Russia.[11]

The lower costs of Russian weapons prompted Arab states to increase weapons purchases in the 1990s and Moscow significantly diversified its customer base to include states such as Kuwait, the United Arab Emirates and Oman. Russia also signed a range of bilateral security cooperation agreements with Middle Eastern states. While Russia's Middle East policy was constrained in the late 1980s and early 1990s due to its internal difficulties, the administration of Boris Yeltsin increasingly devoted more attention to the region which was seen as an area in which Moscow could compete with the US and the European Union. The reassertion of Russian power in the Middle East followed the appointment of Yevgeny Primakov as foreign minister in 1995.[12] Primakov launched a series of commercial and diplomatic efforts to enhance Russia's influence in the region and he was well-received by Arab states and his anti-Israeli stance.

Beginning in the mid-1990s, Russia endeavored to use its security ties in the region to enhance its diplomatic and economic ties. After the Persian Gulf War, Moscow re-established diplomatic ties with Saudi Arabia and continued to improve relations with Iran, including military sales and expanded assistance with Tehran's fledging nuclear program. One result of better Russian-Iranian relations was the withdrawal of Iranian support for Islamic insurgents in pro-Russian regimes in Central Asia.[13] While the United States officially pursued democratization in the Middle East, Russia's embraced a less idealistic goal: stability. Alexei Vassiliev labeled Moscow's new policy as "pragmatism."[14] For instance, in 1994, when Hussein deplored troops along the border with Kuwait, Russia used its influence

---

9   Grimmett, R. (1996), "Conventional Arms Transfers to Developing Nations, 1988–1995," *Congressional Research Service* 96-677 F, Washington, D.C.: CRS, 2.

10   "Land of Crisis and Upheaval," *Jane's Defence Weekly* (July 30, 1994), 29.

11   Heinlein, P. (1999), "Chechnya Update," *Voice of America* (November 28).

12   Feldman, S. (1988), "The Return of the Russian Bear?" *Jaffee Centre for Strategic Studies*, Tel Aviv University, March, available at http://www.tau.ac.il/jcss/sa/v1n1p1_n.html, 1. Yevgeny Primakov was Foreign Minister (1996–1998) and Prime Minister (1998–1999).

13   Naumkin, V.V. (1997), "Russia, the Arms Trade, and Military Political Stability in the Middle East," in J. Pierre Andrews and Dmitri V. Trenin (eds), *Russia in the World Arms Trade*, Washington, D.C.: Carnegie Endowment, 69.

14   See Vassiliev, A. (1993), *Russian Policy in the Middle East: From Messianism to Pragmatism*, Dryden, NY: Ithaca Press.

with Baghdad to resolve the crisis.[15] Moscow later opposed US-led strikes on Iraq in 1998 in response to interference with UN weapons inspections. Russian leaders also denounced the management of Clinton's new policy of regime change in Iraq.

The dual containment policy of the US was perceived as creating trade opportunities for Moscow. Economic relations between Tehran and Moscow increased through the 1990s, while Russian leaders signed a range of economic deals with Iraq to be implemented should sanctions be lifted. Meanwhile, Moscow inked a range of economic agreements with other states in the Middle East, covering sectors from transportation to agriculture.[16] Russia also sought technical assistance and investment from the Middle East in developing its domestic energy production capabilities.[17] In return, Middle Eastern states have provided Russia with considerable loans and underwritten Moscow's foreign debt. Between 1991 and 1995, Kuwait lent Russia more than $1 billion, while other states in the region provided an additional $2 billion.[18] In 1991, the Middle East supplied 5 percent of Russia's total foreign investment, a figure that steadily increased.[19] There was also an increase in private investment by Middle East firms. For instance Gulf Russia, a UAE company, spent $6 million to acquire the rights to develop energy fields in Russia, in the Stavropol region in 1993.[20] In addition, in 1996, an Omani company began working with Russian and Kazakh firms to develop a pipeline from Kazakhstan.[21]

US–Russian Rivalry in the 1990s

Through the Cold War, and once again in the 1990s, US–Russian competition in the Middle East was characterized by the "Great Game" paradigm as described by Vaughn Shannon: "world powers vied for control of vital trade routes, sea lanes, and oil fields in the Middle East."[22] The Great Game continued despite a lack of substantial policy disagreements. The two former Cold War enemies had more commonalities through the 1990s than divergences. Policy toward Iran and Iraq were the notable differences; beyond those two exceptions, the two countries cooperated on a range of issues, including efforts to resolve the Arab–Israeli conflict and suppress terrorism. The US even supported Russia's bilateral security ties with states such as Kuwait

---

15   Gornostayev, D. (1994), "Russia's Difficult Partners," *CDPP* 46/1, 12; and Kondrashov, S. (1994), "Kozyrev's Gulf Diplomacy Gets Differing Ratings; What Russia Wanted to Prove in the Iraq Affair," *CDPP* 46/1, 12.

16   Sigov, Y. (1994), "Russian Business Slowly Moves Toward the Persian Gulf," *Moscow News*, November 1, 8.

17   "Gulf Russia," *The Oil and Gas Journal*, 91(20), May (1993), 27; "Pipes and Drums," *The Economist* (November 23, 1996), 7.

18   Yetiv and Lansford, 79.

19   Skibinskaya, I. (1993), "Arab Petrodollars Flow into CIS," *Moscow News*, August 20.

20   "Gulf Russia," 27.

21   "Pipes and Drums," 7.

22   Shannon, V.P. (2003), "The Politics of the Middle East Peace Process and the War on Terror," in Patrick Hayden, Tom Lansford, and Robert P. Watson, (eds), *America's War on Terror*, Aldershot: Ashgate Publishing Limited, 80.

and Oman. Nonetheless, the mistrust which characterized the Cold War lingered into the aftermath of the conflict and despite a range of incentives for cooperation between the two states, tensions continued.[23]

Through 1993, Russia supported the US containment policy towards Iraq. However, President Boris Yeltsin (under pressure from nationalists and communists in the Duma) dropped his support for the United Nations embargo on the Saddam regime and increasingly criticized the US-led air strikes on Iraq that were prompted by various provocations, including the failed 1993 effort to assassinate former President Bush during a visit to Kuwait. By 1994 Moscow began actively calling for the lifting of UN Security Council sanctions on Iraq and launched a diplomatic effort to gain support for the removal of trade restrictions.[24] Yeltsin had three goals or interests for this Russian policy: 1) to demonstrate to both, the world and the Duma, that Russia was still a major power in the Middle East; 2) to regain or "collect" Iraq's $7 billion debt to Russia; and 3) to expand opportunities for Russian oil and gas companies to acquire business contracts with Iraq. In mid-February 1996, Iraq and Russia signed an agreement for oil and the "training of Iraqi oil specialists."[25] Moscow was initially the main purchaser for Iraqi oil under the UN-sanctioned "Oil for Food" program. In addition, in March 1997, Russian firms reached an agreement on a $3.8 billion contract for exploration of the Western Kurna oil field.[26]

During the Iraqi crisis of October–November 1997, when the Saddam regime refused to allow specific individual UN weapons inspectors into the country because of their nationality, Moscow called for negotiations with the United States and UN. In a success for Russian diplomacy, Russian Foreign Minister Yevgeny Primakov formulated an agreement whereby the US weapons inspectors excluded from Iraq were allowed entry in exchange for a "vague" pledge to lift sanctions if the regime continued to cooperate with the world body. In January 1998, Saddam Hussein repudiated on the agreement and eventually ordered the withdrawal of all weapons inspectors. Russia intervened to solve the crisis, as the US and Great Britain increased troop deployments in the Persian Gulf. Whilst, the UN did allow Iraq to sell more oil, Russian diplomatic activity, as Robert O. Freedman points out, "achieved little in getting sanctions lifted."[27]

The 1998 Iraq crisis highlighted the tensions between presidents Yeltsin and Clinton. Yeltsin increasingly opposed the sanctions against Iraq and sought to bolster

23   Oliker, O. and Yefimova, N., "Carnegie–Rand Workshop on the Future of the Greater Middle East and the Prospects for US–Russian Partnership," Occasional Paper, RAND: Center for Russia and Eurasia and Center for Middle East Public Policy and Carnegie Moscow Center: Carnegie Endowment for International Peace (July 2004), OP-118-CMEPP/CRE, available at http://carnegie.ru/en/pubs/media/88860P118.pdf, 24.

24   Freedman, R.O. (1998), "Russia's Middle East Ambitions," The Middle East Forum: Promoting American Interests, *The Middle East Quarterly* 5/3, available at http://www.meforum.org/article/405, 3.

25   Freedman, R.O. (2001), "Russian Policy Toward the Middle East Under Yeltsin and Putin," in *Jerusalem Letter/Viewpoints: Centre for Public Affairs 461*, September 2, available at http://www.jcpa.org/jl/vp461.htm, 12.

26   Feldman, 4.

27   Freedman, "Russia's Middle East Ambitions," 4.

Russia's influence in the regime. Meanwhile, the US Congress enacted the Iraqi Breach of International Obligations Act in August (1998), which authorized Clinton to take all appropriate action to force Iraq to comply with its international obligations. This was followed on October 31 by the Iraq Liberation Act which made regime change in Iraq a foreign policy goal of the United States. On the eve of Anglo-American air strikes against Iraq in December 1998, Russia criticized the United States' threat of force and called for the removal of sanctions on Baghdad.[28] Following the US attacks, the Duma condemned the strikes as an act of "international terrorism" in a resolution that passed 394 to 1.[29] Russia also recalled its ambassador to the United States, an action not taken since the height of the Cold War. Nonetheless, Moscow's reaction could be mainly viewed as an expression of domestic politics. It also followed the general pattern of response common during the Soviet period. Nikolai Sokov described the Russian response to Iraq in 1998 in the following terms:

> Historically, the Russian reaction to international crises has always been excessively emotional, bordering on overreaction. In this sense, the Iraqi crisis repeats a familiar pattern that is well over a hundred years old: you vent your feelings right away and plan policy later. This means that in a few weeks there will probably be a cooling-off period, when policy will be gauged to match the actual events more precisely. Of course, the political damage will already have been done, and there is little question that succumbing to emotions will be, as always, counterproductive from the standpoint of the long-term interests of Russia.[30]

Tensions over Iran also separated the two countries through the 1990s. Since the death of Ayatollah Ruhollah Khomeini in 1989, US–Iranian relations have been contentious. Iran's mullah's essentially defined their foreign policy through opposition to Washington and successive American administrations. While Tehran has chafed under continuing US economic sanctions, Washington has accused Iran of attempting to undermine the regional allies in the Middle East, including Saudi Arabia, and waging a terrorist campaign against the Israeli-Palestinian peace process. The US has also charged Iran with sponsoring the bombing of the American military housing complex, Khobar Towers, in Saudi Arabia in 1996 in which 20 were killed and 372 wounded.[31]

By 1992, Russia was Tehran's main arms supplier, providing a range of military equipment, including main battle tanks (MBT), armored personnel carriers (APC), and aircraft. Russia even negotiated an agreement to allow Iran to produce local versions of the T-72 MBT and various APCs under a licensing agreement. Russian technicians are employed in Iran's missile program and are reported to have worked on Iran nuclear weapons effort. In 1993, Iran became the first country in the Persian

---

28   Heinlein, P. (1998), "Russia/Iraq," *Voice of America,* (November 11), available at http://www.fas.org/news/iraq/1998/11/12/981112-iraq05.htm.

29   Sokov, N. (1998), "Russian Reaction, Day Two: Recalling the Ambassador," *Iraq Special Collection,* Center for Nonproliferation Studies (December 18), available at http://cns.miis.edu/research/iraq/rus21298.htm.

30   Ibid.

31   Pollack and Takeyh, 20.

Gulf with submarines when it purchased two Russian-made Kilo-class diesel submarines and eight mini-subs (four other submarines, including another Kilo-class vessel, were subsequently purchased). Russia provided training for the crews of the vessels and technical assistance for the Iranian Navy as it began construction of locally built submarine, based on the Kilo subs in 2005.

US–Iranian relations improved briefly in the late 1990s and early 2000s, as Washington and Tehran tacitly cooperated on issues such as the Balkans and Afghanistan, showing that they have the same interest in the war on terror, namely the suppression of Sunni Islamic terrorist groups. However, as Olga Oliker and Natasha Yefimova point out, there are "insufficient grounds for real rapprochement."[32] American and Russian policy differences over Iran remain rooted in Washington's effort to contain Tehran, and Moscow's policy of economic and military engagement. Of particular concern to American policymakers is Russo-Iranian nuclear cooperation. The Clinton administration unsuccessfully attempted to stop the Russia sale of two light-water reactors. Russian policymakers asserted that the sale would not accelerate Iran's nuclear proliferation efforts and could serve as leverage for concessions from the United States in other issue areas.[33] However, with the economic and military sanctions on Iraq, Iran emerged as Russia's main ally in the Middle East. One of Yeltsin's chief political advisers noted that "Iran can be a good and strategic ally of Russia at the global level to check the hegemony of third parties and keep the balance of power."[34]

Putin's Renewed Pragmatism

Russia's guiding policies in the Middle East continued to be based on pragmatism, including its interaction with the United States. This economic and security realism continued, and even expanded, under Putin. From 1999 onward, Putin's Middle East policy was guided by interests and calculated cost-benefit analysis. Oliker and Yefimova assert that Russia had "more limited political, economic, military, and diplomatic tools," and had "much less interest in the Middle East" than the United States.[35] Russia's contemporary interaction with countries in the strategically vital Middle East is based on four main interests: 1) securing its traditional strategic interests; 2) restoring its international diplomatic influence, 3) balancing the United States when appropriate for Russian interests, and 4) pursuing economic development, including energy and trade.

The Middle East is geographically close to Russia. There is the perception in Moscow that the "near broad" (Soviet Union's former republics) directly affect Russian stability and security. Hence, the Middle East can affect the Caucasus and

---

32　　Oliker and Yefimova, 12.

33　　Buszynski, L. (1995), "Russia and the West: Toward Renewed Geopolitical Rivalry," *Survival* 37, 120; or Foye, S. (1995), "A Hardened Stance on Foreign Policy," *Transition* 9, 9 June, 36–40.

34　　Quoted in *Tehran IRNA*, in Foreign Broadcast Information Service (FBIS): *NES*, March 8, 1995, 51.

35　　Oliker and Yefimova, 5.

Central Asia, which then affects Russia itself.[36] Russia's motivation, therefore, is to stabilize both the military-political situation in the Middle East and in the former Soviet Republics. Concurrently, Russia tries to limit Turkey's power and influence in its southern tier near abroad, Central Asia and Caucasus, for the same reason.[37]

Turkey is perceived as a regional threat to Russian influence and a country that cannot be wooed away from the United States because of the long history of the relationship between the two allies. Turkey's control of access to the Black Sea is especially significant to Moscow which continues to seek guarantees for Russian shipping through the Mediterranean and access to the Middle East for Russian goods, including arms and energy supplies to states such as Syria.[38] Russia has also complained of Turkey's arming the Chechen rebels, which has threatened Moscow's control over the entire North Caucasus.[39] Nonetheless, Turkey is Russia's main trading partner in the Middle East; bilateral trade amounts to $10–12 billion annually.

In order to retain its market share in weapons sales and arms transfers, Putin's Russia seeks a role in regional security.[40] Both Yeltsin and Putin envisaged a broad collective security system in the Persian Gulf with involvement by both Russia and the United States. For example, M. A. Smith reminds us that Primakov, in October 1997, "outlined a codex of behavior in the sphere of security" that could form the "basis of such a system."[41] Putin understands the necessity of partnership with the United States on a broad level, as Moscow lacks the influence to resolve the Arab–Israeli conflict without American participation.[42] Moscow also accepts that it will not have the same diplomatic influence with Tel Aviv that Washington possesses. But Russia seeks to bring pressure on the Arab states, mainly Syria and Iran, to participate, or at least not openly undermine, the Arab–Israeli peace process. Involvement in regional negotiations serves as one of means by which Russia can bolster its diplomatic prestige. In addition, the efforts of the United States to maintain stability in the region benefit Russia and other outside powers, such the European Union states, without forcing upon them the diplomatic or fiscal costs of significant military deployments. Meanwhile, Washington has "little leverage" to pressure Moscow to abandon arms sales to the Middle East.[43] Consequently, Russia remains free to pursue weapons sales and arms transfers and rely on the United States to maintain regional peace.

---

36   Grummon, S. (1995), "Russia's Ambitions in the Persian Gulf," The Middle East Forum Promoting American Interests, *The Middle East Quarterly* 11/1, available at http://www.meforum.org/article/247, 1.

37   Feldman, 7.

38   Smith, 21–22; See also Baklanov, A. (1999), "Blizhnyy Vostok; regional'naya bezopastnost' i interesy Rossii," Tsentr Mezhdunarodnykh Otnosheniy MGIMO 15, 7–8.

39   All information from Freedman, "Russia's Middle East Ambitions," 6.

40   Grummon, 1; Russia wants interaction and cooperation, "to ensure security and stability," see Smith, 2–3.

41   Smith, 23–24.

42   Ibid.

43   "Moscow Muscles Its Way Back into the Middle East," *Middle East* 356, 20–21 May 2005.

Russia's Role in the War on Terror

The terrorist attacks of September 11, 2001 focused US foreign and security policy on the Middle East and reenergized the Great Game between Washington and Moscow. Russia's role has been complicated by its history in the region, particularly the legacy of the invasion of Afghanistan. At an official level, many states continue to view Russian interaction in the regimes with suspicion. Al Qaeda leader Osama bin Laden and the leadership of many radical Islamic groups firmly believe they were responsible for the demise of the Soviet Empire, that "the Soviet Union was defeated not in the Cold War waged by the West, but in the Islamic jihad waged by the guerrilla fighters in Afghanistan."[44] Many Islamic radicals believed that the Soviet Union was a more formidable enemy because of its totalitarian nature and, what they perceive as inherent weaknesses of the United States, materialism and unwillingness to tolerate military or civilian casualties. Furthermore, among Islamic fundamentalists, Russia is increasingly viewed as a balancer against American economic and security primacy in the Middle East. This changed view has done little to endear Moscow at the official level; consequently, Russia's motives continue to be viewed warily. However, on the Arab street, Russia is seen as an arbiter, an antidote to US or Western policy against Islamists.

Russia's policy goals reinforce this perception. Moscow does not oppose the US-led War on Terror. Russia has in fact cooperated on a variety of levels, including intelligence-sharing and it even provided weaponry to the anti-Taliban Northern Alliance during Operation Enduring Freedom.[45] Moscow has its own concerns over Islamic terrorism expressed chiefly in the ongoing Chechen conflict and the rising Muslim population in Russia (estimated at 14.8 million in 2005, or 10.2 percent of the population). Russia has also supported American efforts to promote regional stability in the Central Asian Republics, although it opposes the increasing security ties between states such as Uzbekistan and the United States since they threaten to undermine Moscow's traditional influence in the region and supplant Russian economic interests in developing the lucrative energy resources of the area with American companies.[46] In addition, Russia resists American efforts to promote democratization in the Middle East which it perceives as a threat to its relations with key allies, including Syria and Iran.[47] Consequently, the United States and

---

44   Lewis, B. (2005), "Freedom and Justice in the Modern Middle East," *Foreign Affairs* 84/3, 50.

45   Russia provided a significant amount of weaponry to the anti-Taliban Northern Alliance, including 50 older MBTs, 80 APCs and various artillery pieces and small arms. The United States provided Russia with between $40–45 million to underwrite the costs of the equipment; Gertz, B. (2001), "Russia Supplies Tanks," *Washington Times*, October 25; and O'Flynn, K. (2001), "Russia in Multi-Million Arms Deal With Northern Alliance," *The Guardian*, October 23.

46   On US–Russian rivalry in Central Asia, on a country-by-country basis within the broader context of the War on Terror, see Crosston, M. (2006), *Fostering Fundamentalism: Terrorism, Democracy and American Engagement in Central Asia*, Aldershot: Ashgate.

47   Dzieciolowski, Z. (2006), "Russia and the Middle East: Post Soviet Flux," *Open Democracy: Free Thinking for the World*, 3, August 14, available at http://www.opendemocracy.net/content/articles/PDF/3817.pdf.

Russia were on opposite sides of the international diplomacy surrounding the Cedar Revolution in Lebanon in 2005. Russia was specifically accused of undertaking a variety of steps to prevent the rise of democracy in Lebanon in order to maintain Syrian influence over Beirut.[48]

Presidential Relations

Relations between Clinton and Putin continued the estrangement that developed in the final years of Yeltsin's tenure. In the aftermath of the 2001 terrorist attacks, however, the personal relationship between Vladimir Putin and George W. Bush briefly reached a level unseen in Russian-American interaction since the waning days of the Cold War. In the wake of the attacks, Putin offered significant support to Bush and pledged to "profoundly change" the relationship between Russia and the US-dominated North Atlantic Treaty Organization (NATO) in order to suppress global terrorism.[49] In October, the two presidents pledged cooperation in the war on terror during a conference in Shanghai and declared:

> The leaders of the two countries [Bush and Putin] view US-Russian cooperation as a critical element in the global effort against terrorism. They reaffirm their personal commitment and that of their two countries to fight this deadly challenge through active cooperation and coordination, both bilaterally and within the framework of international institutions.
>
> The Presidents note with satisfaction the fruitful cooperation between the United States and Russia in the United Nations and the UN Security Council, in the NATO-Russia Permanent Joint Council, and in the G-8. They also instruct their governments to reinforce bilateral cooperation through the US-Russia working group on countering terrorism and other threats emanating from Afghanistan.[50]

The Bush-Putin relationship reached it peak during a summit at the Bush's Crawford, Texas ranch in November 2001. The Summit provided the two leaders with an opportunity to make progress on a number of issues ranging from cooperation in the war on terror to US efforts on ballistic missile defense.[51]

---

48 The Russian–Syrian Connection: Thwarting Democracy in the Middle East and the Greater OSCE Region, US Congress, Commission on Security and Cooperation in Europe, Hearing before the Commission on Security and Cooperation in Europe, One Hundred Ninth Congress, first session, March 9, 2005.

49 Daley, S. (2001), "NATO Says US Has Proof Against Bin Laden Group," *The New York Times*, October 3.

50 "Joint Statement on Counterterrorism by the President of the United States and the President of Russia," US White House, Office of the Press Secretary, Shanghai, China (October 21, 2001).

51 At the ranch, Bush even taught Putin the Texas two-step to the tunes of Cotton-Eyed Joe; Smith, D.J. (2001), "Presidents get just one chance at the Cotton-Eyed Joe," *Janes.com*, November 19, available at http://www.janes.com.

Iraq War

In contrast, the Iraq War of 2003 was characterized by disagreement between not only the US and Russia, but the US and Europe.[52] Russia opposed US policy in the build-up to the Iraq War because of the potential for regional instability and the possibility of the loss of billions of dollars in debt, and both economic and military agreements between Moscow and the Saddam regime. Putin was willing to support UN weapons inspections, but his government argued that the US did not allow sufficient time for the inspections to work. Putin subsequently called the Iraq War a "big political mistake" which would dissipate any goodwill toward the US from the 2001 terrorist attacks.[53] Russian opposition was mainly based on the destabilizing effect a conflict would have on the stability of the Middle East.[54] Prior to the start of hostilities, officials in Moscow even declared that the US policy was "illegal" since the US and its allies did not gain a UN resolution specifically authorizing the use of force.[55] Nonetheless, Putin allowed traditional American allies such as France and Germany to lead the international effort to prevent the war and refrained from the vitriolic rhetoric which marked the international debate over the war. In the aftermath of the war, Putin supported efforts to stabilize the region. Russia endorsed the failed post-Saddam UN mission and in 2004, Moscow agreed to write off 90 percent of Iraq's debt, reducing Iraq's debt to $3.5 billion. Moscow also promised $4 billion in investments to aid Iraq.[56]

The Arab–Israeli Peace Process

In a speech on June 24, 2002, Bush called for the creation of a Palestinian state in exchange for democratic and administrative reforms, as well as effective

---

52   The second war the US waged against Iraq in 2003, "caused a split in the European security system," to the extent that was an "Old" Europe–"New" Europe divide. For information on the transatlantic security split; convergences and divergences of US and European security policy with particular reference to Russia, see Duric (2005), "Russia and the 'Old' Europe versus 'New' Europe Debate: US Foreign Policy and the Iraq War 2003," in Tom Lansford, Blagovest Tashev, (eds), *Old Europe, New Europe and the US: Renegotiating Transatlantic Security in the Post 9/11 Era*, Aldershot: Ashgate Publishing, 57–77. While the Iraq War of 2003 caused the most serious split in the transatlantic security system, by 2006, there remained a convergence on Lebanon; Gordon, P.H. (2006), "As the Mideast Comes Apart, America and Europe Come Together," *Global Politics*, Spring, available at http://www.brookings.edu/views/op-ed/gordon/2006may_june.htm, 1–2.

53   "Which Way Really?: Sidelined by the War on Iraq, Russia Could Still Win the Crucial Role it Seeks," *The Economist* (April 05, 2003), 44.

54   "Russia in Consultations with US, EU, Arab Countries on Iraq Problem Settlement," *Pravda*, 18(33) (April 30, 2003), available at http://newsfromrussia.com/main/2003/04/46574.html, 1.

55   Paton Walsh, N. and Henley, J. (2003), "Moscow and Paris Issue Dire Warnings: Putin Warns of Gravest Consequences as French Reject Blame for Diplomatic Failure," *The Guardian*, March 18, 2.

56   "Moscow Muscles Its Way Back into the Middle East," 20–21.

counterterrorism policies by the Palestinian National Authority. Bush's Arab–Israeli policy was a continuation of previous administrations' which attempted to balance Israeli security and Palestinian self-determination. However, while Clinton sought to achieve a breakthrough in the peace process, Bush pursued a more multilateral approach, based on a quartet that included the US, Russia, the European Union, and the UN. Russian involvement reflects the commonality of interests in resolving the Arab–Israeli conflict or at least ameliorating the strife. Moscow's participation also serves to confirm the country's importance in international diplomacy.[57] Increased Russian cooperation with the US on the Palestinian issue reflects the impact of the Chechen conflict on the Kremlin. Whilst the communist governments were critical of Israel, contemporary Israeli officials contend that Moscow is more empathetic to Tel Aviv's terrorist threat than Washington.[58] However, Russia continued to offer substantial support for the Palestinian Authority, including extensive financial aid.[59]

Russia continues to have significant interests in Israel. There is extensive trade between the two countries (Israel is Russia's second largest trade partner in the Middle East). The levels of interstate interactions are also important to note. Nearly one million Russian-speaking Jews live in Israel, which has led to cultural exchanges, tourism and remittances. The aircraft industries of the two countries are deeply intertwined.[60] For instance, Russia and Israel jointly produce and sell military equipment.[61] More than 80 percent of Israel's crude oil is imported from Russia. In March 2006, Russia's state energy company, Gazprom signed an agreement to expand energy exports to Israel.

Russia and Israel have cooperated extensively on counterterrorism. In the wake of the series of terrorist strikes in Russia from 1999 onward, Moscow's intelligence services dramatically increased collaboration with their counterparts in Jerusalem, including secretly training together. In addition, in 2006, a joint counter-terrorism working group began the creation of a joint "single database" of international terrorist organizations and their leaders.[62] Such cooperation is viewed by Washington as a positive step and the enhanced bilateral counterterrorism relationship is perceived as an enhancement in the war on terror. Russian policymakers also accept that the US-Israeli relationship will not be superseded by ties between Moscow and Tel Aviv. Israel was concerned with Moscow's ties to Hamas and Russian support to Iran's nuclear program, arms sales to Syria, and rising anti-Semitism.[63] Ilya Bourtman asserts that Vladimir Putin pursues a "non-ideological ... two track policy towards

---

57   All information taken from Oliker and Yefimova, 19.

58   Ibid.

59   This comes as the Americans and Europeans "were cutting off or suspending" their aid; Ibid., 92.

60   Freedman, "Russian Policy Toward the Middle East Under Yeltsin and Putin," 15.

61   Bourtman, I. (2006), "Putin and Russia's Middle Eastern Policy," *The Middle East Review of International Affairs* 10/2, available at http://meria.idc.ac.il/journal/2006/issue2/jv10no2al.html, 5.

62   All information taken from Ibid., 2–5. ; Israel was one of the first nations to offer Russia support after the Beslan tragedy in 2004. Israel has also urged Moscow to reform its intelligence gathering agencies; Ibid., 4.

63   Ibid., 5.

the Middle East" in which he is "allowing Russia to develop friendly ties with Israel while simultaneously nurturing alternative ... interests with Arab countries."[64]

The death of Palestinian Liberation Organization (PLO) chairman Yasser Arafat was perceived as a potential turning point in the conflict. Russia participated in the creation of an initiative, the Forum for the Future, to promote democracy in the Middle East.[65] The Kremlin believed that the new PLO president Mahmoud Abbas would be more likely to restrain terrorist elements among the Palestinians. Abbas did take a number of steps to reduce terrorist attacks, with mixed success, and labeled suicide attacks as "counterproductive."[66] Nonetheless, Abbas' inability to control extreme anti-Israeli groups, such as Hamas, prompted Russia to enhance ties with the group. In March 2006, Moscow hosted a Hamas delegation in contrast to the accepted position of the US and EU based on no negotiations with Hamas until the group denounces terrorism and agrees to recognize Israel.[67]

Russia's role in the Arab–Israeli conflict is complicated by its close relationship with Syria. In 2005, Russia announced that sale of the Strelets mobile SA-18 air defense missile system to Syria. In addition, Moscow agreed to cancel three-quarters of Damascus' $13.4 billion debt.[68] Russia also pledged to protect Syria from US efforts to isolate Damascus.[69] This policy resulted in significant differences between Moscow and Washington over Syria, especially in the aftermath of the summer 2006 Israeli–Hezbollah conflict.

Iran

On February 27, 2005, Putin announced that Russia would deliver nuclear technology to Iran, despite "intense US and Israeli opposition."[70] Investigators from the International Atomic Energy Agency (IAEA) have reported that Tehran is attempting to gain the ability to produce enriched uranium, as well as separate plutonium, which would provide the basis for a weapons program.[71] Russian policymakers have stated

---

64   Ibid., 1.

65   See Ross, 73, 74. For the implications of Yasser Arafat's death see Ibid, 66–74.

66   Makovsky (2005), "Gaza: Moving Forward by Pulling Back," *Foreign Affairs* 84/3, 52.

67   All information taken from Cohen, A. (2006) "US Should Warn Russia Over Its 'Soviet' Middle East Policy," WebMemo # 1007, Research, Russia and Eurasia, The Heritage Foundation, March 6, available at http://www.heritage.org/Research/RussiaandEurasia/wm1007.cfm, 1–2.

68   All information taken from "Moscow Muscles Its Way Back into the Middle East," 20–1.

69   Ibid.

70   Feldman, 4–5.

71   Pollack, K. and Takeyh, R. (2005), "Taking on Tehran," *Foreign Affairs*, 84(2), 20. Iran claims it has an "inalienable right" under the Nuclear Non-Proliferation treaty (NPT) to peaceful nuclear technology. However, this civilian nuclear technology can also be used to make bombs. Iran has a history of deceiving inspectors and concealing its nuclear program and has "redoubled its enrichment efforts and restricted the inspectors work;" "Iran's Nuclear Ambitions: When the Spinning Has to Stop," *The Economist* 380/8492, August 26, 2006, 10.

publicly that the country would not stop nuclear cooperation with Iran, but Russia has since modified its approach, calling for greater transparency in Iran's nuclear program and for greater IAEA regulation.

Putin's position on Iran, which contrasts significantly with that of the Bush administration, reflects Moscow's economic and security interests. Iran is Moscow's ally and a primary military customer. On February 28, 2005, Moscow signed a landmark nuclear fuel agreement with Iran to construct a light-water nuclear power reactor in Bushehr. Negotiations on an additional five reactors also continued despite international concern over Iran's nuclear program. Several hundred Iranian nuclear physicists and engineers were trained in Russia and an unknown number of Russian scientists and technicians are employed by Tehran.[72] In addition to the nuclear relationship between the two countries, Russia has also transferred ballistic missile technology and expertise to Iran, including long-range missile capabilities.[73] This aggravated relations with both the US and Israel who remain resolutely opposed to Iran acquiring missile nuclear weapons and delivery systems. A nuclear armed Iran, allied and armed by Russia, is seen as one of the most significant challenges to the US and itsnkey allies in the region.[74] In January 2006, Russia signed a $132 million agreement with Tehran to design, test and launch the Iranian telecommunications satellite, the Zohreh, and the surveillance satellites Mesbah and Sinah-1.[75]

Russia condemned Iranian President Mahmoud Ahmadinejad's October 2005 statement that Israel should be wiped off the map. The Kremlin asserted that the President's comments were "unacceptable."[76] There are also a number of other problems in the Russian–Iranian relationship, including the fact that Russia's trade with Iran is actually less than with Israel.[77] Furthermore, Russia officially opposes a nuclear armed Iran, since Tehran could become a regional rival to Moscow in the near abroad (especially the Caspian region).[78]

Conclusions

On September 19, 2006, George W. Bush, at the UN General Assembly, spoke of "a world beyond terror, where ordinary men and women are free to determine their own destiny, where the voices of moderation are empowered, and where the extremists are marginalized by the peaceful majority. This world can be ours if we seek it and if

---

For the prospects of a nuclear Iran, see Ross, D. (2005), "The Middle East Predicament," *Foreign Affairs* 84/1, 63–6.

72   Cohen, 1.
73   Feldman, 5.
74   Cohen, 1.
75   "Moscow Muscles Its Way Back into the Middle East," 21.
76   Bourtman, I. (2006), 12. See "Russia Condemns Iranian President's Statements on Israel," Agence France Presse, October 27, 2005.
77   Freedman, "Russia's Middle East Ambitions," 5.
78   Cohen, 1.

we work together."[79] Bush highlighted democratic accomplishments in Middle East, including elections in Bahrain, Egypt, Jordan, Saudi Arabia and Yemen. He declared the following:

> Some have argued that the democratic changes we're seeing in the Middle East are destabilizing the region. This argument rests on a false assumption, that the Middle East was stable to begin with. The reality is that the stability we thought we saw in the Middle East was a mirage. For decades, millions of men and women in the region have been trapped in oppression and hopelessness. And these conditions left a generation disillusioned, and made this region a breeding ground for extremism.[80]

Bush criticized the regimes in Iran and Syria and declared that countries around the world had to end support for terrorism and terrorist organizations.[81] He also underlined the core idealism of American Middle East policy. Successive American administrations have sought, with varying degrees of commitment, to spread democracy in the region as a means to enhance stability and reduce the root causes of terrorism. US Middle East policy is a mix of idealism and political realism based on ongoing strategic interests, including alliances with states such as Israel, Turkey and Saudi Arabia.

In comparison, Russian Middle East policy is based on political realism as expressed through the pursuit of short-term economic, political and security interests. Contemporary Kremlin policy reflects the legacy of the past. Russia's main allies, including Syria, had ties to Moscow during the Cold War. Other Cold War partners, such as Libya and Yemen, have sought closer ties to the US and Europe, while because of the 2003 war, Iraq has moved into the American orbit. In the Great Game for regional supremacy Russia has been forced to seek other allies, including principally Iran. While the Kremlin seeks to compete with the United States in the region, current American primacy allows Moscow to ignore the long-range consequences of its policies and concentrate on immediate gains. Moscow can also act as a balancer against Washington in the eyes of the Arab street. When the Kremlin perceives it to be within its interests, Moscow will cooperate with Washington. Conversely, if Russia can acquire short-term economic or political gains at the expense of the United States, it will do so.

---

79   Bush, G.W., *Address to the United Nations General Assembly, Washington. D.C.*, available at http://www.whitehouse.gov/news/releases/2006/09/20060919-4.html.

80   Ibid.

81   For an analysis of Bush's speech, see Pilkington, E. (2006), "Defiant Bush Appeals to People of Middle East," *The Guardian*, September 20, 16.

SECTION II
The Far East and the US in the Middle East

Chapter 5

China's Middle East Policy Since the Post-Mao Reform

Chunlong Lu and Jie Chen

The Middle East has been the main stage for competitions among great powers. In the era of the Cold War, the United States and the Soviet Union dominated this region, and the struggles between them dictated the politics of the Middle Eastern region. Not until the 1960s did the People's Republic of China (PRC) have any interest in this region. As China's economic and military power has grown rapidly since the late 1970s, its presence in the Middle East has become increasingly influential. This chapter examines the major components, motivations, and impacts of China's policy toward the Middle East.

China's policy toward the Middle East has experienced three phases since the establishment of the PRC in 1949.[1] The first phase (1949–1955) is characterized by the dominance of the Maoist "revolutionary" ideology. While criticizing most Arab state leaders in the Middle East for being "feudal dictators," "imperialist proxies" and "anti-revolutionaries," China supports their people's anti-colonial efforts. None of the Arab state rulers recognized the newly formed PRC, and they still maintained diplomatic relations with the Republic of China (ROC) that had retreated to Taiwan in 1949. In this phase, most Arab state rulers held no trust in the PRC and followed Washington's lead in the United Nations against Beijing's bid for its UN membership.[2] Israel was the only country in the Middle Eastern region that officially recognized the PRC during this period. On January 9, 1949, Israeli Foreign Minister Moshe Sharett sent a cable to his Chinese counterpart, Zhou Enlai, informing him of Israel's de jure recognition of the PRC.[3] Israel would have established diplomatic relations with Beijing if the Korean War had not happened.

In the second phase (1956–1976), Beijing sought to strengthen its ties with anti-Western Arab states and regarded their foreign policies as anti-imperialist. In this phase, the PRC's diplomatic relations with the Middle East Arab countries were paralyzed by the Cultural Revolution within the country for a while, and later resumed on an anti-Soviet imperialist basis in the 1970s. During this period, the Beijing government chose to support the Arab/Palestinian fight against Israel and saw

---

1   See Pan, G. (1997), "China's Success in the Middle East," *Middle East Quarterly* 4.

2   Harris, L.C. (1993), *China Considers the Middle East*, London: I. B. Tauris & Co Ltd.

3   Melman, Y. and Sinai, R. (1987), "Israeli-Chinese Relations and Their Future Prospects: From Shadow to Sunlight," *Asian Survey*, 27, 395–407.

Israel as a proxy of Western imperialism.[4] For the lack of capabilities and resources, Beijing's support for the Arab/Palestinian has been confined primarily to political rhetoric, advocating the "armed struggle" against Israel "until final victory" and implicitly denying Israel's right to exist in the Middle East.[5] Besides the rhetorical (or moral) support, Beijing provided a token of military and financial assistance to the Palestine Liberation Organization (PLO).[6]

In the third phase (from 1978 on), Beijing adopted a less ideological and more practical diplomacy, with the aim of creating a favorable international environment for its own economic modernization.[7] China has no longer based its policy toward the Middle East on revolutionary or anti-imperialist ideologies. National interest now is almost the only guide for China's foreign policy. This third phase is characterized by the normalization of the relations between China and all Middle Eastern countries. In the 1990s, Beijing successfully maintained good relations with all Middle East nations, "ranging from America's close allies (Israel, Saudi Arabia and Turkey) to intensely anti-American states (Libya, Iran, and even Iraq)—a major accomplishment in the history of Sino-Middle East relations."[8]

Since 1978, Chinese leaders have implemented a policy of "Reform and Open" to modernize its economy, and gradually downgraded the importance of traditional Marxist ideology. Thus, the Beijing decision-makers have tried to make its relations with other countries serve the national goal of economic modernization and political stability. As a result, the Chinese leaders have gradually defined a set of substantive and tangible interests in the Middle East region. Among these interests, the quest for oil is the most important one, followed by strengthening economic relations with the Middle East and cooperation with Moslem countries in that region in containing the separatist movement within China.

The PRC's Quest for Oil

At the present time, China's Middle East policy is dictated mainly by its quest for oil. With its rapid economic growth since 1978, the PRC's oil demand has increased significantly and become more and more dependent on foreign oil supply. Currently, around 30 percent of the PRC's oil demand is met by oil imports. Due to the stagnation of domestic oil production and the rapid increase of demand for oil, it is projected that in the next two decades, up to 75 percent of the PRC's oil demand will come from foreign suppliers. Among those foreign suppliers, the Middle East is the largest one. Currently, around 60 percent of the PRC's oil imports are from the Middle East. Moreover, it is predicted that in the next two decades, around 80 percent of the PRC's

---

    4   Rynhold, J. (1996), "China's Cautious New Pragmatism in the Middle East," *Survival* 38/3, 102–16; Melman and Sinai.

    5   Sobin (1991), "The China-Israel Connection: New Motivations for Rapprochement," *The Fletcher Forum of World Affairs* 15, 111–25; Xiaoxing Han (1993), "Sino-Israeli Relations," *Journal of Palestine Studies* 22, 62–77.

    6   Sobin.

    7   Pan.

    8   Ibid.

oil imports may come from this region. The Beijing leadership is now aware that to sustain economic growth, it has to secure the continued access to large quantities of foreign oil. Thus, energy security has become a high priority in the PRC's foreign policy agenda, particularly in its policy towards the Middle East.[9]

Beijing projects that its oil demand will rise to about 5.2 million barrels per day (mb/d) by the year 2010, while the International Energy Agency (IEA) predicts a much larger demand: 7.1 mb/d. Even if we take the conservative figure of 5.2 mb/d, the Chinese Government nonetheless expects to have to import around a half of that amount to meet the country's oil demand, assuming that the PRC will maintain the current level of oil production—3.28 mb/d.[10] There is little possibility that China can increase its domestic oil production substantially in the coming years. As a China energy expert pointed out, "the major oil fields in eastern China, which account for about 90 percent of total crude production, have peaked and are in decline."[11] While the development of oilfields in Xinjiang province in west China and the exploitation of offshore oil ranges in the East China Sea may represent a new hope for the PRC's domestic oil production, both of the sources fall far behind the growing demand.[12] The IEA estimates that, by 2020, the PRC's oil demand will increase to about 10.1 Mbp/days, and thus Beijing will have to import around 75 percent of that oil demand.[13]

In 2002, China's oil demand reached 5.26 mb/d, and China became the world's third largest consumer of petroleum products, ranked only behind the US and Japan. In 2003, China's oil demand climbed up to 5.5 mb/d and surpassed Japan to become the world's second largest consumer of petroleum products only after the US.[14] And in 2004, the PRC's oil demand increased to 6.4 mb/d.[15] It is also worth noting that "during the 1996-2001—the same period in which the Asian financial crisis occurred and, as a result, most East Asian economies sharply contracted—China's net oil imports increased by 50% annually."[16]

Such a dramatic increase of demand for oil and the deepening dependence on foreign supplies makes Beijing concerned about the possibility of an oil supply crisis. Unfortunately, Beijing is not well prepared for such a potential crisis. Unlike Western industrialized countries that have had ample experiences in managing the adverse effects of oil supply disruptions, the PRC is a new consumer in the international oil

---

9   Calabrese, J. (2004), "Dragon by the Tail: China's Energy Quandary," *MEI Perspective*; Middle East Institute, March.

10   See Obaid, N.E., Jaffe, A., Morse, E.L., Gracia, C. and Bromley, K. (2002), "The Sino-Saudi Energy Rapprochement: Implications for US National Security' in *The Gracia Group Report*, Washington, DC: Department of Defense, January 8.

11   Downs, E.S. (2000), *China's Quest for Energy Security*, Santa Monica, CA: RAND Corporation, 7.

12   Troush, S. (1999), "China's Changing Oil Strategy and its Foreign Policy Implications," CNAPS Working Paper, Washington, DC: The Brookings Institution, Center for Northeast Asian Policy Studies.

13   International Energy Agency, *World Energy Outlook 2004*.

14   International Energy Agency, *Oil Market Report*, March 11, 2004, 12.

15   Ibid., p. 43.

16   Calabrese, 2.

market. And the PRC is not a member of the IEA and does not participate in some Western industrialized countries-led multilateral institutions (i.e., Organization for Economic Co-operation and Development) that could be used to deal collectively with an oil crisis. Thus, the PRC cannot use international institutions and multilateral approaches to mitigate its vulnerabilities to an oil supply crisis.[17] Moreover, the PRC has not established a 90-day national strategic oil reserve system and Beijing has not developed any laws and regulations to manage the use of oil under the situation of an oil crisis.[18]

At present, more than half of China's oil imports are from the Middle East region and have to be transported by tanker. Thus, the stability of the Gulf Region and the safe passage of the sea-lanes between the PRC and the Straits of Hormuz are critical to the Chinese national interests. Yet, current Chinese military capability is still too limited to play any significant role in maintaining the stability in the Gulf and safeguarding the oil sea-lanes. Fortunately, the US is taking the chief responsibilities for these areas. As a result, Beijing has enjoyed the benefits of "free-riding" generated by the American protection, even though Beijing apprehends that it might become vulnerable to American pressures.[19]

All in all, energy security is one of the most salient national interests of the PRC. In the PRC's 10th Five Year Plan (2001–05), Beijing authorities explicitly mentioned "energy security" and regarded "energy security" as one of top priorities in the national agenda. And "energy security" has also become one of the "hot topics" among scholars in China.[20] The key of the PRC's "energy security" is to safeguard oil supplies from abroad, especially from the Middle East, and Beijing regards the continued access to these supplies as essential to its economic development.[21]

Securing the Oil from the Middle East

In the future, Beijing will participate in the IEA and develop joint emergency management with the IEA. In addition, the PRC may develop a national strategic oil reserve system. At the present time, however, China has no alternatives but to take measures to secure the oil supplies from the Middle East. To achieve this

---

17   See Myers Jaffe, A. and Lewis, S.W., "Beijing's Oil Diplomacy," *Survival*, 44(1), 115–134; Calabrese.

18   Downs, E.S. (2004), "The Chinese Energy Security Debate," *The China Quarterly* 177, 21–41; Calabrese.

19   Downs, *China's Quest for Energy Security* ; Downs, "The Chinese Energy Security Debate"; Calabrese.

20   See Lei Wu (2003), "China's Oil Safety: Challenges and Counter Measures (Zhongguo shiyou anquan mianlin de tiaozhan yu duice)," *West Asia & Africa (Xiya feizhou)* 4, 17–21; Weijian Li (2000), "Middle East Oil and China's Energy Security (Zhongdong shiyou yu zhongguo nengyuan anquan)," *Journal of Arab World (Alabo shijie)* 75, 4–9; Zhongqian Yang (2001), "China's Oil Security and its Middle East Oil Strategy (Zhongguo shiyou anquan iiqi zhongdong shiyou zhanlue)," *World Economic Studies (Shijie jingji yanjiu)* 1, 19–22, 37.

21   See Downs, "The Chinese Energy Security Debate'; Calabrese; Yang; Li.

current goal, Beijing has used bilateral diplomacy to strengthen its political relations with the Gulf oil-exporting nations. Among those Gulf nations, Beijing is eager to improve ties with two countries—Iran and Saudi Arabia.[22]

In terms of dealing with bilateral relations with oil exporting countries, Beijing believes that "the cultivation of strong bilateral relationships with oil-producing countries in the Middle East can help China secure the oil resources it needs from the region."[23] First, Beijing made efforts to cooperate with the most influential organization in the Middle Eastern region—the Gulf Cooperation Council (GCC).[24] Second, Beijing has substantially improved its relationships with Iran and Saudi Arabia. In 1970, China and Iran established official relations, which had been broken off in 1949 following the establishment of the PRC. But it was not until the early 1980s that these relations improved significantly. High-level diplomatic interaction focused on cooperation in issues including the Iran–Iraq War, arms sales, and balancing global hegemonies.[25] Iran's distance from both the US and the Soviet Union makes it a good candidate for Beijing to form an alliance. Since the 1990s, with the PRC becoming dependent on foreign oil supply, good relations with Iran have become much more important than they were before in the eyes of Beijing decision-makers. Currently, Iran is the PRC's second largest oil exporter, ranking only behind the Saudis.

Sino-Saudi relations have grown significantly since the two countries established full diplomatic ties in 1990. On October 21, 1999, the PRC's President Jiang Zemin officially visited Saudi Arabia and pronounced "strategic oil partnership" relations with Saudi Arabia and underscored that the PRC attached great importance to the development of its relationship with the Saudi Government.[26] The two countries signed a memorandum on petroleum cooperation on October 31, 1999 and agreed to take measures to facilitate investments in refining, petrochemical sectors and petroleum technical services cooperation in their respective countries.[27] Currently, Saudi Arabia is China's largest oil exporter. By year 2005, Saudi Arabia provided China with 14 percent of its imported oil.[28]

After September 11, America became suspicious of the Saudi Government, given 11 out of 19 terrorists in the September 11 attack were from Saudi Arabia.

---

22   Obaid et al. and Blumenthal, D. (2005), "Providing Arms: China and the Middle East," *Middle East Quarterly* 12, 11–20; Jaffe and Lewis.

23   Downs, 48.

24   The six member states of Gulf Cooperation Council are: the United Arab Emirates, Oman, Bahrain, Qatar, Kuwait and Saudi Arabia.

25   See Bates, G. (1992), *Chinese Arms Transfers: Purposes, Patterns, and Prospects in the New World Order*, Westport, CT: Praeger, 96–9.

26   "Chinese President Meets GCC Secretary General," *Xinhua News Agency*, November 1, 1999.

27   *Memorandum of Understanding on Petroleum Cooperation between the Government of the People's Republic of China and the Government of the Kingdom of Saudi Arabia*, The PRC's Ministry of Foreign Affairs (June 5, 2002), available at http://www.fmprc.gov.cn/eng/wjb/zzjg/xybfs/gjlb/2878/2879/t16423.htm.

28   *Chinese Customs Statistical Yearbook 2005* (Beijing: Customs General Administration of the People's Republic Of China).

And American efforts to push democracy in this region have unnerved the Saudis and other regimes, which have received American overtures tepidly. Summing up regional sentiment, Saudi Arabia's Foreign Minister asserted that "reform must stem from the regime itself and not from outside and under foreign conditions."[29] Riyadh has worried that the liberation of Iraq's Shiites from Saddam Hussein's authoritarian rule may ignite pressures for democracy and trigger political turmoil within the Kingdom, which has a substantial Shiite population, most of which resides in major oil producing areas. As repressive societies, China and Saudi Arabia are wary of outside intervention or pressures; in this respect, they have a common set of interests.[30] Along the same line, Iran also shares common interests with the PRC. Tehran has criticized foreign intervention, particularly the US intervention, in the Gulf Region and has been critical of the American "promotion of democracy" in this area.

Lastly, Beijing has consistently supported the Arab states politically and diplomatically in the international arena. For example, China has backed the Palestinian struggle against Israel to win support from the oil-exporting Arab countries. Beijing has used its position and influence in international organizations to lobby for the interests of Iraq and Iran with regard to Iraq's Weapon of Mass Destruction (WMD) and the Iranian nuclear issue. As a permanent member of the United Nations (UN) Security Council, the PRC has enormous influence in the UN bodies, and thus is of exceptional importance in the eyes of the oil-exporting Arab countries.[31]

Strengthening Economic Ties

Over the last decade, China's economic and trade relations with the Gulf Cooperation Council countries have grown significantly. Sino-GCC trade volume has jumped from 1.5 billion dollars in 1991 to 17 billion dollars in 2003, an increase of more than 10 times. In 1992, the GCC-China Trade Conference was established and the main expanding area of cooperation between the Gulf and the PRC is the oil industry.[32] In 1996, the GCC and China established a regular political and economic consultative mechanism that supported increased economic and trade cooperation.[33]

The close economic ties between China and the GCC were strengthened by the establishment of a Free Trade Area (FTA) agreement, which was initiated during a GCC delegation visit to Beijing in July 2004.[34] It represents an important advance

---

29   See News Conference, Dubal Al-Arabiyah Television in FBIS: NES, World News Connection (May 4, 2004).

30   See An, W. (1998), "Stable Development of the Sino-Middle East Friendship and Co-operation (Zhongguo-zhongdong youhao hezuo guanxi wending fazhan)," *West Asia & Africa (Xiya feizhou)* 6, 54–60.

31   Troush.

32   Rynhold.

33   "Chinese President Meets GCC Secretary General."

34   Yan Meng (2004), "Trade to Expand with Gulf Nations," *China Daily*, July 7, 2004, available at http://www.chinadaily.com.cn/english/doc/2004-07/07/content_346037.htm.

on economic, trade, investment, and technological co-operation.[35] This agreement commits all parties to "establish a joint economic and trade co-operation commission and officially launch a bilateral consultative mechanism."[36] 'Currently, the GCC nations have become the PRC's eighth largest trading partner, eighth largest export destination and ninth largest source of import.'[37] It is also worth noting that since the 1990s the PRC's exports to and imports from the Middle Eastern countries have risen quickly, while those of Russia and America have performed less well on average (see Table 5.1).

The main area of the increasing economic relations between the oil-exporting Gulf countries and China is the oil industry. On the one hand, Beijing helped its main oil companies to buy equity stakes in the oil industry of Middle East nations. On the other hand, Beijing encouraged the Gulf oil-exporting countries to invest in its downstream oil industry.[38]

So far, Beijing has shown a strong interest in having major Chinese oil firms participate in oil field development projects in the Middle Eastern region, including Iran, Saudi Arabia, and to some extent Kuwait.[39] Since 1993 when the PRC became a net oil importer, Beijing has planned to secure the continued access to foreign oil supplies by obtaining "around a third of its energy needs through international exploration and acquisition activities."[40] This plan has been strongly supported by the PRC's major oil companies, who are the key drivers of China's investment in overseas oil fields. In the 1980s, Beijing created three major oil companies— the China National Offshore Oil Corporation (CNOOC) that controlled most of the PRC's offshore oil industry, the China National Petrochemical Corporation (SINOPEC) that was in charge of oil refining and oil products marketing, and the China National Petroleum Corporation (CNPC) that was responsible for the PRC's onshore oil exploration and production.

In June 1997, CNPC signed a 22-year production-sharing contract with Saddam Hussein's Iraq to develop half of the al-Ahdab field after the UN sanctions against Baghdad are lifted. Located about 40 miles south of al-Kut in central Iraq, Al-Ahdab was Iraq's second largest oil field.[41] In May 2004, SINOPEC, together with Saudi Arabia Oil Company (ARAMCO), signed an agreement with the Ministry of Petroleum of the Kingdom of Saudi Arabia for natural gas exploration and

---

35   See Wu, Y. (2004), "Pact Ensures Benefits for Both China, GCC," *China Daily*, July 8, available at http://www.chinadaily.com.cn/english/doc/2004-07/08/content_346410.htm; Also see Yan Dai (2004), "Closer Economic Ties with GCC Suggested," *China Daily*, July 8, available at http://www.chinadaily.com.cn/english/doc/2004-07/08/content_346425.htm.

36   Ibid.

37   Rynhold, 110.

38   Xu, X. (1998), "China and the Middle East: Cross-Investment in the Energy Sector," *Middle East Policy* 7/3, 122–36; Calabrese, J. (1998), "China and the Persian Gulf: Energy and Security," *Middle East Journal* 52, 351–66.

39   Obaid et al.

40   Ibid., 18.

41   Given the UN sanctions and the US war in Iraq, CNPC has done little but to survey Al-Ahdab. At present, there is little prospect that CNPC can resume this oil development contract with the new Iraqi Government.

Table 5.1   Exports to and from the Middle East (value in million US dollars)

		1993	1994	1995	1996	1997	1998	1999	2000	2001	2002
The PRC	Exports to the Middle East	2,417.2	2,658.2	3,252.5	3,285.8	3,954.3	4,448.6	4,797.8	6,677.3	7,047.5	9,928.8
	Imports from the Middle East	1957. 6	1604. 3	2,129.4	2,981.3	3,779.3	3,075.1	3,431.3	9,778.7	8,909.6	9,246.9
Russia	Exports to the Middle East	3,081.3	1473. 2	2,483.5	3,110.6	3,565.4	3,573.8	2,921.6	6,141.1	6,147.2	6,385.4
	Imports from the Middle East	1,129.4	400.5	541.5	735.5	994.1	614.0	412.5	478.5	602.3	831.0
USA	Exports to the Middle East	15,991.9	14,002.6	14,787.4	17,067.4	18,712.2	20,313.2	16,620.3	15,194.5	15,194.9	15,203.1
	Imports from the Middle East	13,296.3	13,174.6	13,533.3	14,515.6	16,386.4	14,250.4	19,532.1	30,895.4	29,873.1	26,996.8

Note: Data for this table are drawn from *International Trade Statistics Yearbook*, various issues, New York: United Nations

development in the Rub Alkhali Basin. This is the first public tender hosted by the Saudi Government for its natural gas field exploitation. SINOPEC maintains a four-fifths share. One of SINOPEC officials commented that, "[t]hanks to her fast economic growth, China houses robust demands for energy sources, and petroleum and natural gas in particular. Saudi Arabia is the world's largest provider of oil and gas resources. Hence, the two countries are highly complementary to each other in their drive for economic development."[42]

In October 2004, the PRC and Iran signed a preliminary agreement on oil and natural gas for the potential value of more than billions of dollars. According to the agreement, Iran would allow the PRC's SINOPEC to develop Iran's Yadavaran oil field in exchange for agreeing to buy 10 million tons of Iranian liquefied natural gas annually for 25 years. The agreement was signed by Iranian Oil Minister Bijan Namdar Zanganeh and the head of China's National Development and Reform Commission Ma Kai in Beijing.[43] SINOPEC will have a 50 percent interest in Yadavaran oil field and this deal is the PRC's largest oil investment in the Gulf Region.[44]

The Beijing decision-makers also hope "to establish long-term energy ties with oil-producing countries in the Middle East and has devoted considerable effort to attracting foreign investment from Saudi Arabia, Kuwait, and Iran"[45] in the PRC's energy sector. For example, Kuwait Petroleum Company (KPC) has a 14.7 percent stock in China's Yacheng offshore gas field. This is "the first such project in which China has cooperated with foreign companies since its implementation of reforms."[46] Particularly, at the current stage, the Saudis and Iranians are actively taking measures to be involved in China's oil downstream investments. For example, ARAMCO is involved in the construction of the Qingdao refinery in Shangdong Province in which ARAMCO committed to supply 10 million tons of crude oil over a 30-year period.[47] ARAMCO is now the largest shareholder in the Thalin refinery in Northeast China and is involved in the upgrade of a major Fujian refinery to capture the PRC's south-eastern oil market.[48]

Currently, most of the PRC's existing refineries are unable to process the Saudi and Iranian crude oil since their crude oil has a high sulfur content. In the 1990s, China imported its largest quantity of oil from Oman and Yemen because China lacked capacity to process the high-sulfur crude oil in 1990s and thus China depended heavily on Oman and Yemen for importing low-sulfur crude oil.[49] However, the dramatic growth of China's oil demand cannot be met by Oman and Yemen alone,

---

42   *SINOPEC News* (March 7, 2004), available at http://english.sinopec.com/en-newsevent/en-news/1373.shtml.

43   Pottinger, M. (2004), "China and Iran Near Agreement on Huge Oil Pact," *The Wall Street Journal*, November 1.

44   Jin, L. (2005), "Energy First: China and the Middle East," *Middle East Quarterly* 12/2, 3–10.

45   Downs, 33.

46   Calabrese, 357.

47   Ibid., 358.

48   Obaid et al.

49   Ibid.

and the prospect of the dry-up of Oman's and Yemen's oil reserves is making Beijing turn its interests to Saudi Arabia and Iran. In fact, only Saudi Arabia and Iran can feed the PRC's desperate thirst for oil. Thus, Beijing decision-makers are eager to attract Saudi and Iranian investments in its refining industry.

Meanwhile, both Saudi Arabia and Iran have shown strong interest in expanding their share in the PRC's oil market. "Basically, Saudi Arabia is going to have to invest heavily in Chinese refining upgrades if we're to have a dominant presence in China," said a senior member of the Saudi Consultative Council and a former Deputy Minister of Finance and National Economy.[50]

Beyond the oil-exporting Arab countries, China has improved its economic ties with Israel substantially. Since 1978, Beijing's decision-making was dominated by its drive to modernization. Beijing decision-makers have come to realize the potential benefits of the improved economic relations with Israel. Positive relations with Israel would offer the PRC "the prospect of increased commerce" and "acquisition of high-quality, inexpensive technology."[51] Thus, Beijing discarded its former anti-Israeli policy. In the late 1970s, Beijing moderated its policy on the Arab–Israeli conflict and supported the peace treaty signed by Israel and Egypt in 1979 in Washington.[52] In 1982, the PRC's Prime Minister Zhao Ziyang delivered a statement in Cairo: "all the Middle East countries including Israel should enjoy the rights of independence and existence ... on the basis of the Israeli withdrawal from the territories occupied in 1967 and the restoration of the rights of Palestinian people."[53]

During the 1980s, there were no official diplomatic relations between the two countries. However, bilateral economic, technological, and commercial exchanges grew significantly. The PRC has a special interest in Israel's exportable technology such as solar energy and agricultural fertilization techniques.[54]

After the US-Soviet sponsored Madrid Conference on the Middle East peace, Beijing established full diplomatic relations with Israel in January 1992. And subsequently, Beijing supported the Oslo agreements and the Israel-Palestinian and Israel-Jordan peace processes, backed the concept of "land for peace" as the basis of the Middle East peace, and advocated the creation for an independent Palestinian nation.[55] China also emphasized that Israel's security should be guaranteed, a position that the Beijing government never took before. In the 1990s, economic relations with Israel became vital to China since Israel was an important supplier of high-technological products to the PRC. Israeli Prime Minister Benjamin Netanyahu even told Beijing, "Israeli know-how is more valuable than Arab oil."[56] Currently, Beijing wants to uphold good relations with both the oil-exporting Arab world and Israel and

---

50   Ibid., 14.
51   Sobin, 116.
52   Melman and Sinai, 405.
53   Han, 67–68.
54   Sobin; Han.
55   Rubin, B. (1999), "China Middle East Strategy," *Middle East Review of International Affairs* 3/1, 46–54.
56   Ibid., 51.

thus cautiously maintains a balance from the two sides. For the PRC, the Arab's oil and the Israeli know-how are equally important for its drive to modernization.

Fighting Radical Forces

In recent years, Beijing has also emphasized the cooperation with Muslim countries in fighting radical religious groups in its Middle East policy.[57] This emphasis has been mainly motivated by the increasing agitation of separatist forces for national independence in the so-called minority regions within China, such as Xinjiang. The Chinese central government has been perplexed by the Uygur separatist movement in west China since 1990s. The Uygur, who are of Turkic origin and of Muslim religion, have a population of about 18 million in Xinjiang Province, a very important area which constitutes one-sixth of mainland China and has huge reserves of oil, natural gas and other valuable minerals. Several factors contributed to the rise of the Xinjiang Uygur separatist movement in the 1990s.

First, after the end of Cold War and the collapse of the Soviet Union, the independence of Central Asian Islamic countries set an example for the Uygur to follow and encouraged the Uygur to seek their own national identity. Second, this nationalist tendency among the Uygur has also been reinforced by the Pan-Turkism.[58] The core of the Pan-Turkism is to restore the glory of Turkic Empire. Even though the Turkey government has guaranteed not to support the Uygur separatist movement, the radical forces of Pan-Turkism within Turkey have supported the Uygur separatist forces and been actively exporting the Pan-Turkism ideology to the Uygur population. Finally, the radical Taliban has supported the Uygur separatist forces, such as the East Turkistan terrorist groups, and has exported fundamental Islamism to the PRC's Uygur population. Beijing's support for the American war in Afghanistan since September 11 can be regarded as a reflection of its own security concerns.

The radical Uygur separatist forces have staged a set of terrorist attacks including riots, assassinations, and bombings since 1990s. For example, between 1990 and 2001, "East Turkistan terrorist forces, based in western Xinjiang, staged more than 200 attacks in Xinjiang, killing 162 people of all ethnic groups."[59]

Beijing has put much effort in fighting against the Uygur separatist forces, which also called for much caution in order to not harm the relations with Saudi Arabia and Iran. Both Saudi Arabia and Iran have actively supported Islamic movements abroad and their religious leaders have expressed a special interest in the well-being of Chinese Muslims, and this may create tensions in the Sino-Saudi and Sino-Iran

---

57   Sisci, F. (2002), "China Plays the Middle East Card," *Asia Times Online*, April 23, available at http://www.atimes.com/china/DD23Ad01.html); Parker, T. (2000), "China's Growing Interests in the Persian Gulf," *The Brown Journal of World Affairs* 7/1, 235–43; Jaffe and Lewis; Li; Fangxiao, D. (1995), "Political Situation in the Middle East and China's Middle Eastern Diplomacy (Zhongdong zhenzhi geju yu zhongguo de zhongdong waijiao)," *West Asia & Africa (Xiya feizhou)* 6, 7–12.

58   Pan.

59   Jin, 7.

relations. For example, the late Sheikh Abdulaziz bin Baz, former Grand Mufti of Saudi Arabia said in 1998 that they have a moral obligation to help the Chinese Muslim brothers.[60]

Beijing is conscious about the potential political risks caused by cracking down the Uygur Muslim separatist forces in Xinjiang. In response to the concerns of the Saudi and Iranian Muslim leaders, Beijing leadership also took measures to co-opt local Muslim leaders in Xinjiang. For example, when Iranian President Muhammad Khatami visited Beijing in 2000, the PRC arranged for him to meet with the co-opted Muslim leaders. After a talk with these co-opted Muslim leaders, Khatami declared that Xinjiang Uygur Muslims could work as a bridge connecting China with the Middle East Muslim world.[61] On the other hand, the Beijing leadership insisted that, "we will make sure that Islam is practiced in a way that is line with Chinese culture and tradition."[62] So far, Beijing's co-opting strategy seems to be successful and it has largely appeased the concerns from the Saudis and Iranians. The silent cooperation from the Middle Eastern Muslim countries is of exceptional importance to China, which has taken measures to block the influence of fundamental Islamism from abroad.

After the September 11 terrorist attack, Beijing joined the American-led anti-terrorism camp and insisted that the fight against the radical Uygur separatist forces shall be a part of global fight against terrorism. For example, Chinese Foreign Ministry spokesman Zhu Bangguo stated, "The United States has asked China to provide assistance to the fight against terrorism. China, by the same token, has reasons to ask the United State to give its support and understanding in the fight against terrorism and separatists. We should not have double standards."[63] On the other hand, Beijing kept some distance from the US-led anti-terrorism war. Chinese Government insisted that the root of terrorism is poverty and the deepening gap between the developed and developing countries, and consequentially Beijing suggested that the current war is not the best way to eradicate terrorism. To get rid of terrorism from the Middle Eastern region, Beijing proposed: first, to solve the long-lasting Palestinian/Israeli conflict in a peaceful and fair manner; and second, to help those underdeveloped Arab countries fight against poverty. Beijing's stance is welcomed by the Gulf Muslim countries that have been suspicious of the US-led anti-terrorism war.

On balance, Beijing has been carefully fighting Xinjiang Uygur Muslim separatist movements. So far, Beijing has been successfully winning support from the Middle Eastern Muslim countries, especially Saudi Arabia and Iran, both of which have guaranteed not to intervene in Chinese Muslim affairs. In the words of Mamoun Kurdi, former Saudi Deputy Foreign Minister of Economic and Cultural Affair: "we have been very careful on how we deal with the [Uygurs]. [While] we have a responsibility as the leading and most influential Muslim nation, we also do not want to upset the Chinese."[64]

---

60   Jaffe and Lewis, 126.

61   Blumenthal.

62   Interview in Beijing with the BBC World Service, December 29, 2001.

63   News Conference, Ministry of Foreign Affairs of the People's Republic of China (September 19, 2001).

64   Obaid et al., 37.

The Net Effects of China's Middle East Policy and Implications

The forgoing paragraphs delineate China's Middle East policy since the post-Mao reform: securing the acquisition of oil, expanding economic and trade relations with Middle Eastern countries, and co-operating with Muslim countries in that region in containing the separatist movement within China. What are the effects of China's Middle East policy on this region?

To begin with, Beijing is playing a much more active role in the politics of the Middle East than it ever did before. China's new activism is reflected in the following three aspects:

First, Beijing has used its position and influence in the UN bodies to involve itself in the politics of the Middle East and to increase its political influences in this region. For example, with regard to the post-war Iraqi issue, on many occasions, the PRC has stressed that the UN should play a crucial role in the rebuilding of post-war Iraq.[65] In March 2004, when meeting Bahr Ul-Uloum, the visiting president of the Iraq Interim Governing Council (IGC), Chinese president Hu Jintao said that, "China will consolidate and develop bilateral co-operation with Iraq on the basis of mutual respect, equality and reciprocity" and emphasized again the role of the international community and the idea of "Iraqis governing Iraq."[66] In May 2004, Beijing raised a proposal to enhance the Iraqi interim government's real power by setting a date for a US military withdrawal. In this case, Russia, France, and Germany supported Beijing's proposal, which was included in the final text of the UN Security Council Resolution 1546.[67]

Beijing's strategy is attractive to the Middle East Arab countries which have been resentful of the US Middle East policy.[68] So it is natural for the Middle East Arab countries to look east to the PRC for political allies. Furthermore, Beijing and the Middle East Arab countries realize that their political cooperation may help them counterbalance America's potential political dominance in this region. For example, Iranian leaders even described their relations with Beijing as "fundamental" and "strategic."[69]

Second, Beijing is making efforts to get involved in the Middle Eastern peace process. In November 2002, China decided to dispatch its first Middle East peace envoy—Wang Shijie, a veteran Chinese diplomat who had served as ambassador to Bahrain, Jordan, and Iran. Such action represents Chinese shift toward a more robust, hands-on policy in this region and asserts Beijing's influences in the Middle East affairs.[70] Beijing emphasized that it is unfair to isolate the PRC—one of the permanent members of the UN Security Council—from Middle East affairs. The

---

65   See, for instance, *Beijing Xinhua*, FBIS: CHI, May 27, 2004; also, *Beijing Xinhua*, March 25, 2004 in FBIS: CHI.

66   "HU Offers Help to Iraqi Peace and Development," *China Daily*, March 26, 2004, available at http://www2.chinadaily.com.cn/english/doc/2004-03/26/content_318057.htm.

67   Jin, 6.

68   Li.

69   Troush.

70   Blanche (2003), "China's Mid-East Oil Diplomacy," *The Middle East* 330, 48–51.

US-led Quartet which includes the US, Russia, the European Union (EU), and the UN currently dominates the Middle East peace process.

Third, Beijing has developed an arms relationship with Iraq and Saudi Arabia, as well as with some of the smaller Arab Gulf states, to increase its political influence in this region.[71] China's arms sales to the region expanded significantly during the Iran–Iraq War to the total volume of over $12 billion and after the end of Iran–Iraq War, China's regional arms sales fell by about 40 percent. Currently, Washington suspects that Beijing may work through providing arms (conventional and unconventional) to the Arab oil-exporting countries to secure its oil acquisition.[72] For example, in prepared testimony for a 2003 hearing before the Congressional US-China Economic and Security Review Commission on China's energy needs and strategies, Roger W. Robinson, chairman of the commission, and C. Richard D'Amato, vice chairman, argued that Beijing's relations with the Arab Gulf countries may involve the offer of missile and WMD technologies to these countries for the sake of securing long-term access to oil supplies.[73]

On the other hand, even though much evidence has indicated that China is having more and more of an impact in the region, Beijing is far from becoming a dominant power in the Middle East. At the present time, the US is the main protector of regional stability in the Middle East and free outflow of oil from the Gulf oil-exporting countries. Beijing does not have a strong blue-water navy to project its military capabilities into the Middle Eastern region and to protect the oil sea-lane from the Persian Gulf to China. This sea-lane stretches from the Strait of Hormuz to the Indian Ocean and the Straits of Malacca, and finally to the South China Sea, a total of more than 7,000 miles. At the current stage, Beijing has to rely on the US to protect the safe and free passage of this sea-lane. Even though the PRC has taken measures to develop its blue-water navy forces and to construct "a naval base in Gwadar, Pakistan, not far from the mouth of the Strait of Hormuz, facilities in Myanmar close to the Strait of Malacca,"[74] there are no possibilities that the PRC can protect this sea-lane by itself in the next two decades.

Furthermore, the PRC's strategy to secure the acquisition of the Gulf oil is motivated more geo-economically rather than geo-strategically.[75] In the past, the PRC had no strategic interests in this region and on most occasions only supported the Middle East Arab countries rhetorically and politically. Since the 1990s, the drive for economic modernization and the quest for oil dominated the PRC's foreign policy towards the Middle East. Overall, the China mainly drew upon bilateral diplomacy to enhance its political and economic relations with the Gulf oil-exporting countries to secure the free flow of trade and oil. Geo-political and strategic interests have never become the top priority in the PRC's policy agenda. With respect to the regional stability of the Gulf and the free passage of the sea oil-lane, Beijing would

---

71   See Gill, 96–99.

72   Blumenthal.

73   Jin, 6.

74   Blumenthal, 12.

75   Rynhold; Manning, R. (2000), "The Asian Energy Predicament," *Survival* 42/3, 73–83.

like to take a free ride on American protection. On the other hand, the US tends to encourage the PRC's free-riding behavior for the sake of the regional stability in the Gulf.[76]

In summary, Beijing's Middle East policy agenda is primarily driven by the economic imperatives of modernization, such as the quest for oil and the commercial and trade relations, rather than by the need to challenge the US hegemony in this region. China is cautious about confronting the American interests, and when it does confront the US in this region, Beijing appears to compromise with Washington.

Conclusions

Of all outside powers, the PRC is the most significant newcomer to the international relations of the Gulf Region. In the late 1970s, the PRC's trade and foreign investment in the region was almost insignificant, but had developed significantly by 2005, and it is forecasted to develop much quicker with the establishment of an FTA between the PRC and the GCC.

The current Beijing Middle East policy is primarily driven by the economic imperatives of modernization. Among these imperatives, the quest for oil is the most important. It is estimated that up to 75 percent of China's oil demand will come from foreign supplies in the next two decades and up to 80 percent of such oil imports may come from the Middle East oil-rich nations. Meanwhile, the trade and commercial relations with Israel have become vital to Beijing since the 1990s, and currently, Israel is an important supplier of high-technological products to Beijing.

To secure the free flow of oil and to maintain the trade and commercial relations with both the Arab and Israeli, China has the common interest with the US in preserving Middle East stability and peace. In recent years, Beijing has actively participated in the Israel-Palestinian peace process, post-war Iraqi reconstruction, and Iranian nuclear program. However, it is not likely that Beijing will take a lead in those issues. Rather, the PRC continues to emphasize that all those issues can be solved only under a UN framework with the lead of the Security Council. Given its position and influence in the UN bodies, Beijing hopes that a UN-led framework would increase its political influences in this region.

With regard to the Middle East stability and peace, Beijing prefers to play the role of the "free rider" rather than that of the "protector." Given the increased political relations with the Middle East nations, particularly Saudi Arabia and Iran, it is likely that the PRC is going to play a much more important role. China may not become a dominant power in this region and may not compete directly with the current dominant power—the US. However, the PRC may become a kind of swing power that can be conditionally effectual in influencing the Middle East peace and security.[77]

---

76   Manning.
77   Han.

Chapter 6

Japan between the United States and the Middle East

George Ehrhardt

By the fall of 2004, two foreign leaders had publicly expressed their hopes that George Bush would win the upcoming American election—the prime ministers of Israel and Japan. The Israeli preference is easy to understand, but Prime Minister Junichiro Koizumi's position is more difficult. This chapter seeks to explain his stance, and in doing so, explain how Japan's policy towards the Middle East is tied to its relations with the United States.

Koizumi's support came in spite of how problematic the Iraq War has been for the Government of Japan. Domestically, a dramatic increase in oil prices during the war threatened Japan's fragile recovery from 12 years of economic depression. Sending forces to Iraq required the passage of controversial legislation permitting the overseas deployment of Japanese troops. On top of that, Japan's support for the US made it a possible target for terrorists. So why would Koizumi want another Bush Administration?

The simplistic answer is that Japan was once again hiding "under America's skirts," as the *Economist* snidely noted.[1] Since the end of WWII, the Japanese Government has supported American policy so consistently that its media refers to the Ministry of Foreign Affairs as "the US State Department's branch office in Tokyo." On issues ranging from the status of Taiwan to the first Gulf War, Japanese policymakers have put aside their own preferences to toe the American line. The War in Iraq is just one more addition to that list.

Appealing as this story may be, it misses two crucial points. Japan's short history of foreign relations has been driven by the need to secure resources from abroad, for the rocky island chain offers the Japanese people neither adequate food nor energy. A stable US-led world order awards Japan the chance to acquire these resources peacefully, with no need to risk the terrible consequences of its pre-war unilateral strategy. To Japan, the United States plays two distinct roles: it provides a security umbrella for a liberal trading order that sustains the Japanese economy, but—and this is an important qualification—it is also an economic competitor within that order. The Japanese Government has persistently followed a policy separating political from economic issues (*seikei* bunri); Koizumi's stance in Iraq reflects Japan's support for American security policy, but it conceals a willingness to enact contradictory economic policies.

---

1   "Japan's assertive new prime minister," *The Economist*, September 28, 2006.

These differences emerge clearly in Japanese foreign policy towards the Middle East. Since 1973, when Japanese policymakers began paying attention to Middle Eastern politics, Japan's economic policies, such as an unofficial boycott of Israel, support for the Palestinians, and sustained economic aid to the region, have flown in the face of America's pro-Israel security policy.

The second point missed in the simple version is the function Iraq played in Koizumi's domestic agenda. Both Koizumi and his successor, Shinzo Abe, have insisted that Japan must take a political role commensurate with its massive economy, but they faced domestic opposition. As often happens in Japanese politics, Koizumi used American demands to advance his own agenda for change. Far from "hiding," the dispatch of Japanese Self-Defense Forces (SDF) troops to Iraq was a statement of Tokyo's growing assertiveness.

This chapter proceeds in three parts. In the first, it briefly outlines the trajectory of Japanese foreign relations, explaining the separation of economics from politics and Japan's reliance on American political leadership. The second part takes a closer look at Japanese policy towards the Middle East to see that division in practice. The chapter closes with an insight into ongoing changes in Japanese foreign policy thinking that suggests Tokyo might once again enter the political arena.

Political Passivity and Economic Assertiveness

Japan's defeat in 1945 still reverberates in its approach to the world. From a Japanese perspective, the war occurred as they struggled to answer the question of how a nation with little usable land and few natural resources could prosper in the modern world. During the 1920s and 30s, as Japan lurched towards war with the United States, a bitter conflict emerged in Tokyo over this issue. One faction called for Japan to seize territory in Asia, seeking autonomy through an aggressive foreign policy. The other argued that conflict with the Anglo-American countries would be counterproductive and sought prosperity through closer economic ties. The militarist faction's victory set events in motion that would lead first to *Pearl Harbor*, then to Hiroshima. As John Dower recounts, Japanese citizens saw the totality of Japan's defeat in 1945 as a crushing repudiation of this militarist approach to foreign policy.[2]

In the war's aftermath, Japanese leaders pursued cooperation with their former enemies. This was formalized in the *Yoshida Doctrine*, which still provides the foundation for Japanese foreign policy. It calls for Japan to do three things: make economic growth the government's primary focus, closely follow America's foreign policy lead, and preserve Japan's unarmed pacifism. In other words, Japan abdicated its security to the United States, simultaneously pursuing an active role in the country's foreign economic relations.

Unlike most countries, Japan has only seen two world orders. From Tokyo's opening to the world in 1853 until the Second World War, Japanese leaders saw a savage world in which the strong preyed upon the weak, exploiting others to

---

2   Dower, J. (1999), *Embracing Defeat: Japan in the Wake of World War II*, New York: W.W. Norton & Co.

strengthen their own benefits. Driven by a passion for national independence, Japan launched a series of rapacious wars with China, Russia and the United States to secure the resources it needed.[3] Not only did these wars ravage the Asian continent and earn Japan the lingering enmity of her neighbors, they ended with the destruction of urban Japan at the hands of US bombers. With the creation of the Bretton Woods system and the UN, America offered Japan a different world, one in which overwhelming American military power guaranteed Japan's companies access to the resources and markets they needed. This new American world order offered to meet Japan's foreign policy goals more securely than the Japanese Empire ever had.

This new order resonated with a domestic rejection of militarism, holding it responsible for leading Japan down the path to destruction. US Occupation authorities cooperated with Japanese elites to blame the war on a small group in the military and industry, avoiding any broader sense of responsibility on the part of the Japanese people.[4] While this has prevented any resolution of Japanese war guilt similar to what happened in Germany, it has also conditioned the Japanese against the use of force in foreign policy.

It is in this spirit that Japan has approached the Middle East, uninterested in political questions like the status of Israel or the Suez Canal. Japan fought one devastating war over oil, and has no plans to get dragged into another.

Japanese Policy Towards the Middle East

This attitude may have peaked in 1964, when Prime Minister Ikeda brusquely dismissed visiting Kuwaiti Foreign Minister Al-Sabah, leaving him to wander the hallways alone, looking for an elevator.[5] Prior to 1941, Japanese contact with the Middle East was limited to a small trade in textiles, but the war cut off contact for a decade. Nor did Japan have significant immigrant populations to raise the salience of Middle Eastern issues. It was not until 1953 that a Japanese trade mission traveled to the region to convince governments there to lower the anti-Japanese policies enacted during the war.

What contact occurred in the following 20 years was driven by Japan's need to pay for oil imports in hard currency, leading the government to promote Japanese exports to the region. This included sponsoring trade fairs and providing loans for infrastructure development. In an effort to promote Japanese indigenous refining capabilities, the government did secure oil rights for Japanese companies from Kuwait

---

3   Ironically, witness to Egypt's suffering at the hands of British imperialists served as a powerful warning to the Meiji-era (late 1800s) Japanese elites, spurring them to pursue independence at all costs. See Mizuguchi, A. (2002), "From Ancient to Modern Times: a Retrospective of Japan's relationship with the Middle East," *Asia-Pacific Review* 9/2.

4   Dower, 1999.

5   Al-Sabah's visit appears in Hirokawa, R. (1987), *Hadanso* [*Breaking Faults*], Tokyo: Kondansha.

and Saudi Arabia, but in general, policy-makers did not see the Arab governments as important, focusing on the major oil companies instead.[6]

Unfortunately, this period also saw the beginnings of a persistent misunderstanding between Arab states and Japan over political issues. Anti-Western sentiment in the Arab World after the 1948 war in Palestine left Arabs with a positive impression of non-white, non-Christian Japan, and Tokyo's acceptance of Nasser's plan to nationalize the Suez Canal (plus its economic support for post-independence Egypt) reinforced their impression. What they missed, however, was that, although Tokyo diverged from the American position, Japanese policymakers did not see themselves as taking the Arabs' "side." To them, they were just keeping their nose out from where it did not belong. At the same time, Japanese companies were rejecting American policy on China and exploring trade links to the mainland, but unlike the Middle East, everyone there understood that the economic activity was independent of any political stance on Taiwan.

Seeking Political Neutrality in the 1973 Oil Crisis

Unnoticed by Ikeda and his successor Eisaku Sato, however, the ground was shifting under Japan's feet, making its policy unsustainable. Before WWII, Japan's military was dependent on imported oil, but the national economy ran mostly on coal (which was domestically available). This changed dramatically as the Japanese economy took off. Between 1945 and 1973, its energy use increased tenfold, and the share of oil in its energy budget exploded from 5 percent to 72 percent.[7] By 1973, 77 percent of that oil came from the Middle East, making Japan especially vulnerable to economic pressure from Arab oil exporters.

When the large Middle Eastern producers nationalized production and threatened "unfriendly" nations with boycotts, Japan unexpectedly found itself on the wrong side of the fence. Arab hostility caught the Japanese Government by surprise. Japan had not opposed any Arab initiatives, it had offered economic aid, and it had even worked behind the scenes at the United Nations for the passage of Security Council Resolution 242, calling for the Israelis to withdraw from the territories it occupied in 1967, and for the "land for peace" settlement of the Arab–Israeli conflict.[8] From an Arab perspective, however, Japanese moves were merely gestures to sustain the flow of oil, and did not reflect any commitment to the Arab cause. Both sides were right, of course. Japan was not genuinely committed to the Arab side, because Japanese leaders couldn't see any reason why they should be committed to either side of a political dispute halfway around the world. Still, the new government of Prime Minister Kakuei Tanaka saw little choice but to take a series of small steps to ensure the access to Arab oil production.

---

6   Yoshitsu, M. (1984), *Caught in the Middle East: Japan's Diplomacy in Transition*, Lexington: Lexington Books.

7   Kelly, D. (2005), "Rice, Oil, and the Atom: A Study of the Role of Key Material Resources in the Security and Development of Japan," *Government and Opposition* 40/2.

8   Mizuguchi.

The Japanese Government's initial response was little more than a codification of previous policy: it issued a statement opposing the acquisition of any territory by force, calling for the withdrawal of Israeli forces from the Occupied Territories, and supporting the rights of Palestinians, all of which came naturally from Japan's continuing pacifism and support for the United Nations. When further pressed by Arab states, the Japanese Government announced its intent to work for peace based on an Israeli withdrawal, and deploring its slowness. The next year it expressed its sympathy for the Palestinian situation by recognizing the PLO.

Nevertheless, Japan's relations with Israel saw no significant change. Even before the 1973 crisis, some Japanese firms had respected the Arab demand for a boycott of Israeli business and some had rejected it. Yamaha Motors, for example, refused to sell cars in Israel, even though Yamaha Music (the two companies had a single chairman) maintained its 20 percent share of the Israeli piano market. Unlike that of the United States, the Japanese Government did not take a stance on the boycott, forcing companies to trade with Israel at their own risk.[9] The government, however, maintained diplomatic relations with Israel, effectively preserving the political and economic status quo, nor did its voting on Arab–Israeli issues in the United Nations change.[10]

What did alter was Japan's policy of relying on the United States to deal with Middle Eastern governments. In what came to be known as "oil-begging diplomacy," high-level Foreign Ministry officials shuttled to the Middle East trying to secure oil contracts.[11] This culminated in Prime Minister Takeo Fukuda's visit to the Middle East, the first prime ministerial visit to the region since before WWII.

Along with diplomatic visits, Japan also attempted to use foreign aid to blunt Arab hostility. Before the 1973 crisis, aid to the Middle East was limited to only 0.8 percent of Japan's Official Development Assistance (as a part of Organization for Economic Cooperation and Development program), but by 1977 that figure had jumped to 24.5 percent.[12] This included grants and loans to oil producing countries, as well as government-financed investment in the region.

Japan also took domestic action to protect its economy from further shocks. The Petroleum Supply and Demand Adjustment Law reinvigorated Japan's declining Ministry of International Trade and Industry, giving it extensive powers to force large consumers to implement conservation programs and require producers to keep oil stockpiles.[13] As a result, when the second Oil Crisis occurred in 1979 during the Iranian Revolution, Japan was much better prepared than it had been in 1973. Since

---

9   Shaoul, R. (2004), "Japan and Israel: An Evaluation of Relationship-Building in the Context of Japan's Middle East Policy," *Israel Affairs* 10/1–2.

10   Kuroda, Y. (2001), "Japan's Middle East Policy: Fuzzy Nonbinary Process Model," in Akitoshi Miyashita and Yoichiro Sato (eds), *Japanese Foreign Policy in Asia and the Pacific*, London: Palgrave.

11   Sakai, K. (2001), "Japan-Iraq Relations: The Perception Gap and its Influence on Diplomatic Policies," *Arab Studies Quarterly* 23/4.

12   Kelly. After the price of oil collapsed in the 1980s, ODA to the Middle East dropped to the 10 percent range again.

13   Johnson, C. (1982), *Miti and the Japanese Miracle*, Berkeley: University of California Press.

1973, a nuclear power initiative had built enough reactors to supply 11 percent of the country's electric power, and Japan now had a 102-day strategic reserve of oil. Still, Japanese leaders felt tremendous pressure to secure the country's oil supplies.[14] Using foreign aid as diplomatic tool, just as they did in 1973, they offered Iraq and Mexico large loans in return for stabilizing the flow of oil to Japan.

This strategy of deflecting political demands appeared in Japan's mirror-image rejection of American demands. Shortly after the Arab world announced its embargo in 1973, Secretary of State Henry Kissinger traveled to Tokyo to encourage Japan to support the American position. Fresh from their humiliation over Kissinger's secret visit to China, however, Japanese policymakers were in no mood to listen, and insisted that Japan had to be seen as separate from the US. In his memoirs, Kissinger recounts how Tanaka and foreign minister Ohira insisted that Tokyo had no interest whatsoever in taking sides in a political struggle over the fate of Palestine; rather, it was just doing the minimum it could to ensure its supply of oil.[15]

Japan's stance on the Arab–Israeli issue illustrates the Yoshida Doctrine in action. It combined a non-critical acceptance of American security policy with an independent economic policy and a firm refusal to become involved in American security action. Just as it had on the issues of relations with Mainland China and of rearmament, Tokyo offered its interlocutors compliance in one sphere and determined independence in others.

The 1991 Gulf War and Cracks in the Yoshida Doctrine

This bifurcated strategy of political neutrality and economic engagement survived with little change until 1991, when the first Gulf War occurred. By this time, Japan was the world's largest consumer of Middle Eastern oil, with the most at stake in the struggle for control of Kuwait's oil. Coupled with Japan's alliance to the United States, Washington reasonably expected that Japan would join the international coalition formed to drive Hussein out of Kuwait. The first Bush Administration made no secret of its demands that Japan send naval units to the Gulf under UN authorization. Nevertheless, the Japanese Government refused, citing its constitutional limits on the use of military force.

American negotiators had butted their heads against this argument without success for three decades as they tried to convince Japanese policymakers to rearm, but this time was different. Military action in the Gulf would not entangle Japan in a wider conflict as it might have during the Cold War. UN Security Council authorization for the war meant that by contributing to the coalition, Japan would be fulfilling its treaty obligations under the UN charter, something that Japanese policymakers claimed was a foreign policy priority.

Most importantly, trade conflicts from the 1980s left Americans unwilling to fight a war for Japan's benefit. During the Oil Crises of the 1970s, Americans still saw Japan as a poor country, producing small cars and cheap toys, and they could accept Japan's inability to become involved in foreign disputes. The 1980s, however,

---

14   Klein, D. (1980), "Japan 1979: The Second Oil Crisis," *Asian Survey* 20/1, 42–52.
15   Kissinger, H. (1982), *Years of Upheaval*, Little, Brown & Co.

saw a dramatic reversal of roles: as the American economy struggled to recover from stagflation, the Japanese economy raced ahead. During the "bubble years" of the 1980s, Japanese competition drove American firms out of business, even entire industries, and used the cash to buy up public landmarks like Pebble Beach golf course or the Rockefeller Center. Under the Reagan Administration, high-level security consultation between the two governments broke off completely over the issue of burden sharing—whether was Japan doing enough for its own security.[16] In this new environment, Japan's refusal to participate in the war was no longer peaceful cooperation; it was the action of a selfish parasite. Tokyo was demanding American soldiers fight for oil to supply Japanese companies so they, in turn, could get more money out of those same soldiers' families. At a time when US Congressmen were taking sledgehammers to a Toyota in front of the Capitol Building, this constituted a powerful argument.

In the end, Tokyo coughed up $13 billion to pay coalition expenses, but this came so late that it could only be seen as a last-ditch attempt to buy Japan's way out of trouble, not a willing contribution to international security. American policymakers were caught in the same situation that the Arabs had found themselves in 15 years earlier. Their beliefs about Japan's willingness to be a committed ally ran straight into the wall of the Yoshida Doctrine, which limited action to the economic sphere, not the political one.

But while the Arabs lacked the power to change Japanese policy, and Kissinger had little reason to, the Clinton Administration had both. American officials sent unsubtle hints that unless Japan shaped up, Washington was likely to lose interest in the alliance altogether.[17] After much soul-searching, and further embarrassment during the 1994 North Korean nuclear crisis, Japanese policymakers eventually agreed to revise the guidelines for US-Japan military cooperation, offering the possibility that Japanese forces could support US action in an area roughly 1,000 miles out from Japan.[18] This new policy did not overthrow the Yoshida Doctrine, but did begin to chip away at it, a process that picked up steam after the 9/11 terrorist attacks on the US soil.

Ongoing Change in Japanese Policy and the Middle East

The events of September 11th, 2001 had a powerful impact on Japanese security policy. Recently, elected Prime Minister Junichiro Koizumi introduced legislation that would allow Japan Self Defense Forces (JSDF) to provide logistical support for US forces and security for US bases in Japan, and also send JSDF abroad for humanitarian missions. This led to the immediate deployment of transport aircraft to

---

16   Ehrhardt, G. (2002), *Engagement and Alliances in Northeast Asia: The Role of Security Consultation*, Ph.D. Dissertation, Indiana University.

17   Funabashi, Y. (1999), *Alliance Adrift*, Council on Foreign Relations.

18   Murata, K. (2000), "Do the New Guidelines Make the US-Japan Alliance More Effective?" in Masahi Nishihara (ed.), *The Japan-US Alliance: New Challenges for the 21st Century*, JCIE Press.

Pakistan, naval vessels to the Indian Ocean, and the eventual deployment of combat engineers in the occupation of Iraq.

The legislation enacted in 2003 to permit the dispatches set two important precedents for future Japanese policy. Japanese troops entered a combat zone—even in a rear support capacity—for the first time since 1945. Furthermore, the language of the law empowered them to use weapons not just for self-defense, but for the defense of anyone under their responsibility. Critics envisioned a scenario where Japanese soldiers would find themselves in combat defending a hospital where wounded American soldiers recuperated. None of these would have been possible a decade before, when the 1991 debacle revealed the tight constraints on Japan's security policy.

Domestic Change and Support for American Policy in Iraq

In addition to the fears of US abandonment that emerged after the war, two dramatic shifts in domestic politics set the stage for this reconfiguration of Japan's security policy. The first was the near-disappearance of the long-time socialist opposition. From 1955 until the late 1990s, Japan's Socialist Party (JSP) had been the single largest party after the Liberal Democratic Party (LDP), comprising approximately one third of the Diet. While it remained strong, it consistently opposed any active cooperation with US security policy; although never in power, it was able to constrain LDP decision-making. After a brief flirtation with the LDP in the 1994, coalition government's socialist voter support plummeted and the JSP vanished overnight. Its replacement as leading opposition party, The Democratic Party (DPJ), actually expressed cautious support for Koizumi's actions, allowing him to go further than he would have a decade before.[19]

A similar shift to the right had occurred within the LDP as well with Koizumi's election as party president in April of 2001. While foreign policy did not feature prominently in his election, the contest inadvertently drew a clear line between the old guard, which supported Japan's traditional pacifism and a non-controversial foreign policy, and a new generation of men like Koizumi and Shinzo Abe, who believed Japan should take a more active role in its own security. This battle within the LDP did not climax until the 2005 elections, when the old guard was expelled and defeated, but by September 2001, Koizumi was already pressing hard for domestic reform in Japan's public spending that directly threatened their political supporters. Thus, the old guard had neither energy nor political capital to spend worrying about the foreign policy shift. These changes left Koizumi with a freer hand than any previous Japanese Prime Minister.

More important than the laws themselves, however, was the new spirit in which they were enacted. In contrast to the 1991 Gulf War, the current US Government does not appear to have placed heavy pressure on Japan for assistance, and, in fact,

---

19   Sakai, K. (2003), "11 September and the Clash of Civilizations: the Role of the Japanese Media and Public Discourse," *Arab Studies Quarterly* 25/1–2.

sees such pressure as endangering Koizumi's ability to act.[20] Instead, the laws are a manifestation of a growing sentiment that Japan should play a political role—within some constraints—commensurate with its economic might.[21]

Immediately after the 9/11 attacks, 57 percent of voters agreed that Japan should assist the US military's actions against terror.[22] As the Iraq War loomed, voters in most countries saw it as an American adventure, and raised their voices in protest. In Japan, however, the proportion of people who felt that Japan should support US policy actually *rose*, to 76 percent.[23] Discussion with Japanese voters revealed that this was not support for the war itself, but a belief that this time Japan had a duty to step up and participate in the international effort. Such opinion explains why most of those who supported cooperation with the US in the poll answered that they did so because it was necessary, not because they agreed with US policy itself. This interpretation is further supported by the persistence of public support for JSDF troops in Iraq, despite the escalating violence there, measuring success by the scale of Japanese action than by the results of US efforts in Iraq. A survey done as the ground elements pulled out of Iraq in 2006 found that a significant majority (59 percent) of Japanese still felt the dispatch had been the right thing to do.[24] These numbers demonstrate how public opinion in Japan has shifted to favor a more active and engaged foreign policy.

Part of this change is generational. As those who remember WWII fade from the scene, they are being replaced by younger, more nationalistic generations, who value an increased world role for Japan. Another poll in June of 2006, for example, found that the strongest support for the JSDF mission in Iraq came from voters in their 20s.[25] In the years to come, Japan's role in Middle Eastern security issues is likely to rise, as Tokyo pursues a more activist foreign policy.

Redefining Activism: Differences between Japan and other Great Powers

In a policy book such as this, however, which juxtaposes independent action by international powers and their support for the United States, it is important to distinguish Japan's activism from that of the traditional great powers. Where European countries, broadly speaking, define an active role in world politics as one

---

20   Ishizuka, K. (2004), "Japan and UN Peace Operations," *Japanese Journal of Political Science* 5/1, 137–57. Accusations of US pressure led Koizumi to display his limited command of English by proclaiming in the Diet that America had not asked him to "show the frog [flag]."

21   Hughes, C. (2004), "Japan's Security Policy, the US-Japan Alliance, and the War on Terror: Incrementalism Confirmed or Radical Leap," *Australian Journal of International Affairs* 58/4, 42–45.

22   Shinbun, Y. (October 21, 2001), A larger proportion of respondents (3.6 percent) felt that Japan should join combat operations against terrorists than felt that Japan should not cooperate with the US (2.4 percent).

23   Shinbun, Y. (May 3, 2003).

24   Shinbun, Y. (July 10, 2006).

25   Shinbun, A. (June 29, 2006).

in which they can oppose American policy, Japanese leaders still largely measure activism by the degree of support they can provide to the United States.

This is not a rejection of Japan's own national interest; rather, it is an affirmation of that interest. Japan has prospered under American hegemony more than any other country on the planet. The "Yankee go home" spirit of the 1950s withered away as American policies provided access to the resources and markets that brought Japan wealth beyond politicians' extravagant campaign promises. However intolerable some of the US policies may be, the liberal order sustained by America answers Japan's core needs better than Japanese independent policy. Tokyo leaders also recognize that for the indefinite future, America remains the world's pre-eminent economic and military power, and see no reason to challenge that. This means that for Japan, vigorously pursuing its national interest entails active support for American policy.

In 2004, the national interest triumphed over pacifist norms and a respect for the United Nations in Koizumi's support of President Bush's re-election.[26] For all of its foreign policy failures, the Bush Administration has maintained better relations with Japan than any president since Teddy Roosevelt. From a Japanese perspective, the Bush Administration was worth supporting because, first of all, it dropped long-time American demands for changes in Japanese economic policy, and, second of all, it more broadly respected Japanese preferences.

Unlike President Clinton's hard-line demands for increasing the sale of American products in Japan, or the George Bush's sales job for American auto parts, the current Bush Administration has remained silent on the trade issue. Nor has the Bush Administration simply refrained from demanding Japan to change. In the midst of a Japanese debate about how much of the Anglo-Saxon model it should adopt to pull out of a decade-long recession, President Bush appeared before a joint session of the Japanese Diet, shocking viewers (such as this author) by insisting that Japan look to its own internal tradition to find solutions. These policies are a tacit acceptance of the Yoshida Doctrine's first clause, that Japan should independently pursue its own agenda of economic development.[27]

Ironically—given its reputation elsewhere—the Bush Administration's Asia policy strove to make Japan feel included, rather than ignored. Where Gore and Kerry promised to deal with North Korea one-on-one dialogue, Bush insisted that Japan and other Asian countries be present at the table. Where Clinton stirred unease by flying directly to Beijing without a stop in Japan, Bush made sure Tokyo was his first stop in Asia. Where Clinton and former Prime Minister Hashimoto kept their distance after a number of trade spats, Bush actually seemed to enjoy going out for *yakitori* (Japanese type of grilled chicken) with Koizumi, dropping in for an unscheduled chat with Foreign Minister Makiko Tanaka when she was in

---

26   The strength of these norms is described in Hook, G. et al. (2001), *Japan's International Relations: Politics, Economics, and Security*, London: Routledge.

27   And act independently it has. Resisting American attempts to isolate Iran, Foreign Minister Kawaguchi visited Tehran in 2002 and 2004, as well as signed an agreement to work with Iran in developing a new oil field at Azegedan.

Washington, and his immediate reaction to the *Ehime Maru*[28] tragedy were well publicized in the Japanese media.

Supporting American policy served as an important litmus test for the Bush Administration, and Tokyo felt that passing that test was more important for Japan than principled opposition to the war in Iraq. Koizumi's willingness to take that support to a new level with the dispatch of JSDF units to the Middle East reflects a change in Japan's perception of its role in the world, reflecting a position of a growing majority that agrees Japan must actively cooperate with the United States in providing international security.

Conclusions

While the Middle East has never been at the top of Japan's priorities, events there have thrown its foreign policy into sharp relief.[29] During the 1950s and 60s, Tokyo closely followed the *Yoshida Doctrine*, emphasizing economic links with oil producing countries without attaching any political strings. The 1970s, however, exposed the dangers of this policy, as Japan suffered through the Oil Shocks when the Arabs demanded political action that Tokyo was unwilling to take. Conversely, Japan also refused American demands for political action. These cracks finally splintered open in 1991, when Japan's reluctance to participate in the first Gulf War exposed it to international ridicule and threatened its alliance with the United States.

Japan's actions after 9/11 are more than just a response to terrorism, or to US demands. The support for US action and the dispatch of JSDF troops to Pakistan and Iraq reflect a growing perception among Japanese leaders and the general public that Japan should no longer rely on others to provide the peace it needs to sustain prosperity. Instead, it must do what it can to support the US in its role as guarantor of a liberal world order.

In the most striking acknowledgment of this change to date, the LDP released a draft of proposed revisions to Japan's constitution in November of 2001. The headline grabbing change referred to Article 9, which currently prohibits Japan from the use of military force or even possessing a military. The LDP proposed to amend this to allow Japan a military and permit its use abroad as part of international peacekeeping activities. Where previous LDP Administrations have finessed the issue by referring to the constitution's preamble, which declares support for the United Nations, current Prime Minister Shinzo Abe insists that the constitution itself must be re-written. To

---

28   On February 9, 2001, *USS Greenville* submarine, while surfacing, hit a Japanese fishing vessel *Ehime Maru*, with high school students on board. *Ehime Maru* sank, taking lives of nine crew members, four of which were students.

29   It is curious to note that Abe's new (September 2006) national security adviser has close personal ties to the Middle East. Before becoming a Diet member, Yuriko Koike graduated from Cairo University in Egypt, and worked as a journalist covering the Middle East for Nippon TV. After joining the Koizumi Cabinet in 2003, she made multiple trips to the region, and welcomed Middle Eastern dignitaries to Japan.

allay fears on the Asian mainland, Abe posits that the revisions are not intended to allow Japan to "wage war."[30]

Instead, the changes will smooth the way for Japan to support US and UN action in the model established after 9/11. In 2002, the government explicitly rejected a "special relationship" between the US and Britain, insisting that the two countries "complement" each other's policies.[31] This vision describes what subsequently happened in the Middle East, where Japanese forces supported American ones in non-combat roles, whether surveillance and re-supply at sea, or in reconstruction duties in Iraq. Japan's role in a proposed multinational blockade of North Korea appears to confirm this, with Abe offering to use Japanese naval vessels to support the blockade, although not taking responsibility for the boarding of suspect vessels. What exactly this means for the Middle East will depend on events, but should the US once again feel a need for Japanese rear area support, it is highly likely that JSDF troops will return to the region.

---

30   Prime Minister's Diet Interpellation, October 19, 2006.
31   Mochizuki, M. (2003), "Strategic Thinking under Bush and Koizumi: Implications for the US–Japan Alliance," *Asia-Pacific Review* 10/1.

Chapter 7

At the Crossroads of Foreign Policy Decisions: India in the Middle East

Anna Rulska and David Jackson

India does not currently exercise a great deal of influence in the Middle East, but as a rising economic and political power on the world stage, it will likely play a critical role in the future of the region. New Delhi's engagement with the Middle East, in configuration with its general approach to foreign policy, has been driven by a policy of non-alignment. However, recent dialogue between New Delhi and Washington, which started after the end of the Cold War, challenges this policy. Given the current international configuration of threats, challenges, and power, India finds itself at the crossroads of decisions regarding its foreign policy. In its approach to the Middle East, five factors impact New Delhi's strategy: 1) regional power of China, 2) conflict over Kashmir with Pakistan, exasperated with possession of nuclear weapons by both states, 3) threat of Islamic terrorism, 4) increasing dependency on energy imports, and 5) existential need to uphold friendly relations with the United States—which also serves as the main frame for outlining India's policy in the region.

In order to provide a comprehensive view of India's approach to the Middle East, complimented by an analysis of the above mentioned factors, this chapter starts with a brief discussion of the economic and political position of India in the world, followed by a section delineating the basis of New Delhi's relationship with Washington and its main areas. The third section focuses on the issues of energy and non-proliferation in the context of relations with Iran. In section four, the Arab–Israeli conflict is discussed, followed by a brief analysis of the security threats shared by both India and Israel—namely that of Islamic terrorism. This chapter concludes with a prognosis of what the future holds for India's foreign policy in respect to the Middle East and what degree of influence will New Delhi be able to exercise in the region.

India in the World

The historical and demographic characteristics of India influence its policies toward the Middle East. In order to understand India's position in the world and its influence on international politics in respect to other states, it is also important to provide general information regarding the political and economic conditions.

India achieved independence in 1947, after years of nonviolent resistance led by Mohandas Gandhi and Jawaharlal Nehru. In 2006, India's population was estimated at just under 1.1 billion, with about 81 percent Hindu and 13.4 percent Muslim. About a quarter of Indians live in poverty, although the economy has grown at an average rate of 7 percent since 1994 and the poverty rate has been reduced by about 10 percent in the same time period. While the majority of India's citizens (60 percent) work in agriculture, that industry accounts for only about 19 percent of India's GDP; services account for the majority (54 percent). Approximately 5.1 million Indians live with HIV or AIDS.[1]

India is a federal republic and is the world's most populous democracy. There are dozens of political parties, many of which represent only the interests of one of India's 28 states. In 2006, the Prime Minister Manmohan Singh, whose governing India National Congress Party-headed coalition consisted of 20 parties representing 270 seats out of 545 in the People's Assembly. Under then-Prime Minister Atal Bijari Vajpayee the more conservative Bharatiya Janata Party (BJP) formed a coalition government between 1998 and 2004, and now is the opposition. The Communist Party of India holds 43 seats, and is an important coalition partner of the Congress Party Government.[2]

As is the case with most countries that attempt to achieve a global power status and claim a regional power position, India's most important foreign relations take place with nearby states. India maintains a significant relationship with neighbor and frequent enemy Pakistan—the scope of which also impacts Indian approach to the issues in the Middle East region. Both states possess nuclear capabilities and have gone to war against each other three times over the disputed region of Kashmir. In 1998, India tested three nuclear weapons, first such tests in 24 years, and just three weeks later Pakistan did the same.[3] During the Cold War, the US tilted in favor of Pakistan, but India and the US began to improve relations after the collapse of the USSR in 1991. After the terrorist attacks of September 11, 2001, the US sought closer ties with Pakistan, but it hoped to do so without alienating India.

India's foreign relations reflect a traditional policy of nonalignment, the exigencies of domestic economic reform (privatization and market liberalization) and development, and the changing post-Cold War international environment. While at times India saw itself as the leader of a nonaligned bloc during the Cold War, it also depended heavily on the Soviet Union for trade and weapons. The collapse of communism in Europe and the dismantling of the Soviet Union forced India to look elsewhere for strategic partners and to drift towards the US. "The relationship between our two nations has never been stronger, and it will grow even closer in the days and years to come," President Bush said on July 18, 2005 when Indian Prime Minister Manmohan Singh visited Washington, D.C.[4]

---

1   "India," *The World Factbook*, available at https://www.cia.gov/cia/publications/factbook/geos/in.html.

2   Ibid.

3   Winner, A.C. and Yoshihara, T. (2002), "India and Pakistan at the Edge," *Survival*, 44(3), 69–86.

4   Khanna, P. and Mohan, C..R. (2006), "Getting India Right," *Policy Review*, 135, available at http://www.policyreview.org/135/khanna.html.

The relationship between New Delhi and Washington both impacts and is influenced by the current international challenges and global trends.[5] Global energy security issues, with increasing usage and dependency, did not circumvent India, nor did it avoid affecting India's stance toward Iran—and with that a close collision with the United States, further exaggerated with India's position toward the war in Iraq. Combined with the effort to enhance non-proliferation, counteracted by the neighborhood of China and Pakistan, India finds itself often at the crossroads of decision-making in its foreign relations. As Washington and other western capitals, New Delhi experiences much amplified pressures from and fears of Islamic fundamentalism, which in turn puts India in a position of sympathizing and understanding the travails of Israel. The above mentioned domestic and international factors serve as a fundament to establish the trajectory of India's relationship with the Middle East, positioned in the framework of the relationship with the United States.

India and the United States in Perspective

Relations between India and the US have always been complicated. In the current international arrangement, plagued by issues of nuclear proliferation, undefined security threats and Islamic fundamentalism, New Delhi's dialogue with Washington has gained in importance and significance. "India lost its independence when America gained its own, and when India did become free, it placed itself essentially on the opposite side of the Cold War from the US, leading to decades of mutual suspicion and mistrust."[6] While India took its nonaligned status seriously, for example, bristling at Soviet Premier Nikita Khrushchev's anti-West comments made during a 1955 visit, it relied on the Soviets for military hardware and trade. In 1971, India and the Soviet Union signed a friendship treaty. The same year, the Bengalis of East Pakistan rebelled and the Pakistani military dictatorship crushed the rebellion, leading to charges of genocide.[7] The Indians sided with the rebels, and thus began the pro-Pakistan "tilt" which saw a cut off of US aid to India and military assistance to Pakistan.

Only with the end of both colonialism and the Cold War could relations improve between the US and India. However, the Clinton administration may have lost an opportunity by negatively viewing India primarily as a nuclear proliferation threat, rather than positively focusing on New Delhi's development leading to its emergence as an economically strong, liberal democracy. "We find the Americans over-bearing, preachy and sanctimonious ... insensitive to our needs, aspirations, challenges and threats," Congress Party minister Jairam Ramesh said of the Clinton administration's approach to India prior to the Musharraf coup in Pakistan. This,

---

5   Mohan, (2002), "A Paradigm Shift toward South Asia?" *The Washington Quarterly* 26/1, 141–155.

6   Khanna and Mohan.

7   Paterson et al. (1995), *American Foreign Relations*, New York: Houghton Mifflin, Volume 2, 254.

along with the Kargil War and both countries' testing nuclear weapons changed the context of US-subcontinent relations.[8]

President Clinton visited India in March of 2000 (the first visit of an American President since Jimmy Carter's visit in 1978), spoke before the Indian parliament, and signed a "vision statement" for future cooperation.[9] In contrast to his actions in India, when Clinton flew to Pakistan, he criticized the coup and later he directly intervened to end the Kargil War, which Pakistan had initiated in 1999 in the disputed Kashmir region.[10] The relationship changed again dramatically after the terrorist attacks of September 11, 2001.[11] The US needed the assistance of the Pakistanis to root out al-Qaeda cells on the rugged border between Pakistan and Afghanistan, and so US criticism of military rule in Pakistan subsided. As Khanna and Mojan put it, "indeed, it is now said that India and Pakistan are ... 'America's two new best friends'."[12] That might have been putting it a bit too nicely, as India did not immediately view closer US-Pakistan relations as a positive development. Then-Secretary of State Colin Powell visited India in October 2001 to assure the leadership in New Delhi that closer US ties with Pakistan would not mean more distant relations with India. "The United States and India are united against terrorism and that includes the terrorism that has been directed against India," Powell said, as he also reaffirmed that solving the Kashmir conflict was essential for bringing stability to the region.[13]

Moreover, the sudden warming of relations with Pakistan required the ignoring or downplaying of certain unwelcome actions by Pakistan in the past.[14] In a December 2002 *New York Times* editorial, Howard French wrote: "Few countries have improved their standing in American eyes as dramatically as Pakistan has in the past two years," yet the editorial went on to criticize past technology exchanges between North Korea and Pakistan that saw Pyongyang provide missile technology to Pakistan in exchange for nuclear weapons technology.[15] Further, French argued, such exchanges may have gone on longer than Pakistan admitted, and he maintained that such behavior was unacceptable from a reliable international partner. The US's changed attitude toward Pakistan after September 11th underscores the importance

---

8   Khanna and Mohan.

9   Ibid.

10   Limaye, S.P. (2002), "Mediating Kashmir: A Bridge Too Far," *The Washington Quarterly* 26/1, 157–167.

11   Raja Mohan, C. (2002), "A Paradigm Shift toward South Asia?" *The Washington Quarterly* 26/1, 141-155.

12   Khanna and Mohan.

13   Tyler, P.E. and Dugger, C. (2001), "Powell's Message: America's Courting of Pakistan Will Not Come at India's Expense," *New York Times*, October 18.

14   Schaffer, T.C. (2002), "US Influence on Pakistan: Can Partners Have Divergent Priorities?" *The Washington Quarterly* 26/1, 169–183.

15   "Nuclear Duplicity from Pakistan," *The New York Times* (December 2, 2002), A20, column 1. *The Times* also reported that, "Not only has Pakistan cooperated closely on its nuclear and missile programs with North Korea, experts say, but also with Iran and Syria, countries that the Bush administration said this week could someday put weapons of mass destruction in the hands of terrorists." French, H.W. (2002), "In Pakistan, US Embraces Friend of a Foe," *The New York Times* (May 25), A8.

of shifting circumstances in relations and the difficulties the US will continue to face as it tries to maintain friendly relationships with both India and Pakistan.

The Bush administration has been able to maintain and improve relations with both Pakistan and India, despite those two countries' antipathy toward one another, and the Congress Party-led government's reliance on the Communist Party as a coalition partner. Nevertheless, India voted with the US against Iran at the IAEA in 2005 and the US and India signed a nuclear accord in 2006. The agreement would allow India access to US civilian nuclear technology, India would open 14 of its 22 nuclear facilities to inspections, and India would not transfer nuclear technology to other countries.[16] IAEA Director General Mohamed ElBaradei strongly supported the accord, saying, "this agreement is an important step towards satisfying India's growing need for energy, including nuclear technology and fuel, as an engine for development. It would also bring India closer as an important partner in the non-proliferation regime."[17]

India's massive population and strong economic growth have compelled the country to consider any energy sources available. Currently, India relies on imports for about 70 percent of its oil needs.[18] India has limited coal and uranium reserves and currently derives about 3 percent of its electricity supply from nuclear power.[19] By 2050, India hopes to provide 25 percent of its electricity with nuclear power.[20] Procuring large amounts of energy from stable resources is likely to remain an Indian foreign policy interest for the foreseeable future. Friendly relations between India and some of the countries on which it relies for oil—for example Venezuela and Iran—could strain relations between India and the US in the future.

One particular area of disagreement between India and the US relates to India's energy needs and plans to build a 1,674 mile pipeline to carry liquefied natural gas from Iran to India. The pipeline would run through Pakistan (an undersea route that India would prefer is not technologically feasible), in particular the province of Baluchistan, which is hardly under the central government's control.[21] The US disapproved of this plan because it contradicts the administration's goal of pressuring and isolating Iran.[22] But if India's energy needs outweigh concerns they might have with running a pipeline through a country with which it has gone to war, it should

---

16   *US and India Seal Nuclear Accord*, BBC News, available at http://news.bbc.co.uk/go/pr/fr/-/2/hi/south_asia/4764826.stm.

17   *IAEA Director General Welcomes US and India Nuclear Deal*, available at http://www.iaea.org/NewsCenter/PressReleases/2006/prn200605.html.

18   *Prime Minister Dr. Manmohan Singh's Interview on Charlie Rose Show*, New Delhi: Ministry of External Affairs (February 27, 2006).

19   "US and India seal nuclear accord."

20   Ibid.

21   "Condoleezza's Spanner in Indo-Iran Gas Pipeline," *India News Online,* March 28, 2005, available at http://news.indiamart.com/news-analysis/condoleeza-s-spanner-9122.html.

22   Nunan, P., "US Concerned About India-Iran Pipeline Project," *Voice of America,* March 17, 2005, available at http://www.voanews.com/english/archive/2005-03/2005-03-17-voa35.cfm?CFID=34035824&CFTOKEN=66837617.

not be surprising that it would be willing to test relations with the US for the same reason, even though now the pipeline deal is stalled.

As this section indicates, the relationship between the United States and India focus on the necessity of cooperation and friendliness, despite challenges, disagreements, and diverging preferences. Recent embracing of Pakistan by Washington places New Delhi in a situation of uneasiness, further complicated by India's energy needs. However, common values of democracy and security serve as links between the two states, and provide necessary basis for increased cooperation between Washington and New Delhi.

Energy and Non-Proliferation: India and Iran

India's relations with Iran concern more than just the issue of the gas pipeline. While the nuclear-armed India is not a signatory of the Nuclear Non-Proliferation Treaty, Iran acted as one of the original signatories, committing to the NPT in 1970, and signing the renewal of the treaty in 1995.[23] On February 4, 2006, the IAEA voted to refer Iran to the United Nations Security Council because of its suspected nuclear weapons program. The IAEA Board of Governors voted 27–3 in favor of referring Iran to the Security Council, with five abstentions. India joined the US in support of this measure, while only Cuba, Syria and Venezuela voted against.[24] Prime Minister Singh has tried to put a positive spin on India-Iran relations after the vote by saying, "our relations with Iran, we relish a great deal. We have civilizational links. We are in the same region as Iran. And our concern with regard to Iran is that Iran is a signatory to the NPT. Iran must, therefore, have all the rights—which go with its being a member of the NPT. But it—it has also certain obligations, which it has voluntarily taken."[25] After a September 24, 2005 vote in the IAEA that found Iran in non-compliance with the NPT and called on Iran to return to the negotiating process (the vote was 22 in favor, one against (Venezuela) and 12 abstentions), more than a million Indian workers took to the streets to protest downsizing and privatization, but also to denounce India's IAEA vote. The protesters were led by four left-wing political parties the governing coalition relies on for support.[26] Some university professors condemned the decision as well. "By taking this disgraceful step, India is indicating that it has become a camp-follower of Washington," said Gulshan Dietl, a West Asia expert at the School of International Studies at Jawaharlal Nehru University in New Delhi.[27]

---

23   Chubin, S. and Litwak, R.S. (2006), "Debating Iran's Nuclear Aspirations," *The Washington Quarterly*, 226(4), 99–114.

24   Saikal, A. (2006), "The Iran Nuclear Dispute," *Australian Journal of International Affairs* 60/2, 193–199.

25   "Prime Minister Dr Manmohan Singh's Interview on Charlie Rose Show."

26   Hallinan, C., "India, Iran and the United States," *Foreign Policy in Focus* (October 19, 2005), available at http://www.fpif.org/fpiftxt/2890.

27   Bidwai, P. (2005), "India ditches Iran and Nonalignment," www.antiwar.com; (September 28), available at http://www.antiwar.com/bidwai/?articleid=7423.

The criticism against the 2005 decision appears in a piece entitled "India Ditches Iran and Nonalignment," and asserts that through the vote, "India has signaled the collapse of its long-standing policy of nonalignment."[28] Not only is the title quite telling, but it also points out the drastic shift in the steeple of Indian foreign policy, namely the nonalignment.

First, the nonaligned movement has hardly been alive and well since the collapse of the Soviet Union. This policy was not intended to be an anti-US movement, but instead to represent a bloc of nations who wanted to pledge their allegiance to neither the Soviets nor the Americans. India, moreover, had been doing quite a bit of signaling since the collapse of the Soviet Union in 1991, implying that closer strategic ties with the US were part of its plan. New Delhi is probably less interested in maintaining the romantic notion of the nonaligned movement than it is in the very practical problem of how to balance the interests of two countries whose significance for India cannot be underestimated: the US and Iran.[29] This explains that while India did not contribute troops to the US-led coalition that invaded Iraq in March 2003, it also did not condemn the decision as strongly as many countries did, including many of America's traditional European allies.[30] While India did not assist in the US-led Iraq invasion, it shares with the US a concern over the spread of Muslim fundamentalism, which also allows India to better understand the issues with which Israel struggles.

India and the Arab–Israeli Conflict

India and Israel's relationship has improved since the early 1990s as well. New Delhi opposed the creation of Israel in 1948, and the Indian National Congress adopted a pro-Arab stance in the Arab–Israeli conflict because of Mahatma Gandhi's attempts to woo Indian Muslims for the sake of Hindu–Muslim unity, Jawaharlal Nehru's[31] opposition to basing a state's existence on one religion and perception of similarities between Zionism and imperialism.[32] Throughout the Cold War, India followed a pro-Arab policy, motivated in part by the government's concerns for the sentiments of Indian Muslims, deference to Arab sensibilities and belief in nonalignment.[33] In fact, while India eventually recognized the existence of Israel, New Delhi and Jerusalem did not normalize diplomatic relations until 1992.[34]

---

28   Ibid.

29   See Mitra, P. and Hate, V. (2006), "India–Iran Relations: Changing the Tone?," *South Asia Monitor*, Vol. 92 (Center for Strategic and International Studies).

30   Khanna and Mohan.

31   First Prime Minister of India, in office from 1947 until 1964.

32   Kumar, D. (2001), *India and Israel: Dawn of a New Era* (Jerusalem; Institute for Western Defense) December. Available at: http://www.westerndefense.org/bulletins/Dec-01.htm.

33   Ibid.

34   Rubinoff (1995), "Normalization of India-Israel Relations: Stillborn for Forty Years," *Asian Survey* 35/5, 487–505.

Much changed in the early 1990s to alter India and Israel's relationship. First, of course, was the collapse of the Soviet Union, which eroded the relevance of the nonaligned movement. Depressed oil prices in this era somewhat reduced India's dependence on oil from Arab countries. The Organization of the Islamic Conference repeatedly passed pro-Pakistan resolutions on Kashmir and, by 1991 the PLO itself was negotiating peace with Israel. The rise of Islamic fundamentalism in this period worried India as well, and after the Gulf War, public opinion in India demanded a different attitude toward Israel. These developments changed political and economic circumstances which allowed for initial small steps toward improved economic and cultural ties between the two countries.[35]

The two countries exchanged high-level government visitors and in 1998 Israel celebrated "Shalom India" to mark India's 50th year of independence. These early steps were soon followed by increased economic and strategic cooperation. According to Kumar, "Israel's main considerations are the huge Indian market with more than 200 million middle class consumers, a link to the Far East and arms sales."[36]

Arms sales have taken off in the past several years. As Ninan Koshy pointed out in 2003: "The alliance between India and Israel … is based predominantly on military and intelligence cooperation. Israel has become the second-largest supplier of arms for India, next only to Russia."[37] India is the third largest importer of Israeli weapons (after China and Turkey) and Israel has supplied India with such diverse weapons systems as sensors to monitor the Line of Control along the India–Pakistan border, radar systems, attack boats and upgrades for Indian Air Force planes.[38]

India and Israel have been co-operating with regard to nuclear weapons as well. While the US sponsored sanctions and an arms embargo against India after their nuclear test in 1998, Israel did not react to the tests.[39] Neither country is a signatory of the NPT and each benefits by supporting the other's placement outside the NPT regime. Moreover, Israel may enjoy Pakistan's preoccupation with India because Pakistan is the only Muslim country with nuclear weapons.[40] Iranian Foreign Minister Kamal Kharrazi said during his visit to Islamabad, soon after the Pakistani nuclear tests, that "Muslims feel more secure from any Israeli threats under the Pakistani nuclear umbrella."[41] This is not, however, how the Pakistani nuclear program has progressed. It does not appear that they have shared nuclear technology with terrorist groups or their supporter governments in the Middle East and there is really no incentive for Pakistan's leadership to supply nuclear arms to groups who would not mind seeing his government overthrown.

---

35   Kumar.
36   Ibid.
37   Koshy (2003), "Sharon is Coming to India," *Foreign Policy in Focus*, May 27.
38   Kumar.
39   Koshy.
40   See Walker (1998), "International Nuclear Relations after the Indian and Pakistani Test Explosions," *International Affairs* 74/3, 505–528.
41   Kumar.

Issues of Islamic Terrorism

As mentioned above, a driving force behind many changes in India's foreign policy has been the fear of Islamic terrorism. In March 1993, coordinated terrorist bombings killed 257 people in Bombay. According to the BBC, the bombings were carried out in retaliation for anti-Muslim riots which earlier in the year had killed hundreds of both Muslims and Hindus.[42] The Indian Government also believes, however, that the mastermind of the plot is criminal underworld figure Dawood Ibrahim, who was believed to be living in Pakistan in 2006.[43] Terrorist attacks in India have become relatively commonplace. In July 2006 commuter trains were attacked in Bombay, killing 200. Bombay police officials blamed the Islamic militant group Lashkar-e-Toiba (which opposes Indian control of Kashmir and wants Islamic rule over India), based in Pakistan, for the attacks, and asserted the attacks were planned by Pakistan's intelligence agency.[44] The threat of fundamentalist Islamic terrorism thus colors many of India's most important relationships.

India and Israel share the desire to stamp out fundamentalist Islamic terrorism. The very existence of Israel is at stake, as Islamic terrorists view Israel as the "eternal enemy."[45] Of course, there is much diversity in the goals and tactics of Islamist terrorist groups, and while some organizations have recognized Israel's right to exist and support a two-state solution of the Israel–Palestine conflict, dozens of Islamist terrorist groups swear they will wage jihad until Israel is eliminated and Islamic law (as they interpret it) reigns in vast areas of the Middle East and South Asia. Israel, therefore, has an existential interest in defeating Islamist terrorism.

In contrast, India's problem with terrorism begins with Kashmir, which is controlled by India, Pakistan and China. India has fought three wars with Pakistan over the territory (in 1947, 1965, 1971, and 1999) and one with China (in 1962). The populations of the Pakistani and Indian-controlled portions of Kashmir are majority Muslim. The Pakistani portion nearly 100 percent Muslim, while the Indian section is more mixed.[46] According to the *New York Times*, "During Pakistan's last confrontation with India over Kashmir, American intelligence agencies found 'disturbing evidence that the Pakistanis were preparing their nuclear arsenals for possible deployment', according to a recent paper by Bruce O. Riedel, a former member of the Clinton administration's National Security Council."[47] A nuclear confrontation between India and Pakistan over Kashmir would most likely force the US to condemn the party that struck first, and collapsed relations between Pakistan and the US would hamper the war against terrorism and may increase the likelihood

---

42   *1993: Bombay Hit by Devastating Bombs*, (BBC) (July 26, 1994), available at http://news.bbc.co.uk/onthisday/hi/dates/stories/march/12/newsid_4272000/4272943.stm.

43   *Four Guilty of 1993 Mumbai Blasts*, (BBC) (September 12, 2006), available at http://news.bbc.co.uk/2/hi/south_asia/5335760.stm.

44   *Pakistan's Role in Mumbai Attacks*, (BBC) (September 30, 2006), available at http://news.bbc.co.uk/2/hi/south_asia/5394686.stm.

45   Kumar.

46   Limaye.

47   French.

of nuclear weapons technology ending up in the hands of fundamentalist Islamic terrorists.

India and Israel have mutual political and strategic interests in combating Islamist violence which are magnified by the geopolitical fact that Israel and India are placed at either end of the central Arab/Islamic bloc.[48] But the nature of the threat Islamist ideology poses to each country influences its reaction. Israel is a Jewish speck in an Arab-Muslim sea while India is the dominant economic, political and military power on the sub-continent. New Delhi certainly does not want to harm its relations with Syria and Iran by seeming too close to Israel. "India's threat is mainly from Pakistan, Afghanistan and some fundamentalist groups active in the Arab Gulf states," writes Kumar.[49] Despite India's potential rise to global power, it will likely remain preoccupied with the terrorist threat in its neighborhood.[50]

Difficult Decisions: India in Iraq

India has long-term strategic interests with regard to the situation in Iraq. In March 2003 the US and United Kingdom-led coalition invaded Iraq and overthrew the regime of Saddam Hussein. India did not participate in the coalition, but as mentioned previously, Indian criticism of the invasion was more muted than that of some historic US allies. On the other hand, as the situation in Iraq worsened in the summer of 2003, India considered sending troops to Iraq to assist in quelling violence and restoring law and order. New Delhi indicated it would only be willing to send troops if they were under the United Nations umbrella, a situation which became impossible when the UN Security Council passed Resolution 1483 on May 23, 2003 which stated that the US and UK acted as occupying powers and the authority in Iraq.[51] Participation by any nation's troops would place them under US and UK authority and not that of the UN.

India faced a complicated strategic choice in the debate leading up to the 2003 Iraq War. Since September 11, 2001, India has seen the US become ever closer to Pakistan. At the same time, India found itself searching for its place in the global order following the end of the Cold War. Would it remain active with the non-aligned movement, or would it push for closer ties with the US? The decision to participate in or oppose the war in Iraq tested India in ways it had not been tested since the end of the American-Soviet conflict. To support the US and provide troops would mean a total rebuke by India of the nonaligned movement, which condemned the war. On the other hand, to oppose the war publicly and to condemn the US action would threaten India's standing with the US. In the early stages of the engagement in Iraq, opposition to the US action was believed to threaten the acquisition of lucrative contracts from the US to rebuild the Iraqi infrastructure. "Prime contracts for reconstruction funded by US taxpayer dollars should go to the Iraqi people and those

---

48   Kumar.

49   Ibid.

50   Kumar (2002), "Religious Fundementalism in India and Beyond," *Parameters* 32.

51   United Nations Security Council Resolution 1483, available at http://daccessdds. un.org/doc/UNDOC/GEN/N03/368/53/PDF/N0336853.pdf?OpenEleme.

countries who are working with the United States on the difficult task of helping to build a free, democratic and prosperous Iraq," according to White House spokesman Scott McClellan.[52] Refusing to participate in the war might also exclude India from a place at the table when the contours of power in the new Middle East are being created. Now that the Iraq operation has gone poorly for the US, these concerns seem less important, but at the time they factored into India's concerns as a rising global power.

One should not underestimate the difficulty of the choices India had to make relative to the Iraq War and its aftermath. "Earlier, careful consideration had been given to the question of sending Indian troops to Iraq, keeping in mind our longer-term national interest, our concern for the people of Iraq, our long-standing ties with the Gulf region as well as our growing dialogue and strengthened relations with the United States," said External Affairs Minister Natwar Singh in late 2003.[53] But India did not participate. Even after the invasion, India did not send troops to restore law and order because they would not be under UN mandate. The foreign minister suggested a number of factors contributed to India's decision, saying, "India's approach takes into account a number of relevant factors such as the ground realities, the political roadmap for Iraq, the role of the UN, public perceptions in Iraq and the national sentiment."[54] These factors did not work out to compel India to send troops to Iraq even after the invasion. Contributing troops might never have been politically feasible, as in April 2003 the Indian parliament voted unanimously to "deplore," the war in Iraq and to declare that the war was "without the special permission of the UN and is against the UN charter."[55] The wording of the resolution was considered something of a victory for the BJP government, however, it did not use the stronger word "condemn."

The decisions regarding the war in Iraq challenged India's relationship with the United States. New Delhi had to balance its hesitancy to join the "coalition's of the willing" actions in Iraq with its need to preserve a close and friendly relationship with Washington. India's stance toward American engagement in Iraq impacts the future of its position in the world—although the strength and direction of this impact remain to be determined.

Conclusions: The Future Path of Indian Foreign Policy in the Middle East

What might the future hold for India's foreign policy, especially with regard to the Middle East? A number of important changes in the context of India's place in the world are occurring. According to the CIA National Intelligence Council

---

52   *US Ban on Iraq Contracts Angers Canada*, CTV (December 11, 2003) Available at http://www.ctv.ca/servlet/ArticleNews/story/CTVNews/1071057620405_15/?hub=TopStories.

53   *Interview of India's External Affairs Minister to IANS*, (New Delhi: Ministry of External Affairs) (December 31, 2003), available at http://mea.gov.in/interview/2003/12/31in01.htm.

54   Ibid.

55   "Parliament Deplores American Invasion," *Financial Express*, April 8, 2003.

report *Mapping the Global Future*, by 2020 "India's GNP will have overtaken or be on the threshold of overtaking European economies."[56] This could make India's the third largest economy in the world (behind only the US and China) and would magnify the importance of India as a global power. "The likely emergence of China and India, as well as others, as new major global players—similar to the advent of a united Germany in the 19th century and a powerful United States in the early 20th century—will transform the geopolitical landscape with impacts potentially as dramatic as those in the previous two centuries."[57] More countries are going to want access to India's markets, which should supply India with additional leverage. A state with the third largest economy in the world is unlikely to be content as a regional player. India's growing economy will permit it to continue with military modernization as well, which will increase its ability to project its influence around the world. But the fast-growing economy presents as many challenges as it provides benefits. India already imports 70 percent of its oil, and continued rapid economic expansion will force it to seek new sources, which is certain to require India to become ever more deeply involved in the politics of the Middle East.

India's foreign relations, however, are about more than trade and force. As Khanna and Mohan put it, "the perceived distinction between India's nonaligned past and alliance-oriented future is a complex one. At one level, India continues to cling to a cherished Nehruvian ideal of autonomous action based on democratic right and self-defined interest. At the same time, India has shown increasing flexibility in engaging the major powers and has expanded cooperation with the United States even in areas of prime security concern to itself."[58] This means that while India may retain a romantic attachment to the old nonaligned ideals, circumstances have so changed that India's interests are best protected by pursuing a series of strategic alliances rather than seeking to be the leader of a great nonaligned bloc. Instead, these entangling alliances require constant maintenance and often contradict one another. Prime Minister Manmohan Singh has stated, "We should develop friendly relations with as many major powers as possible. This will help in securing wider international support when we need it most."[59] Such a position, however, incites natural contradiction. For example, it is difficult for a state to simultaneously improve relations with Iran and Israel, or the US and Iran. As the IAEA votes on Iran, India's desire to build a pipeline for liquefied natural gas conflicts with its increasing strategic cooperation with the US, indicating clearly that developing friendly relations with as many major powers as possible is much more difficult than it sounds. In the end, it depends in part on which states India defines as major powers, and which may be relegated to lower status. New Delhi, however, is likely to be inclined to juggle relations with the US, Israel, and China as it grows into a global power, while it also continues to deal with the threat of Pakistan and what it believes is Pakistani-supported terrorism.

---

56   *Mapping the Global Future*, available at http://www.foia.cia.gov/2020/2020.pdf.
57   Ibid.
58   Khanna and Mohan.
59   Ibid.

SECTION III
The Middle East and the US

Chapter 8

The United States and Israel:
The Implications of Alignment

Daniel J. Graeber

The modern Jewish state in biblical Palestine is inextricably linked to moral and ancient religious attitudes that became favorable at the beginning of the twentieth century. The United States shares this approach which is reflected in its vital role in the creation and existence of the modern Jewish state.[1] Washington feels morally obligated to Israel and this stems, in part, from the strong influential domestic Jewish lobby, concerns regarding strategic US interests in the Gulf Region, and subsequent interests in stability in the oil rich Middle East. The US and Israel, therefore, share a special relationship that exists on a moral, strategic, and regional level. Although limited disagreements on detailed policy initiatives may emerge from time to time, US foreign policy in regards to Israel remains relatively static. Regional clashes, such as the war between Hezbollah and Israeli Defense Forces (IDF) in 2006, or the situation in Palestine, may strain this special relationship, but the strategic cooperation between the two powers remains relatively unwavering and strong. Yet, while US foreign interests are often expressed and maintained through its relationship with the State of Israel, the nature of this relationship may also be detrimental to US national security. This chapter examines the nature of US alignment with Israel and the regional implications of that alignment by way of historical assessment.

Evolution

Historically, a well funded and influential voice supporting the interests of a Jewish state rang loud in the international community. On November 2, 1917, British Foreign Secretary, Arthur James Balfour, echoed an emerging regional sentiment regarding the British Mandate for Palestine. In a letter to the Zionist banking mogul, Lord Walter Rothschild, Balfour expressed Her Majesty's "declaration of sympathy" for "a national home for the Jewish people" established in the region.[2] In part due to rising anti-Semitic sentiments in Europe, this "declaration of sympathy" concerning

---

1   Moore notes that religious dogma and shared moral convictions greatly influenced the relationship between the United States and Israel during the Truman administration. Moore, J. (2002), "Destabilizing the Middle East: US policy toward Palestine, 1943–1949," *Journal of Church and State* 43/1, 115–34.

2   The Balfour Declaration, November 2 1917, available at http://www.yale.edu/lawweb/avalon/mideast/balfour.htm.

the British Mandate for Palestine was seen to extend British influence over the Suez Canal and establish ballast against French influence in the Middle East.[3] The Balfour Declaration was controversial in regards to the level of endorsement perceived in Her Majesty's "declaration of sympathy." Several British White Papers emerged after the Balfour Declaration stating that it was not an assertion of British support for an actual Jewish state, only an expression of "sympathy" regarding anti-Semitism. In 1939, a policy paper was issued by the British Colonial Secretary stating that the Balfour Declaration "could not have intended that Palestine should be converted into a Jewish State against the will of the Arab population."[4] The MacDonald White Paper of 1939 expressed concerns to that regard and called for the limit of transfers of Arab lands and spoke out against increases in Jewish immigration to the area.[5]

American sympathy towards the Zionist movements increased as uprisings became more violent in the British Mandate of Palestine. Beginning in the late 1920s, frustrations with the uncertainties of the region led to boycotts and expressions of civil unrest. The death of the Muslim preacher, Izz ad-Din al-Qassam, at the hands of British police led to loss of Her Majesty's control over the region. In response to a British commission recommending partitioning the Mandate into separate Jewish and Arab states, armed revolts erupted between British supported Jewish forces and the Arab Palestinians. This was in-step with regional expressions emerging from the Arabs, notably, Saudi Arabia, whose King warned President Teddy Roosevelt that support for the Jewish cause would lead to regional violence.[6] Regional sentiment by all sides suggested that the situation between the Jews and Arab Palestinians would be best settled by dividing the territories into separate entities.

The regional circumstances were changing, as developments leading to existence of the Israeli state were taking place: Lebanon gained independence in 1943; the Arab League, coordinating the policies of the Arab states, formed in 1945 at the behest of the British crown; also in 1945, Syria was granted independence from the French. Continuing with that momentum, the UN General Assembly passed Resolution 181 on November 29, 1947, stating that "[i]ndependent Arab and Jewish States and the Special International Regime for the City of Jerusalem ... shall come into existence in Palestine."[7]

Members of the Arab League had expressed their displeasure with the formation of a Jewish state to the US Secretary of State, James Byrnes, in 1945. Yet despite

---

3   See Macintyre, D. (2005), "The Birth of Modern Israel: A Scrap of Paper that Changed History," *The Independent*, May 26, available at http://www.aljazeerah.info/ Opinion%20editorials/2005%20Opinion%20Editorials/2005%20Op%20Ed%20Links/May %202005%20Opinion%20Links.htm.

4   The MacDonald White Paper of 1939, available at http://www.yale.edu/lawweb/ avalon/mideast/brwh1939.htm.

5   Ibid.

6   Moore notes that "The King of Saudi Arabia warned President Roosevelt that America's support for 'unreasonable' Jewish immigration would lead to great bloodshed and disorder throughout the Middle East." Moore, 118.

7   United Nations General Assembly Resolution 181, "Future government of Palestine," Resolution adopted on the Report of the Ad Hoc Committee on the Palestinian Question, 1947, 131, available at http://www.alhaq.org/etemplate.php?id=121.

the regional discontent, but in the spirit of Resolution 181, Israel declared itself an independent state on May 15th, 1948. The Truman administration had originally intended to consult Arab states regarding the official US position on Palestine. In part from pressure from Jewish Americans, the Truman administration decided to cancel this discussion. Ignoring opposition from the region, the advice of Secretary of State Marshall, the newly founded Central Intelligence Agency, and the National Security Council, President Truman recognized the new Israeli Government within minutes of the declaration of its establishment.[8] In response, members of the Arab League expressed their intention to intervene and reiterated a general consensus viewing the new State of Israel as an expression of Western colonialism. The Arab League refused to accept the legitimacy of the Jewish state and, as promised, launched military strikes against Israel sparking the Arab–Israeli War of 1948.

In response to escalating regional conflict with Israel over the Sinai Peninsula, the United Nations established a peacekeeping force in 1956 in order to keep the border between Egypt and Israel demilitarized. Countering the Egyptian declaration calling for the destruction of Israel and the subsequent disbanding of the UN peacekeeping force monitoring the Sinai Peninsula in 1967, the Israelis were forced to convey a defensive posture. The decision to close the Straits of Tiran to Israeli vessels also provoked the Israelis against what it perceived to be an imminent Egyptian attack. Seeing the United States pre-occupied with the situation in Vietnam, the Israeli strategists viewed a preemptive attack to be both strategically advantageous, as well as geopolitically beneficial and launched the opening salvos of the Arab–Israeli War of 1967. The United States saw Israel as the aggressor and expressed frustrations over the attacks and the long terms consequences to Arab/Israeli relations. Yet, in previous diplomatic consultations prior to the conflict, the Johnson administration was concerned over Soviet intervention in the region, especially regarding Egypt, which it perceived as a proxy of the Soviet Union in the Cold War setting, much as it regarded the Soviet invasion of Afghanistan a decade later.

The conclusion of the Arab–Israeli War of 1967 resulted in a major victory for Israel. It had gained control over Egyptian, Syrian, and Jordanian lands in the Sinai Peninsula, the Gaza Strip, the Golan Heights, and the West Bank respectively. In regards to US relationships, the situation was exacerbated by the sinking of the USS *Liberty*, an intelligence gathering vessel patrolling international waters off the Sinai Peninsula.[9] Internationally, the conflict resulted in the unanimous adoption of United Nations Security Council Resolution 242 in November 1967, recognizing some territorial adjustments as a result of the conflict, but also emphasizing the right of "every state" to "work for a just and lasting peace."[10] Resolution 242 would be referred to as the "land for peace" contingent in later negotiations.

The regional implications of the Arab–Israeli War of 1967 resulted in Israel being recognized as a regional power broker in the minds of the Arab states. The

---

8   Moore.

9   Bailey, C.E. (1990), *US Policy Towards Israel: The Special Relationship*, Marine Corps University Command and Staff College, available at http://www.globalsecurity.org.

10   United Security Council Resolution 242. November 22, 1967, available at http://daccessdds.un.org/doc/RESOLUTION/GEN/NR0/240/94/IMG/NR024094.pdf?OpenElement.

repercussions of this acknowledgment altered US foreign policy towards Israel as well. Many American foreign policy officials began to see Israel as an emerging asset for expressing US interests in the Middle East, much in the fashion of the British in the 1920s. Enhancing the emerging US relationship was the French embargo on arms trades with Israel, leaving the United States as the sole supplier of strategic equipment to the Israelis following the 1967 War. While the US maintained strategic and diplomatic interests in the region after the war, notably with Egypt, the US pledged to grant Israel a "qualitative edge" in military capabilities.[11]

The passage of *Resolution 242* signified the first regional recognition of the State of Israel with an "acknowledgement of the sovereignty ... of every State in the area."[12] Egypt, especially, began to distance itself from regional discontent regarding the Jewish state, moving away from Soviet influence, and establishing closer ties with Western powers.[13] This relationship with Egypt would prove influential in negotiations between the United States, Israel and Egypt at the Camp David summits during the Carter administration. Following the 1967 War, the interests of Israel and the United States developed into something of a regional partnership, as the United States increasingly viewed Israel as an agent for US interests. Following the Camp David talks, the United States extended its strategic benefits to Israel, increasing the level of loans and gifts and decreasing the level of direct purchases by the Israeli Defense Forces. The period after the Camp David summits saw Israel as the largest recipient of US aid, with levels reaching into the $1.8 billion mark by the late 1970s.[14]

For its part, Israel viewed itself somewhat intertwined with US strategic and regional policies. The Israelis perceived coordinating with US regional policy as a means to secure economic and military aid. It also served to advance their defensive posture in the region. The dynamics of regional conflict also pressured other aspects of international relations. Israel became a buffer against Soviet interests in the region, as well as the embodiment of Arab resentment. The Arab oil embargo of 1973 also reflected regional tensions, highlighting the conflict of interests between securing Israel's "qualitative edge" while maintaining formal relations with the oil rich Persian Gulf states.

The Camp David Accords of 1978 had several regional effects. It established a framework for the implementation of Resolution 242, in effect calling for an autonomous Palestine in the Gaza Strip and the West Bank. It also launched diplomatic relationships with Israel and Egypt, culminating in a peace treaty negotiated between the two parties, which carried implications effecting regional dynamics, with Egypt absolving decades of hostility toward Israel and aligning itself with pro-Western

---

11   Steinberg, G.M. (1998), "Israel and the United States: Can the Special Relationship Survive the New Strategic Environment?," *Middle East Review of International Affairs* 2/4, 1–16.

12   Unscr, 242.

13   Telhami notes that the Egyptians were among the first of the Arab states to signal a willingness to recognize the State of Israel in accordance with UNSCR 242. Telhami (2001), "The Camp David Accords: A Case of International Bargaining," *Columbia International Affairs Online*, available at http://www.ciaonet.org/casestudy/test01/index.html.

14   Steinberg.

interests. The Camp David Accords made headway in resolving the conflicts between the Arabs and the Israelis. The intimate involvement of United States, by way of direct involvement by President Jimmy Carter, was seen as integral to the level of progress made in negotiations with regional partners. During the Carter administration, the United States served largely as a regional moderator for peace.

War between Iran and Iraq erupted in 1980. The US, still harboring resentment over the hostage crisis in Iran, provided military and intelligence support to Iraq. Israel, however, although officially neutral, gave its support to the non-Arab Iranians. The government in Jerusalem also maintained relations with the Iranians in order to provide a safeguard against Soviet influence. In addition, Israel engaged in arms negotiations with the Iranians during the war. The Iraqi invasion of Kuwait, however, provoked a dramatic policy change by the George H. W. Bush administration, as it responded with resounding military force against its former ally, Saddam Hussein, in order to liberate Kuwait. Despite its earlier preemption against the Osiraq nuclear facility in Iraq, Israel displayed a great level of restraint during the first Persian Gulf War at the behest of the United States, as the US cautioned that Israeli engagement would result in a regional conflict spiral. The Israelis did not respond militarily to the repeated bombardments from Iraqi Scuds, choosing instead to place a greater emphasis on maintaining a cooperative defense relationship with the United States. It marked the first time Israel had placed its strategic and defensive posture in the hands of the United States. Ultimately, the Israelis traded their right to retaliation in exchange for US pledges to destroy Iraqi weapons facilities and WMD capabilities.[15]

The clash between the Israelis and the Palestinians intensified, as regional conflicts boiled over to encompass other areas, notably Lebanon in the 1980s. In an effort to influence the conflict, foreign policy advisers in Washington sought to engage the Israelis and Palestinians in high profile negotiations. Secretary of State James Baker persuaded the Israelis and Palestinians to engage in diplomatic wrangling rather than armed conflict to mediate the situation. He sought to tie both sides up in negotiations, which at least had a moderating effect on the state of affairs. Baker advanced a decidedly Palestinian perspective in his diplomatic strategy in order to more effectively sell the Israeli position to the Arabs.[16]

The subsequent American show of force in Iraq crippled Saddam's military, although it left his regime largely intact. The American action alleviated Israel from one of its primary security threats. Secretary Baker perceived this as a vital breakthrough, as the thumb of external pressure exerted by Saddam was removed. This opened the door for regional players to hazard a greater role in moderating the

---

15　Ibid.

16　Baker is quoted to have said to Prime Minister Yitzhak Samir: "We want to take what you have and market it with the Arabs." Dennis Ross called this "selling" and stated that "Selling became part of our modus operandi—beginning a pattern that would characterize our approach throughout the Bush and Clinton years. We would take Israeli ideas or ideas that the Israelis could live with and work them over—trying to increase their attractiveness to the Arabs while trying to get the Arabs to scale back their expectations." Haley, P.E. (2006), *Strategies of Dominance: The Misdirection of US Foreign Policy*, Baltimore: Johns Hopkins University Press, 34.

region. Baker also hoped that his Arab diplomatic perspective of Israeli positions would portray the Israeli's as flexible and appeasing, garnishing reciprocity from the Arab constituency. Furthermore, he saw an opportunity to sideline Arafat's PLO from any negotiations, segregating any voice of belligerence in the wake of the first Gulf War. Yet, Baker was a pragmatist. Keeping with his Arab perspective, he expressed to the American Israel Public Affairs Committee (AIPAC) that hopes for a "Greater Israel" in the region were unattainable.[17] The victory against Iraq reinforced American hegemony with Israel as its partner in the Middle East, yet Israel remained unrepentant and hesitant to moderate its regional posture. The first Bush administration left the Israelis in a position relatively similar to which it started.

The Clinton doctrine was largely centered on domestic priorities. By keeping domestic agendas on track and in order, America's overall policy initiatives seemed more attractive to the international audience. Keeping with this approach, the Clinton administration chose the role of facilitator in its relationship with the Israelis. This was especially applicable to the Palestinian situation. Continuing where Carter had left off, Clinton embraced the theme of "selling" the Israeli position to the Arabs, specifically to Arafat himself. Also from the Carter playbook was the direct involvement of President Clinton in the negotiations between the Israeli and the Palestinians. Both sides reciprocated by showing military restraint that may not have been the case otherwise. This was similar to effects seen by Secretary Baker during the first set of negotiations at Camp David.

The Israeli/Palestinian negotiations surrounding the Oslo Accords during the Clinton administration were not without complications, however. It soon became apparent that Washington was becoming a mouthpiece for the Israelis. The Israeli Prime Minister, Ehud Barak, expressed erratic behavior during negotiations and insisted that there be no written record of agreements or disagreements between the parties. This, in effect, left the Clinton administration with few negotiating tools, save the promise of peace. The US also lost valuable time by allowing the Israeli Government to approach Syria regarding regional issues before dealing with the Palestinians which reflected an apprehension by the Israelis to engage in comprehensive mediation with her neighbors. Finally, unlike talks during the Carter administration, the negotiations under Clinton took place behind closed doors, leaving acrimony due to the lack of transparency.

In the end, Clinton's promise to not hold Arafat responsible for any failures proved empty, suggesting the US had surrendered its negotiation strategy to appease the Israelis. Despite gracious accommodations to the Palestinians, issues regarding Israeli settlement activity in the Palestinian territories remained unresolved, raids and assassinations went unrelented, and militant attacks continued unabated. The very public failure of the negotiations surrounding the Oslo Accords discredited, in many ways, elements of direct presidential involvement, incremental augmentations, extended frameworks, and confidence building measures. The response by Arafat and Barak only encouraged resentment from both sides, resulting in a rise in the popularity of militant groups such as Hamas and increased IDF incursions into

---

17   Baker said before AIPAC: "For Israel, now is the time to lay aside once and for all the unrealistic vision of a Greater Israel." Ibid., 36.

the Palestinian territories. This affected the policy of George W. Bush extensively, especially considering the shadow cast by the al-Qaeda attacks of 9/11 against the United States.

The absence of any resolution to the Israeli/Palestinian conflict left both sides in a state of discontent. From the Palestinian side, the frustration with check points and Developing World conditions only increased the appeal of groups such as Hamas and emboldened anti-US sentiment in the region. From the Israeli perspective, increased terrorist activity drew on the need for increased IDF actions and penetration into the Palestinian territories. Following the attacks of 9/11, escalations between the Israelis and Palestinians had grown to such an extreme that Israel's Arab neighbors, such as Egypt and Saudi Arabia, insisted on US involvement to moderate the situation. Yet with the failure of Oslo setting precedent with the second Bush administration, direct involvement was eschewed in favor of a policy of detachment. In effect, the US would not use its influence to either offer incentive or incur penalties on either side to resolve the conflict.

The lack of a direct negotiating partner, the United States, left the Israel/Palestinian situation with no clear direction, no benchmarks, and no framework in which to operate. The Bush administration repeatedly refused to meet with Arafat and voiced little opposition to continued Israeli settlement activity in the Palestinian territories. The Israeli besiegement of Arafat's compound in Ramallah in 2002 provided further evidence of US ambivalence to Israel's regional aggression and signified a certain freedom of action for the Israelis.

The Bush administration released the details of "a performance based 'Roadmap' to a permanent two-state solution to the Israeli-Palestinian conflict" in April 2003.[18] The "Roadmap" was a multi-phased process with the objective of establishing an independent Palestinian state, securing Israel's safety, and terminating Israeli settlement activity in the Palestinian territories. Consistent with the post-9/11 doctrines of the second Bush administration, the "Roadmap" also called for regime change in the Palestinian territories in exchange for independence, effectively sidelining any progress until Arafat was removed from power. The contributing goals of the Quartet, an international compendium coordinating with the "road-map," called for further goals of moderating the militant group, Hamas, and creating conditions for political progress in Palestine.[19]

Just as Baker viewed the victory in the first Gulf War as an opportunity for an assertive Middle East policy, the George W. Bush policy team saw the complete elimination of Saddam Hussein as a grand opportunity for regional peace. The road to peace, Bush presumed, led through Baghdad. Eliminating the strategic threat from Iraq left Israel's eastern border relatively secure and opened regional avenues to a more aggressive peace initiative. It also increased anti-Western sentiment and the

---

18   *A Performance-Based Roadmap to a Permanent Two-State Solution to the Israeli–Palestinian Conflict*, US (US Department of State) (April 30, 2003), available at http://www.state.gov/r/pa/prs/ps/2003/20062.htm.

19   International Crisis Group, "Israel/Palestine/Lebanon: Climbing Out of the Abyss," Crisis Group Middle East Report No. 57, July 25, 2006, available at http://www.crisisgroup.org/home/index.cfm?id=4282&l=1.

subsequent attraction of militant groups, such as Hezbollah, as the US follies in Iraq continued throughout the war. Backing Israel's strategic aggression, rather than encouraging diplomatic integration, suggests US perceptions may be out of step with the region. A US led effort to integrate Israel into the region and solve the Palestinian conflict addresses many of the complaints of the militant organizations, but it also positions the United States in a more permanent role in the region.

The post-9/11 Middle East political environment was exemplified by moderate democratic reform. Although officially prohibited from participating, members of the Muslim Brotherhood gained several parliamentary seats in Egyptian elections in 2005.[20] The death of Arafat in November 2004 eliminated a major obstacle to the progress of the "road map". In the fall of 2005, the Bush administration indirectly targeted foreign aid money to assist the Palestinian Authority with increasing voter turn out and optimism in face of strong opposition from the militant Hamas.[21] Regional elections a year after Arafat's death resulted in a dramatic victory for Hamas, yet the United States, Israel, and members of the Quartet refused to recognize it as the ruling party of the Palestinian territories which was inconsistent with the rhetoric of spreading democracy in the region.

This further cast the Israelis as the only legitimate partner to the US for regional stability. Democratic and regional reform may be acceptable to the United States only if groups with policies consistent with the US are elected. The post-Arafat elections in the Palestinian territories served as a model for regional democratic processes, yet the results brought a US Department of State designated terrorist group to power. In this sense, despite international support for the "road-map" and various other frameworks, the US relationship with Israel, and with the region as a whole, only strengthened the appeal of radical Islam.

Israel and Lebanon embarked in all out war following the kidnapping of Israeli soldiers by the military wing of Hezbollah in July 2006. Hezbollah showed surprising staying power with its mostly rudimentary weapons system, even claiming victory over Israel. In the fall of 2006, Hamas formally renounced its ceasefire with Israel, sending the region into turmoil, as Palestinians wrangled with internal power struggles and international sanctions. IDF air raids in November 2006, on the Palestinian territories have resulted in Gazans resorting to human barriers to deter Israeli attacks. And in the wake of political assassinations, Lebanon once again teeters on the brink of civil war. Secretary of State, Condoleezza Rice, has referred to this as "the birth pangs of a new Middle East."[22] Yet this new Middle East may have a marked anti-Western slant.

---

20   Haley. Open elections in a region historically plagued by autocracy often result in success at the polls for the political wings of many militant organizations.

21   Wilson, S. and Kessler, G., "US Funds Enter Fray In Palestinian Elections," *Washingtonpost*, January 22, 2006, available at http://www.washingtonpost.com/wp-dyn/content/article/2006/01/21/AR2006012101431.html.

22   *Special Briefing on Travel to the Middle East and Europe*, US (US Department of State) (July 21, 2006), available at http://www.state.gov/secretary/rm/2006/69331.htm.

The Military Relationship

The US and Israel had no military or strategic relationship for the first 20 years of Israeli statehood.[23] The strategic relationship between the two states developed after the 1967 War, as Israeli emerged as a victorious regional power. Washington saw Israel as an asset with the capability of extending US interests in the Middle East. The French arms embargo against Israel after the 1967 War positioned the US as the sole weapons supplier to Israel. The escalation of the Cold War, the Islamic Revolution in Iran, and the Soviet invasion of Afghanistan resulted in the elevation of Israel to a strategic asset to the US military posture in the Persian Gulf.

Regarding autonomous deterrent capabilities, Israel maintains a de facto nuclear weapons status. Its position of nuclear ambiguity has caused some regional anxiety and exists as a source of tension for the United States. Israel argues that ambiguity exists as an effective deterrent, although it is mindful to minimize the damage to its strategic relationship with the United States. In this light, Israel has not tested its weapons systems, although it continues as a non-signatory to the Nuclear Non-Proliferation Treaty. In 1969, the Israelis and the United States reached an agreement in which Israel would not test its nuclear capabilities in exchange for US assurances of Israel's "qualitative edge" in its regional defense posture, enforcing the nuclear ambiguity as a deterrent protecting not only Israeli but also Western interests in the region.[24]

Israel's military and strategic relationship with the United States has several regional implications. Israeli intelligence services offer a unique perspective in the US led war on terror, providing the US with vital information on militant activities in the region.[25] As the US/Israeli strategic partnership evolved after the 1967 War, and as the US sought greater advantages to the unique strategic vantage point of the IDF, Washington was also obliged to provide the Israelis with pledges to protect their vital security interests. As a result, US military assistance and arms sales increased significantly and the IDF was gradually more equipped with and dependent upon American weapons platforms and technology. Regionally, Israel has continued to exemplify US military proficiency by its use of the Apache gunship, yet the conflict in Lebanon in the summer of 2006 may signify a departure from the relevance of that relationship as the nature of warfare has evolved in the twenty-first century.

The Periscope of the West

The United States is one of the most abundant consumers of oil in the world and one of the most influential markets in the world economy. Interruptions to either would have a ripple effect internationally. One of the vital interests of the United States is access to oil at a stable price in the Persian Gulf. Political and military turmoil in the Gulf Region disrupts not only the price, but the accessibility to oil reserves. This was made all too clear during the oil embargo in the 1970s. In order to sustain at

---

23   Moore.
24   Steinberg.
25   Bailey.

least some control over its vital interests, it is advantageous for the United States to remain in a largely hegemonic position regionally.[26]

Israel is often seen as a client of the United States. Yet, Israel simultaneously seeks significant influence over US policy, and is constrained by appeasing policy makers in the United States. The sentiment in the Arab community is that Israel, first with the British during the Mandate in Palestine, and now with the United States since the Arab–Israeli War, is an extension of Western imperialism. This imperialism continues, according to the Arab perspective, to maintain its colonial influence in the region.[27]

The reciprocal strategic relationship between the United States and Israel is founded on common regional interests concerning security objectives and political interests in the Middle East. The 1967 War brought the United States and Israel into a unique relationship after the French arms embargo. Israel also provided a bulwark against the spread of Soviet influence during the Cold War. The interdependent affiliation between Israel and the United States was further strengthened by the escalation of anti-Western violence in the region during the 1980s. Israeli appeasement of US interests in exchange for security agreements continued, as did US dependence on Israel to bolster its regional interests. The Israeli Government often seeks to involve the United States in its regional affairs, including the *Israeli/Palestinian* conflict, in an effort to retain Israeli's security network. Yet, the Israelis often make concessions for that support. The relationship is one of strategic mutual reciprocity.

The regional threat environment has also undergone a dramatic shift after the Cold War. No longer was Israel seen as a fortification against Soviet influence, as Israel's Arab neighbors, notably Jordan and Egypt, have taken a decidedly Western tilt as the Soviet influence dissolved. Peace treaties have been established between the Egyptian Government and the Israelis. Iraq no longer poses the threat to Israel's national security that it did under Saddam Hussein. And the Iranians do not have a tested weapons system capable of reaching Israel. This leaves Islamic fundamentalists as the primary threat to Israeli security. With the establishment of the US as the dominant military power in the world following the success of the first Gulf War, the strategic partnership between the United States and Israel may hold less importance.

Perhaps considering its proximity to the Middle East and the subsequent threat environment, the Israelis perceive Wilsonian ideology of democratic peace[28] as

---

26   Art, R.J. (2004), "The Strategy of Selective Engagement," in Robert J. Art; Kenneth Waltz (eds), *The Use of Force*, London, UK: Rowman and Littlefield Publishers, Inc.

27   Doran notes that "[a]ccording to a commonly held version of history, the Western powers (especially the United Kingdom and the United States) planted Israel in the Arab world and then nurtured it with the intention of using the Jewish state as an 'imperialist base', a bridgehead for dominating the entire region." Doran (2003), "Palestine, Iraq, and American Strategy," *Foreign Affairs* 82/1, 1–9.

28   Woodrow Wilson implanted the democratic peace theory of Immanuel Kant into the foreign policy of the United States. The democratic peace theory states that democratic societies do not go to war with one another. The administration of George W. Bush has embraced this policy, seeking democratic reform, either through influence, such as in Saudi Arabia, or by regime change, such as Iraq. Israel and the United States, however, differ over

a largely utopian concept that is out of step with their security demands. Israel's primary concern is survival in a community relatively hostile to its very existence. The US desire to spread democracy to the Middle East is not a vital concern to the Israelis. The Arab world, according to the Israelis and several others in the region, is not conducive to Western notions of democracy. Furthermore, the US record with regime change, both in Iran and Iraq, does not sit well with a nation living amongst its enemies, as Israel currently does. Israel's foreign policy is based on survival, not democratization or regime change.[29]

Some ideologues of Israeli foreign policy, notably Ariel Sharon's ultra-nationalist party, have indicated a reluctance to associate too closely with United States foreign policy. These policy makers see strategic dependence on United States as detrimental to an image of self-reliance in a hostile neighborhood. On the other hand, the conservative party of notables such as former Prime Minister Binyamin Netanyahu sees a strong relationship with the United States as a means to strengthen the deterrence capabilities of Israel. By embracing the US as a partner for peace, the Israelis ensure any regional negotiations will emphasize, or at least tend towards, Israeli objectives. Conversely, the Progressives, the party of Shimon Peres, see the American regional posture as something of a part of a reciprocal partnership, viewing concessions to US interests as a means of securing a sponsor to the Israeli vision of the region.[30] Inevitably, however, with the continuation of the ultra-nationalist Likud party maintaining key positions in the Israeli Government, the political relationship with the United States may be faltering, as it did militarily after the first Gulf War.

Regional Implications

Access to Persian Gulf oil at a stable price is of vital interest to the United States. A volatile political and military climate in the region has an effect on the oil market, and subsequently, US interests. It is, therefore, advantageous for the United States to maintain a dominant position, both politically and militarily, in the Persian Gulf. Israel is integral to that position. At the onset of US/Israeli relations, however, unified support for Israel among US policy makers was notably absent. Initially, the State Department had warned President Truman that rhetoric supporting the creation of a Jewish state would hinder regional stability. Congress, however, saw the creation of Israel as an opportunity to extend an arm of US interests into the Middle East and express support for the Jewish state.[31]

---

the prevalence of democratic peace. Washington sees the spread of democracy as a vital element to its national security. Israel sees stability and security as the primary principles of national security; not governmental reform. With the incorporation of militant groups such as Hezbollah and Hamas into the political fray, Israel sees free elections and democracy for its Arab neighbors as a strategic threat.

29   Benn, A. (2005), "Israel and Arab Democracy," *National Interest* 80, 44–48.

30   Rynhold, J. (2000), "The View from Jerusalem: Israeli–American Relations and the Peace Process,' *Middle East Review of International Affairs* 4/2, 1–14.

31   Moore.

Prior to the Arab–Israeli War of 1967, there was prevalent Soviet influence among Israel's neighbors, notably Egypt. During the prelude to the 1967 conflict, President Johnson had warned the Soviets of the dire consequences of acting through the Egyptians against the Israelis. After Israel's victorious emergence as a regional power in 1967, the strategic and regional relevance of the US/Israeli partnership increased. Instability in the region was detrimental to the vital interests of both countries, and the benefit of a partnership in the region had obvious implications. From the US perspective, the Israelis may be seen as one of the first lines of defense in securing American interests in the region. Considering the subtext of US/Israeli relations regarding military technology, the general perception among Western powers in the region is that the United States must maintain the dominant role. The Israelis rely on the United States to supply, or at least influence, their defense posture. Yet, in order for Israel to be effective in the region, the US must be acting effectively as well. The strength of Israel in the region depends on the relative strength of the United States.

Israel may be more comfortable with the United States as an ally rather than a moderator for peace in the area. US as an ally has witnessed the Palestinian intifada, the emergence of political Hamas, and the war between Hezbollah and the IDF. Categorizing Israel as a strategic asset may be advantageous to US interests, and vice versa. But, US as a broker for peace has faired better in the past, as both the Carter and the Clinton administrations have testified. Ultimately, Israel as a partner works better than Israel as an ally, as gains toward regional moderation and incorporation could lead to a cooperative, rather than openly hostile, region.[32]

The Palestinian territories, for all intents and purposes, exist in Developing World conditions. Parallels have been drawn between the current state of the Palestinians to that of Jews during the founding movements of Israel.[33] In that regard, the continuation of the Israeli/Palestinian conflict poses a direct threat to the strategic and national interests of the United States. The raison d'être of many militant organizations, including al-Qaeda, centers on a decidedly anti-Israeli sentiment. Anti-Israeli sentiment translates into anti-American sentiment due to the nature of US strategic partnership with Israel. The US tends to prefer bilateral relationships in its affairs throughout the world. Israel and the US, therefore, often share the brunt of each others regional resentment. Most Arabs disapprove of the situation in which the US and Israeli policy has left the Palestinian territories.[34] The American refusal to call for an Israeli ceasefire during the war with Lebanon in the summer of 2006 is indicative of US unconditional support of Israeli military activity in the region. Conversely, anti-Western sentiment was reflected at Hezbollah rallies following the war, as they declared victory over the US backed IDF. As Israeli military forces may

---

32　　Judis, J. (2006), "Apocalypse Now: Bush's Failed Israel Strategy," *The New Republic*, available at http://www.carnegieendowment.org.

33　　Moore goes so far as to cite a study by L. Carl Brown that "credibly portrays the displaced Palestinians as victims and suggests some parallel between their plight and the Holocaust." Moore, 115.

34　　Van Evera highlights Zogby poll numbers regarding Arab sentiment that give an indication of the general anti-Western sentiment in the region. Van Evera, S. (2005), *Why US National Security Requires Mideast Peace*, MIT Center for International Studies.

be seen as an extension of the US military, a victory over the IDF is a victory over the United States in the eyes of the Arabic community.

The alignment of Israel with the United States casts Israeli actions as parallel with Western interests. The Palestinian intifada is generally an anti-Western reaction. Revolt in the Palestinian territories may be perceived as a surrogate war against the Americans. However, a resolution to the Palestinian conflict would also solidify the presence of the United States in the region. The Israeli/Palestinian issue simultaneously serves as the cynical cause celebre of militant organizations and the primary regional dilemma for Western powers. For all parties involved, the situation is a zero-sum game.

Much of the recruitment propaganda emerging from militant organizations, such as al-Qaeda, uses the Palestinian cause as inspiration. The anti-Western sentiment that is embodied in the Israeli/Palestinian cause is used to define the ideology and recruitment base for militant organizations. In the first statements following the attacks against the United States on September 11, 2001, Osama bin Laden stated that "neither America nor anyone who lives in America will ever dream of peace until we experience it as a reality in Palestine."[35]

The foreign policy of the United States in the Middle East is driven to some extent by the regional policies of Israel. The *Israeli/Palestinian* conflict provides a lens through which to examine the conflict between Western and Arab countries. Resolving the *Israeli/Palestinian* conflict settles many regional issues,[36] while siding with Israel encourages anti-Western response. Incorporating regional issues to address grievances will eliminate much of the raison d'être of anti-Western sentiment, despite the inevitable integration of the United States in the region. An incorporated approach will encourage engagement rather than isolation, bringing holistic moderation to mitigate regional conflict. The US relationship with Israel should not drive a regional policy towards peace in the region.[37]

The US/Israeli relationship is centered on securing Israel and securing vital US interests in the region. Political reform has been sidelined for security issues in the region. Strategic prevention of anti-Western violence has taken precedence over addressing the root cause of unrest in the region. The United States and Israel have a unique relationship. The Israelis need US adherence to its own interests in the region and therefore answers calls for restraint in its policies regarding its neighbors. The United States needs Israel to serve as its beacon in the region. This dual policy has been the consistent factor in the special relationship between the United States and Israel.

Special thanks to Chelsea Gruber and Peter O'Toole for their help with this project.

---

35   Doran, 4.
36   Judis.
37   Bailey.

Chapter 9

Realpolitik and Religion: The Twin Sources of Saudi Arabia's Foreign Policy

Evan Campbell and Steve A. Yetiv

Saudi Arabia plays a critical role in world politics. Sitting atop the largest proven oil reserves in the world, it supplies the bulk of the oil exported from the Persian Gulf, amounting to about a quarter of the world's supply. Moreover, Saudi Arabia possesses the largest excess production capacity of any country in the world, which enables it to raise or lower production at a moment's notice—and by enough of a margin to have a serious impact on world oil prices and, hence, the global economy. It is, therefore, a major player on the global stage, even if many indicators would rank it among the world's developing countries.

This chapter characterizes Saudi Arabia as having two parallel foreign policies: one secular and one religious. Since its founding, and even before, it has sought to tread a line between maintaining its security while retaining its religious respectability. Evidence suggests, of course, that religion alone is not the guiding light of Saudi foreign policy. 'While Islam has often been an ingredient in both domestic politics and external conflicts ... policy decisions have generally been made and implemented in the light of national, rather than religious, considerations.'[1] At the same time, it is clear that Saudi Arabia is in many ways limited in its alignment choices by the bounds of Islamic (and Arab) respectability.

While scholars differ on the relative weight Riyadh's policy elite gives to the dual considerations of security and religion, this chapter argues that since the Islamic Revolution of 1979 and especially since the end of the Cold War, it has become ever more difficult to find any harmony between the two central elements of Saudi foreign policy.

The Saudi definition of security has two overlapping components: foreign and domestic. In the foreign sphere, Riyadh acts to prevent the appearance of a regional hegemon. It typically uses economic weapons and, when necessary, foreign assistance to do this. Historically, Saudi Arabia has used these forms of balancing to blunt the hegemonic designs of Nasser's Egypt, Saddam Hussein's Iraq, and Iran under both Shah Pahlavi and the Islamic Republic. Given the unstable nature of the

---

1   Landau, J. (1990), *The Politics of Pan-Islam: Ideology and Organization*, Oxford: Clarendon Press, 253.

regional balance of power, it is not surprising that realist predictions fare so well in the Saudi case.

Islamic solidarity is a major legitimating force for Saudi foreign policy. For instance, it remains essentially antagonistic to Israel despite a paucity of direct military threat, systematically resisted the influence of the atheist Soviet Union in the region, undertakes major humanitarian efforts to protect Muslims around the world (for example in the Afghan Civil War or in the former Yugoslavia), funds Islamic education in Indonesia, and builds Mosques in Africa. These goodwill measures, moreover, are only the public face of Saudi Arabia's campaign for Islamic unity. Its leaders are also working at the highest levels as founding members of the World Muslim League and the Organization of the Islamic Conference (OIC) in order to "enhance Saudi Arabia's aura of leadership throughout the Islamic world."[2] By all these means, Saudi Arabia hopes to build on its innate status as guardian of the holy cities and secure a long-lasting position of moral leadership in the Islamic world.

This leadership, in turn, serves the domestic security interests of the regime. Maintaining strict control over the ideas of its population is critical for the Saudi state, and closely related to its relations with foreign powers, since, as Mamoun Fandy noted, "outside powers traditionally have manipulated [Saudi opposition] groups to their own ends, and in turn the internal opposition has made use of global movements to enhance their local standing."[3] It is here that foreign and domestic security, and the secular and religious foreign policies overlap. Saudi Arabia is often described as an "omnibalancer," using the term coined by Steven David, meaning that it sometimes designs its foreign relations in order to protect itself from internal threats as well as external ones.[4] The primary tool of Saudi omnibalancing is religious and Arab appeal. For instance, Saudi Arabia's primary method of distancing itself from the United States is by publicly championing causes that are popular among Muslims, such as solidarity with Palestine, stating that "we do not accept the presence in our country of a single soldier at war with Muslims or Arabs"[5] at the beginning of the War on Terror, or seeming to support Iran's nuclear energy program in 2006 (but not nuclear weapons—see below).

This is broadly true of Saudi Arabia's relations with most Muslim states; it is rather loathe to arouse the ire of the "Arab street" abroad, at least when its vital

---

2   Peterson, J.E. (2002), *Saudi Arabia and the Illusion of Security*, London: Oxford University Press for the International Institute for Strategic Studies, 33.

3   Fandy, M. (1999), *Saudi Arabia and the Politics of Dissent*, New York: St. Martin's Press, 5.

4   For the definitive statement of omnibalancing, see David, S.R. (1991), *Choosing sides: alignment and realignment in the Developing World*, Baltimore: Johns Hopkins University Press; Nonneman, G. (2005), "Determinants and Patterns of Saudi Foreign Policy," in J. Aarts and Gerd Nonneman (eds), *Saudi Arabia in the Balance*, Washington Square, NY: New York University Press, 315–351; Gause III, G.F. (2002), "The Foreign Policy of Saudi Arabia," in Anoushiravan Ehteshami and Raymond Hinnebusch (eds), *The Foreign Policies of Middle East States*, Boulder, CO and London: Lynne Rienner. Nonneman and Gause have both applied the term to Saudi Arabia.

5   "Blow for Bush as Saudis Deny Use of Bases," *The Daily Telegraph*, October 1, 2001.

security interests are not at stake. By earning the goodwill of the domestic and foreign *Umma*, in turn, Saudi leaders seek to lessen both domestic and international pressures on the regime. The quest for domestic, or regime, security, causes Saudi Arabia to put an Islamic face on many of its international efforts, and simultaneously fuels its rivalry with ideologically divergent Muslim states and its notorious domestic human rights abuses.

The most important foreign policy challenges Saudi Arabia faces relate to its relations with the United States, Iran, Iraq, and Israel. While there are numerous issues that do not seem to fit a state-level analysis (such as terrorism), even these are largely connected with Saudi Arabia's relations with these four powers. The purpose of this chapter is to ask how Saudi Arabia's "religious foreign policy" impacts the choices available to it when dealing with these three challenges. Increasingly, Saudi Arabia finds itself politically unable to pursue policies that would enhance its security or position in world politics because its policy choices are limited by the bounds of Islamic (and Arab) respectability. This is a pattern demonstrable in the history of the Kingdom of Saudi Arabia, and one that has a critical impact on its relations with the four powers mentioned above.

Religion and Security as Historical Factors

Despite its immense wealth, Saudi Arabia is a small state in a volatile and fractious region, surrounded by hostile neighbors and restive populations. In addition, it was cobbled together in the three decades between 1902 and 1932 from numerous formerly independent sheikhdoms and Bedouin territories, and as such from the beginning the principal goal of the House of Saud was to give off the appearance of being legitimate rulers, rather than the usurpers. Luckily, their initial primary source of funds, tolls from the annual *Hajj*, was soon replaced with profits from the Kingdom's massive petroleum deposits, which the Arab-American Oil Company (ARAMCO) originally discovered and drilled in the late 1930s. The new source of income bestowed the new country's absolute monarchy with that most fungible of power assets: money. The position Saudi Arabia soon came to enjoy brought new challenges, as suddenly the Kingdom's rulers realized that their investment might be at risk from envious and unfriendly neighbors.

At the same time, the House of Saud finds itself in the unique position of being in control of the Hejaz, home to the Muslim holy cities of Mecca and Medina. As mentioned, the Kingdom's initial importance in international politics derived from its position as protector of these sacred places. However, this role bore certain responsibilities, especially for what is still a deeply traditionalist and pious dynasty concerned above all with defining its legitimacy in religious terms.

This conception of legitimacy is the result of the historical evolution of the Saudi dynasty itself. In the eighteenth century, the ancestors of Saudi Arabia's present rulers adopted the radical teachings of Muhammad ibn Abd al-Wahhab, who spread his message throughout the eighteenth century until his death in 1787. In 1744, he made an alliance with Muhammad ibn Saud, a local ruler of a small Arabian oasis town, who received the reformer and gave him protection.[6] One and a half centuries later, the relationship was still strong. The brutal fundamentalist Wahhabi tribesmen known as the *Ikhwan* proved central to the military conquests of ibn Saud, the founder and first King of Saudi Arabia, including the capture of Islam's two holiest sites at Mecca and Medina in the 1920s, and to the formation, contrary to what most might have predicted, of the Saudi nation.[7] The alliance between ibn Saud and Abdul Wahhab was congealed through generations of inter-marriage and would offer the royal family a religious legitimization of its rule.[8] Descendants of the royal family and those of Abdul Wahhab would rule the governmental and religious dimensions, with a symbiosis between them.

Wahhabism takes different forms, but prominent among them is the notion that non-Muslims should not be present on Saudi soil, and that aggressive jihad against them can be justified, even mandated. This does not mean that Wahhabism should necessarily spawn terrorism, a notion widely rejected by Saudi authorities whose brand of Wahhabism differs from bin Laden's Salafi Islam, despite the fact that in interviews bin Laden quoted generously from Wahhab's teachings.[9] There is little doubt that it shaped and possibly drove his views and actions.

Wahhabism serves a political purpose, and, to this end, the Saudi ruling family sought from its very beginnings to justify its rule at home by reference to Islamic and Wahhabist orthodoxy. "The legitimacy of the Saudi regime has always been based on its religiosity, which the royal family has used purposefully to secure geopolitical ends."[10] In the earliest days of the Kingdom's existence, the regime sought Islamic respectability abroad to buttress the regime's legitimacy at home. After securing control of the Hejaz in 1926, ibn Saud convened a Muslim World Conference in order to "secure Islamic international approbation of his control of the formerly Hashemite territory."[11] By earning the support of the Muslim world, ibn Saud calculated, he could assure the security of his new regime at home. Islam, then, was the crucial element by which ibn Saud legitimated Saudi Arabia's appearance on the international scene and among the disparate Arab tribes that suddenly found themselves its subjects.

In this sense Islam is the force by which the regime justifies itself—if it can retain the respect of other Arab and Muslim states, it will retain the respect of its own people. At the same time, it feels compelled to seek the approval of its domestic

---

6   Al-Rasheed, M. (2002), *A History of Saudi Arabia*, Cambridge and New York: Cambridge University Press, 15–20.

7   The Ikhwan helped him expand the kingdom but eventually turned on him. He defeated them in the 1920s.

8   See Helms, C.M. (1981), *The Cohesion of Saudi Arabia*, Baltimore: Johns Hopkins University Press; Safran, N. (1985), *Saudi Arabia: The Ceaseless Quest for Security*, Cambridge, MA: Harvard University Press.

9   See Fandy, 190–192.

10   Bronson, R. (2005), "Rethinking Religion: The Legacy of the US-Saudi Relationship," *Washington Quarterly* 28/4, 121–37, 127.

11   Piscatori, J. (1983), "Islamic Values and National Interest: The Foreign Policy of Saudi Arabia," in Adeed Dawisha, *Islam in Foreign Policy*, Cambridge, New York: Cambridge University Press, 35.

ulama. Thus, even in more recent times, when Iraq invaded Kuwait, King Fahd turned to and gained reluctant support from the Wahhabi clerics, as he had several times in past situations, for his considered decision to allow non-Muslim troops on Saudi soil. The clerics, meanwhile, have benefited from largely free reign in religious practices—an arrangement that was shaken by the effects of 9/11.

US–Saudi Relations

Security and religious factors have been critical in shaping the Saudi approach toward US–Saudi relations. The Saudis have been unable to escape their dependence on America as a security guarantor; at the same time, this very dependence has sometimes run counter to maintaining their Islamic credentials. Roughly speaking, this balancing act has become harder to execute over time.

US–Saudi relations have been a composite of unspoken agreements, cautiously cooperative interactions, and hidden resentments, enmeshed in mutual dependencies that are sometimes obfuscated for political reasons. Deciphering them can at times be akin to breaking special codes. Thus, assessing them over a long period of time is critical.

Israel represents one area of major difference in bilateral relations. The Saudi position on Israel has fluctuated from maximum hostility, to the notion that Israel has a right to exist, if it meets certain conditions that Israel has viewed as largely unreasonable. Within these parameters, the Saudis have seen Israel as an occupier, a foreign entity in the land of Islam. As the caretakers of Mecca and Medina, they have felt obligated to promote Muslim causes like the plight of the Palestinians. Obviously, assailing Israel has also served local politics. Naturally, the Saudi position has contrasted starkly with that of the United States. It has deep religious, political, and strategic ties to the Jewish state, which it sees as an important democratic ally in a region hostile to democracy. Washington has viewed Arab hatred of Israel as counter-productive and unacceptable. Behind a generally pro-Israel public, it has been willing, certainly since the 1967 Six Day War, to countenance tensions with Arab states that arise from its support of Israel.[12]

US–Saudi differences over Israel began to develop when Israel became a state in 1948, but clearly expanded only after the 1967 War when Israel, in what the United Nations determined to be an act of self-defense, attacked Arab states that appeared poised to launch war. Israel gained control of key territories, including the West Bank and Gaza Strip, and the US–Israeli relationship would soon become a *de facto* alliance.

On June 6, the second day of that war, the Saudi regime, partly in response to popular demonstrations, asserted that it would cut off oil supplies to any state that aided Israel. The Saudis stopped oil shipments to the United States and Britain, but a market glut undermined the boycott which was abandoned by early September when it become too burdensome on oil producers. Thereafter, the United States and

---

12   Quandt, W.B. (2001), *Peace Process: American Diplomacy and the Arab–Israeli Conflict since 1967*, Washington, DC: Brookings Institution Press.

Saudi Arabia managed their differences over Israel fairly well, until the 1973 oil embargo.

Relations were mended in the mid-to-late 1970s, but the embargo left an unpleasant residue in its path, and, in any event, problems recurred in bilateral relations in 1978–1979. Yet, subsequent security threats helped re-strengthen mutual relations. The 1981 US sale of AWACS aircraft to Saudi Arabia was one of several developments during the Iran–Iraq War which served to build US–Saudi mutual trust. Although US interest in the AWACS sale, as implied by several US officials,[13] was related to the Soviet threat from Afghanistan, the Saudi interest in co-operating with America was motivated by the Iranian threat; in the same time, however, both Riyadh and Washington were equally concerned with security challenges at the regional and global level. The AWACS sale improved Saudi security and US intelligence and reconnaissance reach, and mutual cooperation.

The AWACS sale was related to the Saudi agreement to build huge underground strategic facilities,[14] which were intended to support a massive US deployment in the event of a major Iranian or Soviet threat. Oddly enough, they were used not against Iran or Moscow but against Iraq in 1990. Such forces were a sine qua non for mounting Operation Desert Shield and Storm in 1990–91.[15] For its part, Washington also reacted favorably to Saudi requests for US arms and military backup support against real and perceived threats from Iran. While the AWACS package, to some extent, improved US–Saudi security relations, the RDF, which in 1983 transformed into CENTCOM, enhanced US regional credibility, as did US defense efforts throughout the 1980s, such as the reflagging of Kuwait tankers in 1987. Problems in US–Saudi relations did not disappear, but the cooperation catalyzed by the Iran-Iraq conflict contrasted starkly with the less than cooperative relations that existed prior to it.

The 1990–91 Gulf crisis motivated the highest level of US–Saudi cooperation to date. Even during the US reflagging of Kuwaiti tankers in 1987, Riyadh was concerned about identifying with Washington only to have it curtail the mission if events went awry. In 1990, Riyadh was initially nervous about requesting US support after Iraq's invasion. The fear was that such support would agitate religious elements in the Kingdom, and in fact it was one of the key reasons that bin Laden turned against the Al Saud and launched terrorism against the United States. But the 1990–91 crisis spurred unprecedented US–Saudi cooperation, gave both states invaluable political and military experience, and represented a significant break with the past. The Saudis became convinced of US staying power and vice versa.

Throughout the 1990s, Saudi leaders managed reasonably well the competitive pressures of preserving tradition amid change; and leaning in a pro-American direction, while not alienating domestic constituents. They have realized that they

---

13   For example, see Secretary of State Haig (1981), "Saudi Security, Middle East Peace, and US Interests," *Current Policy* 323, 1–3.

14   Armstrong, S. (1981), "Saudis' AWACS Just a Beginning of a New Strategy," *Washington Post*, November, 01. He broke this story.

15   For details on this infrastructure, see *Conduct of the Persian Gulf War: Final Report to Congress*, Washington, DC: GPO, April 1992, Appendix F.

need the United States to ensure against any major future threat to their survival. As then Crown Prince Abdallah asserted in 1998, US–Saudi ties were "deep and strategic and in the long term, this fact will only increase in importance."[16] The Al Saud also depended on the United States to help them diversify their economy, because Washington played, and still plays, a central role in international organizations and serves as gatekeeper to the global economy.[17] Of course, economic dependence is not a one-way street. The United States benefits from Saudi investment and needs Riyadh to provide oil and to increase its production when crises or global demand require it, and also to play a cooperative role in providing for regional stability.

US–Saudi relations were shaken by the September 11 terrorist attacks. The view emerged in the United States that the 9/11 hijackers were at least affected, if not indoctrinated, by an extremist brand of Islam taught in Saudi religious schools. The royal family, after all, created the broad system of mosques, bureaucracies, and schools run by religious leaders, and they sustain, finance, appoint, govern and sometimes even sanction or fire them. Over time, in fact, the regime has gained more influence over religious leaders and their activities, and has bureaucratized the religious establishment.[18] It is, therefore, clear that the regime has influence over what is taught to Saudis about the West, and especially, the United States.

In addition, September 11 put a disturbing spotlight on the regime. The number of news stories flowed without end. The regime was increasingly seen as corrupt in some circles in Washington, tied to terrorism by the American public, and as lagging far behind Kuwait, Qatar and Bahrain in moving towards democratic practices, much less democracy.

Moreover, 9/11 forced a serious reconsideration about how public and intense US–Saudi military cooperation should be. Saudis, including those in the royal family, began to question whether the security benefits of an American connection were worth the potential domestic costs of increasing opposition to the regime from religious and other elements, as reflected in the al-Qaeda threat. Some observers went so far as to say that public anger in Saudi Arabia at both the monarchy and the United States threatened to tear apart their strategic alliance.[19]

For their part, scores of Saudi religious scholars and academics did issue a manifesto in spring 2002 which suggested that Muslims might find common ground with the West, and liberal strains could be identified within the Kingdom.[20] But, at

---

16   At a meeting with US oil executives one of whom reported it. Quoted in Obaid, N.E. (2000), *The Oil Kingdom at 100: Petroleum Policymaking in Saudi Arabia*, Washington, DC: The Washington Institute for Near East Policy, 8.

17   The diversification plan appears to be initially successful, though not without potential pitfalls. See Ibid.

18   See Gause III, G.F. (1994), *Oil Monarchies: Domestic and Security Challenges in the Arab Gulf* States, New York: Council on Foreign Relations Press, 12–16. Also, Kechichian, J.A. (2001), *Succession in Saudi Arabia*, New York: Palgrave, ch. 3. Al-Yassini, A. (1985), *Religion and State in the Kingdom of Saudi Arabia*, Boulder, CO: Westview Press, 70–6.

19   This broader sentiment was captured in Rouleau, E. (2002), "Trouble in the Kingdom," *Foreign Affairs* 81.

20   On these strains, see Dekmejian (2003), "The Liberal Impulse in Saudi Arabia," *The Middle East Journal*, 57.

the same time, immoderate forces were at play who heavily and openly criticized their counterparts. In one such rebuke, the writer, reflecting some broader sentiment, praised the war on America as giving Muslims a "sense of relief" that action was taken against Americans who have oppressed the Islamic world.[21] Many in Saudi Arabia saw the US war on terrorism as a war to enhance American power at the expense of Muslims. Anti-Americanism was heightened by views that the United States had sought to strangle the Iraqi people with economic sanctions, and then to take their oil in war; that Riyadh was too dependent on a manipulative and intrusive America for security; that it was in bed with Washington economically; and that pro-Israel Washington was either against or neglectful of the Palestinians.[22] The US decision to withdraw key forces from Saudi Arabia in the summer of 2003 may well appease some discontents in the Kingdom, but that remains to be seen.

As the events clearly showed, Riyadh was confronted to a greater extent than in the past with the problem that even if mutual interests strengthened bilateral relations, US–Saudi relations were a subset of, and had to consider, US-Muslim world relations. The regime became intimately aware of the trade off between its US connection and good standing with actors that resented it in and outside the Kingdom,[23] and the diminished threat from Iran and Iraq over time allowed Riyadh to distance itself more from Washington, although only so far. Perceptions that the Saudis wanted US forces to leave were repeatedly dispelled by Saudi leaders,[24] but reflected real concerns.

On the American side, 9/11 elevated the question of the proper US security role in Saudi Arabia to a national debate, with a number of senior officials in Congress and The Pentagon even asserting that a US military withdrawal from Saudi Arabia should be considered,[25] and with alleged claims that the Saudis sought such action as well.[26] American forces eventually did withdraw from the Kingdom in 2003.

Furthermore, some US officials were unhappy with the lack of Saudi military support following 9/11. Although Riyadh broke diplomatic relations with the Taliban, it refused to allow America use of its bases in the war which removed the Taliban from power. This raised questions about whether Riyadh felt under pressure to distance itself from Washington after 9/11. However, the arrangement was not without reason. The United States did not want to destabilize the Saudi regime, especially if it could meet particular strategic goals without basing in Saudi Arabia. And, in fact, as former CENTCOM leader, General Anthony Zinni, pointed out:

---

21   Quoted in MacFarquhar, N. (2002) "A Few Saudis Defy a Rigid Islam To Debate Their Own Intolerance," *New York Times*, July 12, A1, 10.

22   Yamani, M. (2000), *Changed Identities: The Challenge of the New Generation in Saudi Arabia*, London: Royal Institute for International Affairs, esp. 35, 71.

23   This paragraph is based partly on an interview with former US Ambassador to Saudi Arabia, Chas W. *Freeman* Jr, by phone, January 17, 2003.

24   See "Iran and Saudi Arabia Are Watching In the Middle Of The Devil's Triangle," *APS Diplomat News Service* (January 28, 2002).

25   On this debate, see MEED 46, January 25, 2002, 2; *APS Diplomat News Service* 55, December 10 2002; *The Economist*, January 26, 2002.

26   Crown Prince Abdallah Subsequently Refuted these Claims. See "Abdullah speaks out," *Meed* (February 1, 2002).

Washington had been taking action even before 9/11 to develop other basing options so that it would not become "totally dependent on one place."[27]

The issue of Israel arose anew as well. The Saudis, perhaps to shore up their Islamic credentials challenged by al-Qaeda, repeatedly expressed disappointment with the generally pro-Israel US position in the wake of Palestinian-Israeli violence. This anger was reflected in an August 2001 letter from Crown Prince Abdallah to President Bush alerting the United States to the potential for a serious rupture in relations.[28]

But, despite such differences and recriminations, the two sides sought to preserve relations. Indeed, until September 15, 2002, the Saudi public position on Iraq fell far short of what the United States sought, although it is likely that the private position was at least somewhat more forthcoming. Riyadh refused to allow invading US forces to use Saudi bases such as the sophisticated Prince Sultan Air Base Command Center south of Riyadh, which was designed and built by the United States to house the air staff of the Central Command in wartime, and argued that the use of force was not warranted. In mid-September, however, the Saudis changed public course and indicated that the United States could use military bases in an attack on Iraq, if the UN Security Council passed a resolution backing military action.

To some extent, the lagged effects of 9/11 continued to plague relations between Washington and Riyadh. In late 2002, for the first time, the Al Saud initiated a zealous defense of their efforts to fight terrorism and crack down on Saudi charities. They sought to convince Americans that they were important and useful allies, to counter anti-Saudi sentiment that might hurt relations, and to distance themselves from international terrorism. On December 3, 2002, Saudi Foreign Policy Advisor Adel al-Jubeir discussed with the media a summary Saudi report outlining how much it had done to fight terrorism and argued that Saudi Arabia had been "unfairly maligned" based on misunderstandings and deliberate lies about what Saudi Arabia has done on terrorism.[29] In some measure, the regime was misunderstood. After all, most high-ranking members of the royal family—at least those who do not want to challenge the leadership for internal political reasons—do not sympathize with al-Qaeda, and see Osama bin Laden as a threat. Saudi Arabia withdrew his citizenship in 1994 and subsequently he became an increasingly harsh critic of the regime and has sought its demise, with the hope of replacing it with a Taliban-like Government. Those who sympathize with him in Saudi Arabia are not fans of the regime.

But while at least most in the House of Saud do not support al-Qaeda, the real question has been whether the regime would aggressively fight terrorism even at the risk of alienating influential Saudi businessmen, elements of the public, and of course, the clergy which lent it credibility and support. A harsh response could even

---

27 Quoted in Sciolino, E. and Schmitt, E. (2002), "US Rethinks Its Role in Saudi Arabia," *New York Times*, March 10, 24.

28 "Saudi–US Ties Set To Change As War On Terror Spreads Across The Middle East," *APS Diplomat News Service* (February 25, 2002).

29 The transcript appears in "Adel Al-Jubeir Holds News Conference," Federal Document Clearing House, December 3, 2002, available at http://web.lexis-nexus.com/universe/document.

alienate Mullahs and others who are not extremist, but who nonetheless resent royal family interference, especially under perceived pressure from Washington. Riyadh has shown some recognition that changes are needed in Saudi religious schools,[30] and has taken some steps to curb its own radical Islamists.[31] It has also moved to freeze suspected terrorist holdings, to police local charities and financial institutions more vigorously,[32] and to provide some intelligence assistance to Washington.[33] The al-Qaeda threat in the Kingdom has also pushed Saudi authorities to crack down on militants and to increase their cooperation with Washington.[34]

However, many observers believe that the regime could do much more to fight terrorism. Since 9/11, US federal officials sent hundreds of written requests for specific information to their Saudi counterparts and have expressed frustration that many of them have gone unanswered.[35] Yet, the regime has also had to take into account its own constituents. If the US and Saudi publics were voting after 9/11, they may very well have chosen a divorce based on irreconcilable differences.[36]

The 9/11 attacks, of course, cannot be de-linked from the Iraq War of 2003. This is because the war was treated by the Bush administration as part of the broader assault on terrorism sparked by 9/11. The fall of Saddam's regime made Washington less critical to Riyadh in the security arena. In the broader scope of time, it cannot be lost on any Saudi leader the fact that of the three Saudi states that have existed since 1744, the first two collapsed not as a result of internal developments, but chiefly from external invasion.[37]

On the whole, war and transnational terrorism made it harder for the Saudis to reconcile religious and security considerations in their foreign policy. The departure of American forces from Saudi Arabia may ease this problem to some extent, but continuing demands from Washington that Riyadh step up its anti-terrorism efforts may well continue to force the Al Saud to balance between preserving their American strategic connection and challenging the domestic bargain set up in 1744, on which their legitimacy rests.

---

30   See "Saudi–US Relations Are Running Through Lengthy Turbulence," *APS Diplomatic News Service* (December 10, 2001).

31   Saudi foreign minister Faisal indicated at least that the regime had taken measures to remove anti-American teachings from its madrasas. Interviewed on CBS, September 15, 2002.

32   "Riyadh Cracks Down On Terrorists Assets," *APS Diplomat Recorder* (October 27, 2001).

33   See Lorenzetti, M. (2002), "US firms say timetable may slip on Saudi gas deals," *Oil & Gas Journal*.

34   Interview with Energy Information Administration Director, Guy Caruso, August 8, 2003, Washington, DC.

35   Sanger, D.E. (2002), "Bush Officials Praise Saudis For Aiding Terror Fight," *New York Times*, November 27, 2002.

36   On polls showing anti-Americanism, see the results of a survey of nine Muslim countries. The USATODAY/GALLUP poll was released on February 27, 2002, available at http://www.usatoday.com/news/attack/2002/02/27/usat-pollside.htm.

37   Fandy, 248.

Saudi Relations with the Islamic Republic of Iran

Historically, relations between Saudi Arabia and Iran have always been uneasy. Owing perhaps to the age-old Arab-Persian dichotomy or to the mere fact that both states seek to control the oil resources of the Persian Gulf, their foreign policies have often been at odds with one another. This situation has been especially pronounced since 1979, despite a *rapprochement* in the wake of the Persian Gulf War. However, Saudi Arabia often pursues a line towards Iran far more conciliatory than one might expect, especially given the demonstrated desire of the Islamic Republic to destabilize and undermine the Saudi monarchy. This chapter argues that this phenomenon is the result of Riyadh's fear of falling afoul of global Islamic opinion; hence, Tehran actively positions itself as a global Islamic leader, generating a considerable amount of empathy, especially in the non-monarchical and non-Arab Muslim states. A hard Saudi line on Iran might jeopardize the Kingdom's religious legitimacy, and hence is often eschewed.

This phenomenon has a complicated history. The Islamic Revolution of 1979 was radicalizing in a way perhaps not even fully appreciated today. For the first time in modern history, Saudi leaders had to contend with a vibrant and polarizing rival that specifically challenged the Kingdom's pride of place in Islam. The leader of the Iranian revolution, Ayatollah Khomeini, presented a direct challenge to the cultural appeal of Saudi Arabia by trying to position Iran as the true standard-bearer of political Islam in the late twentieth century.

As one scholar put it in the 1980s, "in the ... Gulf states [Iran's radical interpretation of Islam] is perceived as a menace to their security and stability partly because in [Khomeini]'s Islam there is no room for monarchical systems. Furthermore, Iran's militant non-alignment policy runs counter to the close ties that exist between conservative Gulf states and the United States."[38] Iran during Khomeini's reign also sought to undermine Saudi Arabia's system of foreign relations, sought to rouse its minority Shi'a population against Riyadh, and supported violent demonstrations and even attacks against pilgrims at the annual *Hajj*. Chubin has described this relationship as an "Islamic Cold War." However, it should be noted that the Islamic dimension of Iran-Saudi relations is one where Iran, since the 1980s, proves a major irritant rather than an alternative center of gravity.

> [Iran] retains its attraction as a revolutionary model and as a source of funds for oppositions groups. Unable to attract others by example or ideology, Iran can nonetheless tap into the discontent of other societies, eroding the legitimacy of their governments by alluding to their dependency, materialism and cultural contamination.[39]

Iran has made and makes a major issue out of Saudi Arabia's marriage of convenience with the United States, arguing that no state can claim a special position within

---

38   Ramazani, R.K., "Khumayni's Islam in Iran's Foreign Policy," 26 in Dawisha (ed.).

39   Chubin, S. and Tripp, C., *Iran-Saudi Arabia Relations and Regional Order: Iran and Saudi Arabia in the Balance of Power*, Oxford and New York: Oxford University Press for the International Institute of Strategic Studies, 61.

Islam that relies on Americans and Zionists for its security. The centrality of this reasoning to Iranian official discourse is clear enough from Khomeini's last will and testament.[40]

Tehran targets dissident elements at the domestic level of Saudi society as well. A good example exists in Iranian propaganda materials produced for foreign consumption. One, "characteristically entitled [Horizons of Islamic Unity], an 85-page book in Arabic, published in 1982 by Iran's Ministry for Islamic Guidance, quoted the views of the major revolutionary leaders ... striving to minimize the significance of Shiite-Sunnite doctrinal differences."[41] At the time, this was a slap in the face of Saudi Arabia, which both practiced harsh discrimination against its Shi'a populations. As late as 1991, high-ranking members of the Saudi Higher Council of Ulama were denouncing Shi'a as enemies of Islam on the level of Jews and even issuing *fatwa* calling on Sunnis to murder them.[42]

The Shi'a of Saudi Arabia were a major target for Iranian propaganda in the 1980s and 90 s—Khomeini, for instance, called for the unity of all Shi'a and spoke of the damnation awaiting the House of Saud in his will. The Iranian revolution sparked civil unrest among Saudi Shi'a in 1979 and 1980 in the oil-rich Eastern Province town of Qatif.[43]

Another major point of contention between Iran and Saudi Arabia is the annual pilgrimage to Mecca, the *Hajj*. Saudi Arabia had traditionally used the annual event to cultivate its moral position in the Muslim world. Beginning in the 1980s, however, the mullah regime in Tehran began to use it as a platform to agitate for revolution and thus enhance its own international Islamic appeal. To that end, Iran has ostentatiously sponsored radical demonstrations during the *Hajj*, which notoriously turned violent in 1987 and 1989. To counter the emerging Iranian ideological threat during the annual pilgrimage, Saudi authorities have relied on ever-greater controls to prevent anti-regime sentiments or materials from filtering in with the waves of pilgrims. However, Saudi authorities have tended to tread lightly around this issue—too much repression could stimulate resentment both internationally and domestically. Iran has retorted that the Saudi goal of separating politics from religion during the *Hajj* reveals that Riyadh is a tool of the superpower agenda.[44] Saudi Arabia has therefore been reticent to clamp down too hard on *Hajj* demonstrations, while simultaneously aware that their goal is to undermine the Saudi state. The answer since 1996 has been to prohibit pilgrims from carrying literature deemed threatening into Saudi Arabia, while allowing demonstrations to take place in specified areas. The *Hajj* remains a

---

40   "The Last Message: The Political and Divine Will of his Holiness Imam Khomeini," available at http://www.irna.ir/occasion/ertehal/english/will/index.htm

41   Landau, 259.

42   Fandy, 206. See also "The Shi'ite Question in Saudi Arabia," International Crisis Group Middle East Report 45, September 19, 2005, 9–13.

43   Quandt, W.B. (1981), *Saudi Arabia in the 1980s: Foreign Policy, Security, and Oil*, Washington, D.C.: Brookings Institution Press.

44   Ramazani, R.K. (1983), "Khumayni's Islam in Iran's Foreign Policy," in Dawisha, (ed.), *Islam in Foreign Policy*, 27.

sticky issue in Saudi-Iranian dealings, since "when relations deteriorate, Iran can use this issue to apply pressure and reach a broader audience."[45]

Iran has also tried to use the Arab–Israeli conflict as a wedge against Saudi Arabia. For Tehran, it is an Islamic issue, not an Arab one, which also constitutes the approach taken by Riyadh. Iran criticizes Saudi Arabia's acceptance of talks, claiming that it does so at Zionist and American bidding.[46] The effect of this rhetoric is easy to overestimate. However, it demonstrates that Islamic issues are an important dimension of the relations between Saudi Arabia and Iran.

Saudi Arabia was careful during the Iran–Iraq War to avoid direct involvement. While it secretly supported Iraq with financial and other resources, it refused to contribute any forces and, except a 1984 incident in which a Saudi F-15 shot down an Iranian F-4 Phantom, generally refrained from retaliating against consistent Iranian attacks on its oil tankers.[47]

Scholars tended to see the 1990s as a sort of cooling-off period in Saudi-Iranian relations. Saddam Hussein's ambitions against both had been checked, and for the moment much of the international community's focus was on him. The start of the Second Palestinian Intifada in 2000 also gave Iran and Saudi Arabia common cause, at least momentarily. While there were whispers of Iranian involvement in the Khobar Towers bombing of 1996, relations were much more tranquil than they had been in the preceding decade. The attacks of September 11, 2001, however, brought Saudi Arabia's controversial alliance with the United States back into the forefront of regional politics, and the launching of the War on Terrorism further complicated matters as the United States forcibly toppled the governments of two states bordering on Iran. Operations Enduring Freedom and Iraqi Freedom have heightened Iran's perceptions of threat from the United States. As long as Riyadh maintains close military ties to Washington, its relations with Iran will be more complicated, due to widespread mistrust of the Americans in Iran and the broader Muslim world.

The withdrawal of most American military personnel from Saudi Arabia in 2003 does not mean that that relationship is at an end. Since the original purpose of that deployment was to deter Saddam Hussein, it has in a sense served its purpose. In any case, it appears that the United States will remain in the region for some time, albeit with its base of operations moved out of Saudi Arabia.

Iran's pursuit of uranium enrichment presents a further challenge. For security reasons, Saudi Arabia is uncomfortable with a nuclear-armed Iran. However, concern about religious legitimacy prevents Saudi Arabia from actively opposing Tehran's nuclear program. Not only could Tehran apply more diplomatic pressure against Saudi Arabia and other states in possession of a nuclear deterrent, but its ties to Islamist radical groups opposed to the Saudi monarchy could heighten the level of terrorist threat to the regime. However, Saudi Arabia does not wish to appear to favor the American and European position on Iran's nuclear program, since doing so might invite reaction on the Islamic front abroad and at home. Prince Turki bin-

---

45   Chubin, 56.
46   Ibid., p. 58.
47   "Attack in South Persian Gulf said to threaten New Phase in War," *New York Times*, June 12, 1984.

Faisal, the Saudi ambassador to the United States, clearly stated the Saudi position in February 2006 when he said that Iran's nuclear program "escalates the tensions, and brings about competition which is unneeded and unnecessary and uncalled for." At the same time, however, he was careful to frame the debate in less polarizing terms, by making a general call for a nuclear-free Middle East, an obvious jab at Israel. "They [Iran] see the US government negotiating with North Korea ... and they see the US signing a nuclear peace agreement with India ... and they see the US turning a blind eye completely to Israel, although Israel has the most nuclear weapons in our part of the world."[48] At the same time, the Islamic dimension of Riyadh's policy compels it to appear supportive of Iran. Saudi leaders have repeatedly stated that they believe Iran's nuclear program to be peaceful and have criticized the West's accusations, while at the same time favoring a diplomatic solution. This is likely a play to a Muslim audience, since if it made statements in line with its security interests, Riyadh might risk being undercut by Ahmadinejad's attempts to mold Iran into a martyr of the West.

With the defeat of Saddam Hussein, Iran remains the single largest state-level threat to Saudi Arabia. It entertains regional hegemonic ambitions, and has set itself on a collision course with the United States, the guarantor of the Kingdom's security. It is militarily powerful and ideologically hostile. It challenges the legitimacy of the Saudi regime. It is supportive of international terrorism, Saudi dissident groups, and aims to offset the regional balance of power by possessing nuclear weapons. Yet Saudi Arabia has been and is constrained in its rivalry with Islamic Iran by its potent desire to remain the spiritual leader of the global *Umma*.

Saudi Relations with the New Iraq

Not unlike the case of Saudi-Iranian relations, the Kingdom's relations with Iraq have also been buffeted by events in the region. Beginning with Saddam Hussein's invasion of Kuwait and culminating in the US-led invasion of Iraq in 2003, these events made it more difficult for the Saudis to reconcile their pursuit of security with their religious legitimacy.

The Iraq War that began in 2003 was a watershed moment in the politics of the Middle East. Not only was one of the Gulf's titans removed from the equation, but the role of the United States, and Saudi Arabia with it, came into serious question. Many met the invasion and fall of Saddam Hussein with jubilation, others with uncertainty and apprehension about America's intentions in the region. As regards Iraq we have two principal arguments. First, the religious aspect of Saudi foreign policy made it infeasible for Riyadh to support the removal of one of its principal threats, as much a boon to its security as that might have been. The situation of 2003 therefore stands in sharp contrast with that of 1990–91, at which time Arab and Muslim opinion was largely divided, if not in Riyadh's favor. By 2003, however, the Kingdom's mercurial relationship with the United States and its "beholden-ness" to Islamic opinion contributed to the ground swell of criticism of Riyadh that led it

---

48   "Saudi Prince Slams Iran's Nuclear Program," *The Daily Star*, February 10, 2006.

to a fundamental reassessment of its partnership with America. Second, the results of the Iraq War were more or less deleterious to the interests of Saudi Arabia, as the outcome of the war would most likely draw Iraq away from the Saudi orbit and intensify sectarian divisions in the region—something against which Saudi Arabia's Wahhabist appeal can do little.

Saddam's ouster revolutionized Saudi Arabia's relations with its northern neighbor. The change, however, is not necessarily for the better. This is because historically, Saudi Arabia has had two major interests in its relationship with Iraq. First, Iraq must be strong enough to stand on its own. A militarily and socially weak and fractured Iraq does little for Saudi Arabia but place a cauldron of unrest on its northern border. Second, Saudi Arabia is part of a triangular balance of power in the Persian Gulf with Iran and Iraq. Iraq must at the very minimum, therefore, be kept out of the Iranian camp, just as the reverse is true. Saudi Arabia has historically used Iraq to balance Iran, displayed through its tacit support for Saddam during the Iran–Iraq War.

Before 1990, Saudi leaders were suspicious of Iraq because of its military strength and its ties to the Soviet Union. Moreover, Iraq's Ba'athism presented an Arab socialist alternative to Saudi conservatism, and Saddam had pretensions of making himself a new Nasser. Saudi Arabia and Iraq, even as they shared common cause in opposing the regional designs of revolutionary Iran, were also at odds over a number of other issues. While Saudi Arabia was willing to offer "peace initiatives" to Israel and to eventually normalize its relations with Egypt after Camp David, for instance, Iraq remained resolute in its total rejectionism and presented enough of a threat to Israel that Begin felt the need to attack Iraqi nuclear facilities in 1981. The Saudi *ulama*, including the Grand Mufti ibn Baz, at the same time, regarded "Arab nationalism in its Ba'athist version a form of *jahiliyya* (pre-Islamic age of ignorance) to be fought alongside Communism and Westernisation.'[49] Siding with Saddam's Iraq to balance Iran, then, further complicated the Saudi position since whatever it gained in traditional security, it could lose in domestic legitimacy.

The American-led campaign in Iraq has numerous implications that relate to the two key factors—religion and security—shaping Saudi Arabia's foreign policy. The first argument posits that the Iraq War demonstrates the difficulty Saudi Arabia faces in reconciling its quest for security with its religious legitimacy. The Iraq War was and is deeply unpopular in Saudi Arabia. The Saudis, accordingly, have been careful to avoid publicly supporting the American war effort in Iraq, even if they were pleased that Saddam was eliminated. As such they publicly and stridently denounced the invasion but "quietly allowed US Special Forces to mount ground operations out of bases in northern Saudi Arabia and allowed command and control, surveillance, refueling, and other logistical support to be carried out at Prince Sultan Airbase."[50]

---

49   Al-Rasheed, M. (2005), "Circles of Power: Royals and Society in Saudi Arabia," in Aarts and Nonneman, 195.

50   Alterman, J.B. (2005), "Don't Stand so Close to Me," in Daniel Benjamin (ed.), *America and the World in the Age of Terror: A New Landscape in International Relations*, Washington, D.C.: Center for Strategic and International Studies Press, 165.

In one sense, then, Saudi Arabia supported the invasion. Reticence to *appear* pro-American, however, best defines the Saudi position.

The heady days following September 11, 2001 were ones of extreme polarity in the global community—George W. Bush's axiom "with us or against us" turned out to be largely accurate in the case of the Middle East. The Muslim world, for its part, came down overwhelmingly against the American-led War on Terrorism. Saudi Arabia was therefore presented with a choice between supporting the defeat of its principal foe and standing in solidarity with the *Umma*. The difficulty of the choice, and the ambiguity of Saudi Arabia's ultimate answer, reflects once again that harmony between *realpolitik* and religion is becoming an ever scarcer commodity.

Second, the war in Iraq threatens to lead to an increase in Iran's influence in the region. The power vacuum that followed Saddam's reign resulted in the ascendancy of the formerly oppressed Shi'a majority. This ascendancy of course accompanies the fall of the Sunnis from power, and sectarian tensions there have tended to widen the rift in other parts of the Muslim world, including Saudi Arabia.[51] This could give an advantage to Iran. The ascendancy of Shi'a politicians in Iraq is threatening to Saudi Arabia, if only because the former's sectarian identity might make them less likely to directly oppose Tehran. A 2006 Center for Strategic and International Studies (CSIS) report indicates a high degree of Iranian interference in Iraq, especially through its influence over the Supreme Council of the Islamic Revolution in Iraq (SCIRI) and by providing training and financial support to Shi'a militias in the country.[52] Iran has also sought to use the machinery of the nascent democracy in Iraq to bolster its own interests there, laboring, for instance, to keep more "pro-Iranian" candidates in office.[53] Put bluntly, from the Saudi perspective Saddam Hussein was replaced with an uncertain power vacuum that threatens to leave behind a Shi'a-dominated Iraq that will draw closer to Iran, hence threatening Saudi influence in the region. As one analyst put it, "Tehran now sees an opportunity to fulfill one of the most cherished aims of the Iranian revolutionary experiment, 'to export the revolution.'"[54]

The worst-case scenario, sectarian civil war in Iraq, could prove disastrous for Saudi Arabia, as it would threaten to draw in Iran and likely Saudi Arabia as well, further exacerbating the tensions in that relationship. In addition, it would produce a new generation of battle-hardened radicals, many of whom, both Sunni and Shi'a, might make the Kingdom their next target. As Jon Alterman has argued, the strife in Iraq has also complicated Saudi Arabia's relations with the United States, which in turn could threaten its ability to lobby for greater American assistance on security matters.[55] The Bush Administration and the coalition militaries, for instance, have repeatedly suggested that the insurgency in Iraq is comprised largely of "foreign

---

51   There is some fear of a spillover, as occurred on a limited basis after the Iranian revolution, but the Shi'a minority in Saudi Arabia is too small to pose a real threat to the regime. See "The Shi'ite Question in Saudi Arabia" and Fandy, 174.

52   Obaid, N., *Meeting the Challenge of a Fragmented Iraq: A Saudi Perspective,* (Center for Strategic and International Studies).

53   See, for instance, "In Iraq's Choice, a Chance for Unity," *Washington Post*, April 26 2006.

54   Ibid., p. 18.

55   Alterman, 165.

fighters" from numerous Muslim countries, especially Saudi Arabia.[56] This view, however, has recently been challenged.[57] Regardless of the actual composition of the insurgency, the possibility of widespread Saudi involvement only compounds American resentment of Saudi Arabia, home to 15 of the nineteen 9/11 hijackers.

Most predictions of the future of Iraq appear grim, but it is useful to dwell for a moment on the possibility that the coalition will succeed in its goal of leaving behind a stable Iraq with a representative government. George W. Bush has stated that the coalition seeks to build democracy in Iraq in the hopes that it will spread to other countries, especially since his re-election in 2004. Even before then, he stated in a radio address that "the success of Iraqi democracy would send forth the news, from Damascus to Tehran, that freedom can be the future of every nation."[58] While Bush was careful not to mention Riyadh, it is clear that democratization of the region would pose a major threat to the Saudi monarchy. As such, it has attempted to pay some lip service to democratic practice, holding largely token local elections in 2005, won easily by Islamist candidates.[59] If Iraq is democratized and if the phenomenon manages to spread through some kind of grass roots action, the Saudi regime could find itself in serious trouble.

The Arab–Israeli Conflict in Saudi Foreign Relations

Saudi Arabia has two major interests in the Arab–Israeli conflict: to appear hostile enough on the one hand not to lose either the support of the *ulama* at the domestic level or the approbation of world Muslim opinion, but on the other hand appear to accept Israel enough to abide by Riyadh's increasing commitments to the international community. Israel is a case where Saudi Arabia must choose between its religious foreign policy and its goal of taking on a greater role in international politics. While Saudi Arabia's security goals are not directly related to its position on Israel, the same basic phenomenon shows itself—in keeping with the central argument of this chapter, these goals are in large part contradictory and, given the escalation of the Arab–Israeli conflict in the early twenty-first century, the rise of Hamas to power, the War on Terrorism, and a host of other factors, the reconciliation of these two goals is becoming increasingly more difficult.

Gawdat Bahgat has described Saudi Arabia's position on Israel as one of "cautious acceptance."[60] Saudi Arabia, while never at the forefront of the Arab–Israeli conflict, has long been indirectly involved, in some ways on both sides of the conflict. Nonetheless, Israel is at the forefront of Saudi foreign policy calculations because it represents the most visible dividing line in global politics. It is here that

---

56   See "Saudi Fighters 'are Leading the Surge in Attacks on British Troops'," *Daily Telegraph*, (May 31, 2006).

57   See Cordesman, A. and Obaid, N., *Saudi Militants in Iraq: Assessment and Kingdom's Response*, (Center for Strategic and International Studies).

58   President George W. Bush, Radio Address, May 1, 2004.

59   "Islamists win Saudi Elections," CBSNews.com, (February 11, 2005).

60   Bahgat (2006), *Israel and the Persian Gulf: Retrospect and Prospect*, Gainesville, FL: University Press of Florida, 128.

Saudi Arabia's religious foreign policy is most important—a hard line on Israel can do more to project an image of Islamic and Arab solidarity than most other issues combined. At the same time, Saudi leaders have sometimes taken unpopular positions on Israel, for instance offering "peace plans" in 1981 and 2002.

The Arab–Israeli conflict, ironically, works as a tool of Saudi omnibalancing in both directions. As mentioned, Saudi Arabia extends financial support to the Palestinians despite no direct military threat from Israel, but Riyadh also mediates its policy toward Israel to extract concessions from the West. As Joseph Kostiner has argued, Saudi Arabia extended its 2002 peace plan to Israel in order to cauterize the wounds to its partnership with the United States opened by the trauma of 9/11.[61] At the same time, then-Crown Prince Abdullah was careful to advocate a peace plan that demanded too many concessions for Israel to accept—one that urged them to give up all their gains since the Six Day War.

Nonetheless, Saudi Arabia generally tries to maintain an image of enmity to Israel and is actually supportive of its enemies. Saudi Arabia has traditionally used non-conventional means to express its opposition to Israel, such as boycotting the Camp David negotiations, funding the Palestinian authorities and neighboring Arab states and applying economic sanctions (oil embargoes) to punish Israel's supporters, as in 1967 and 1973.

Riyadh's allies among the *ulama* would abandon it very quickly if it appeared to support Israel in any way, a factor that seriously complicates Saudi Arabia's security policy. The Saudi alliance with the United States, while protecting the Kingdom in times of dire need, has also offered critics of the monarchy the opportunity to denounce it as little more than a tool of Zionists. In order to allay these accusations, Saudi Arabia has always provided the Palestinians with monetary support, despite its nervousness about, for instance, Arafat's prominent leftist tendencies and his public denunciation of the Kingdom's cooperation with the United States in 1990–91.[62] Similarly, Saudi authorities seem to ignore their fears of Arab and Islamist radicalism in the case of the Hamas government in the Palestinian territories, continuing to grant it financial and logistical support and even calling on others not to cut it off.[63]

Saudi Arabia's commitments to Palestine and refusal to accept Israel as a member of the international community tend against its desire for greater participation in international politics. Saudi Arabia's hands are in a sense tied by its commitment to maintaining Islamic respectability with regard to Palestine. This much is evidenced by the accession of Saudi Arabia to the World Trade Organization (WTO) in 2005 and its subsequent foot-dragging over dropping some elements of its boycott against Israel, as required by WTO bylaws. To drop the boycott, however, would jeopardize

---

61   See Kostiner, J., "Coping with Regional Challenges: A Case Study of Crown Prince Abdullah's Peace Initiaitve," 352–371 in Aarts and Nonneman.

62   See Ibid., pp. 137–138.

63   "Saudi Warns against Isolating Hamas," *Washington Post*, May 18, 2006 ; The pro-Israeli think-tank, Washington Institute for Near East Policy, also charges that Saudi Arabia operates training facilities for Hamas radicals, see Levitt, M. (2005) "A Hamas Headquarters in Saudi Arabia?" Washington Institute for Near East Policy Peace Watch #521, September 28.

the Kingdom's carefully–crafted aura of legitimacy. In the WTO case, however, Saudi policymakers have seemed to speak out of both sides of their mouths. For instance, Dr Hashim Yamani, Saudi Minister of Commerce and Industry said on September 12, 2005 that Saudi Arabia would deal with all members of the WTO, a clear allusion to questions about the status of Israel.[64] US officials seemed to think (at least publicly) that they could be held to their word. Trade Representative Rob Portman seemed optimistic, testifying in February 2006 to the House Ways and Means Committee that "[Saudi Arabia] will abide by their WTO commitments."[65]

Saudi Arabia, however, since joining WTO on November 11, 2005, has failed to comply with the WTO rules regarding trade restrictions with other members. The US House of Representatives passed a resolution condemning this failure to comply in March 2006.[66] Saudi Arabia further aroused doubts that it ever had any intention of complying with the pledges it made before accession to the WTO when it hosted the "Ninth Meeting of the Liaison Officers of Islamic Regional Officers for the Boycott of Israel" in Jeddah in March 2006. Though OIC and Saudi officials described the summit as just a routine annual meeting to discuss the long-standing boycott, some observers, especially the Israeli media, were skeptical.

One possible reason for Saudi Arabia's acceptance of the Israeli limitation on its policy is the intensifying polarization of the Muslim and Arab worlds since the beginning of the second Intifada in 2000. Ahmadinejad's Iran, moreover, has begun to take anti-Israeli rhetoric to seemingly new heights (or depths), further radicalizing a region already tense from years of war. Unwilling to appear supportive of the state, Iran's president said he would wipe Israel off the map. Saudi leaders, therefore, may be wary of entering into new territory in order to join the WTO, admittedly a bastion of "Western" respectability.

The fact that Iran now seeks to radicalize the debate over Israel could have serious implications for the foreign policy of Saudi Arabia. Its tendency is not to oppose the majority of other Middle Eastern states with regard to Israel. As such, Ehud Olmert's more conciliatory approach—withdrawal—may not elicit a favorable response from Saudi Arabia. This, combined with Riyadh's ongoing support for Hamas, means that Saudi Arabia will likely not back down on the WTO, and will not back any peace plan that is more moderate than those that require Israel to withdraw to its 1967 borders, if any at all.

Conclusion

The foreign policy of Saudi Arabia, like that of all states, is shaped by myriad of factors. But as with other states, some factors predominate over others. In the Saudi case, security is crucial because the Al Saud operate in a neighborhood which presents them with either existential threats or the possibility of existential threats, a situation which can be contrasted sharply with the condition of Western European states, for instance. Moreover, while religion affects the behavior of many states in

---

64   Kuwait News Agency (KUNA) (September 13, 2005).

65   "Saudi Arabia to Host Israel Boycott Event," *Jerusalem Post*, March 7 (2006).

66   House Concurrent Resolution, 370; Introduced March 29, 2006.

world politics, it is fundamentally and historically tied to the very legitimacy of the Saudi regime, which cannot be said of democratic states in this sense.

This chapter showed how the factors of religion and security impact Saudi foreign policy, and how it has become harder for the Saudis to reconcile these sometimes competing factors. Some scholars believe that the Saudi regime is vulnerable to decline. Such views have been aired for decades and have thus far proven premature or false. But the strength of the regime is likely to be linked to how it handles the challenge of meeting its security goals, while not weakening its religious legitimacy. That balancing act is not only important for the Al Saud—it may affect the global economy as well. Indeed, until the world takes more serious and responsible measures in decreasing global oil dependence, the world's economic health will be tied to the fate of Saudi Arabia.

Chapter 10

The Centrality of Egypt to the Future of the Greater Middle East

B.J. Jordan and Robert J. Pauly, Jr

Introduction

Al-Qaeda's attacks on the United States on September 11 2001 affected America's policy toward one region of the world—the Greater Middle East—more significantly than any other. In response to the attacks, the United States carried out two military operations—Operation Enduring Freedom in the fall of 2001 and Operation Iraqi Freedom in the spring of 2003—designed to eliminate the existing regimes in Afghanistan (the al-Qaeda-harboring Taliban) and Iraq (President Saddam Hussein's repressive Baathists) and lay the foundation for the development of enduring liberal democratic institutions in those states and in the broader Arab and Muslim Greater Middle East. In addition to the daunting challenges in implementing that strategy on the ground in Afghanistan and Iraq—challenges that have grown ever more evident in US-led nation/state-building efforts in each of those contexts—the George W. Bush administration's grand strategy to transform the Greater Middle East involves a delicate balancing act given the existence of a string of long-standing American alliances with authoritarian governments in the region. Understandably, those governments are reluctant to support US efforts to promote democratization generally and freedom of political expression specifically because such developments would likely undermine their own control over their populations.

One such relationship is that between the United States and Egypt. Put simply, Egypt is crucial to the development and implementation of US foreign policy in the Greater Middle East. Knowledge of the geography of the area is necessary to fully understand this importance. Egypt is located in Northern Africa, bordering the Mediterranean Sea, between Libya and the Gaza Strip, and the Red Sea north of Sudan, and includes the Asian Sinai Peninsula. By comparison, Egypt is slightly more than three times the size of New Mexico.[1] More broadly, the Middle East is a region comprising the lands around the southern and eastern parts of the Mediterranean Sea, a territory that extends from the Eastern Mediterranean Sea to the Persian Gulf. The Middle East is a sub-region of Asia and sometimes North Africa. The area is comprised of several ethnic and cultural groups, including the Persian, Arabic, and Turkish cultures. Egypt, with its Sinai Peninsula in Asia and the rest mostly in North

---

1   "Egypt," *CIA World Factbook*, available at https://www.cia.gov/cia/publications/factbook/geos/eg.html.

Africa, is also considered a Middle Eastern state. The term Middle East defines a cultural area, so it does not have precise borders. It is generally taken to include Bahrain, Egypt, Turkey, Iran, Iraq, Israel, Jordan, Kuwait, Lebanon, Oman, Qatar, Saudi Arabia, Syria, the United Arab Emirates, Yemen, and the Palestinian Territories of the West Bank and the Gaza Strip.

Some scholars have criticized the term *Middle East* for its perceived Eurocentrism. The region is only east from the perspective of Western Europe. To a person from India, it lies to the west. To a Russian, it lies to the south. The description *Middle* has also led to some confusion over changing definitions. Before the First World War, the term *Near East* was used in English to refer to the Balkans and the Ottoman Empire, while the term *Middle East* referred to Persia, Afghanistan and sometimes Central Asia, Turkmenistan and the Caucasus. By contrast, *Far East* refers to the countries of East Asia: China, Japan, North Korea, South Korea, Taiwan, and Hong Kong. With the disappearance of the Ottoman Empire after the First World War, *Near East* fell out of common use, while *Middle East* came to be applied to the re-emerging countries of the Arab world.

Egypt is an especially significant state within the Middle East for a number of reasons. Egypt has the largest population in the region, one estimated at 69.5 million. It also has a long history of leadership in the region, starting with the rise of the Pharaonic civilization and peaking from 1250 to 1520 CE when Egypt became the most influential Islamic center in the Muslim world. The cultural influence of Egypt lessened with the rise of the Ottoman Empire in the sixteenth century. However, with the exception of Anwar Sadat, Egyptian presidents since 1954 have been slowly re-establishing Egypt as a powerful cultural force in the Middle East. Egypt's capital city, Cairo, is the home of al-Azhar, the world's first and most respected Islamic University. Egypt has also become the music and film capital of the Arab world.[2]

Egypt has a great deal of importance in the Middle East because of its military strength. Second only to Iran, Egypt has the largest army in the Middle East and the 13th largest army in the world. Cairo receives $1.3 billion annually in military aid from the United States, a practice that commenced under the auspices of the Camp David Peace Accords between Egypt and Israel via mediation by the James E. Carter administration in 1979. It is in America's interest to maintain Egypt as an ally to help ensure the maintenance of US influence in the Middle East.[3]

If Egyptian policy toward Israel were to shift negatively, the West could possibly face an Egyptian-led war against Israel that could include the use of nuclear, chemical, or biological weapons. Since the United States is seen as an ally of Israel, there would also be the possibility of an oil embargo against it. Middle Eastern and North African countries contain 70 percent of the world's known oil reserves with forecasts of an even greater market share in the future. Such an embargo would have a devastating effect on the world's economies, especially those of Europe and Japan which are heavily dependent on Middle Eastern oil imports.[4]

---

2   *SIPRI Yearbook 1997: Armaments, Disarmament and International Security*, Stockholm International Peace Research Institute, Oxford: Oxford University Press, 40–41.

3   Ibid.

4   Ibid.

It is clear that Egypt has the vast potential to influence the rest of the Middle East and the entire Arab world. In more ways than one, Egypt is the heart and the mind of the Arab world, as well as the political center of Arab consciousness. In essence, without Egyptian leadership, the Arab world would be rudderless. Discourses emerging from Egypt, both secular and Islamic, have shaped the framework of references employed by Arabs elsewhere. It should come as no surprise that there has been no Arab–Israeli war ever since Egypt made peace with Israel.[5]

In the past 50 years, two powerful and antithetical ideas emerged from Egypt, both of which continue to influence the rest of the Middle East. These two ideas are Arab socialism and Muslim brotherhood, both of which constitute the backbones of Arab politics today. Arab socialism is embedded in the state machinery, while Islamic resurgence is taking a strong foothold in civil society. As a general rule of thumb, Egypt's strengths are Arab strengths and Egypt's weaknesses are Arab weaknesses.[6]

The Palestinian cause has literally been surrendered by the Arab world since the Camp David Accord. Today, Egypt plays the role of the moderator. Every time an Arab state determines to take punitive action against Israel, Egypt's leadership call for a summit to promote a moderate response. The primary role of Egypt is to keep the Arab response to Israel atrocities within acceptable limits. In effect, making Egyptian foreign policy means shaping Arab foreign policy. Neither Arab socialism nor Islamic revivalism has succeeded in addressing the many problems of Egypt as well as the rest of the Middle East. The consensus is that Islam will play a central role.

The balance of the chapter is designed to address each of these issues—and their impact on US foreign policy toward Egypt and the Greater Middle East through the presentation of six sections that unfold in the following manner. The first section examines the impact of Islamic fundamentalism on Egyptian politics and society. The second section looks at the foreign policy of the regime of Egyptian President Hosni Mubarak. The third section discusses the human rights record of the Mubarak regime. The fourth section analyzes the role of oil in Egypt's economy and its impact on Cairo's policies toward its neighbors on one hand and the United States and the West on the other. The fifth section examines the impact of the events of September 11, 2001 and the resulting Global War on Terrorism (GWOT) on the relationship between Egypt and the United States. The sixth section offers a set of concluding observations on Egyptian–American relations at present and in the future.

Egypt and Islamic Fundamentalism

Many Western scholars consider Islamic fundamentalism to be a politically motivated phenomenon rather than a religious phenomenon. The general consensus is that Islamists use religion as a tool to attract and control followers. This would seem to be a very plausible explanation for the source of Islamic fundamentalism.

---

5   Khan, M., "Egypt's Lead in the Arab World," *The Globalist* (August 31, 2003).
6   Ibid.

However, to Islamists, there is no separation between church and state. As Mary Anne Weaver notes, "Islam is very different: it covers every aspect of life, politics and economics, religion and social issues, science and knowledge. Therefore, it is not possible to differentiate between religion and politics. In Islam, you cannot be a Muslim unless you know politics. We do not follow your axiom 'Leave what is for Caesar for Caesar and what is for God for God'."[7]

Radical Islamists are willing to use violence to establish an Islamic state in accordance with the Shariah (Islamic Law). Moderate Islamists desire to legally and peacefully establish a state based on a combination of man-made laws and the Shariah. However, the moderate Islamists are no less a threat in Egypt and elsewhere to Western interests because they wish to strengthen their state in Islamic, not Western terms.[8] The Muslim Brotherhood, the major moderate Islamic group in Egypt, clearly reflects this sentiment in its goals. Its members desire to create an Islamic order as determined by the supremacy in all questions of law, politics, and society. They reject what they consider to be corrupt Western ideologies and place an emphasis on a strong moral component, which stresses the needs of individuals at the expense of traditional commercial elites and foreign interests.[9]

For the very reason that Islamists make no distinction between religion and politics, the West would no longer be able to rely on Egyptian support and cooperation and would lose its major sphere of influence in the Middle East if Islamists took control of Egypt's government. The popularity of Islamic fundamentalism is rapidly growing in Egypt. Most Egyptians have turned to the moderate Islamic groups, although the radical groups do hold appeal for some. The enhanced influence of the Islamists is evident not only in the poorer classes, but also in the relatively small middle class. The very poor look to Islam as it gives their lives purpose and hope.[10]

Interestingly, Islamic fervor is also steadily expanding in the Egyptian student population. Although the government bans forming religious and political groups on university campuses such as al-Azhar, students are defiantly establishing underground Islamic organizations. The growing influence is also clearly evident in elementary schools and in high schools. Islamic rhetoric is increasingly dominating school curricula as many teachers are sympathetic to the Islamic cause. It is even common to see young school girls wearing the *hijab*, a veil covering a woman's hair. A class of religious scholars, the al-Azhar ulama, is challenging government policies; its members have established themselves as Egypt's political and moral caretakers.[11]

The rising popularity of Islam can be traced back to Gamal Abdul Nasser, the Egyptian President who disappointed middle class professionals who hoped to be the country's economic driving force during the 1960s. Nasser strove to educate the

7   Weaver, M.A. (1999), *A Portrait of Egypt: A Journey Through the World of Militant Islam*, New York: Farrar, Straus and Giroux, 117.

8   Abdo, G. (2000), *No God but God: Egypt and the Triumph of Islam*, New York: Oxford University Press, 2000.

9   Ibid.

10   Ibid., p. 96.

11   Ibid., p. 5.

masses and provide them with the same opportunities only the rich had previously enjoyed. Secondly, he followed political policies of pan-Arabism and anti-colonialism. Thirdly, Nasser created a socialist state. These policies failed and left the Arab world divided. Egypt's expanding weaknesses were obvious in battlefield losses to Israel in the Jewish state's war for independence in 1948 and in the June 1967 Six Day War. All of these factors caused Egyptians to look back to a time when Egypt dominated the Islamic world. This reasoning especially appealed to the middle class whose origins were somewhat humble, and rooted in Islam.[12]

The middle class professional groups began to establish syndicates, and their members freely elected Islamic leaders. These syndicates offered social assistance not only to their members, but to the general populace as well. For example, shortly after the 1992 earthquake the syndicates provided money, food, clothing, shelter, medicine, and structural advice for those in need more efficiently than did the government. As a result of their growing popularity and increasingly Islamic character, the Egyptian Government outlawed most of the syndicates. Nevertheless, the syndicates demonstrated to the Egyptian people that Islam and modernity could be compatible.[13]

Islamism is also growing in popularity with Egyptian women from all economic classes. An increasing number of women in Egypt are adopting the veil and embracing their roles as both mothers and wives, the perpetuators of Islamic culture. Some Egyptian women feel liberated by their veils, not oppressed by them. These "Islamic feminists" believe that Western ideologies have failed the Arab world and are turning to Islam for their identities. These women believe Islamic values promote respect and equality for women.[14]

The expanding Islamic tide in Egypt greatly affects the rest of the Greater Middle East and the West. As more and more Egyptians turn to Islam and away from the Egyptian Government that has dually failed and disappointed them, the more they turn away from the West generally and the United States specifically. The United States supports the Egyptian Government with massive annual aid programs. This American aid is designed to help Egypt bolster its military capabilities and combat the rising tide of Islamism, but is failing to do so. Instead, Islamist groups such as the Muslim Brotherhood are gaining in popularity as a result of the social services they provide to lower class Egyptians at the grass roots level.

The Foreign Policy of President Mubarak

Geopolitics have inevitably shaped Egypt's foreign policy. Egypt occupies a strategic position as a land bridge between two continents and a link between two principal waterways, the Mediterranean Sea and the Indian Ocean. It must therefore be strong enough to dominate its environment or risk becoming the victim of outside powers, such as Israel, Libya and the Sudan and powerful actors at the broader regional level,

---

12   Ibid., pp. 75–82.
13   Ibid., p. 105.
14   Roded, R. (ed.) (1999), *Women in Islam and the Middle East: A Reader*, London: I.B. Tauris & Co., 16–1.

including Iran, Saudi Arabia and Syria. Its security is also linked to control of the Nile, on whose waters its survival depends.[15]

Even with the rise of Islamic fundamentalism in Egypt, President Hosni Mubarak has enjoyed more than 25 years of popular support. Some of his tangible achievements include creating job opportunities through huge national projects, raising the standard of living, and improving sectors such as housing, water, electricity, communications, and roads. Focusing on domestic issues is a general feature of legislative and presidential campaigns worldwide. However, this does not indicate and sort of separation between Mubarak's foreign and domestic policies, which are closely related.[16]

Egypt's foreign policy, unlike its domestic policy, is not an area of much conflict between the government and the opposition. The main features of Mubarak's foreign policy are approved by the majority of Egypt's political parties regardless of their ideological and religious philosophies. The basic traits of Egypt's policies, applied for the past two and a half decades, are all but certain to remain intact. The main feature of the Mubarak regime's foreign policy is its strong link to national economic interests. Economists and businessmen now play a vital role of every Egyptian delegation that accompanies the president on his foreign visits. A most remarkable feature of Egypt's foreign policy since 1922 is that it has remained independent in the face of various superpowers and foreign alliance, particularly since the July 1952 national revolution.[17]

Since the 1990s, there have been drastic changes in the world order, with the end of the bipolar international system and the collapse of the Soviet Union and the communist bloc. These changes have affected the way Egyptians perceive and practice their foreign policy, although they have not influenced core values on which these policies are based. Egyptian diplomacy and foreign policy have continually aimed to consolidate Egypt's regional and international role. Egypt is one of the few countries whose foreign role surpasses its human and material potential. This factor can be attributed to Egypt's long history, its prime geographical position, and its mixing of eastern and Western cultures. On balance, Egypt has also succeeded in blending the traditional and the modern while eliminating hostility, fanaticism, and extremism and embracing tolerance and moderation.[18]

These characteristics come forward in some of the main aspects of Egypt's foreign policy. Foremost of these is Egypt's strong desire to consolidate the Arab–Israeli peace process. Mubarak assumed power in 1981, two years after the signing of the US-brokered Egyptian-Israeli peace treaty, and before full Israeli withdrawal from the Sinai Peninsula. Because of the treaty, there was considerable Arab hostility toward Egypt and a complete economic boycott of the country. Mubarak had to lead Egypt's diplomacy and foreign policy along two parallel tracks: complete respect of

---

15   *The Determinants of Foreign Policy*, available at http://reference.allrefer.com/country-guide-study/egypt/egypt 144.html.

16   Osama Al-Ghazali, H. (2004), "Egypt's Foreign Policy in Mubarak's Fourth Term," Historical Society of Jews from Egypt, August 16.

17   Al-Ghazali, 2.

18   Al-Ghazali, 4.

the peace treaty and commitment to completion of the peace process, while at the same time exerting relentless efforts to restore Egyptian-Arab relations.[19]

Mubarak's policies and leadership succeeded. In April 1982, the Sinai was restored to Egypt after a full Israeli withdrawal. Mubarak then began a combative legal battle over the possession of Taba, which it recovered in September 1987. Mubarak fully respected all of its commitments with Israel, leaving the process of normalization to develop according to the will of Egypt's people and civil institutions. Mubarak was also able to differentiate between Egypt's peaceful relations with Israel and its condemnation of the acts of violence and aggression that Lebanon and Palestine were subjected to during the 1980s. Therefore, he succeeded in restoring good relations with the Arab states and, in returning the Arab League to its Cairo headquarters, initiated a new era of Arab reconciliation.[20]

In August 1990, the Iraqi invasion of Kuwait wrecked all Arab hopes of unity and led to an unprecedented lack of Arab cohesion. Yet it also constituted a catalyst for more international efforts to resume the Arab–Israeli peace process, leading to the 1991 Madrid peace conference, which was sponsored by the United States on the heels of its successful leadership of the broad coalition of state that successfully expelled Iraq from Kuwait in the 1991 Persian Gulf War. Since then, Egypt has taken on the responsibility of sponsoring the peace process. Even after the 1993 Oslo agreement between Israel and the Palestine Liberation Organization (PLO), and the 1994 Jordanian-Israeli peace treaty, Egypt sustained its efforts despite then Israeli Prime Minister Binyamin Netanyahu's negative policies on all tracks of the peace process.

The secondary aim of Egypt's foreign policy is to maintain good relations with the United States, based on the principle of equality rather then dependence, and without conceding the independence of Egypt's decision making. This sort of relationship seems logical between a Middle Eastern regional power and a superpower at the top of the world order. This relationship is affirmed by the coordination between both countries over vital regional issues. During Mubarak's presidency, there have been many differences of opinion between Egypt and the United States, on issues such as nuclear armament in the Middle East and around the world, the details of the peace process with Israel, and Egypt's policy toward Libya, Iraq, and Sudan. Nevertheless, these disagreements help highlight the independence of Egyptian foreign policy.[21] Most recently, the independence was evident in Cairo's lack of support for the US-led Second Iraq War in the spring of 2003 and the nation/state-building process America has attempted in Iraq in the time since then.

The third important dimension of Egypt's foreign policy is its stance against terrorism and the violence and its call for peace. This can be seen in two of Mubarak's initiatives: his bid to rid the Middle East of nuclear weapons; and his call for coordinated efforts to confront international terrorism. Although the latter initiative was well received in the United States and around the world, the special relationship binding Washington and Tel Aviv placed many reservations and obstacles on the

---

19   Ibid.
20   Al-Ghazali, 5.
21   Ibid.

road to regional nuclear disarmament. Mubarak saw this policy as a double standard which encouraged violence and increased feelings of oppression in the Developing World. Egypt's foreign policy under Mubarak has definitely expanded in the Middle East and elsewhere and is likely to expand even more.[22]

Egypt's foreign policy at the outset of the 1950s, under Nasser's leadership, focused mainly on Arab, African, and Islamic matters. However, in the 1980s and 1990s, Egypt began to focus on new areas, including Asia and the Mediterranean. The interest in Asia came as a response to the significant developments there, specifically the increasing role of China in international politics and the emerging economic impact of Japan and India. The interest in the Mediterranean region was a response to the perceived future challenges to regional Middle Eastern cooperation. In a world of ever-increasing economic groupings, it is considered inevitable that there will be an agreement between the countries north and south of the Mediterranean.[23]

The Human Rights Record of the Mubarak Regime

Egypt has shown little improvement in the area of human rights under President Mubarak. In 2004, the Egyptian Government set up a National Council for Human Rights and appointed several respected independent activists to its board, but serious issues like routine torture of persons in detention and suppression of non-violent political dissent remain unaddressed. Women and girls face systematic discrimination under personal status and other laws, and violence directed at women and girls frequently goes unpunished.[24]

One of the tools used by Mubarak to violate human rights is the tradition of "emergency rule." The rule allows arbitrary arrest and indefinite detention without trial, and creates an atmosphere of impunity in which torture and ill-treatment flourish. In February 2003, the government extended 22 years of continuous emergency rule for another three years. Mubarak's government has used the rule to criminalize political dissent at will, and will defer civilian defendants to military courts or to state security courts in which trials do not meet international standards of fairness.[25]

In 2004, it was estimated that 15,000 persons are being detained without charge, many for prolonged periods of time. Also, in 2004, the Human Rights Association released a list of 75 attorneys who have been held without charge or trial, some for as long as 16 years.[26] More broadly, in its most recent annual report on the issue, which was released in March 2006, the US Department of State noted that, in 2005, the Mubarak "government's respect for human rights remained poor, and serious abuses continued in many areas." Most significantly, according to the report, those abuses included limitations on the right of citizens to change their government; existence of the state of emergency, which has been in place almost continuously since 1967;

---

22   Ibid.
23   Ibid.
24   *Human Rights Watch: Egypt*, January 13, 2005.
25   Ibid.
26   Ibid.

torture and abuse of prisoners and detainees, including the deaths in custody; poor conditions in prisons and detention centers; impunity; arbitrary, sometimes mass, arrest and detention, including prolonged pretrial detention; executive influence on the judiciary; denial of fair public trial and lack of due process; the holding of political prisoners; restrictions on civil liberties, including freedoms of speech, press, assembly, and association; some restrictions on freedom of religion; and corruption and lack of governmental transparency.[27]

Security forces and police routinely torture and mistreat detainees, particularly during interrogations. Torture in the past was used primarily against political dissidents, especially Islamists, but in recent years it has become rampant in ordinary police stations as well. Torture and ill-treatment are known or suspected to be the cause of at least 17 deaths in detention in 2002 and 2003, and many more in 2004. Ironically, Ministry of the Interior officials confirmed that there had not been a single criminal investigation of SSI officials for torture or ill-treatment in the past 18 years.[28]

In 2002, Egypt instituted a new law governing associations, Law 84. This law severely compromises the right to freedom of association, giving the government unwarranted control over the governance and operations of non-governmental organizations (NGOs). The law provides for criminal penalties for unauthorized activities, such as, engaging in political or union activities reserved for political parties and authorized syndicates.[29] Mubarak's government also maintains strict control over political associations. The official Political Parties Affairs Committee, comprised almost entirely of government officials and traditionally headed by the chairman of the ruling National Democratic Party, routinely rejects applications to form new political parties, based on broadly worded criteria such as whether the party's program "constitutes an addiction to public life." On October 27, 2004, the committee, for only the third time since 1977, approved a new party, al-Ghad.[30]

Egypt, the Middle East and Oil

World oil production and reserves have witnessed a steady increase in recent years while consumption and prices have fluctuated up and down. The Arab region produces approximately one-third of the world's oil and includes about two-thirds of its reserves. Egypt, the first Middle Eastern state where petroleum was discovered, continues to be a significant producer of that resource.[31] Oil is one of the most important factors driving the Egyptian economy as well as its foreign policy. Egypt produced an average of about 700,000 barrels/day of crude oil in 2005, down

---

27   *Country Report on Human Rights Practices,'* (Egypt: US Department of State), March 2006, available at http://www.state.gov/g/drl/rls/hrrpt/2005/61687.htm.

28   *Human Rights Watch: Egypt.*

29   Ibid.

30   Ibid.

31   "The Egyptian Petroleum Industry", *American Chamber of Commerce* in Egypt (June 06, 2005).

sharply from its peak of 922,000 barrels/day in 1996.[32] In addition to its role as an oil exporter, Egypt has strategic importance because of its operation of the Suez Canal and Suez-Mediterranean Pipeline, two routes for export of Persian Gulf oil.[33]

Oil prices fell sharply after the terrorist attacks of September 11, 2001, but rebounded in early 2002 and 2003. Between 2004 and 2006, prices increased sharply in the face of limited OPEC spare production capacity and rapid world oil demand growth. Egypt's economy was hurt following the terrorist attacks on the United States because of the lowered oil prices. Since then, Egypt's economy has grown slowly. Cairo's earnings from oil revenues have declined by over 50 percent from 1996 to 2006. For 2005 and 2006, Egypt's real GDP growth increased by 5 percent and is expected to continue in 2007. Besides oil imports, the other major source of income in Egypt is so-called "remittances" from Egyptian workers in the oil-rich Persian Gulf states. Increased oil prices tend to help remittances.[34]

Although the income from oil has dwindled in recent years, it still is the most important industry in Egypt and the Middle East, and Egypt is instrumental in the Middle Easters oil policies because of its leadership role in the region's affairs, as well as its control of the Suez Canal and corresponding pipelines. Egypt's Oil Minister, Sameh Fahmy, aptly summarized this relationship: "Oil is the backbone of economic and social growth in Egypt and the Middle East."[35]

Egypt and the Global War on Terrorism

The most striking effect in the battle against Muslim extremists was the September 11 2001, attack on the United States. Mubarak, who has first-hand experience having fought Islamic terrorism at home through much of the 1990s, strongly condemned the attacks. He has generally supported the US-led GWOT, including the prosecution of Operation Enduring Freedom in the fall of 2001 in Afghanistan. However, he did not support the US-led Second Iraq War. The lead hijacker in the 9/11 attacks, Muhammed Atta, was Egyptian. Osama bin Laden's al-Qaeda terrorist network grew in part out of Egyptian extremist groups, and many of its leaders are Egyptians, including his second-in-command, Ayman al-Zawahiri.[36]

As it is for much of the Middle Eastern world, the Egyptian public is hostile to the US policy on terrorism. However, because of its alliance with Mubarak, the United States considers Egypt a bulwark of stability and an important voice of moderation in the Middle East. There is friction in American-Egyptian relations. The United States has often criticized Egypt's human rights record, and has recently linked future American aid to an improvement in human rights. The United States is also

---

32   "Egypt," *CIA World Factbook.*

33   Energy Information Agency, Official Energy Statistics from the United States Government, Egypt, available at www.eia.doe.gov/emeu/cabs/egypt.html.

34   "Egypt," *CIA World Factbook.*

35   Fahmy, S., "Egypt's Oil and Gas Products," *Egypt's Economics* (December 28, 2004).

36   "Terrorism: Questions and Answers," *Council on Foreign Relations* (May 2005).

concerned over anti-American and anti-Israeli pieces that are commonly published in Egypt's government-controlled press.[37]

As a leader of the Middle Eastern world, excluding Israel, Egypt is the second largest recipient (after Israel) of US aid. Egypt gets $1.3 billion annually in military aid and about $600 million per year in economic assistance, which amounts to about 10 percent of the total US foreign aid budget of approximately $14 billion. Even with the assistance from the United States, Egypt's economy remains weak, with population growth far exceeding economic input.[38]

US officials are pleased with Egypt's cooperation in the war on terrorism, however limited, because it sets a good example for the rest of the Middle East. Mubarak has also stepped up arrests and prosecutions of Islamist militants. However, while Egypt supported the US-led war in Afghanistan, it did not join the effort, nor did it support the US-led Second Iraq War. Egypt's two largest Islamic terrorist groups are Jamatt al-Islamiyya and Egyptian Islamic Jihad, both of which have ties to al-Qaeda. These two groups draw lower- and middle-class followers from the country's south and from Cairo's slums. Leaders from both groups fought alongside the Afghan *mujahedeen* against the Soviet occupation of Afghanistan in the 1980s. Most Egyptians have expressed revulsion for the groups' terrorist attacks, which have decimated one of Egypt's most important sources of income, its tourism industry. Both of these Islamic terrorist groups desperately want to overthrow Mubarak, which they see as corrupt and repressive, and replace his government with an Islamist state.[39]

Much of the Middle Eastern feelings against the West come from bitter memories of imperialism. Most Arabs are very concerned about the spread of Western culture, which they view as a type on imperialism. These anti-imperialist feelings affect the foreign policies of the Middle Eastern states in two distinct ways. Initially, relations between Arab and Western states are undermined by mistrust. Secondly, anti-imperialistic policies often put Middle Eastern state in opposition to Western ones.[40]

Arab regional organizations, such as the Organization of the Islamic Conference and the Arab League, actively strive to promote regional cooperation and struggle against heavy Western influence. As Egypt is a member of both organizations and was a British colony from 1882 to 1952, its foreign policy reflects Egypt's desire for a united Arab front that follows a distinctly Arab, not Western, ideology. Also, the Egyptian Government often turns a blind eye to some Islamist activities in order to gain legitimacy and approval from the populace and other Arab states.[41]

The Organization of the Islamic Conference (OIC) is an important Islamic organization that affects Egypt and the Middle East. The OIC has 56 members,

---

37   Ibid.

38   *US Foreign Assistance Reference Guide*, (US Agency for International Development) (January 2005), available at http://pdf.usaid.gov/pdf_docs/PNADC240.pdf.

39   "Jamaat al-Islamiyya, Egyptian Islamic Jihad," *Council on Foreign Relations* (May 2005).

40   Islam, S. (2004), "Far from Making the World a Safer Place," *Yale Global* (April 16).

41   Ibid.

including all members of the Arab League, and is headquartered in Jeddah, Saudi Arabia. Its purpose is to coordinate the member states' foreign policy on Islamic issues in order to keep Arab interests safe and secure. This organization pressures Egypt to resist Western influence and to shape its foreign policy so that it reflects shared Islamic principles.[42]

Two points from the OIC's Charter particularly demonstrate how Egypt is torn between the influence of Western and Arab/Islamic organizations. The OIC calls on its members to support the Palestinians against the Israelis. Egypt defends the rights of the Palestinians, but it has been at peace with Israel since 1978. In this respect, Egypt's foreign policy is torn between promoting Western/Israeli and Arab/Islamic interests and provides a compromise reflecting both sets of interests. The second point attempts to end all forms of colonialism. Egypt is sensitive towards an encroaching Western culture, but it is also heavily reliant on Western aid. Egypt is therefore pressured to find a balance between promoting *Western/Israeli and Arab/Islamic* interests.[43]

The purpose of Arab League is to provide consensus on the major issues that face its 21 members, which includes the "state of Palestine" as of 1989. The main idea is that if all the member states can coordinate their foreign policies, the Arab League will act as a United Arab Front that would presumably be strong enough to counter Western influence.[44] The emphasis that the Arab League puts on creating a united Arab Front serves as evidence of its desire to become a strong international force that is representative of Arab interests. Currently, the Arab League, headquartered in Cairo, strongly influences Egypt to remain in solidarity with its Arab neighbors. Again, Egypt is very closely tied to the West both economically and politically and cannot commit itself entirely to a united Arab Front when it conflicts with Western interests. Therefore, Egypt's foreign policy must balance between Western influences and the influences of the Arab League.[45]

When Egypt signed the Camp David Accord with Israel, the Arab League revoked Egypt's membership and moved its headquarters out of Cairo. Egypt was only allowed back into the Arab League in 1989 after Mubarak worked very hard to win back the League members' confidence. Today, Egypt continues to formulate its foreign policy under this tension. The Arab League clearly pressures Egyptian foreign policy-makers to support it in condemning Israel. However, since 1989 Egypt has had to balance its relationship with Israel between making it too confrontational and too friendly to appease both the Arab League and the United States.[46]

---

42   *The Permanent Delegation of the Organization of the Islamic Conference*, available at http://www.oic-un.org/about/over.htm.

43   Ibid.

44   *League of Arab. States*, European Institute for Research on Mediterranean and Euro-Arab Cooperation, available at http://www.medea.be/en/index101.htm.

45   Ibid.

46   "Arab League Calls on Arab States to Sever Relations with Israel According to Summit Resolutions," *ArabicNews.com*, October 26, 2000, available at http://www.arabicnews.com/ansub/Daily/Day/001026/2000/02606.htm.

Conclusions

Egypt's foreign policy operates along a non-aligned level. Factors such as population size, historical events, military strength, diplomatic expertise, and a strategic geographical position give Egypt extensive political influence in the Middle East. Cairo has found itself at the crossroads of Arab commerce and culture for hundreds of years, and its intellectual and Islamic institutions are at the center of the region's social and cultural development.[47]

The Arab League's headquarters is in Cairo, and the Secretary General of the League is traditionally an Egyptian. Former Egyptian Foreign Minister Amr Moussa is the present Secretary-General of the Arab league. Egyptian Deputy Prime Minister Boutros Boutros-Ghali served as Secretary-General of the United Nations from 1991 to 1996.[48]

Egypt is a key partner in the search for peace in the Middle East and resolution of the Israeli-Palestinian conflict. Then Egyptian President Anwar Sadat's ground-breaking trip to Israel in 1977, the 1978 Camp David Accords, and the 1979 Egypt-Israel Peace Treaty represented a fundamental shift in the politics of the region, from a strategy of confrontation to one of peace. Egypt was subsequently ostracized by other Arab states and ejected from the Arab League from 1979 to 1989. As Cairo played an important role in the negotiations leading to the Madrid Peace Conference in 1991 under US and Russian sponsorship, it brought together all parties in the region to discuss Middle East peace.[49] This support has continued to the present, with Mubarak often intervening personally to promote peace negotiations.[50]

Egypt is often described as a country on the brink of an Islamic revolution. Even if this is not entirely accurate, it reveals the growing popularity of Islam in Egypt. American foreign policy-makers do not fully understand the nature or appeal of Islamic fundamentalism and American aid is not effectively countering the rising tide of Islamism. It may be quite possible that American foreign policy-makers may be too confident that Egypt is a reliable ally to the West. Clearly, Egypt is influenced by Islamic elements and is continually compromising American interests and desires in order to appeal to the Islamic aspirations of both Egypt and the Middle East. Since the Egyptian Government under Mubarak controls American aid, much of the aid has not reached many Egyptians. This factor only makes the appeal of the Islamists continually stronger.

---

47   "Egypt," *CIA World Factbook*.
48   Ibid.
49   Ibid.
50   Ibid. In 1996, Mubarak hosted the Sharm El-Sheikh "Summit of the Peacemakers" attended by then American President William J. Clinton and other world leaders. In 2000, he hosted two summits at Sharm El-Sheikh and one at Taba in an effort to resume the Camp David negotiations suspended in July of 2000. In June 2003, Mubarak welcomed President George W. Bush for another summit on the Middle East peace process. Another summit was convened in Sharm El-Sheikh in early 2005, which was attended by Egypt, Israel, the Palestinian Authority, and Jordan. The Egyptian Chief of Intelligence, General Omar Suleiman, has played a substantial role in negotiations between the Israeli and Palestinian sides and is highly respected on both sides.

The Islamist revolution which is occurring from the bottom up will likely continue to gain more strength in the coming years. Since the American Government does not totally understand even the basic nature and appeal of Islamic fundamentalism, US policies, which are based on secular Western assumptions, will not effectively counter it. Egypt will therefore remain an unreliable ally in the region, with American interests being jeopardized.

As a rule of thumb, Egypt is approached as a barometer in the Middle East region and often used to sound out reactions and proposed policies. If Cairo is on board with a coalition to drive Iraqi troops out of Kuwait, other Middle East Arabs will be there too. If Egypt refuses to join a military coalition to strike against the Taliban in Afghanistan, it is unlikely that any Arab country would send troops there. As a central power in the Middle East, Egypt serves as a political umbrella for Arabs and Muslims.[51]

Ultimately, the success or failure of American-led efforts to promote liberal democratic reform in the Greater Middle East will depend not only on the extent of progress (or lack thereof) in Afghanistan and Iraq, but also on relations between the United States and its allies in the region, most of which do not have governmental systems in place that allow full freedom of expression for their citizens. Egypt is perhaps the most significant of such states given the generally cooperative relationship it has had with the United States since Mubarak first came into office a quarter century ago. While Mubarak's decision to allow opposition candidates to contest him in the 2005 national elections—which he won overwhelmingly nonetheless—represented a step forward in terms of political freedom, it was a marginal one at best. For America's vision of a more democratic Egypt and broader Greater Middle East, it must continue to strike a balance between maintenance of its alliance with Cairo, while applying steady but subtle pressure on Mubarak and his advisers to allow more room for the citizens they to express themselves more freely. Given the limited progress on that front to date, any such reforms will necessarily remain a long term objective, one that must be pursued consistently by American Presidents to come.

---

51   Khalil, N., "Steering a Steady Course," *Al-Ahram Weekly,* October 17, 2001.

Chapter 11

Iran and the Middle East: The Pursuit of Security and Legitimacy in the American Age

Vaughn P. Shannon

Introduction

For much of 2006, Iran commanded the attention of US, European, and regional pundits and politicians. Despite the raging civil chaos in Iraq three years after the US-led ousting of Saddam Hussein, Iran seemed to figure more prominently in the world spotlight for its perceived nuclear ambitions and support for Middle East groups Hezbollah and Hamas. In 2002, the Bush Administration had demarcated the nexus of "terror" and WMD as the number one threat to a post-9/11 America, and placed Iran with Iraq and North Korea on an "axis of evil" confronting the world.[1] The 2005 election of controversial Iranian President Mahmoud Ahmadinejad, the 2006 rise of Hamas to power in the Palestinian legislature, the Hezbollah kidnappings of Israeli soldiers that sparked a brief war the same summer, and the IAEA's finding that Iran was in violation of its NPT obligations, created new salience on the issue of Iran's role in the Middle East.

Indeed, Iran's regional position has ironically improved under the Bush administration's tenure and war on terror, however unintended. The US elimination of the regimes of the Taliban and Saddam Hussein left Iran in a position of regional prominence and security, with the potential to assert unprecedented influence in a Shi'a dominated post-Saddam Iraqi Government. A new confidence appeared in Iranian diplomacy and the brash assertion of the right to enrich uranium even in the face of IAEA, UN, and bilateral pressure to the contrary. Yet despite the new opportunities afforded Iran by the elimination of its neighboring rivals, Iran also faces a US-dominated region, with American forces occupying those neighboring states, while continuing to assert the right to preemption and regime change. While Iraq's capabilities have been reduced, a nuclear Israel remains as a regional player for influence both directly and as a perceived extension of US influence.

The crux of the debate, as is often the case in international relations, is about motives more than power. What drives Iran's behavior? Do they want nuclear weapons and, if so, for what purpose? Are they driven by fear or ambition? Do

---

1   *2002 State of the Union Address*, available at http://www.whitehouse.gov/news/releases/2002/01/20020129-11.html.

they mean to export revolution, destroy Israel and take over the Middle East? Or do they seek mere security in a US-dominant region in which the lone superpower fosters anti-Iranian opposition and regime change? Or is all politics local, with Iran's actions aimed at shoring up domestic legitimacy? The answers to these questions are key to understanding how the world responds to Iran.

This chapter seeks to situate this debate and provide some clarity in the most difficult of questions about Iran's foreign policy and motivation. Iran is a divided society whose regime faces twin challenges of internal legitimacy and external pressure from the US. Moderates and hardliners have pulled and hauled the Iranian ship of state on different tacks in the areas of security, economy, and ideas. Hardliners have generally kept the upper hand in steering this ship, but under constraints of regional and US threats and an increasingly reform-minded domestic population disenchanted by the promise of its revolution. Iran's policy has thus reflected the attempt to navigate these twin pressures, asserting its potential externally, while attempting to deflect the energy of domestic criticism away from Tehran toward Tel Aviv and Washington, DC. In its own form of face nationalism, Iran's dangerous game of scapegoating and brash independence may invite unwanted US, Israeli, regional or global reprisals. Thus, while Iran may not be on the path of genuine aggression and expansionism, its motives of domestic and regional legitimacy-building in the face of American regional hegemony may unwittingly bring its own demise.

This chapter proceeds with a general overview of the modern Islamic Republic of Iran and the factors influencing its policies, distinguishing issues of religion, economics, geopolitics and domestic legitimacy. Focusing on the last of these influences, the essay then describes and analyzes Iranian foreign policy trends, with particular focus on its nuclear program, terrorism, and its position on the question of Israel. The chapter then assesses the repercussions of the Iranian position vis-à-vis US and the region.

The general thesis, that in its search for security and legitimacy Iran's bark is worse than its bite, flies in the face of much pop media analysis in American circles, which tends to portray as foregone fact that Iran is pursuing nuclear weapons and takes at face value translations of Iranian claims to seek to wipe "the Zionist entity" off the map. Iran's face politics, coupled with the seeming belief in Tehran that the US will not attack while mired in Iraq, is a dangerous combination in the enduring tendency in international relations to underestimate the effects of one's actions on the perceptions and insecurities of one's rivals. By the time this volume is in print, there may very well have been a strike on Iranian nuclear facilities, or even war, led by anxious Israeli and American leaders reading the worst-case scenario into Iranian actions and intentions. As happened with Iraq's Saddam Hussein, a misperception of US intent to act is a disaster for the lesser power, even if it also spells further trouble for a stretched-thin superpower. Whether such an unnecessary clash of mutual harm can be averted depends on the understanding of both sides, to which this chapter hopes to contribute.

Iran in Regional and Global Context

Iran's relationship within the region designated as "Middle East" has long been complex. As a Shi'a country amid a Sunni region and a Persian country amid an Arab region, Iran has stood apart in its identity, interests and role in the politics of the area. Iran's relationship with the Arab world before the revolution was, in the words of historian George Lenczowski, "altogether correct and friendly but not devoid of moments of tension and suspicion."[2] But it has been the Iranian revolution, which ushered in an Islamic Republic of Iran seeking to "export revolution," that has raised regional and global concerns about the Persian state.

Iran is seen in contrast to Western views of competitive electoral democracy and human rights. This is not to say that democracy is foreign or nonexistent in Iran or to Iranians. The majlis and president are popularly elected, though candidates are vetted through a screening process. As for human rights, Zachary Karabell notes that "Iran does not possess a strong domestic legacy of human rights".[3] This goes for the era of the Islamic Republic, as well as the Pahlavi regimes that preceded it. Iran's approach to human rights has been characterized as nationalist, stressing Islamic rights in the face of perceived international—and especially US—attempts to impose outside norms that threaten the status quo erected by the Islamic revolution.

Iran also swims against the global tide regarding a two-state solution for the Israel-Palestine issue, part of a shrinking camp of rejectionists once popular in the Middle East. Iranian support for groups such as Hezbollah and Hamas, which are hostile to Israel and designated terrorist organizations by the US State Department, creates an awkward dynamic in the region sympathetic to the Palestinian cause but increasingly under the pressure of a post-9/11 US war on terror. To the extent that Iran engages in a nuclear energy program and is suspected of seeking nuclear weapons, regional and global concerns over Iran will continue. Before turning to Iran's behavior in detail, let us consider the different factors that shape our understanding of those policies.

Factors Influencing Iranian Foreign Policy

This section assesses the relative influences of geopolitics, economics, religion, and domestic politics on Iranian foreign policy.

Geopolitics and Security

The geopolitical calculus is certainly another factor driving Iranian behavior. Until the Iraq War of 2003, the Persian Gulf area had been a bipolar balance of power between Iraq and Iran. The two countries were comparable on several dimensions

---

2   Lenczowski, G. (1980), *The Middle East in World Affairs*, Ithaca: Cornell University Press, 219.

3   Karabell, Z. (2000), "Iran and Human Rights," in David Forsythe (ed.), *Human Rights and Comparative Foreign Policy*, Tokyo: UN University Press, 209.

and at the same time both far exceeded all other regional players.[4] This regional competition preceded, but was exemplified by, the Iran–Iraq War, in which an anxious Iraq supported by the Arab Gulf states warred with the newly revolutionary Iran.[5] The global stakes in this balance of power were clear in the number of states backing one or both sides, including the United States. Iraq's invasion of Kuwait ended Western and Soviet sponsorship of the Baghdad regime, as Saddam appeared more threatening and destabilizing to the regional balance of power than earlier presumed. The defeat and subsequent containment of Iraq in the Gulf War degraded Baghdad's capabilities and, coupled with the end of the Cold War, permitted the US to fill the security vacuum as Gulf protector against Iraqi or Iranian designs. The US policy of "dual containment" projected US power into the region to deter regional threats directly through a series of bases, sanctions and, in the case of Iraq, no-fly zones.[6]

With Iraq out of the strategic equation, the new Middle East can be seen as a balance of power between Iran and Israel, with weaker Arab and Gulf states sandwiched in between. Table 11.1 shows the various dimensions of the military balance, in which Iran has more troops but Israel more tanks and aircraft. Of course, two vital components of the military balance are unreported here:

Table 11.1   The Iran-Israel Military Balance, 2004[7]

Country	Regular Troops	Reserve Troops	Total	Tanks	Aircraft*
Israel	186,500	445,000	631,500	3,930	798
Iran	518,000	350,000	868,000	~1,700	335

Israel's nuclear weapons and alliance with the global superpower, the United States. Israel's policy of "nuclear opacity" notwithstanding, it has been known for some time that the tiny country has possessed nuclear weapons capability since the

---

4   This is an overall assessment based on armed forces personnel, armor, artillery and helicopters. There are more dimensions than are shown here, and in a few categories Saudi Arabia and UAE compete. For a full array, see the "Middle East Military Balance," Jaffee Center for Strategic Studies, available at http://www.tau.ac.il/jcss/balance/gulfCharts.html.

5   See Karsh, E. (1987), "Military Power and Foreign Policy Goals: The Iran–Iraq War Revisited," *International Affairs*, 64/2, 83–95.

6   Herrmann, R.K. and Ayers, R.W. (1997), "The New Geo-Politics of the Gulf: Forces for Change and Stability," in Gary Sick and Lawrence Potter (eds), *The Persian Gulf at the Millennium*, Basingstoke: Macmillan; Pollack, K. (2004), *The Persian Puzzle*, New York: Random House, 259–65.

7   Feldman, S. and Shapir, Y. (eds) (2004), *The Middle East Military Balance*, Cambridge: MIT Press; Cordesman, A. (2003), "Syrian Military Forces and Capabilities," Center for Strategic and International Studies, April 15, available at http://www.jewishvirtuallibrary.org/jsource/Threats_to_Israel/milbal.html.

late 1960s, with estimates ranging from 100 to as many as 400 warheads.[8] Iran's threat environment, then, includes a nuclear adversary backed by the world's pre-eminent military power whose military forces occupy the countries book-ending the Persian state. Under dual containment, Iran also had to contend with an America whose forces were now stationed in proximity to the Islamic Republic.

But such conditions of threat and opportunity could logically lead to different policy prescriptions, of bandwagoning with the US or balancing it. Systemic security dynamics constrain but are ultimately indeterminate of Iranian behavior and choices. Particularly since there has been evidence of accommodation and mischief since the 1990s, as recounted above, a fuller explanation of Iran's behavior must be found. It is in Iran's domestic politics that the incongruous and mixed signals of Iranian foreign policy in the security realm achieve more focus.

Economics

A second approach to Iran's behavior is economic. Iran is a substantial economic regional actor. In 2004, Iran's proven crude oil reserves amounted to 132,460 (mb), the second largest reserves in OPEC and the world behind Saudi Arabia.[9] While oil is key to Iran's economic health, Walid Khadduri notes that "oil alone cannot help" Middle East states carry out "sustained and balanced development" without diversification and reform.[10] Iran has the makings of a more diversified economy that has yet to reach its potential. Unlike Kuwait and other Gulf states dependent on oil for generating revenue and development funds, Iran's economy retained some diversity, cultivated by policies of import substitution industrialization.[11]

Iran's post-revolution economy stumbled under the converging pressures of population swelling, stagnating output and falling oil prices in the 1980s, leaving 1992 per capita income at about 38 percent of the level of 1979.[12] Combined with the bloody stalemate of war with Iraq, the Khomeini revolution had lost its initial sheen of popular enthusiasm. As Jahangir Amuzegar notes, "the revolutionary fervor has been replaced by concern over inflation, unemployment, pollution, traffic congestion and daily discomfort."[13]

Iran thus began an era of pragmatism and reform to adapt to its internal and external complications, although such reforms have been inconsistent and met with resistance in Iranian society. A resurgence in oil prices bolstered Iran with upwards of $40 billion in foreign exchange reserves, but problems of unemployment and

---

8   Broder, J. (2001), "Israel's Nuclear Blind Spot," *The Washington Post National Weekly Edition*, March 19–25, 22.

9   *OPEC Annual Statistical Bulletin, 17*, available at http://www.opec.org/library/Annual%20Statistical%20Bulletin/interactive/2004/FileZ/Main-Dateien/ASB.pdf.

10   Khadduri, W. (1996), "Oil and Politics in the Middle East," *Security Dialogue* 27/2, 155–66.

11   Richards, A. and Waterbury, J. (1996), *A Political Economy of the Middle East*, Boulder: Westview Press, 23–7.

12   Ibid., p. 241.

13   Amuzegar, J. (1995), "Islamic Fundamentalism in Action: The Case of Iran," *Middle East Policy* 4/1–2, 28.

stagnation persist.[14] As for Iran's claim to be developing civilian nuclear energy, many Western critics dismiss the need for such a source given Iran's wealth of petroleum reserves. Nonetheless, the economic case for nuclear energy has some merit. According to one analysis, "substituting Iran's domestic oil demand partly with nuclear power" creates "a win-win situation" of cheaper nuclear energy and increases in oil exports.[15]

One reason for continued Iranian economic woes beyond state inefficiencies is the sanctions levied by the US since the days of the revolution, and strengthened in the 1996 Iran-Libya Sanctions Act. Iran's plan to open its own oil exchange—the Iranian Oil Bourse (IOB)—may make Iran a dominant center of the Middle East's oil trade, which some say will trade for oil in euros, circumventing US sanctions and potentially causing a drop in value for the American currency.[16] In this way, domestic economic forces and broader geopolitics may both be served by the same policy. But the sways between engaging the West and taking independent stands on issues like nuclear energy, point to a crucial need to understand the conflicting decision imperatives coming out of Tehran. Sometimes simultaneously, there are pushes in both directions and this reflects the divided nature of the regime and its country.

Religion

Arguments of a religious influence on foreign policy have simplistic and nuanced variants. The simplistic view of a clash of civilizations offered by Samuel Huntington posits a transnational Islam pitched against "The West" and its ascribed values of secularism, liberty and democracy.[17] Some argue that Islamic Sharia is opposed to the norms of democracy, religious tolerance, political pluralism and numerous components of the Universal Declaration of Human Rights; others suggest Islam is a heterogeneous theological tapestry aimed at ordering a moral society, with facets compatible with modernity and democracy.[18]

Before the revolution, Islam and Iranian nationalism have had what Barry Rubin describes as a "complex relationship" from the pre-Islamic Zoroastrianism, through the Abbasid caliphs, to the Safavid dynasty that introduced an "Iranian interpretation of Islam in the tradition of its Shi'a branch."[19] Religion affects Iran's foreign policy as Iran affects religion in the region. The Iranian revolution is widely viewed as the impetus to the modern resurgence of political Islam. Toppling a Western-supported

---

14   *CIA Worldfactbook*, available at https://www.cia.gov/cia/publications/factbook/geos/ir.html#Econ.

15   Straka, T. (2005), "Killing the dollar in Iran," *Asia Times*, August 26, available at http://www.atimes.com/atimes/Global_Economy/GH26Dj01.html.

16   Boghrati, N. (2006), "Iran's Oil Bourse: A Threat to the US Economy," Worldpress. org, (April 11), available at http://www.worldpress.org/Mideast/2314.cfm.

17   Huntington, S. (1996), *The Clash of Civilizations and the Remaking of World Order*, New York: Simon and Schuster.

18   Amuzegar, 22–23.

19   Rubin, B. (1980), *Paved with Good Intentions: The American Experience and Iran*, New York: Penguin Books, 5; see also Mortimer, E. (1982), *Faith and Power: The Politics of Islam*, New York: Vintage, chapter 9.

regime emboldened the Muslim world of the potential and pride of Islam as a political force.[20] Iran is seen as the head of a movement to remake regional, if not world, order under a fundamentalist vision of Islam. This spread is perceived through direct influence in Shi'a Iraq and through proxies Hezbollah and Hamas.

Although religion matters to Iranian leaders and policy-makers, however, some decry the tendency to "overstate the influence of Islamic ideology" in Iranian foreign policy, noting the "dynamic context and multiple influences" on decision-making.[21] Some suggest that especially after Khomeini's death and the withering nature of the war with Iraq, Iran became a "status-quo power" and gave up ambitious, zealous designs. The invocation of Islamism has been inconsistent in the face of "the realities of international politics," and Iran's Islamist identity co-exists with a more nationalist and anti-Western facets.[22] It also co-exists with a prominent pro-Western pragmatist segment of Iranian society, creating a rift in the legitimacy of the state that must be handled delicately by the governing elites. As with economics and security, then, domestic politics is an important piece of the puzzle of Iranian identity and policy.

Domestic Politics and Legitimacy in Post-Revolutionary Iran

Post-revolutionary Iran possesses what Mohsen Milani calls "limited popular sovereignty" and "primitive pluralism," borne out of the revolution's populist and Islamist themes.[23] Attempting to give voice to those oppressed under the Shah, but within an Islamist framework, Iran has direct elections for its parliament (Majlis) and President within the confines of candidates vetted by the Council of Guardians. The Islamic nature of the state was codified in its Constitution, passed by referendum in 1979, but the plebiscite was boycotted by nationalists, liberals and leftists opposed to both the Shah and the emerging Islamist state.[24] With the degree of freedoms constrained under a regime in which laws, candidates and liberties can be controlled by unelected clerics, the legitimacy of the Iranian regime remains questionable for at least some of the population.

A more sophisticated argument for the role of religion in Iranian foreign policy recognizes that the regime's legitimacy stems substantially from the ideals and promise of the revolution. Legitimacy, or the relationship between ruler and ruled in which the latter accept the rightness of the former's authority and power to govern, has long been in short supply in the Middle East.[25] On the legitimacy criteria of

---

20   Mortimer, 296–297; Palmer, M. and Palmer, P. (2004), *At the Heart of Terror: Islam, Jihadists and America's War on Terrorism*, Lanham: Rowman and Littlefield Publishers, 91–2.

21   Maloney, S. (2002), "Identity and Change in Iran's Foreign Policy," in Shibley Telhami and Michael Barnett (eds), *Identity and Foreign Policy in the Middle East*, Ithaca: Cornell University Press, 115.

22   Ibid., pp. 109–112.

23   Milani, M. (1997), "Political Participation in Revolutionary Iran," in John Esposito, ed., *Political Islam: Revolution, Radicalism, or Reform?* Boulder: Lynne Rienner, 78-88.

24   Ibid., p. 82.

25   See Hudson (1977), *Arab Politics: The Search for Legitimacy*, New Haven: Yale University Press, 1977, 1–2; Rachel Bronson (1996), "Cycles of Conflict in the Middle East

identity, authority and equality, the Shah failed on the latter two dimensions at least. As Bronson suggests, in the absence of genuine freedom and democracy to bestow legitimacy upon a state, "nationalism, ethnicity, or religion tend to be relied on."[26] As a modern Islamic regime, Tehran's legitimacy rests substantially on the fate of its myth and message of Islamism, infused with themes of utopianism and justice against external oppression.[27] Thus, gestures must be made to prop up this myth and message, and conservatives, hardliners and pragmatists alike are constrained to make gestures for Islam (their interpretation) and against the scapegoats of Iranian and broader Muslim problems (namely Israel and the USA).

Both crusaders and pragmatists are as well constrained by domestic divisions and the external geopolitical realities of American primacy and Israeli and Arab rivalry which effectively check the dream of Iranian regional hegemony. At home, an undercurrent of liberalism and reform-minded elements in society continue to challenge the regime.[28] Iran had abandoned (or at least suspended) the dream of the Ayatollah by the end of the 1980s; what persists is the mirage of identity for an increasingly skeptical domestic population. Like China and the Soviet Union before them, Iranian domestic legitimacy is challenged by promises unfulfilled.

Foreign policy, then, confirms that "all politics is local," in the search for legitimacy. Peter Gries identifies "face nationalism" as a commitment to a collective identity and the reflection of the "elite-mass legitimacy dynamic that is central to" nationalist politics. He further notes a desire in China "to reorder extant hierarchies," a sentiment he claims is "common throughout the Third World." The question is not the existence of anger and desire for superiority, but the intensity of these sentiments. Intensity is related to whether or not anger is acted upon.[29] That intensity, and the approach to projecting Iranian identity to a domestic and world audience, however, is handled differently by hardliners and moderates. Iran's political system has allowed both elements to be heard, often simultaneously and in contradiction with one another.

In some matters, there is consensus and common ground in Iran. For example, a 2006 *Reader's Digest*-Zogby International survey found that 56 percent of Iranians polled believe their country should lead the region "diplomatically and militarily," while only 12 percent said their country should not be the dominant regional power.[30] But divisions in Iranian society remain as to the course of Iranian

---

and North Africa," in Steven Brown, ed., *International Dimensions of Internal Conflict*, Cambridge, Mass.: MIT Press, 212-3. On legitimacy, see Max Weber (1947), *The Theory of Social and Economic Organization*, New York: Oxford University Press, 124–6.

26   Bronson, 212.

27   Maloney, 97–102.

28   On Iran's Liberalism and Domestic Legitimacy Crisis, see Danny Postal (2006), *Reading Legitimation Crisis in Tehran*, Prickly Paradigm Press. The role of legitimacy in the nuclear crisis is covered well by Shahram Chubin (2006), *Iran's Nuclear Ambitions*, Carnegie Endowment for International Peace.

29   Hays Gries (1999), 'A China Threat?' *World Affairs* 162/2, available at http://www. findarticles.com/p/articles/mi-m2393/is_2_162/ai_58243521/pg_7.

30   *Inside Iran—Exclusive Reader's Digest/Zogby International Poll of Iranians Reveals a Society in Flux* (July 13 2006) Available at http://www.zogby.com/news/ReadNews.

society, with the Zogby poll finding nearly equal percentages of respondents wanting Iran to become more secular and liberal (31 percent) versus more religious and conservative (36 percent).[31] Domestic agitation for reform led to the surprise election and reelection of moderate Mohammed Khatami in 1997 and 2001. The Majlis was likewise rocked by reform-minded candidates that included the defeat of conservative Speaker Ali Akbar Nateq-Nuri.[32] Considered by some to be a "new stage in Iran's political evolution," the victories reflected and seemingly would advance political reforms hinting at a pluralization of political parties unseen since a 1981 law banned and restricted various organizations deemed a threat to the revolution.[33] The hardliner fear of Western influence is seen in several restrictions in 2006, from limiting broadband internet access, seizing illegal satellite dishes, and closing down Iran's leading reformist newspaper, *Shargh*.[34] Such measures by hardliners are met with condemnation and petitions from reformist and moderate MPs, and Iranians alike.

The two camps have competed in the case of the regional approach to the US as well. Ahmadinejad's hardline approach was to enlarge the conflict and make Israel a critical and visible part of the international debate. Renewing the debate of Israel's right to exist and questioning the Holocaust and its consequences, they thought, bought domestic and regional legitimacy and, in Trita Parsi's words, "reveal the impotence of the pro-US Arab regimes, who would be in equal parts pressured and embarrassed."[35] Moderates favored invoking the suffering of the Palestinian people but worried that the hard line rhetoric would backfire at Iran's expense.[36]

While legitimacy in Iran is tenuous, it can be replenished to the extent that the US and others can be ascribed blame for such promises. Israel and the United States remain the external scapegoats Iranian leaders turn to in rhetoric and policy to bolster their regional and domestic credentials. This has led to activities in the realm of nuclear politics and terrorism that, in a post-9/11 world, have raised Western fears about Iran's intentions, given its mixed signals and vitriolic rhetoric. The result may be alienation, an arms race, or even war. With these concerns in mind, and the thesis of domestic division and legitimacy in hand, we now turn to describing and interpreting Iranian foreign policy.

---

dbm?ID=1147.

31   Ibid.

32   Fairbanks, S. (1988), "Theocracy versus Democracy: Iran Considers Political Parties," *Middle East Journal* 52/1, 17.

33   Ibid., pp. 22–24.

34   Tait, R., "Iran Bans Fast Internet to cut West's Influence," *Guardian Unlimited*, October 18, 2006, available at http://technology.guardian.co.uk/news/story/0,,1924637,00. html?gusrc=rss&feed=1.

35   Parsi, T., "Under the Veil of Ideology: The Israeli–Iranian Strategic Rivalry," *Middle Eastern Report Online*, (June 9, 2006), available at http://www.merip.org/mero/mero060906. html.

36   Ibid.

Iranian Designs in the Middle East: Words versus Deeds

Mahmood Sariolghalam divides Iran's foreign policy into "pre-ceasefire" and "post-ceasefire" periods, referring to its involvement in the Iran–Iraq War waged through much of the 1980s. The former period constituted the revolutionary period of trying to bring about a regional Islamic order; the latter became a period of reassessment and moderation.[37]

The "pre-ceasefire" phase of Iranian foreign policy was captured in the rhetoric of "neither east nor west" and "exporting revolution."[38] Each concept can and has been broadly defined in practice, but the underlying theme in the early years was a new independent path for Islam against the conventional choices of pro-US westernization and pro-Soviet communism. Iran became an advocate for not just Iranians or even just Muslims: Khomeini argued "we want to export our revolution to all Islamic countries as well as to the oppressed countries," defining the "export of our revolution" as helping "nations grow aware and save themselves."[39] Very early, then, there was reason for regional suspicions of Iran's agenda, and vice versa.

While Iran possesses a regular armed forces charged with defending the country, Ayatollah Khomeini also established the Revolutionary Guard to protect and assist the ruling clerics in the enforcement of Islamic code. Among the Iranian Revolutionary Guard Corps is the Qods (or Jerusalem) Force, responsible for extraterritorial operations, training and intelligence gathering. There is also an Office of Liberation Movements, which has established a Gulf Section to which globalsecurity.org attributes the objective of destabilizing "Arab Gulf states by supporting fundamentalists with military, financial, and logistical support."[40] The Iranian Revolutionary Guard Corps has been accused of plotting a violent coup in pro-American Bahrain, as well as creating Hezbollah groups in Bahrain, Kuwait and Saudi Arabia.[41]

Among the ambitious early machinations of Khomeini's regime was anti-Saddam and anti-Baathist rhetoric and propaganda streaming along the radiowaves of Iraq in early 1980.[42] This fueled Saddam Hussein's perception of Iran's intentions to destabilize the Shi'a-dominant Iraq, contributing to the decision to attack Iran later that year. Successfully deflecting Saddam's aggression, however, the leadership of the ruling Islamic Republican Party (IRP) pushed for an offensive against Iraq in

---

37   Sariolghalam, M. (1996), "The Future of the Middle East: The Impact of the Northern Tier," *Security Dialogue* 27/3, 309–10.

38   Behrooz, M. (1990), "Trends in the Foreign Policy of the Islamic Republic of Iran, 1979–1988," in Nikki Keddie and Mark Gasiorowski (eds), *Neither East Nor West*, New Haven: Yale University Press, 14–5. On the tendency for headiness and conflict following revolution, see Walt, S. (1996), *Revolution and War*, Ithaca: Cornell University Press.

39   Behrooz, 14.

40   *Qods (Jerusalem), Force—Iranian Revolutionary Guard Corps (IRGC—Pasdaran-e Inqilab)* available at http://www.globalsecurity.org/intell/world/iran/qods.htm.

41   Clarke, R. (2004), *Against All Enemies: Inside America's War on Terror*, New York: Free Press, 112–3.

42   *The Iran-Iraq War*, Library of Congress Country Study, available at http://memory.loc.gov/cgi-bin/query/r?frd/cstdy: @ field (DOCID + ir0151).

1981,[43] alarming regional and world powers of the prospect of military victory by the new Islamic power.

Instead, the war became a bloody stalemate that would ultimately reign in the revolutionary fervor of Tehran. The post-ceasefire phase reflected a new status quo largely along the same geographical lines that preceded the war. This conflict had drained Iran of its early optimism and confidence, and threatened the legitimacy on which the regime was built. As Maloney argues, "having described the war with Iraq in terms of morality" to "mobilize popular support and military zeal, Iranian leadership thus incurred a substantial cost in terms of its own legitimacy in acknowledging the futility of the war's continuation."[44] Khomeini died not long after "drinking a bitter chalice of poison" that was peace with Iraq, helping to demarcate a new era of Iranian foreign policy as successors strove for redefinition of goals and reintegration into the regional and global community.[45]

To be sure, a strain of activism continued in Iranian foreign policy into the 1990s. From funneling arms to Bosnian Muslims to challenging the United Arab Emirates over disputed Gulf islands, Iran continued to engage in activities some characterize as mere "status buys" rather then revolution-export.[46] Despite some evidence of continued export and influence peddling abroad, the 1990s reflected a moderation in response to this new domestic, regional and global environment. Iran affirmed it would "tolerate no alteration of the political geography of the region," suggesting an abandonment of revolution or at least that Iran was now playing defense.[47] Seeking normalization with Saudi Arabia and others in the region, President Rafsanjani's "nationalist pragmatism" extended as far as the United States, who offered US Conoco Corporation a $1 billion offshore development deal in 1995.[48] Reformist President Mohammed Khatami offered the olive branch of dialogue with the US in the late 1990s, calling for a "dialogue of civilizations" and publicly apologizing to the American people for the hostage crisis of the revolution. The US responded with a call for "a road map leading to normal relations" and waived sanctions against foreign companies that picked up on the scuttled Conoco deal.[49]

But despite calls from analysts and task forces for normalization and a move from "dual containment" to "differentiated containment,"[50] both Iranian and US hardliners opposed Khatami's reform-minded moderating trends, with Ayatollah Khamenei's revolutionary Khomeini's ruling out of ties with the US.[51] News about secret 1995

---

43   Pollack, 188–189.

44   Maloney, 108.

45   Sariolghalam, 109.

46   Bazargan, D. (1997), "Iran: Politics, the Military and Gulf Security," *Middle East Review of International Affairs* 1/3; Maloney, 112.

47   Maloney, 111.

48   Herrmann and Ayers.

49   Sick, G. (1999), "Iran Has Changed, Why Can't We?," *Washington Post National Weekly Edition,* April 5, **23**.

50   See Independent Task Force (1997), *Differentiated Containment: US Policy Toward Iran and Iraq*, Washington, D.C.: Council on Foreign Relations Press.

51   Barraclough, S. (1999), "Khatami and the Consensual Politics of the Islamic Republic," *Journal of South Asian and Middle Eastern Studies* 22/2, 11–12.

appropriations by the Republican Congress to fund CIA covert action to "overthrow" Iranian regime "set off alarms throughout the Iranian hierarchy" and prompted a symbolic reciprocal move by the Majlis to fund covert operations against the US.[52] In November 1995, the US military training headquarters in Riyadh, Saudi Arabia, was bombed, killing five Americans. On June 25, 1996, a truck bomb detonated at the US Air Force complex in Khobar, Saudi Arabia. Given Iranian connections to regional groups, suspicion of their role in the bombings mounted in the United States. Yet the Saudis executed the alleged conspirators of the Riyadh bombing, and denied the US access to suspects or information on either event. US leaders debated a response against Iran but, short of evidence implicating the Tehran regime, deferred action.[53] A 1994 bombing of a Jewish communal center in Argentina raised similar claims of Iranian complicity, despite Tehran's repeated denials.[54]

Other attempts at rapprochement occurred in the post-9/11 climate, but were similarly unsuccessful in no small part due to hardliners on each side. In 2003, Iran's moderate reformist regime, supposedly with the blessing of the spectrum of "major political players in the Iranian regime, approached the US via contacts in Switzerland. The offer allegedly was that Iran would raise the possibility of cutting Iran's support for Hamas and Islamic Jihad, helping to pacify and disarm Hezbollah, and address US concerns about its nuclear program.[55] It could be that Iran was ready to play ball in the face of US determination and the domestic impulse to grow economically. According to this telling, there was a missed opportunity for dialogue and diplomacy.

It could be that the US rebuffed Iran in the early days of the war on terror, when regimes were toppling within a month with little apparent effort. Or it could be that the US did not trust the ambiguous promises of the Tehran proposal. Secretary of State Colin Powell and his deputy, Richard Armitage, were reportedly in favor of engaging the Iranian offer, but the offer was rebuked as a result of opposition by Vice President Cheney and officials in Under Secretary of Defense for policy Douglas Feith's Office of Special Plans—hardliners interested in regime change in Iran.[56] Attempts to reestablish the "Geneva channel" were scuttled by "neocons" who demanded from Iran full information on any high-ranking al-Qaeda members in their possession, but were unwilling to reciprocate with Iran's request for names of Mujahideen–e Khalq (MEK) members held by US forces in Iraq.[57] By 2005, hardliners recaptured the presidency and a spiral of confrontation sent relations on a collision course to be discussed below.

Iran did not altogether oppose the US led invasion of Iraq. In fact, one of the sources for much (dis)information in the buildup to war, Ahmed Chalabi, had open

---

52   Clarke, 103–104.

53   Ibid., pp. 112–121.

54   Perelman, M., "Argentina Issues Iran Indictment", *Forward* (October 25, 2006), available at http://www.forward.com/articles/argentina-issues-iran-indictment.

55   Porter, G. (2006), "Neo-con Cabal Blocked 2003 Nuclear Talks," *Asian Times*, March 30, available at http://atimes.com/atimes/Middle_East/HC30Ak01.html.

56   Ibid.

57   Ibid.

ties to Iran, including a US-funded branch office of the Iraqi National Congress based in Tehran.[58] Iran's government spokesman Abdullah Ramezanzadeh deplored the US for commencing the war but also vowed neutrality and impartiality rather than support "the belligerent parties."[59] For Iran, the deposing of Saddam Hussein posed an opportunity to bring Shi'a influence to Iran's western neighbor, and with it, Iranian influence as well. Nonetheless, while Iran did not mind US forces coming in, Iran did worry about US forces staying—particularly in a post-9/11 context in which the US lumped Iran into the Axis of Evil and embraced preventive war without UN approval. Given US fears of terrorism and nuclear weapons, and given US support for Israel in the region, Iran's positions on these issues becomes all the more critical to understand.

Terrorism and the Palestinian–Israeli Conflict

Iran's involvement in terrorism raises concerns at the regional and global level. The State Department asserts that Iran supports the Lebanese Hezbollah, as well as Palestinian rejectionist groups Islamic Jihad and Hamas, groups labeled as foreign terrorist organizations (FTOs) by the US State Department.

Prior to the overthrow of the Shah, Iran and Israel enjoyed a natural regional alliance faced with common Arab threats, forging close security ties that even survived the Islamic Revolution.[60] Post-revolutionary Iran, for all its bluster aimed at Israel, was quite tame in its opposition to the Jewish state. Ayatollah Khomeini introduced the ritual of observing an al-Qods Day—Jerusalem Day—in 1981, according to one analysis, to "pay lip service to the Palestinian cause at the same time that his regime was scheming to buy arms from the state it denounced as the 'occupier of Jerusalem'."[61] Khomeini was cool to PLO leader Yasir Arafat given his leftist tendencies, and refused to send F-14 fighters to Lebanon, where the PLO battled Israeli forces.[62]

Of course, while cold to Arafat's PLO, Iran *has* supported Islamist anti-Israel groups like Hamas and Hezbollah, and Iran is firmly in the "rejectionist" camp on the Israel-Palestine question, opposed to recognition of the Jewish state. To the extent that Hamas and Palestinian Islamic Jihad have served as "spoilers" sabotaging peace talks in the 1990s, Iran's complicity has been directly or indirectly implicated.[63] Iranian Foreign Minister Manuchehr Mottaki reiterated that "the declared and specific policy

---

58   Hosenball, M., "Intelligence: A Double Game", *Newsweek*, May 10, 2004, available at http://www.msnbc.msn.com/id/4881157/.

59   "Iran: Government spokesman reiterates Tehran's neutrality in US war on Iraq," *Tehran IRNA* (March 20, 2003), *World News Connection,* FBIS Transcribed Text, document # FBIS-NES-2003-0320.

60   Bahgat (2005), "The Islamic Republic and the Jewish State," *Israel Affairs* 11/3 (2005), 517–34; Parsi.

61   Parsi.

62   Ibid.

63   On the role of extremist violence disrupting Palestinian-Israeli peace negotiations see Kydd, A. and Walter, B. (2002), "Sabotaging the Peace: The Politics of Extremist Violence," *International Organization* 56/2, 263–96.

of the Islamic Republic of Iran" is that "we don't recognize the Zionist regime and don't consider it legitimate."[64] The revolution changed Iran's position dramatically, with Iran joining other rejectionist elements in the region declaring Israel's existence to be illegitimate. Ayatollah Khomeini's successor, Ayatollah Khamenei, has called Israel a "cancerous tumor" to be "removed from the region," and in 2005, Iranian President Mahmoud Ahmadinejad called for the "Zionist entity" to be wiped off the map.[65] This position minimally reflects an opposition to recognizing Israel, but such rhetoric raises fears in Israel and the West that Iran harbors aggressive intentions towards Israel.

Such fears are backed by support for anti-Israel groups, Hezbollah and Hamas. Through these groups, Iran spreads its political influence into non-contiguous parts of the Middle East, and adds to its deterrent capability against Israel and the US. Some US officials suspect that Iran encouraged Hezbollah's kidnapping of two Israeli soldiers, an operation that provoked the Israeli campaign, in hopes of distracting the United States and its allies from their drive to win UN sanctions against Tehran for its nuclear activities.[66]

If this was the goal, it seemed to backfire. As Parsi and Porter suggest, "[o]n the contrary, the effect of the current escalation has intensified pressure in Washington to take far harsher measures against Iran, including military action."[67] American hardliners and neoconservatives took these events as indicators of the need for direct confrontation with Iran. William Kristol's view connects a few simple dots:

> No Islamic Republic of Iran, no Hezbollah. No Islamic Republic of Iran, no one to prop up the Assad regime in Syria. No Iranian support for Syria…, little state sponsorship of Hamas and Hezbollah.[68]

Such a view grossly oversimplifies the independent role and nature of Hamas and Hezbollah. Others agreed to Iran's role but concluded time for a new approach in order to avoid the mess of confrontation. Others questioned Iran's role altogether.[69] But it is clear that Iranian support for Islamist groups poses a challenge to Israel and reflects Iran's agenda in contrast to the US-led alternative view of the region.

At issue is whether Iran's positions reveal a true desire to unmake or destroy Israel or serve as more "status buys" for an Islamic regime seeking to bolster its legitimacy and credentials at home. Trita Parsi suggests that both Iran and Israel

---

64   "The Zionist Entity and Israel," *Globalsecurity.org*, available at http://www. globalsecurity.org/military/world/iran/zionist-entity.htm.

65   Ibid.

66   McManus, D. (2006), "Iran is Bush's Target in Lebanon," *Los Angeles Times*, July 30, available at http://www.latimes.com/news/nationworld/world/la-fg-usmideast30jul30,0,5289218.story.

67   Parsi, T. and Porter, G., "Is Iran Behind the War in Lebanon?" *NIAC Issue Brief*, July 24, 2006, available at http://www.niacouncil.org/pressreleases/press399.asp.

68   Kristol, W. (2006), "Why Bush Should Go to Tel Aviv—and Confront Iran," *Financial Times*, July 16, available at http://www.ft.com/cms/s/d1e9154e-14e0-11db-b391-0000779e2340.html.

69   Parsi and Porter.

possess "a critical common interest" in the need to portray their strategic conflict as an ideological clash in an effort to isolate one another regionally and globally.[70] Israel and its supporters pushed the image of "the sole democracy in the Middle East and an illiberal theocracy that hated everything the West stood for," while Iran sought to unite Muslims against the Zionist entity and undermine Arab governments who did not tow the hard line on Israel.[71] Kaveh Afrasiabi insists that the rhetoric is just that, and that Iranian policymakers consider Israel "not germane to Iran's national security worries."[72]

Iran's policy is a dangerous balance to maintain its influence against US-Israeli dominance without provoking US-Israeli (and world) retaliation that would undo the regime. Parsi and Porter note that "Tehran has consistently challenged US red lines on its nuclear program, but has done so while maintaining the ability to make concessions when it had to in order to avoid a military confrontation with the West that it knew it could not win." They add that, "it has been a primary interest of Iran to negotiate for security guarantees and a new status as a legitimate regional power, while avoiding moves that could risk trapping Iran in a military confrontation with Washington."[73]

Beyond the question of Israel, some wonder about Iran's broader ties to terrorism. At least eight of the hijackers passed through Iran in 2000–2001, but there is no evidence of involvement. Iran has arrested some al-Qaeda elements in the country; it also claims arrested and repatriated hundreds of al-Qaeda suspects, including Khaled al-Harbi.[74] Iran has detained al-Qaeda operatives since 9/11, and the Iranian Government indicated support for the Iraqi Governing Council and promised to help Iraqi reconstruction.[75] However, CIA chief Porter Goss reportedly handed over three dossiers to Turkish security officials that contained evidence that Tehran is co-operating with al-Qaeda.[76]

The uncertainty surrounding Iranian involvement with al-Qaeda or other terrorist activities is not comforting to an insecure United States. If the US is operating under what has come to be known as the Cheney Doctrine or "1 Per Cent Doctrine," then if there is a 1 percent chance of a country passing WMD to a terrorist, the US must act.[77] An important question, thus, becomes: what are Iran's nuclear ambitions?

---

70   Parsi.

71   Ibid.

72   Afrasiabi, K.L. (2005), "The Myth of an Israeli Strike on Iran," *Asia Times*, April 7, available at http://www.atimes.com/atimes/Middle_East/GD07Ak01.html.

73   Parsi and Porter.

74   Johnston, J. (2004), "Regime Change in Iran now in Bush's Sights," *Sunday Herald*, July 18, available at www.sundayherald.com/print43461.

75   Qods (Jerusalem) Force—Iranian Revolutionary Guard Corps (IRGC—Pasdaran-e *Inqilab*).

76   "Is Washington Planning a Military Strike?" der *Spiegel* (December 30, 2005), available at http://www.spiegel.de/international/0,1518,392783,00.html.

77   Suskind, R. (2006), *The One Percent Doctrine*, New York: Simon and Schuster; Gardinier, S. (2006), "The End of the "Summer of Diplomacy': Assessing US Military Options on Iran," *A Century Foundation Report*, 6.

The Nuclear Question

Well before 9/11 and the war on terror, some Western analysts speculated that Iranian civilian nuclear energy programs merely "serve as the foundation for a nuclear weapons program."[78] Kemp and Harkavey reported in 1997 that Iran was "assumed to be moving toward nuclear acquisitions" and "appears to be striving mightily to acquire nuclear weapons," confidently asserting that "it will if it can."[79] Evidence of the Shah's pursuit of nuclear weapons exists, and the question is whether Khomeini revived this program. Most evidence of nuclear activity, however, relates to the acquisition of reactors and centrifuge technology that is compatible with a peaceful civilian nuclear energy program as well as an enrichment program for weaponization. The former is NPT compliant; the latter is not.

The nuclear question gained international attention in 2002–2003, when the International Atomic Energy Agency (IAEA) found Iran in violation of the NPT and related safeguards agreements pertaining to undeclared activity. Iran had not revealed certain past nuclear activities and sites, and the IAEA identified additional undeclared parts of the Iranian nuclear program and encountered problems in obtaining Iran's cooperation in resolving a number of issues.[80] In 2003–2004, the IAEA reported trace elements of Highly Enriched Uranium (HEU) in an Iranian nuclear facility, and that Iran had withheld from inspectors blueprints for an advanced centrifuge design usable for uranium enrichment.[81] By 2006, the IAEA could not conclude that Iran's nuclear program is "exclusively for peaceful purposes."[82]

After alternating between promises to freeze enrichment plans and asserting a sovereign right to do so, Iran broke the UN seals on their nuclear facilities and resumed uranium conversion at their facilities in Isfahan in August 2005.[83] Iran announced simultaneously in April 2006 that they had successfully enriched uranium for the first time and that the country had no intention to develop nuclear weapons. The UN Security Council demanded that Iran stop enrichment activity by April 28, but Iran continued while asserting its right to do so under the NPT. Iran claimed it wanted to operate its nuclear program under supervision by the International Atomic

---

78   See for example the testimony of Michael Eisenstadt, "Iran Under Khatami: WMD, Terrorism, and the Arab–Israeli Conflict", Statement before the US Senate Foreign Relations Committee, May 14, 1998, available at http://fas.org/spp/starwars/congress/1998_h/s980514-eisen.htm.

79   Kemp, G. and Harkavy, P. (1997), *Strategic Geography and the Changing Middle East*, Washington, D.C.: Carnegie Endowment/Brookings Institution, 270–1.

80   Albright, D. and Shire, J., *Iran's NPT Violations: Numerous and Possibly On-Going?* September 29, 2006, avaiable at http://www.isis-online.org/publications/iran/irannptviolations.pdf.

81   *Nuclear Weapons: Recent Developments*, Federation of Atomic Scientists, available at http://www.fas.org/nuke/guide/iran/nuke/index.html; see also Allison, G. (2004), *Nuclear Terrorism: The Ultimate Preventable Catastrophe*, New York: Times Books, 161–2.

82   *Implementation of the NPT Safeguards Agreement in the Islamic Republic of Iran,'* (IAEA Reports) by the Director General, GOV/2006/14, February 4, 2006; GOV/2006/53.

83   Rodgers, W., *Iran Breaks Seals at Nuclear Plant*, CNN, available at http://www.cnn.com/2005/WORLD/europe/08/10/iran.iaea.1350/index.html.

Energy Agency and within its rights and regulations under the regulations of the Nuclear Non-Proliferation Treaty.[84]

In a diplomatic gesture, the United States offered to lift some of its trade sanctions against Iran as part of a package of benefits the EU will deliver to get Tehran to guarantee it will not make nuclear weapons. The incentives offer from six world powers was accompanied by a threat of UN Security Council penalties if Iran fails to halt enrichment.[85] Iran's supreme leader Ayatollah Ali Khamenei said that his country would not give in to "threats and bribes."[86] In response, the UN Security Council passed a resolution that gave Iran until August 31, 2006, to halt uranium enrichment or face potential international sanctions.[87] Iran condemned the resolution, asserting that Iran "will not accept unfair decisions, even in the framework of resolutions by the international bodies."[88] At the time of this writing, the UN was deliberating on how to respond to Iran's behavior.

Two questions arise in the case of the nuclear crisis: what are Iran's weapons capabilities and intentions? UN and US intelligence, and nuclear experts, point out that there's little evidence Iran is anywhere near producing weapons-grade uranium and will not be able to produce a nuclear weapon until about 2010 at the earliest, and perhaps not until 2015.[89] The question of Iran's intentions weighs heavy in response to its behavior. The spectrum of opinion is from those who believe it is purely a civilian energy program overblown by a paranoid West, to a nuclear-weapons aspiring Iran seeking deterrence against perceived US and Israeli power, to desire to assert a regional dominance and aggressive designs to export revolution and Islamicize the region and even "destroy Israel."[90] The US and Israel tended toward the latter worst case scenario in confronting Iran in 2006. Iran's leadership has pledged that Iran will remain a non-nuclear-weapon party to the Nuclear Nonproliferation Treaty, and Ayatollah Khamenei issued a fatwa asserting that the "production, stockpiling and use of nuclear weapons are forbidden under Islam and that the Islamic Republic of Iran shall never acquire these weapons."[91]

Who is right, and what explains Iran's behavior in the nuclear crisis? Tehran has said that Western incentives to halt its nuclear program were an "acceptable basis" for talks, and that it is ready for negotiations. At the same time, Iran has said it will

---

84   Dareini, A.A. (2006), "Iran Hits Milestone in Nuclear Technology", *Associated Press* (April 11), available at http://news.yahoo.com/s/ap/20060411/ap_on_re_mi_ea/iran_nuclear;_ylt=AvGqov52DfEd2bzmYZuSEX0LewgF.

85   Adler, M., *US Sweetens Offer to Iran: Diplomats*, *Yahoo News* Available at http://news.yahoo.com/s/afp/20060605/wl_afp/irannuclearpoliticseusolanaoffer;_ylt=AuUaVfRcl3Yz3jgLBkRpqp0LewgF;_ylu=X3oDMTBjMHVqMTQ4BHNlYwN5bnN1YmNhdA.

86   Ibid.

87   UN Security Council, Resolution 1696 (S/RES/1696), July 31, 2006, available at http://daccessdds.un.org/doc/UNDOC/GEN/N06/450/22/PDF/N0645022.pdf?OpenElement.

88   *U.N. Demands That Iran Suspend Nuclear Work by Aug. 31*, *Global Security Newswire* Available at http://www.nti.org/d_newswire/issues/2006_7_31.html#CC0EB72D.

89   Hosenball, M. (2006), "How Close Is Iran to Having Nuclear Weapons?" *Newsweek*, 25 September, available at http://www.msnbc.msn.com/id/14870327/site/newsweek/.

90   See *Newsweek* (July 24, 2006).

91   Rodgers.

never give up its right under the Nuclear Nonproliferation Treaty to enrich uranium and produce nuclear fuel, while indicating it may temporarily suspend large-scale activities to ease tensions and warning that UN action and sanctions "mean blocking and rejecting talks."[92] If domestic and regional politics is considered, these are not irreconcilable behaviors and requests. If Iran is seeking nuclear weapons, it is clear why they seek to press on. Economic diversification in nuclear energy may be their true end, but Iran asserts the right to enrich in the name of sovereign independence against perceived Western threats and bullying. This plays well domestically even while raising tensions abroad.

But the mix of nuclear ambiguity, defiance of the UN, support for terrorist groups, and at least rhetorical opposition to Israel's existence, is a dangerous brew to concoct in the name of domestic legitimacy and deterrence. Analysts concluded that the summer of 2006, with Hezbollah, Hamas and Iraqi Shi'a agitation destabilizing areas important to US foreign policy, provided an Iranian warning to Washington via proxies and without firing a gun. But an overconfident Iran seeking to tweak the United States is playing a dangerous game that could provoke a regional backlash.

Repercussions of Iranian Policy

What do these foreign and domestic policy positions in the name of domestic legitimacy and regional influence mean for regional and US policy? This section examines the repercussions of Iran's nuclear posturing, support for terrorism and opposition to Israel on regional and US policy.

Regional Response

Since the revolution, Arab states had to reconsider their regional security situation. Iran-Saudi relations have been competitive since the Revolution, as two states vying for authentic Islamic leadership in the Muslim world.[93] This competition led to Saudi support for Iraq in the Iran–Iraq War.[94] They backed Iraq against Iran in the 1980s, despite Iraq's aggression, out of fear of a victory for revolutionary Persian Shi'a Islam under the banner of exporting revolution.

With the defeat and subsequent containment of Iraq under Operation Desert Storm, the Arab states lost one safeguard against Tehran's influence. With the demise of the Soviet Union, the Arab world lost another option for international protection. With Israel and Iran as bookends to the post-Cold War Arab world, the many Arab states substituted US protection, arms purchases and weak attempts at self-sufficient security measures. The Gulf Cooperation Council (GCC) serves as a collective security institution, but the combined capabilities of the oil states do not compare to that of Iran or Iraq. A short-lived "Damascus Declaration" called for an all-Arab

---

92   Dareini, A.A. (2006), "Iran Calls Western Incentives Acceptable," *Associated Press* (July 16), available at http://news.yahoo.com/s/ap/20060716/ap_on_re_mi_ea/iran_nuclear.

93   Mortimer.

94   Al-Mani, S. (1996), "Of Security and Threat: Saudi Arabia's Perception," *Journal of South Asian and Middle Eastern Studies* 20/1, 75–77.

military force from Syria, Egypt and GCC nations, but the plan dissipated amid Iranian objections and internal fights over force structure and implementation.[95]

With the exception of Syria, which has exhibited cordial relations with Iran, regional states already concerned about the Iraq War for their own reasons and consequences, also rue the advantage granted Iran under the new Gulf environment.[96] Iran is in a new position of influence in Iraq and the region as well. Iran's "pro-Palestinian" reputation, renewed confidence and nuclear games have unsettled Arab leaders, who increasingly issue anti-Iranian statements of Iranian power in the region.[97] There is concern that Iran wants to create a "Shi'a crescent' of Iranian-influenced regimes through Iraq, Syria and Lebanon, as well as dominate the Persian Gulf. The US hopes to use such fears to gather Arab support for a hard line on Iran as well as to get regional powers to end support for Hezbollah and other terrorist groups.[98]

Despite concerns about Iran, there is also regional concern about proposed strikes against Iran. The Turkish Government has stated that it opposes military action against both Iran and Syria, but if the United States attacks Iran, some say Turkey will have no choice but to jump on board.[99] Regardless of Iran's intentions, numerous studies warn of a nuclear-weapons-armed Iran as a threat to regional, if not world, security. Fearing nuclear dominoes, there is concern that an Iran with nuclear weapons would "almost certainly give rise to similar programs in other Middle Eastern states."[100]

US Response

The nexus of terrorism and potential nuclear weapons programs is the cause for US concern about Iran. Hardliner US critics suggested that Iran has succeeded in deferring international action and while undercutting "what little international credibility the US retains."[101] There is a sense that Iran may be duly overconfident, perceiving that US power has "waned with its troops bogged down in Iraq."[102]

---

95   Burke, J. and Abernethy, J. (1994), "The Middle East: The Security of a Region", in Douglas Murray and Paul Viotti (eds), *The Defense Policies of Nations*, Baltimore and London: Johns Hopkins University Press, 492.

96   El-Hokayem, E. and Legrenzi, M. (2006) "The Arab Gulf States in the Shadow of the Iranian Nuclear Challenge," The Henry L. Stimson Center, May 26, available at http://www.stimson.org/swa/pdf/StimsonIranGCCWorkingPaper.pdf.

97   Parsi.

98   Rubin, T. (2006), "Time for US to Change the Way it Thinks of Iran," *The Philadelphia Inquirer*, July 17, available at http://www.belleville.com/mld/belleville/news/editorial/15057478.htm.

99   "Is Washington Planning a Military Strike?" der *Spiegel* (December 30, 2005), available at http://www.spiegel.de/international/0,1518,392783,00.html.

100   Perkovich et al. (2005), *Universal Compliance: A Strategy for Nuclear Security*, Washington, DC: Carnegie Endowment for International Peace, 169; see also Feldman (1997), *Nuclear Weapons and Arms Control in the Middle East*, Cambridge: MIT Press.

101   Rubin, M. (2006), "Damage is Done: The Bush Administration's Bad Iran Move," *National Review Online* (June 1), available at http://www.meforum.org/article/939.

102   Parsi and Porter.

Observers noted that US options for responding were "limited," citing the end of "cowboy diplomacy."[103] President Bush has said military force should be the last resort in the effort to prevent Iran from acquiring a nuclear bomb, yet he insists the US would not tolerate an Iranian nuclear arsenal.[104] Pentagon plans are in the works for bombing raids backed by submarine-launched ballistic missile attacks against Iran's nuclear sites to block Tehran's efforts to develop an atomic bomb.[105] Claims were made as early as 2004 that a second Bush administration would include more intervention in the internal affairs of Iran.[106] A January 2005 report claimed that clandestine American commando groups had already infiltrated Iran in order to mark potential military targets, and another suggested that CIA Director Porter Goss asked Turkish Prime Minister to provide support and intelligence for a possible air strikes against Iranian nuclear and military facilities.[107]

The summer 2006 conflict between Israel and Hezbollah has been considered part of a larger struggle between the US and Iran for influence across the Middle East. Bush himself suggested "the stakes are larger than just Lebanon ... [which] I firmly believe is backed by Iran and encouraged by Iran" and "that Iran would like to exert additional influence in the region. A theocracy would like to spread its influence, using surrogates." One official called the conflict "a proxy war," with Israel fighting for one side and Hezbollah for the other.[108]

Beyond the balance of power, the US also seems bent on regime change, with Bush calling Iran "a nation now held hostage by a small clerical elite that is isolating and repressing its people."[109] One obvious question posed by this analysis is that: if Iran faces a domestic legitimacy problem, does that translate into mass support for regime change by the hands of the US? William Kristol optimistically claims that "the Iranian people dislike their regime" and that political and military pressure "could cause them to reconsider whether they really want to have this regime in power."[110]

---

103   Wright, R. (2006), "Options for US Limited as Mideast Crises Spread," *Washington Post*, July 13, A19, available at http://www.washingtonpost.com/wp-dyn/content/article/2006/07/12/AR2006071201557.html; Allen, M. and Ratnesar, R. (2006), "The End of Cowboy Diplomacy," *Time*, July 9, available at http://www.time.com/time/magazine/article/0,9171,1211578,00.html.

104   Bender, B. (2006), "Iran is Prepared to Retaliate, Experts Warn," *Boston Globe*, February 12, available at http://www.boston.com/news/world/middleeast/articles/2006/02/12/iran_is_prepared_to_retaliate_experts_warn?mode=PF.

105   Sherwell, P. (2006), "US Prepares Military Blitz against Iran's Nuclear Sites," *Telegraph*, February 12, available at http://www.telegraph.co.uk/news/main.jhtml?xml=/news/2006/02/12/wiran12.xml&sSheet=/portal/2006/02/12/ixportaltop.html.

106   Johnston, J. (2004), "Regime Change in Iran Now in Bush's Sights," *Sunday Herald*, July 18, available at www.sundayherald.com/print43461.

107   "Is Washington Planning a Military Strike?"

108   Trudy Rubin.

109   President Addresses American Legion, Discusses Global War on Terror, February 26, 2006, available at http://www.whitehouse.gov/news/releases/2006/02/20060224.html.

110   "Kristol Suggests People of Iran Would Embrace US Attack, Triggering Regime Change," *Think Progress* (July 19, 2006), available at http://thinkprogress.org/2006/07/19/

After similar predictions of being greeted as liberators in Iraq, it is important not to confuse internal divisions about a regime for widespread support for foreign, western military intervention. Iranians are divided on many political issues, but have more common shared views of the history of US and other meddling in their country. The United States in 1953 supported the deposing of elected Iranian Prime Minister Mohammed Mossadeq by elements of the Iranian army.[111] The restored Shah of Iran became a "pillar" in the US strategy of stabilizing the status quo in the strategically vital region after the UK's withdrawal.[112] But US meddling in Iranian politics, from the ouster of Mossadeq to support for the often ruthless Shah, was to lose the Iranian population. Despite an infusion of aid and assistance in the 1960s and 1970s, one Iranian critic of the Shah suggested that the US had become "distrusted by most people, and hated by many."[113] The Iranian revolution was as much a repudiation of the US as it was the Shah. Seen as the "Great *Satan*" by fundamentalist elements of the revolution for having supported the Shah and "corrupted" Iran with Western influence, the US became an early scapegoat for the new regime's consolidation of legitimate power, abetting the hostage crisis at the US embassy until early 1981.[114] Decrying both "Eastern and Western colonialism," the new regime asserted the charge that both sought to undermine "the Islamic and independence-seeking movements" of the world.[115]

The Future of Iran and the Middle East

This chapter has sought to provide some clarity about Iran's foreign policy and its motivation. It argued that Iran is a divided society whose regime faces twin challenges of internal legitimacy and external pressure. Iran's policy has sought to shore up domestic and regional legitimacy while balancing the influence of Israel and the US in a new security environment in which neighboring threats—Saddam Hussein and the Taliban—have been conveniently removed by nemesis United States. Iran's dangerous game of scapegoating may invite unwanted US, Israeli, regional and global reprisals. While not on a genuine path of aggression and expansion, others have concluded it to be so and, in the final analysis, perceived reality that drives behavior regardless of what is "objectively" true. Robert Jervis warns all policymakers of the common misperception that others will understand "that you

---

kristol-iran/.

111   Gavin, F. (1999), "Politics, Power, and US Policy in Iran, 1950–1953," *Journal of Cold War Studies* 1/1.

112   Little, D. (2004), *American Orientalism: The United States and the Middle East since 1945*, University of North Carolina Press, 140.

113   Bill, J. (1988), *The Eagle and the Lion*, New Haven: Yale University Press, 130.

114   For numerous in-depth and excellent treatments of US-Iranian relations at the time of the revolution, see Sick, G. (1985), *All Fall Down: America's Tragic Encounter with Iran*, IB Tauris and Co., Ltd.; Rubin; Bill, Chapter 7; Cottam, R. (1988), *Iran and the United States: A Cold War Case Study*, Pittsburgh: University of Pittsburgh Press, Chapter 6; and Pollack, Chapter 6.

115   Behrooz, 15.

are not a threat," suggesting that self-righteousness and a lack of understanding leads to a belief that "the other knows he is not hostile."[116] Further, believing oneself to be peaceful, for another to respond with hostility feeds a perception that the "other is aggressive and must be met with strength and firmness."[117] Thus, the world witnesses in the early twenty-first century a classic security dilemma, by which Iranian nuclear programs—which may well be peaceful—provoke fear and escalation by the US-led west, which demands that Iran cease activities Tehran feels are safeguarded by international law and the NPT.

This dilemma is of course working in both directions. Critics have questioned the utility of threats in bringing about acquiescence, suggesting that the hard line against Iraq may have accelerated Iranian and North Korean nuclear programs "because of the Bush bellicosity, the Bush Doctrine, and the Bush war."[118] Because of American talk of an "axis of evil," US activities to foster anti-Iranian groups, and US demonstrated willingness to overthrow regional regimes, Iran may conclude an unjust and imperial America means it harm, requiring measures in response to deter such an eventuality. These measures, such as defiant continued nuclearization and indirect agitation in the Levant and Iraq, only confirm Washington's beliefs of hostile intent in a perceived resurgent revolutionary Iran.

Instead of trusting in deterrence and diplomacy, the US, at the pinnacle of world power, seems more skittish of minor rogue powers than it ever was of its rival Soviet behemoth. The language of elevated alarm at the prospect of minor powers of 20–60 million rivals that of Cold War fears, on the flimsy "worst case" reasoning that such minor powers would dare threaten or use WMD against the US directly or through terrorist operatives.[119]

Yet the coming battle would be costly on both sides. US intelligence assessments warn that Iran is prepared to use long-range missiles, secret commando units, and terrorist allies around the globe in retaliation for any strike on the country, and could use missiles and gunboats to shut off access to the economically vital Persian Gulf, sparking an oil crisis.[120] Iraqi Shi'ite cleric, Moqtada al-Sadr, whose militia has clashed with US troops before, vowed to defend Iran if it were attacked.[121]

Because of this prospective crash-course, in which the US perhaps overestimates Iranian actions and threats, while Iran underestimates US resolve and seriousness, Trudy Rubin argues that the US must test whether Iran is serious about dialogue and compromise because it is in America's interest to find out whether Iran is willing to play a constructive regional role and at what price.[122] The need for flexibility is particularly crucial given the domestic face politics being played in Iran. A senior Iranian official said: "The United States has problems in Iraq, Lebanon, Syria, and

---

116   Jervis, R. (1976), *Perception and Misperception in International Politics*, Princeton: Princeton University Press, 354–5.

117   Ibid., 355.

118   Buchanan, P. (2005), "Bye-Bye, Bush Doctrine: It's back to deterrence," www.antiwar.com; (May 04) available at http://www.antiwar.com/pat/?articleid=5829.

119   Suskind; Gardinier, 6.

120   Bender.

121   Ibid.

122   Trudy Rubin.

Afghanistan," and that "Iran is the one who can help (in all those places). The United States needs Iran's help, not confrontation."[123] The priority in the West should be recognizing the politics behind the rhetoric, the fear behind the behavior, and on identifying and cultivating those in Tehran who offer the pragmatic vision for its divided country. Neither religion, oil, nor geopolitics make war inevitable—only leaders can choose that course.

---

123   Ibid.

SECTION IV
International Organizations and the US in the Middle East

Chapter 12

NATO and the Middle East:
The Road to Greater Engagement

Chris Zambelis and Eva Svobodová

During the Cold War, NATO's direct interest and involvement in the greater Middle East was limited in scope and, at best, peripheral to its immediate mandate to defend Western Europe from a Soviet invasion. That changed with the break up of the Soviet Union and, most recently, following the September 11 attacks against the United States. The greater Middle East now figures prominently in NATO's evolving strategic vision and outlook as the Alliance expands and its transformation from a Cold War-era institution continues to develop and progress.[1] By default, the post-9/11 security environment characterized by international terrorism, the threat of the proliferation of weapons of mass destruction (WMDs), transnational crime, and instability emanating from weak and failed states, has forced the Alliance to reevaluate its posture towards the greater Middle East on a multitude of levels. This is demonstrated by NATO's efforts to engage the region through cooperative frameworks and direct involvement in Afghanistan, Iraq, Sudan, and other theaters.

NATO's increased "rapprochement" with the Middle East represents a radical departure from its previous policy of limited engagement. At the same time, however, it is a logical development arising from NATO's need and desire to adapt to the post-Cold War era. Upon cursory examination, NATO's growing interest and active involvement in the Middle East, and in out of area operations more generally, appears to stem from the need to confront international terrorist threats and related contingencies in the post-9/11 security environment. However, since the fall of the Soviet Union, NATO's most high-profile missions have involved peacekeeping and stability operations, humanitarian and relief contingencies, and crisis response measures outside of the Alliance's traditional European theater of operations, to include the Middle East.

Given this context, the question begs as to what extent NATO is willing and capable of engaging the region—be it through cooperative security frameworks or military campaigns. Considering the limited capabilities of the Alliance and often divergent interests of the individual members, combined with a generally negative perception of NATO in the Arab and Muslim world, among other things, it is clear

---

1   The greater Middle East encompasses the Arab world, Afghanistan, Pakistan, Iran, Turkey, and Israel. Some definitions include the former Soviet Central Asian Republics, but this chapter will refer to the former definition.

that NATO faces a series of formidable obstacles to making a credible contribution to the security and stability of the greater Middle East.

Despite these obstacles, this chapter argues that the Alliance does have a large part to play. Based on the Alliance's experience and efforts in the former Yugoslavia and elsewhere in Eastern Europe and the former Soviet Union, it has the capacity to contribute to peacekeeping and stabilization operations in the region. NATO diplomacy can also help defuse regional tensions and facilitate the creation of cooperative frameworks for counter-terrorism and other security exchanges. The Alliance can also help promote political reform, especially in the security sector, and play a constructive role in humanitarian affairs.

NATO and the Middle East: Pre-9/11

As a defensive Alliance designed to repel a Soviet invasion of Europe, NATO has traditionally had little formal contact with the greater Middle East. It did not establish official ties with the region until December 1994, when it launched the Mediterranean Dialogue (MD), in conjunction with the Partnership for Peace (PfP) Programme for countries of Central and Eastern Europe. The MD, defined as a "forum for political consultations and practical cooperation, which includes a bilateral and a multilateral component and involves countries of the Mediterranean area," was born of the idea that security of Europe is closely tied to stability and security in the Mediterranean region.[2] The Dialogue's primary objectives include "contributing to regional security and stability, achieving better mutual understanding and dispelling any misconceptions between NATO and its Mediterranean partners."[3] However, unlike the PfP Programme that has over the course of a decade developed into a genuine partnership culminating in two rounds of enlargement, the Dialogue has had much smaller expectations on both sides and has demonstrated only relatively small achievements.

As of today, 30 countries have joined the PfP Programme since 1994, with 10 becoming members of NATO during the 1999 and 2004 enlargements.[4] By signing the Partnership for Peace Framework Document, NATO and the partners pledge to achieve transparency in national defense planning and budgeting processes; democratic control over armed forces; capability and readiness to participate in operations led by the United Nations (UN) and the organization for Security and Cooperation in Europe (OSCE); cooperative relations with NATO in the areas of joint planning, training, and exercises, enabling the participants to engage in

---

2   "NATO's Mediterranean Dialogue & Istanbul Cooperation Initiative: Questions and Answers," *NATO Handbook* (February 18, 2005), available at http://www.nato.int/med-dial/qa.htm.

3   "A More Ambitious and Expanded Framework for the Mediterranean Dialogue," *NATO Policy Document* (July 9, 2005), available at http://www.nato.int/docu/comm/2004/06-istanbul/docu-meddial.htm.

4   "The Partnership for Peace," *NATO Topics* (December 18, 2006), available at http://www.nato.int/issues/pfp.

peacekeeping, search and rescue, and humanitarian operations; and development of forces capable of operating with those of full members of the Alliance.[5]

Thus, while PfP's aim and scope essentially involved bolstering security cooperation and enhancing interoperability between NATO members and participating partner countries, in many respects it has provided a framework for facilitating political reform in countries undergoing transitions from authoritarianism, especially in encouraging transparency in the armed forces and more extensive reform in the area of civil-military relations.[6] Moreover, PfP served as a vehicle to check Russian power in its former sphere of influence. As a result, it is no surprise that most of the former Eastern bloc nations welcomed participation in the PfP and formal contacts with NATO because they saw the Alliance as a guarantee of security against future Russian expansion. Moreover, NATO membership has also been seen as an important step towards membership in the European Union (EU).

Based on the Alliance's success with the PfP, many observers support the establishment of a similar program in an effort to engage the greater Middle East and, by extension, expand NATO's scope and presence in a region that is increasing in strategic significance.[7] However, the initial scope of the MD, and its subsequent achievements, has thus far been far more modest compared to those of the PfP Programme. Unlike the progressive scope of the PfP conditions, the key principles of the Dialogue—a non-discrimination" and "self-determination"—encourage a relaxed approach to cooperation by both parties. The MD countries select activities in which they want to be actively involved and determine their level of involvement. To date, only seven countries have signed up to participate in the Dialogue; the original five—Egypt, Israel, Mauritania, Morocco, and Tunisia—were joined by two more nations: Jordan in November 1995 and Algeria in February 2000. Consequently, cooperation between the seven Mediterranean countries and NATO was limited largely to political consultation and information exchange prior to the 9/11 attacks. Dialogue partners, for instance, participated in NATO-led seminars, conferences, and courses and observed NATO/PfP exercises. Even though military cooperation between NATO and the Dialogue members has taken place, as exemplified by Egyptian, Moroccan, and Jordanian participation in *IFOR/SFOR* and Jordanian and Moroccan involvement in KFOR, it has been outside of the Dialogue framework.

There are several reasons for the timid engagement. First, many governments in the region and Arab and Muslim public opinion more generally harbor deep suspicions of NATO's ultimate motives. In general, much of the region sees the

---

5   Ibid.

6   See *The Path to Partnership for Peace,' report of the Defense Reform Commission for Bosnia and Herzegovina* (September 23, 2005), available at http://www.ohr.int/ohr-dept/pol/drc/pdf/drc-eng.pdf; Ratchev, V., Shalamanov, V. and Tagarev, T., *Defense Sector Reform and the Challenge of Membership: Reshaping Bulgarian Armed Forces for the 21st Century*, available at http://www.iris-bg.org/publications/chapter4.pdf; Michev, O., Ratchev, V. and Lessenski, M. (2002), *Bulgaria for NATO 2002* (Sofia, Bulgaria: Institute for Regional and International Studies).

7   Cagaptay, S., "NATO's Transformative Powers: Opportunities for the Greater Middle East", *National Review,* April 2, 2004, available at http://www.nationalreview.com/comment/cagaptay200404020907.asp.

Alliance as an extension of US foreign policy rather than a multilateral coalition of independent democracies that operate through a consensus framework. Significantly, these feelings prevail even in countries with longstanding and multifaceted strategic ties to the United States, such as Egypt. This poses a problem for NATO's image because popular opinion in the region is deeply resentful of American foreign policy in the greater Middle East.[8]

In general, Arab and Muslim grievances towards American foreign policy center on three main issues: staunch US support for Israel as it continues to occupy and expand settlements on Palestinian land, the war in Iraq, and Washington's longstanding support for authoritarian regimes in the region.[9] Given this background, it is important to emphasize that many Arabs and Muslims do not differentiate between NATO and the United States, although they do distinguish between individual European members and Washington. These sentiments are further influenced by the region's experience under the colonial authority of a number of key NATO members and foreign meddling in their local politics by the superpowers during the Cold War.

While NATO membership topped the list of foreign policy priorities in most of the former communist Eastern bloc after the fall of the Soviet Union, NATO does not have this kind of pull in the Middle East. In fact, NATO does not offer the region anything comparable to the benefits of membership enjoyed by current members. Secondly, the authoritarian regimes in the region are sensitive to foreign pressures to reform. Incumbent autocrats see NATO's increasingly vocal stance on political liberalization and democratization and criticism of international human rights abuses as a threat.[10] As a result, they have no interest in selling NATO to their already skeptical publics. Therefore, unlike their East European counterparts, Arabs and Muslims know little about NATO and what it represents.

Finally, the unique political dynamics of individual Alliance members, which often diverge from each other, will present a series of obstacles that will require lengthy debates and compromises before achieving substantive results. Much of the region already maintains staunch bilateral ties with key NATO members that are mutually beneficial to all parties. Therefore, either side may not see a need for expanding relations under the auspices of NATO. The EU's interests in the region will also influence debate in NATO, especially as European Alliance members seek to balance their commitments with Brussels and the trans-Atlantic partnership.

---

8   See *Impressions of America 2004: How Arabs View America, How Arabs Learn about America,'* (Arab. American Institute and Zogby International, Online). Available at http://www.aaiusa.org/PDF/Impressions_of_America04.pdf; *Arab Attitudes Towards Political and Social Issues, Foreign Policy and the Media*, Public Opinion Poll conducted by the Anwar Sadat Chair for Peace and Development Studies at the University of Maryland and Zogby International (May 2004), available at http://www.bsos.umd.edu/SADAT/pub/Arab%20Attitudes%20Towards%20Political%20and%20Social%20Issues,%20Foreign%20Policy%20and%20the%20Media.htm.

9   See Lynch (2004), "Losing Hearts and Minds," *Foreign Affairs* 28; Marc Lynch (2003), "Taking Arabs Seriously," *Foreign Affairs* 82.

10   Khouri, R.G. (2005), "NATO Parliamentarians Engage Arab World," *The Daily Star*, November 29, 2005.

NATO and the Middle East after 9/11

The attacks of 9/11 against the United States and the growing threat of terrorism have served as a catalyst for NATO's expanded engagement in the greater Middle East on both diplomatic and military levels. NATO has realized that the radical changes in international security require that it can no longer afford to be a defensive pact limited to the Euro-Atlantic theater of operations.

The prevailing social, political, and economic conditions in the greater Middle East and the geographic proximity to Europe make it imperative that the Alliance engages the region. Despite a series of ongoing political reforms that feature greater openness and liberalization on a number of levels, authoritarian rule continues to dominate the area, albeit in varying degrees. The persistence of authoritarianism in the region has contributed to a status quo that is unsustainable and unacceptable, given the incumbent autocratic regimes' inability to address social and economic concerns and meet the basic demands of their people.[11] Moreover, regional autocrats have succeeded in rooting out secular-minded democratic opposition movements and moderate Islamists, leaving no room for a viable political opposition to emerge.[12] The Middle East also lags behind other parts of the Developing World when it comes to a number of key socioeconomic indicators. This climate is contributing to the spread of radical Islamist ideology as a vehicle of protest among the region's frustrated masses and a growing sense of instability.[13]

At this stage, NATO does not have the capacity to address the above mentioned issues substantively. However, the Alliance recognizes that instability in the Middle East poses a direct threat to security on both sides of the Atlantic. Moreover, the simmering conflicts in Iraq, Palestine, Western Sahara, Ethiopia-Eritrea, Somalia, and Sudan provide NATO with a rich "menu" for more crisis response, humanitarian, and stability operations in the greater Middle East.

Since September 11, 2001 NATO has, among other things, worked to expand the scope of the Mediterranean Dialogue, created new initiatives to engage other nations in the region, participated in counterterrorism and WMD-nonproliferation activities, launched operations in Afghanistan, trained Afghan and Iraqi security forces, and provided logistical support to The African Union Mission in the Sudan (AMIS). These activities demonstrate the Alliance's changing focus towards the greater Middle East.

---

11   Ottaway and Carothers (2004), "Think Again: Middle East Democracy", *Foreign Policy* 145.

12   Fuller (2003), *The Future of Political Islam*, New York: Palgrave Macmillan.

13   According to the UNDP, the combined GDP of the 22 Arab League countries is smaller than the GDP of Spain; about 40 percent of adult Arabs are illiterate, two-thirds of whom are women; regional unemployment might rise to 25 million if the current rate does not slow down; and 51 percent of Arab youth said they would consider emigration to other countries, primarily European. See "G-8 Greater Middle East Partnership," *Al-Hayat*, February 13, 2004, available at http://english.daralhayat.com/Spec/02-2004/Article-20040213-ac40bdaf-c0a8-01ed-004e-5e7ac897d678/story.html. These data were adopted from the 2002 and 2003 "Arab Human Development Report" by UNDP.

NATO's Enhanced Engagement of the Region

The November 2002 Prague Summit saw further transformation of the Alliance, as exemplified by the decisions to accept seven new members,[14] enhance NATO's military capabilities and create the NATO Rapid Reaction Force (NATO Response Force (NRF)), and streamline military command structure. NATO members' heads of state and government also agreed to strengthen relations with third countries by upgrading both the political and practical dimensions of the Mediterranean Dialogue. This included, among other issues, a new formula for meetings between NATO and MD countries;[15] involving the MD countries with selected activities of the Euro-Atlantic Partnership Council (EAPC)[16] and PfP; and widening and deepening of practical cooperation on all levels, ranging from education, training, and exercise through consultation on terrorism, proliferation of weapons of mass destruction (WMD), and defense reform.[17]

While the scope of the Prague agenda *vis-à-vis* the MD was impressive, its implementation lagged behind. It suffered from uneven interest on part of the MD countries, their and NATO's "lack of initiatives", insufficient funding, and problems related to the sharing of classified information.[18] The voices calling for an expanded framework were heard on both sides of the Atlantic. The proponents included many prominent figures, such as US Senators Richard Lugar and Chuck Hagel, and the then German Foreign Minister Joschka Fischer.[19] At a Summit in Istanbul that took place on June 28–29 2004, NATO leaders agreed to not only enhance the Mediterranean Dialogue into a "genuine partnership" but also to launch a new initiative—the Istanbul Cooperation Initiative (ICI)—targeted at selected countries in the greater Middle East, starting with the countries of the Gulf Cooperation Council (GCC).[20]

---

14   At the Prague Summit, Bulgaria, Estonia, Latvia, Lithuania, Romania, Slovakia, and Slovenia were invited to join the Alliance.

15   The traditional model of meetings of "19+1" and "19+7" was expanded to "19+*n*", allowing NATO to work with several MD countries on a specific project at the same time.

16   The Euro-Atlantic Partnership Council was set up in 1997 to enable political negotiations on all aspects of NATO-Partner cooperation. It meets once a month at the level of ambassadors; one a year on the level of foreign and defense ministers; and sometimes of heads of state at NATO Summits.

17   "Upgrading the Mediterranean Dialogue Including an Inventory of Possible Areas of Cooperation," *NATO Issues*, available at http://www.nato.int/med-dial/upgrading.htm.

18   Monaco, A. (February 2004), "NATO's Outreach to the Mediterranean: From Dialogue to Partnership?' in *Isis Europe 6/1*, Notes, NATO (ed.) available at http://www.isis-europe.org/ftp/download/nato%20notes%20v6n1.pdf.

19   Fiorenza, N., "A Greater NATO Role in the Greater Middle East?", *NATO Notes*, ISIS Europe 6/1, available at http://www.isis-europe.org/ftp/download/nato%20notes%20v6n1.pdf.

20   "NATO elevates Mediterranean Dialogue to a genuine partnership, launches Istanbul Cooperation Initiative," *NATO Update* (June 29, 2004), available at http://www.nato.int/docu/update/2004/06-june/e0629d.htm. The GCC includes Bahrain, Kuwait, Qatar, Oman, Saudi Arabia, and the United Arab Emirates; see http://www.gcc-sg.org/index_e.html for more information.

According to NATO, MD and ICI are "individualized, but complementary."[21] There are two main differences between the two frameworks: 1) the MD is both bilateral and multilateral; the ICI is bilateral only; and 2) the MD involves Mediterranean countries or countries directly related to the Mediterranean; the ICI is for any Middle Eastern country (including the Palestinian Authority) that is willing to subscribe to the principles of the Initiative. Nevertheless, the MD and ICI are similar in terms of practical cooperation.[22]

Most recently, NATO Secretary-General de Hoop Scheffer stressed the need for closer cooperation between NATO and the Middle East Gulf states during his visit of Doha, Qatar, on December 1, 2005 on the occasion of a conference entitled "NATO's Role in Gulf Security." The presence of Mr Scheffer at the conference marked the first time in NATO's history that a Secretary-General visited the Gulf Region.[23] It also underlined the importance of the area to NATO's strategic thinking as well as the organization's significance in the strategic thinking of the GCC.

The Alliance's interaction with the GCC is an example of NATO's success in engaging the region through effective diplomacy. Unlike other parts of the Middle East, the Alliance's overtures are met with strong support among the Council's members, who are eager to cultivate closer security ties with NATO to include multilateral military exercises and other exchanges. The GCC, which includes Saudi Arabia, Kuwait, Bahrain, Qatar, Oman, and the United Arab Emirates (UAE), has even gone as far as to call on NATO to take the lead in pressing for the elimination of nuclear weapons in the Middle East, a direct reference to Israel and, more recently, Iran.[24] The oil- and gas-rich GCC members fear the rise of Iran as a regional hegemonic force, especially as Tehran comes closer to acquiring a nuclear capability. GCC members have traditionally sought security guarantees from the United States in order to check Iranian influence. Interestingly, the GCC is now looking to enhance its security by enlisting NATO, along with the United States, as a counterbalance to Tehran.

---

21 "NATO's Mediterranean Dialogue & Istanbul Cooperation Initiative: Questions and Answers," *NATO Partnerships*, available at http://www.nato.int/med-dial/qa.htm.

22 The areas of cooperation include advice on defense reform and civil-military relations; promoting military interoperability; counterterrorism; counter-WMD; cooperation on border security to help prevent illicit trafficking of drugs, weapons, and people; disaster preparedness and civil emergency planning; training and education; and participation in NATO exercises. The ICI is designed to complement initiatives developed by other international actors operating in the region. See "Istanbul Cooperation Initiative," *NATO Policy Document*, available at http://www.nato.int/docu/comm/2004/06-istanbul/docu-cooperation.htm; "A more Ambitious and Expanded Framework for the Mediterranean Dialogue," available at http://www.nato.int/docu/comm/2004/06-istanbul/docu-meddial.htm; and "Istanbul Summit Communiqué," *Press Release* 96, June 28, 2004, available at http://www.nato.int/docu/pr/2004/p04-096e.htm.

23 See *NATO's Role in Gulf Security*, available at http://www.nato-qatar.com/security/index.php.

24 "GCC presses NATO for nuclear-free Middle East," *Agence France Presse (AFP)* (December 3, 2005).

Nevertheless, despite all the measures described above, the enhanced MD and ICI have not led, so far, to radical increase in cooperation between the Alliance and the region. Unlike the PfP Program that is directly tied to democratic requirements, the MD and the ICI do not call on the partners to implement democratic measures.[25] In this respect, the difference between the pre- and post-September 11 Mediterranean Dialogue is minimal. Once again, it all boils down to the lowest common denominator to ensure at least minimal cooperation that would allow to bridge the lack of shared strategic vision on part of the 26 NATO members on how to address the problems plaguing the Middle East while circumventing the realities in the region. NATO is aware that placing high importance on democratization would likely lead to a complete halt to cooperation on part of the Middle Eastern governments, which NATO simply cannot afford. As a result, NATO has stayed away from applying pressure on its partners in the region to speed up their political reform initiatives. To illustrate, the enhanced MD calls for mere "promoting" of democratic control of armed forces and transparency in national defense;[26] and the ICI offers assistance in security field in support of democratization efforts of other international bodies.[27]

It is important to mention, however, that practical cooperation has increased after September 11, with Operation *Active Endeavour* serving as the primary example. The Operation, directed from Allied Naval Forces South (NAFSOUTH) in Naples, Italy, aims at providing maritime surveillance and escort in the Mediterranean. Initiated on October 6, 2001, the operation has since then expanded both geographically and task-wise. It now entails escorting merchant ships from Alliance member states in the Straights of Gibraltar, which is widely recognized as an important trade route and a potential terrorist target,[28] and boarding suspect ship in accordance with international law. In March 2004, NATO enlarged the area of operation to cover all of Mediterranean. Finally, the Alliance decided to encouraged PfP Partners and Mediterranean Dialogue members to actively support the operation at the June 2004 Istanbul Summit. The operation has marked particular success in the area of intelligence sharing, with the MD partners providing the Alliance with information on suspicious shipping activities. Algeria, Israel, and Morocco have been in the forefront of countries interested in contributing to the operation.

The Istanbul Summit was crucial for NATO's further involvement in the greater Middle East also because the NATO heads of state and government reached an agreement to expand the role of the International Security Assistance Force (ISAF) in Afghanistan. NATO became involved in Afghanistan when it took command of ISAF on August 11, 2003.[29] Four months after taking command of ISAF, NATO

---

25   See "The Membership Action Plan", *NATO Handbook* (October 8, 2002), available at http://www.nato.int/docu/handbook/2001/hb030103.htm.

26   "A More Ambitious and Expanded Framework for the Mediterranean Dialogue".

27   "Istanbul Cooperation Initiative".

28   The escorts were terminated in May 2004 for the lack of requests. However, they be reactivated if needed.

29   ISAF was created in accordance with the Bonn Conference on December 6, 2001 following the fall of the Taliban regime in Afghanistan. It is mandated by UN Security Resolutions (1386, 1413, p. 1444), and 1510. It is not a UN force; rather, it is a "coalition of the willing," currently composed of 36 nations and providing about 12,000 troops. The

made another step towards greater involvement in rebuilding Afghanistan. By establishing a successful Provincial Reconstruction Team (PRT) in Kunduz province in northern Afghanistan in December 2003, NATO embarked on a gradual expansion of its presence in the country.[30] In 2004, NATO took over four more PRTs, thus contributing to improved security in nine provinces in the north of the country. The trend of expansion continued in 2005, with NATO moving into western provinces of Afghanistan. As of December 2005, NATO had command of nine PRTs and served as a security guarantor in close to 50 percent of Afghanistan's territory. Through its command of ISAF and the PRTs, NATO has also contributed to the successful completion of the first ever democratic elections into the Afghan National Assembly on September 18, 2005.

Most recently, NATO announced it would expand its mission into Southern Afghanistan in May 2006 by sending up to 6,000 additional troops into the country, thus raising the total number to some 16,000 troops and providing security to about three-quarters of Afghanistan.[31] This is a major move for NATO considering the fact that Afghanistan's south, together with its eastern part, has been experiencing an increase in insurgency, headed primarily by the Taliban.[32] It also raises several important issues: the fact that the additional troops will be Canadian and European will challenge the reluctance of most European governments to put their armies in harm's way; moreover, NATO members have so far refused to engage in counter-narcotic operations.[33] With opium being identified as the primary financial source for the insurgency, it remains to be seen how long this separation of tasks will be possible without diminishing the value of NATO's contribution to Afghanistan's security and development.[34]

---

original mission was to "assist the Islamic Republic of Afghanistan in creating a stable and secure environment in Kabul and its vicinity," at least until a country-wide parliamentary elections are carried out. See "History of the International Security Assistance Force," ISAF, September 14, 2005, available at http://www.afnorth.nato.int/ISAF/about/about_history.htm.

30   PRTs are "civilian-military partnerships" geared towards the reconstruction of Afghanistan; only the military elements of PRTs fall under ISAF command. The PRTs are to help strengthen the authority of the Afghan Government, contribute to security, and support activities geared at security sector reform. See "NATO in Afghanistan: Press Factsheet," *Topics*, available at http://www.nato.int/issues/afghanistan/050816-factsheet.htm#troop_contributions.

31   Ames, P., "NATO plans to increase its forces in Afghanistan," *Associated Press* in Boston *Globe* (December 2005), available at http://www.boston.com/news/world/europe/articles/2005/12/09/nato_plans_to_increase_its_forces_in_afghanistan/?rss_id=Boston+Globe+--+World+News..

32   To illustrate, 59 American troops and almost 1,500 Afghans have been killed in the south and east of Afghanistan between January and November 2005; the number of casualties for ISAF was one in the same time frame. See "Southward, ho!" *The Economist*, November 5–11, 2005, 47.

33   It is important to stress that Britain is the lead nation for counter-narcotics in Afghanistan.

34   Felbab-Brown, V. (2005), "Afghanistan: When Counternarcotics Undermines Counterterrorism," *The Washington Quarterly* 28/4, 55–74.

NATO and Bilateral Relations

NATO and the Middle East: Clash of Cultures?

Many observers exaggerate the cultural differences between NATO members and their counterparts in the Middle East as a stumbling block to closer ties, especially in the context of Muslim-Christian relations. However, cultural differences between individual Alliance members and their counterparts in the Middle East have not precluded multifaceted strategic partnerships on a bilateral level and in other frameworks, including international peacekeeping missions. If a clash in culture does exist, it lies in the persistence of authoritarianism that characterizes much of the region, despite widespread political liberalization, compared to the liberal democracies that comprise the Alliance. At the same time, these obstacles have not prevented NATO from engaging the former Eastern Bloc countries during their periods of transition from authoritarianism. Moreover, the Alliance also engages authoritarian regimes throughout the former Soviet Union in a number of capacities.

The stagnant social, political, and economic environment in the Arab world in particular is driving frustrated young Arabs and Muslims to leave in droves for Europe and the United States in search of a better life and a way for supporting their families in their home countries. In general, Arab migrants tend to fall into two categories: production and service sector labor and trained specialists, often with American and European degrees.[35]

Many Arabs are already fluent in English, French, and other European languages and are regularly exposed to American and European media and culture through the rapid spread of satellite television in the region, even in impoverished rural areas. Significantly, popular resentment towards US and Western policy in the region is not driving away economic migrants. This trend is likely to continue in the foreseeable future and could be used by NATO to bolster its case as a viable partner in the region.

Iraq

After much political and diplomatic wrangling, NATO agreed to assist US-led coalition forces by training and equipping the Iraqi security and armed forces. To date, NATO's involvement in Iraq is limited to a support role and there are no plans for a robust expansion. The Alliance created a Training Mission in Iraq just outside of Baghdad to train Iraqi security officials. NATO is also providing support to the 17 member nations participating in the Polish-led multinational division in Iraq.[36] The debate over NATO's involvement in Iraq not only reflects the inherent obstacles of Alliance-based institutions, but also the complexity of inter-Alliance

---

35   See Arab Inter-Parliamentary Union report on the Euro-Arab Parliamentary Dialogue (Brussels), June 20–23, 2002, available at http://www.arab-ipu.org/english/news/eurodialog.html.

36   See statement by Ambassador R. Nicholas Burns, US Ambassador to NATO, "NATO and the Greater Middle East," Brussels, May 18, 2004.

politics, namely the divergent interests and foreign policy orientations of individual member states. Although a number of NATO members, primarily the United States and Great Britain, sought a greater role for NATO in Iraq after the fall of Baghdad, the national interests of other Alliance members clashed with those of Washington and London, ultimately limiting formal NATO involvement.[37] These rifts did not preclude individual members such as Poland and Italy, among others, to join the US-led Coalition in Iraq independent of NATO.

As mentioned earlier, as far as the Middle East in general and the Arab world in particular are concerned, NATO represents an arm of US foreign policy. At the same time, some countries in the region see NATO's reluctance to agree to Washington's request for a more expansive role in Iraq as a sign that the Alliance is capable of acting independent of US foreign policy.[38] Arab countries in particular have, in varying degrees, sought a greater international role for multilateral organizations, such as the UN, EU, the OSCE, and other bodies in local affairs, especially regarding issues such as the Israel-Palestine conflict and other disputes.[39] This serves mainly as an effort to balance Washington's perceived dominance in the region. Ironically, many countries may start to see greater NATO involvement as a means to constrain American inroads into the region.

Ultimately, NATO's position on the Iraq War and its subsequent decision to support the stabilization effort mirrors that of many of Washington staunchest allies in the region who initially opposed the war in the first place but have since contributed funding and resources in areas such as training and logistics.

Iran

NATO's relationship with Iran is receiving more attention of late given the Alliance's recent involvement in Iraq and growing presence in Afghanistan. Iran's energy wealth and its influence in the strategically vital Persian Gulf and Caspian regions, coupled by its nuclear aspirations, make Tehran a key player in NATO's strategic calculus in the Middle East.

On the surface, Iran perceives NATO as a US-dominated Alliance and an extension of US foreign policy. Given the simmering tensions between Washington and Tehran, most recently due to Iran's nuclear weapons program, it is no surprise that Iran is concerned about increasing NATO involvement in the region. Tehran worries that NATO's presence in what it considers its own sphere of influence is part of a US-led strategy to encircle Iran. Iran also fears that the Alliance's presence

---

37   "NATO Divided," *The Economist*, February 12, 2003.

38   See BBC News, Report on Arab and Muslim Media Reaction to the Rift between NATO Members over the War in Iraq, "Arab press welcomes NATO split," *BBC News* (February 12, 2003), available at http://news.bbc.co.uk/1/hi/not_in_website/syndication/monitoring/media_reports/2753137.stm.

39   Per Stig Møller, H.E., Marwan Jamil Muasher, H.E., Foreign Ministers of Denmark and Jordan, "Middle East Roadmap Must Not Fail," *Alshrq Alawsat*, November 16, 2003; also see Blanche, E., "Enter NATO as Middle East peacekeeper: stationing Alliance troops between Israelis and Palestinians is an idea whose times has come," *Lebanese Daily Star*, August 25, 2003.

will grow, along with its capacity to project power, limiting its room to maneuver in the Persian Gulf. NATO has made extensive inroads along Iran's northern borders in the former Soviet Caucasus states of Armenia, Azerbaijan, and Georgia. All three countries are members of the PfP and Azerbaijan and Georgia are outspoken advocates of NATO membership.

NATO has also held talks regarding security cooperation with the GCC, which is seen in Tehran as a US and Saudi-led effort to counter Iranian power in the Persian Gulf.[40] Most importantly, NATO troops have been operating in Afghanistan and specifically in the western provinces that are directly adjacent to Iran's borders.

However, the ties between the Alliance and Tehran are far more complex and require closer examination. Although Iran is concerned about a long-term US presence in Iraq, it also worries about the ongoing instability and the potential spread of the conflict within its own borders. Iran also understands that the US-led Coalition presence in Iraq operates independently of NATO and, at the moment, the Alliance's involvement is quite modest. In fact, there are signs that Tehran, which sent observers to the Alliance's 2003 summit in Munich, is aware of NATO's complex post-Cold War transformation, leaving open the possibility for expanded security cooperation in the region. In other words, Tehran may be getting over the idea that NATO acts as an extension of US foreign policy.[41] Because Tehran enjoys longstanding ties with many key NATO members, especially in the area of trade and energy, it may start to see the Alliance as a way to constrain American influence in the region.

Relations between Iran and NATO are also affected by Tehran's relationship with the EU. Brussels has been in negotiations with Tehran over its nuclear program, under the leadership of Germany, France, and Britain (EU trio). Tehran worries that the break down of negotiations over its nuclear program will lead to a referral to the UN Security Council for possible sanctions. Nevertheless, Iran is well aware of the divergent interests among and between the EU trio and their commitments to Brussels and NATO and feels that it could effectively maneuver this divide to its advantage.

Egypt

NATO's complex relationship with Egypt is indicative of the vast array of opportunities available for forging closer ties to the Middle East. It also demonstrates the inherent obstacles preventing a stronger relationship. As the most populous Arab country, Egypt represents the political and cultural center of gravity of the Arab world. Egypt already maintains staunch political and strategic ties to the United States, Israel, and Europe and is increasingly using its regional clout to bolster its case as the leading advocate for issues affecting the Middle East. Among other things, Cairo is a vocal proponent of reforming the UN Security Council and has expressed its interest to represent the Middle East, Africa, and the greater Islamic world alongside the five

---

40   See "NATO's Evolving Role in the Middle East: The Gulf Dimension," *Conference Organized by the Southwest Asia Project at the Henry L. Stimson Center, with the Cooperation of NATO's* (Washington, DC: Public Diplomacy Division) (June 3, 2005).

41   Afrasiabi, K.L. (2004), "Iran Warms to the NATO Card," *Asia Times*, June 30.

permanent members.[42] Indeed, Egypt's prominent position makes it a vital part of NATO's strategy in the Middle East.

Despite these factors, NATO's relationship with Egypt has been problematic. The results of NATO Secretary General Jaap de Hoop Scheffer's visit to Cairo in October 2005 shed light on the scope of the issues and differences that divide the Alliance and Egypt.[43] Although Scheffer emphasized that NATO and key regional players, such as Egypt, face many of the same threats in the form of radical Islamist terrorism, transnational crime, and other security concerns, making closer cooperation beneficial for all parties, Cairo continues to harbor deep suspicions towards the Alliance. This is rooted in NATO's increasingly active role in advocating democratic reforms in its partner nations in venues such as the 2004 Istanbul summit, an issue that is very sensitive in Cairo. Although NATO is adamant that it does not plan to impose its will on its Middle East counterparts in the area of political reform, skepticism in Cairo and the rest of the region runs deep.

Egypt is critical of United States for its disapproval of the stagnant pace of political reforms and poor human rights record, all of which have gained more exposure in line with Washington's push to promote political reform and democratization in the Arab and Muslim world. Given its experience dealing with the United States on this issue, it is no surprise that Cairo is wary of the Alliance's overtures, especially as advocacy for political reform gains prominence in NATO circles.[44] Egyptian democratic opposition figures often look to Washington and Europe for support when taking on the incumbent regime. The last thing Cairo wants is to answer to NATO on related issues.

In this context, countries such as Egypt welcome NATO cooperation when it comes to collaboration in the security arena, especially in the areas of counter-terrorism, non-proliferation, and joint exercises. Cairo feels it has much to gain from and offer to NATO. And Egypt is open to the idea of increased NATO involvement in the Israel-Palestine conflict, including the possible deployment of Alliance peacekeepers to police any future peace settlement. At the same time, Egypt wants to pick and choose when and in what capacity it will cooperate with the Alliance, according to the stipulations outlined in the MD and ICI.

Israel-Palestine

NATO has historically steered clear of the conflict between the Israelis and Palestinians. Although Israel is a partner in the Mediterranean Dialogue, and the Palestinian Authority was granted observer status in Brussels, the Alliance has nevertheless treaded carefully when it came to engaging both sides. However, because of the centrality of the Israel-Palestine conflict and its implications for the

---

42   El-Ghitany, M., "Eye on the Prize," *Al-Ahram Weekly*, May 12–18, 2005, available at http://weekly.ahram.org.eg/2005/742/eg4.htm.

43   "Cairo presses NATO Chief on post-Cold War role: Alliance faces tough questions over attitude Muslim world," *Lebanese Daily Star*, October 14, 2005.

44   Zambelis, C. (2005), "The Strategic Implications of Political Liberalization and Democratization in the Middle East," *Parameters* (Autumn).

region, NATO is going to have to address the issue as it increases its involvement in the region.

Significantly, many observers suggest that NATO could provide a peacekeeping force to enforce any future settlement between the Israelis and Palestinians, possibly under UN auspices. Given the Alliance's instrumental role in peacekeeping and stability operations in the Balkans and Afghanistan, it is no surprise that NATO is being mentioned as a possible guarantor of any future peace settlement.[45]

Key regional players have long sought greater international involvement in solving the conflict between the Israelis and Palestinians. There is a consensus in the region that only the United States is capable of facilitating a lasting peace between the warring sides. However, due to Washington's staunch ties to Tel Aviv, the United States is viewed as reluctant to pressure Israel on making what are perceived as necessary concessions. The United States is also seen as an obstacle for greater international involvement to facilitate initiatives such as the Road Map. To date, international engagement, including European Alliance members acting unilaterally and under EU auspices, have borne little in the form of concrete results.

Israeli settlement expansion and the controversial construction of a 10-meter high concrete wall to separate Israelis and Palestinians continue unabated in the Occupied Territories which Palestinians and the international community envision to be part of a future independent Palestine. Palestinian attacks against Israelis and Israeli military incursions into the Occupied Territories continue to dash hopes for a lasting peace in the foreseeable future.

Arabs and Muslims in the region criticize the United States for its handling of the peace process and are convinced that that Washington is not a fair broker when it comes to negotiations between the Israelis and Palestinians. Europe, on the other hand, including key Alliance members, is seen as a potential check on US influence in the region and, by extension, Israel. Unlike the United States, key European NATO members often criticize Israel's human rights record, settlement expansion policy, and the legality of the separation wall. This dynamic is another example whereby individual Alliance members could exploit their differences with Washington in seeking a compromise, ultimately bolstering NATO's prestige in the region and paving the way for greater involvement. Significantly, a possible peacekeeping role for NATO is gaining currency in the Middle East, including influential countries such as Egypt.

The Maghreb

NATO's ties with the Maghreb, a geographic region that encompasses the North African countries of Morocco, Algeria, Tunisia, Mauritania, and Libya, are most developed in the Alliance's portfolio. Morocco, Algeria, Tunisia, and Mauritania all participate in regular military exercises with NATO members under the auspices of the Mediterranean Dialogue framework. The Alliance is also involved in supporting counter-terrorism operations and military training and exchanges through the US-

---

45   Monaco, A., "NATO Peacekeepers in the Middle East," *International Security Information Service, Europe* 3/4, April 29, 2003.

led Trans-Sahara Counter-Terrorism Initiative, formerly known as the Pan-Sahel Initiative, that includes the states of the Maghreb (minus Libya) plus Niger, Mali, Senegal, Ghana, and Nigeria.[46]

NATO's interface with the Maghreb is indicative of the diverse strategic and political outlook within the greater Middle East. Despite their common Arab and Muslim linguistic and cultural heritage in relation to other parts of the region, the states of the Maghreb are at the same time detached from the immediate issues affecting countries such as Egypt, Israel, and the Persian Gulf. Morocco, Algeria, and Tunisia maintain close ties with European Alliance members under EU auspices, which include extensive cooperation in the security arena.

The level of US engagement with the region was relatively modest prior to the September 11 attacks, since Washington considered the Maghreb to be lying outside its immediate interests and within the European sphere of influence, especially that of France and, to a lesser extent, Spain. In fact, many proponents of an EU-led security force, independent of NATO, argue for the region's integration through a formal security framework. Europe sees the oil- and gas-rich states of the Maghreb as vital to the continent's economic livelihood and a way to decrease its dependence on Persian Gulf energy sources.

The Tasks Ahead, the Resources at Hand, the Will to Advance

NATO's growing involvement in security, transition, and reconstruction operations in the greater Middle East and elsewhere have been underlined by the organization's desire to contribute to the fight against terrorism and proliferation of WMDs. This raises questions as to how the Alliance should deal with the myriad of challenges presented by such engagement. NATO has adopted several significant counterterrorism and counter-proliferation measures designed at enabling the Alliance to tackle the security threats in the post-September 11 environment. Moreover, it has taken steps to improve the military capabilities of its individual members, create mobile and well-equipped forces, and streamline its military command structure to make decisions in a more efficient manner.

Counterterrorism and Counterproliferation

Counterterrorism and counterproliferation are directly tied to the greater Middle East, since the region has served both as a source and a target of terrorist attacks. Prior to September 11, NATO accepted the threat posed by post-Cold-War security environment, characterized by such issues as illicit trade with "loose" nuclear weapons abundant in Russia and the post-Soviet republics, increased availability of chemical and biological agents, and diffusion of WMD know-how. These issues, combined with events such as Saddam Hussein's use of chemical weapons against the Kurdish minority in Iraq and North Korea and Iran's nuclear weapons programs

---

46   Koch, A., "US to bolster counter-terrorism assistance to Africa," *Jane's Defense Weekly* October 1, 2004.

were reflected in NATO forming the Senior Political-Military Group on Proliferation and the Senior Defense Group on Proliferation in 1994 in order to establish and implement an Alliance-wide policy on WMD proliferation. At the Summit in Washington in April 1999, NATO launched the Weapons of Mass Destruction Initiative (WMDI), aimed at better understanding of WMDs, improving ways of responding to them, sharing intelligence, and increasing the ability of Allied forces to operate in environment affected by WMDs. The Initiative was enhanced by the opening of the Weapons of Mass Destruction Centre at NATO Headquarters in Brussels, Belgium in 2000 with the goal of coordinating efforts related to threat assessment as well as development of responses. The Alliance made an additional step towards strengthening its contribution to security at the November 2002 Summit in Prague and the June 2004 Summit in Istanbul.

The initiatives after September 11 have reflected a joint approach towards counter-proliferation and counterterrorism, as the issues are closely connected. At Prague, the Alliance endorsed a Military Concept for Defence against Terrorism, in which NATO recognized the danger of the terrorist threat and agreed to support its members' efforts in defending their populations and critical infrastructures.[47] It also initiated a new missile defense feasibility study, aimed at better protecting NATO forces, populations, and territory.[48] Moreover, it launched the Prague Capabilities Package that served as a basis for the so-called Prague Capabilities Commitment (PCC)[49] and gave impetus for streamlining NATO's military command structure[50] and creating the NATO Response Force (NRF). Finally, NATO asserted it would need to be ready to engage terrorist groups "as and where required, as decided by the North Atlantic Council," thus allowing for out of-area operations.[51] At the Istanbul Summit, NATO agreed to, among other issues, enhanced package of anti-terrorism measures and establish the position of a Counterterrorism Technology Coordinator

---

47   In the concept, NATO determined it would carry out the following four tasks in defense against terrorism, either as a lead organization or in support of other international organizations of coalitions: antiterrorism, consequence management, counterterrorism, and military cooperation measures, with force protection being imbedded in all of them. See "NATO's military concept for defence against terrorism", International Military Staff, October 2003, available at http://www.nato.int/ims/docu/terrorism.htm.

48   "Improving Capabilities to Meet New Threats," in NATO Publications, *December 2005*, 4, available at http://www.nato.int/docu/briefing/capabilities/briefing-capabilities-e.pdf.

49   Through the PCC, Alliance members pledged to improve their capabilities to face new threats. Defense against WMD attack, strategic air and sea lift, air-to-air refueling, and combat effectiveness were some of the areas identified as needing improvement. See "Prague Summit Declaration," *NATO Press Releases* 127, November 21, 2002, available at http://www.nato.int/docu/pr/2002/p02-127e.htm.

50   In 2003, two new commands were created: an operational command, Allied Command Operations (ACO), located in Brussels, Belgium, and a functional command, Allied Command Transformation (ACT), in Norfolk, Virginia. While ACO oversees operations, ACT is tasked with continuous transformation of the Alliance. See "Improving capabilities to meet new threats," 10–11.

51   Ibid.

and created a Counterterrorism Technology Unit in order to coordinate efforts in developing new technologies.

The Alliance has also been actively involved in counterterrorism and counter-proliferation at sea, as demonstrated by Operation *Active Endeavour*. The Operation fits very well into wider non-proliferation initiatives, such as the US-led Proliferation Security Initiative (PSI), launched by President Bush in 2003 and designed to stem the flow of WMDs, their delivery systems, and related materials, be it at sea, in the air, or on land.[52] By conducting *Active Endeavour*, participating NATO nations have gained valuable skills and capabilities that contribute to counterterrorism and counter-proliferation efforts worldwide. To illustrate the scope of *Active Endeavour*, as of September 15, 2005, close to 69,000 ships had been "hailed" and 95 boarded, and 488 non-combatant vessels had been escorted through the Straits of Gibraltar.[53]

Capabilities

The expanding list of NATO's new tasks has demanded improved capabilities. In this respect, the Rapid Reaction Force is the embodiment of NATO's transformation from a static defense alliance to a dynamic peacemaking and peacekeeping organization. Launched at the Prague Summit in November 2002 and approved by Ministers of Defence in June 2003 in Brussels, the NRF is envisioned as "a highly ready and technologically advanced force made up of elite land, air, sea and special forces components that the Alliance can deploy quickly wherever needed."[54] In October 2003, it reached initial operational capability of approximately 17,000 troops in October 2004, and it is scheduled to attain full operational capability by the fall of 2006 with about 25,000 troops that will be able to deploy on a five-day notice and be self-sustaining for operations lasting 30 days and longer if resupplied.[55]

The NRF has deployed twice so far—both time for emergency relief operations. The first such deployment took place in the aftermath of Hurricane Katrina's devastating impact on the US Gulf Coast in September 2005, and it consisted of the airlift of 10 tons of supplies.[56] The second operation went much further. On October 24, the NRF arrived in Pakistan at the request of the Pakistani Government with the mission to deliver assistance to the survivors of the October 2005 earthquake in Kashmir which has claimed at least 80,000 lives and rendered some 3.5 million

52   *The Proliferation Security Initiative*, (US Department of State) (June 2004), available at http://usinfo.state.gov/products/pubs/proliferation.

53   Cesaretti, R. (2005), "Combating terrorism in the Mediterranean," *NATO Review*, Autumn, available at http://www.nato.int/docu/review/2005/issue3/english/art4.html.

54   "The NATO Response Force: At the centre of NATO transformation," *NATO Topics*, available at http://www.nato.int/issues/nrf.

55   Ibid.; See also: "The NATO Response Force: The driving force behind transformation," Federal Ministry of Defense, June 30, 2005, available at http://www.eng. bmvg.de/C1256F1200608B1B/CurrentBaseLink/N268RHS7925MMISE.

56   Hoagland, J. (2005), "A Transformative NATO," *The Washington Post*, December 4, available at http://www.washingtonpost.com/wp-dyn/content/article/2005/12/02/AR2005 120201750.html.

people homeless.[57] As of December 8, 2005, NATO has airlifted more than 3,000 tons of relief supplies to Pakistan on 150 flights.[58] Moreover, the 1,000-member contingent of NATO engineers and paramedics rebuilt roads, schools, and medical facilities, provided water-purification technology, and treated those injured during the earthquake. While both of these missions were humanitarian in nature, they have served as an example of NATO's future operations and demonstration of the potential of NFR's capability.

The NATO Chemical, Biological, Radiological and Nuclear (CBRN) battalion, created in response to the PCC and based in the Czech Republic, is yet another sign of NATO's improved capabilities. Designed to respond to a WMD attack and manage its consequences, "both inside and beyond NATO's area of responsibility," the battalion achieved its initial operational capability on December 1, 2003.[59] As with the NRF, even though the battalion has undergone only a symbolic deployment by providing protection during the 2004 Olympic Games in Greece, it offers a powerful tool of high relevance vis-à-vis the current spectrum of threats.

Conclusion

NATO's growing interest and presence in the Middle East is indicative of a larger trend rooted in the Alliance's post-Cold War transformation. This pattern will continue to influence the Alliance's outlook *vis-à-vis* the Middle East in the twenty-first century. It also demonstrates that NATO's understanding of security has changed dramatically since the end of the Cold War, as the Alliance attempts to redefine and broaden its priorities beyond the defense of Western Europe and peacekeeping in Eastern and Central Europe, and move southward towards the Middle East. The September 11 attacks instilled a sense of urgency among Alliance members regarding the need to confront a wide spectrum of threats, especially terrorism and the potential use of weapons of mass destruction on NATO territory. In doing so, NATO has acknowledged the need to adopt a more pro-active approach in how it deals with potential security threats.

At the same time, NATO does not have the capability nor the political will to implement a robust initiative designed to bolster regional political reform efforts in the Middle East. Unlike the case of the PfP participants, NATO is not in the position to call for democratization, as it cannot use the possibility of future membership within the greater Middle regional partners. Moreover, official and public opinion continues to harbor suspicions about the Alliance's ultimate motives. At the same time, this should not preclude NATO from expanding the scope of its engagement in the

---

57   "Pakistan: Thousands still without basic shelter two months after quake," *ReliefWeb* (December 9, 2005), available at http://www.reliefweb.int/rw/RWB.NSF/db900SID/EVOD-6JWHB3?OpenDocument&rc=3&emid=EQ-2005-000174-PAK..

58   These flights delivered about 16,000 tents, 500,000 blankets, close 7,000 stoves, more than 17,000 beds or mattresses, tons of medical supplies, and other items. See "NATO continues relief efforts by its mandate," *SHAPE News*, December 8, 2005, available at http://www.nato.int/shape/news/2005/12/051208b.htm.

59   Launch.

region to include more joint training and exercises, peacekeeping and humanitarian missions, and joint security initiatives with the EU and regional governments.

NATO's engagement of the greater Middle East and its operations in the region more generally demonstrate where the Alliance sees its future role. It remains to be seen, however, whether NATO members will be able to match their improved capabilities with a political consensus to allow the Alliance to become more actively involved in the region.

At this stage, the Alliance has its work cut out. The possibilities for cooperation are extensive. Among other things, NATO has a long way to go before it wins over public opinion in the region. Indeed, the popularity of the Alliance in the former Eastern Bloc was critical to its success in the PfP. If NATO hopes of replicating these results in the Middle East, it is going to have to improve its image among Arabs and Muslims. One strategy may be to become involved in helping resolve the Israel-Palestine conflict as an active participant in negotiations or as a peacekeeper charged with monitoring a future settlement.

Furthermore, there is room for expanded cooperation in other areas. For instance, the terrorist attacks in Spain in 2004 and Great Britain in 2005 on the one hand, and Morocco in 2003 and Jordan in 2005 on the other, provide ample space for more formal ties. However, individual NATO members already maintain close relations with their counterparts in the Middle East on a bilateral level, to include high-level security and intelligence cooperation and collaboration. The Alliance must provide a greater incentive for regional players to be more open to engaging NATO in a multilateral context. Without such incentives, NATO will be hard pressed in making greater inroads into the region.

Chapter 13

The United States and the Arab League

Jack Kalpakian

Before 9/11, modern United States policy towards the Middle East has been characterized by three main goals. These goals included: Middle Eastern support for the United States and its Western allies during the cold war, the unhindered flow of oil at market rates, the resilience of Arab states allied with it, and the security and well being of Israel. To some extent, these goals were contradictory and at times the United States failed to make gains in all four categories.[1] Policy in the wake of 9/11 attempted to address the shortcomings of policy the Cold War and its immediate aftermath. In a rare episode of self-criticism, US Secretary of State Condoleezza Rice acknowledged that the United States has not achieved the stability it desires in the Middle East by ignoring democracy in the region:

> We should all look to a future when every government respects the will of its citizens—because the ideal of democracy is universal. For 60 years, my country, the United States, pursued stability at the expense of democracy in this region here in the Middle East—and we achieved neither. Now, we are taking a different course. We are supporting the Second Inaugural Address: 'America will not impose our style of government on the unwilling. Our goal instead is to help others find their own voice, to attain their own freedom, and to make their own way.'[2]

The speech was part of an overall strategy called the Middle East Partnership Initiative (MEPI). While the conflict in Iraq is not a part of this program, it is particularly important to the Arab League, because it represents one of the few US initiatives that treat the region collectively. The program has had its shortcomings and is not without its faults. It represents one of the few tangible ways the United States has tried to alter the institutional culture of the region.

This paper evaluates the relationship between the Arab League and the United States. To that end, the first two chapters explain the political context of the Arab Middle East and the nature of the Arab League. The third section discusses MEPI and the Arab League's response to the program. The fourth section outlines the League's position on Iraq. The fifth and final section discusses the future of the League's relationship with the United States and includes some reflections on America's tragic entry to the Middle East and its long-term consequences for the United States and the Arab world.

---

1   Shlaim, A. (1988), "The Impact of US Policy in the Middle East," *Journal of Palestine Studies* 17/2, 15.

2   Rice, C., *Remarks at the American University in Cairo*, available at http://www.state.gov/secretary/rm/2005/48328.htm.

The basic argument expounded in this paper is that the United States does not appreciate the vast gap between its aspirations for the region and the hopes, fears and dreams of the peoples and elites of the region. Despite its numerous shortcomings, the Arab League was and remains one of the few positive institutions in the region. It did attempt to create circumstances under which it can move away from its earlier mistakes concerning Israel, despite the similarity of that effort to the legal dilemma of "un-ringing" a bell. To the extent that the League cannot accomplish the tasks it assigned itself, it will continue to disappoint both the Arab elite as well as the street, but then again, its goals are not what they are said to be. The motivating anima of the Arab League's founding were British fears of a Soviet thrust into the oil fields and the Suez Canal. The League was formed at British insistence, but the United Kingdom's erstwhile Egyptian allies did wish to compromise their hard-won autonomy if not independence. They did not want a trans-national organization to have influence on Egyptian policy, because the government in Cairo operated within a state system that lacked many of the certainties enjoyed by other regions in the world, including Latin America and South-East Asia.

The Political Environment of the Middle East

The Middle East is not known for the co-operative behavior of its states. Indeed, Stephen Walt used the region as a case study to revive neo-realism in his book *The Origin of Alliances*. Middle Eastern wars have seen the deaths of hundreds of thousands of people since 1955. Wars over territory, oil, resources, Israel's right to exist, and the assertion of one country's hegemony has taken a toll on the Middle East both materially and psychologically. Consequently, foreign policies in the Middle East have been very realistic, following certain approach to national interest definition and negotiation style. The diplomatic style of the Middle East includes three touchstones:

> 1) The rhetoric of Middle Eastern diplomacy embraces certain trans-state ideologies (the most pervasive being Arabism) that would seem to be in accord with collective security thinking at least as a normative rule, but, 2) the reality of daily diplomacy is one in which states (or, more accurately governments) act in a very Machiavellian balance-of-power fashion, and 3) that balancing always presupposes the intervention of outside powers.[3]

The basic Middle Eastern approach to diplomacy is that of a zero sum game: one country's loss is regarded as another's gain. Golda Meir, the late Israeli Prime Minister, once stated that if the Palestinians accept any peace proposals, such proposals are by definition harmful to Israel. There is also tendency to refuse discussing major or "essential" issues separately from minor, unrelated points of disagreement. In addition, there is a tendency to use fait accompli politics to secure gains perceived to be at the expense of others. Vast differences exist between Middle

---

3   Brown (1994), "The Middle East after the Cold War and the Gulf War: Systemic Change or More of the Same?" in George W. Downs (ed.), *Collective Security Beyond The Cold War*, Ann Arbor, MI: University of Michigan Press, 198.

Eastern, including Arab, states in terms of size, population, wealth, and military power; these differences create structural conditions that make friction inevitable. The largest three states, Turkey, Egypt, and Iran, have, from time to time, attempted to dominate the region. Nasser and Khomeini, for example, tried to impose their systems on the region. This lead the smaller states, such as Saudi Arabia, Israel, Syria, and Jordan, to use balancing, bandwagoning, and buffer politics. While this system superficially resembles the world of Thucydides and that of Europe between 1815 and 1914, its best historical parallel is that of Machiavelli's Italy. The overall picture is further complicated by the alliances of these states with outside powers such as the United States, the Soviet Union/Russia, and in former times Czarist Russia, Britain and France.[4]

The Arab states' jealous defense of their sovereignty is not only due to fears of losing one's autonomy and independence to one's neighbors, but it is also due to the overall lack of legitimacy suffered by many Arab states internally. In a region that was, until recently, dominated by tribal, ethnic, and communal divisions, there are two alternative loci of individual loyalty that offer alternatives to the state. At a lower level, the individual can be loyal to his or her clan, tribe, ethnic or religious community. Even in states where tribal and sub-national identities are weak, people tend to identify themselves with the towns and villages of their origin, even if they have not lived there for decades. At a higher emotional plane, Islam and Pan-Arabism provide an alternative to the state as the focus of an individual's identity. In that context, Nasser saw his effort to "unite" the Arab states under Egyptian leadership as a natural restoration of an artificially shattered Middle Eastern system. Faced with competitors for its citizens' loyalty, and challenges appealing to Islam or Pan-Arabism, the Arab state has had to assert itself in two ways: first, it had to adopt Islamic and Pan-Arabist discourse to appease its population and blunt the threat posed to its independence; second, it sought to make alliances with powerful states that can deter its regional rivals. With Israel and Palestine a part of the daily emotional lives of its populations, the list of dilemmas it faces becomes even more complex.

Nevertheless, the Arab world still reflected the Cold War. Early on, Western analysts detected the classical split in the Arab world between pro-Western states led by Saudi Arabia and pro-Soviet states then led by Egypt. Yet, there were major differences between the Soviet/United States bipolarity and the state system in the Arab world. While deterrence and limited escalation were the rule of the day between the United States and the Soviet Union, the Arab states and Israel took risks that their super-power patrons would never take under Cold War rules.[5] Wars and skirmishes between Arab states included full-scale invasions, attempts of annexation, subversion of the sovereignty of neighboring states, and failed attempts at empire-building. The League reflected all the weaknesses of the United Nations and then some. Needless to add, Israel stood as a complicating factor that could not be easily integrated into the system.

---

4   Ibid., pp. 203–207.

5   Binder, L. (1958), "The Middle East as Subordinate International System," *World Politics* 10/3, 426–9.

The Nature of the Arab League and the Centrality of the Palestinian Issue

The Arab League was created in this complex Machiavellian context. Like so many things in the Middle East, it is a direct result of British foreign policy. The League was originally championed by Britain to gain access to foreign policy in the newly independent states of the Levant and Saudi Arabia. The League's British backers envisioned it as an anti-Soviet Arab alliance led by their Arabic-speaking client— Egypt.[6] While Britain was satisfied with Egyptian leadership of the Arab League, Nahhas Pasha's Egypt feared the possible evolution of the League into the sort of federation advocated by Iraq's Nuri al-Saʿid. In 1945, Egypt was the wealthiest and the most advanced Arab state, and it feared having to give its resources and, above all, its sovereignty, such as it was under British influence, to a federative structure. Acting in a manner that can easily be ex-post facto "predicted" by any realist, Nahhas sought to weaken the Arab League as much as possible. In accordance with Egypt's demands, Article 7 of the League's pact states that "unanimous decisions shall be binding upon all member states of the League; majority decisions shall be binding only upon those states that have accepted them. In either case, the decisions of the Council shall be enforced in each member state according to its respective laws."[7] In essence, Nahhas made sure that the League cannot force Egypt or any other member state to act against its interests.

As a result of Article 7, the Arab League has not been able to prevent the dozens of inter-Arab wars that have occurred since 1945. The "aggressor," whoever that may be in any given conflict, was entitled, according to the League's pact, to disregard its decisions. Early functionalist students of the Middle East believed that the Arab League's performance against Iraq in the Kuwaiti crisis of 1961 was a reason to be hopeful.[8] A closer examination, however, reveals that they were celebrating prematurely. One reason that the League seemed to work was the unusual congruence of British and Egyptian interests.

Egypt dominated the League in the sixties. The Egyptian leader, Nasser, had reversed Nahhas' policy and sought to use the Arab League as a tool for expanding Egyptian power in the Arab world. Egypt's wealth was being eclipsed by the oil revenues of Saudi Arabia and Iraq, and Nasser's expansionist tendencies may have been fueled by a desire for oil. Unlike Egypt's Nasser, who favored an all-Arab union, the Iraqi president, Abd al-Karim Qasim, favored *watani* (local) nationalism over *qawmi* (*Pan*-Arab) nationalism. Many in the new "republican" ruling regime sympathized with the idea of unity with Nasser's Egypt, but Qasim did not want to serve Nasser. He did not want to compromise Iraq's sovereignty, a policy practiced by those who had supported union with Egypt. Britain, Kuwait's patron, found itself in a rare tacit alliance with Nasser against Qasim. While the Arab League did

---

6   Hasou (1985), *The Struggle for the Arab World: Egypt's Nasser and the Arab League*, Boston, MA: Routledge, 1–13.

7   Salafy, A. (1988), *The League of Arab States: Role and Objectives* (Washington, DC: Arab. Information Office), December, 28.

8   McDonald, R.W. (1965), *The Arab League: A Study in the Dynamics of Regional Organization*, Princeton, NJ: Princeton University Press, 234.

help end the crisis by admitting Kuwait as a member and replacing British soldiers with Egyptian peacekeepers, it was British military power, and not Arab League displeasure, that deterred Iraq from taking Kuwait in 1961.[9]

Legally, incapable of preventing inter-Arab conflict, the Arab League attempted to unite against Israel. The Joint Defense and Economic Cooperation Treaty adopted in 1948 was designed to enhance Arab power. Under Article 2 of the treaty, an act of aggression by a state (whether a member or not) against a member state of the League is considered aggression towards all members of the League. Article 6 of the treaty made Joint Defense Council decisions binding on all member states, if they are adopted by a two-thirds vote.[10] Israel acquired the role of the primary central antagonist of the Arab world. It was demonized. As Robert W. McDonald put it, "from a Westerner's point of view, it is a regrettable but indisputable fact that during most of its history the Arab League has been obsessively convinced that the only threat to peace in the Arab region comes from Israel."[11]

The August 1967 Khartoum Summit conference solidified the anti-Israeli perspective by rejecting peace, recognition and relations with Israel. But that stance did not eliminate inter-Arab disputes with regard to alliance against Israel or, for that matter, most inter-Arab fighting. The greatest failure of the Arab League was its inability to act against Saddam Hussein after he annexed Kuwait. In 2002, the League revived its efforts at un-demonizing Israel through an offer of normalization of relations in return for an Israeli withdrawal to the 1967 frontier.[12] Under the Saudi-sponsored Beirut Summit conference declaration, the Arab world would normalize its relations with Israel in return for land. Specifically, the Arab League's price for normalization of relations is the territories occupied in 1967, including East Jerusalem, the Golan Heights, the West Bank and the Gaza Strip.

The possibility of Israel to take the Saudi proposals seriously in the wake of Saudi Arabia's recent actions in relation to the Arab League's boycott of Israel is difficult to see. The economic boycott of Israel began with the independence of the Jewish state and continues in a more limited form to this day. A specialized organization, called the Arab League Boycott Office, was created to prevent trade with Israel, Israelis, and with third-country firms that engage in any kind of economic activity with Israel or Israelis—secondary and tertiary boycotts. With the signing of their respective peace treaties with Israel, Egypt and Jordan have ended their participation in the boycott. Several other Arab states have dropped the secondary and tertiary boycotts. In order to make progress in its negotiations for admission into the World Trade Organization, Saudi Arabia suggested that it no longer observed the secondary and tertiary boycotts.

---

9   Farouk-Slugett, M. and Slugett, P. (1987), *Iraq Since 1945: From Revolution to Dictatorship*, New York: KPI, 56–8.

10   Pognay, I. (1987), *The Arab League and Peacekeeping in the Lebanon*, New York: St. Martin's Press, 13–4. See also Ali Salafy, 36–7.

11   McDonald, 239.

12   Khalidi, W. (2003), "The Prospects of Peace in the Middle East," *Journal of Palestine Studies* 32/2, 60. Taylor, A.R. (1982), "The PLO in Inter-Arab Politics," *Journal of Palestine Studies* 11/2, 74. The texts of the Khartoum and Beirut declarations can be accessed online in Arabic at the Arab League's website http://www.arableagueonline.org.

But with the advent of the latest *Intifada* in 2000, Saudi Arabia began enforcing the boycott again, in probable violation of its GATT and WTO commitments.[13]

The MEPI Program

The tragicomedy of the continued boycott aside, the League was responding to the dramatically altered environment of the post-9/11 world with its offers of normalization of the relationship with Israel. The US invasion of Iraq and the growing instability in the region may have led the Arab League to make that dramatic gesture. Perhaps the same motives drove the United States towards attempting to alter the nature of both the political culture and political economy of the Arab World. The Middle East Partnership Initiative is perhaps best understood as part of a whole process of dramatically increased US engagement with the Middle East. The Bush administration signed a Free Trade Agreement with Morocco, Jordan, and Bahrain in the years following 9/11. It is currently negotiating Free Trade Agreements with the United Arab Emirates and Oman. But these initiatives are bilateral and do not reflect Arab League's involvement as a whole.[14]

The MEPI remains the only program that is designed to be pan-Arab in scope and reach. It deals with issues that are traditionally considered "low" politics by realist thinkers, and it seems to aim at no less than the transformation of Arab political culture. It is not a big-budget program but it addresses problems that the United States had not addressed since it imposed democratization and decolonization on European states. While modestly funded at about $100 million a year, the program represents an American attempt to engage Arab public directly over the heads of leaders and opinion makers. It is centered on five pillars of action: political reform, economic development, educational reform, women's equality and the "cross" pillar which establishes networks of alumni and the development of civil society.[15] The goals of each of these pillars entail profound changes in the way the Arab world has traditionally functioned.

The political pillar is also called the "Democracy" pillar in the US State Department's materials. It is perhaps the most important pillar of the MEPI program. It focuses on enlarging the political space available to parties and individuals in the Middle East by supporting elections, legal reforms, free speech and press, and the nascent Lebanese democracy. The stated goals for this pillar are:

> In the democracy pillar, MEPI programs seek to develop the institutions that are essential to active citizenries and accountable, representative government; to strengthen democratic practices, electoral systems, and civil society, including political parties; to promote the rule of law and an autonomous judiciary; and to enhance the role of an independent, professional news media.[16]

---

13   Kontorovich, E. (2003), "The Arab League Boycott and WTO Accession," *Chicago Journal of International Law* 4/2, 268–8.

14   William, H.C., *Free Trade Agreements* (CRS Report for Congress), 7.

15   Department of State, *Middle East Partnership Initiative*, available at http://mepi.state. gov/mepi.

16   Ibid.

Needless to say, this pillar represents a direct challenge to the authoritarian governments that have been the mainstay of the region. There are governments that were embarking on reforms for internal motives such as Jordan, Morocco and Yemen, but while these countries did benefit from MEPI support for their activities, they remain in the minority with most Arab states viewing program as intrusive at best. The United States is deeply mistrusted by the Arab states it regards as allies, precisely because its values differ so widely from their own. Asking the Arab world to become more democratic does, in some ways, present many Arab states with an existential threat. According to Marina Ottoway, a leading scholar at the Carnegie Endowment for International Peace, the democratization pillar may actually lead to outcomes unfavorable to the United States:

> Arab governments and commentators received the Broader Middle East Initiative badly. The opposition was not on content, but due to the fact that, first, the initiative came from the US and, second, that the Arab countries had no initial input in shaping it. The final G8 communiqué endorsing the initiative does not have much content for Arab governments to worry about, as it is simply a statement of intent. An indication that there might not be any significant follow-through is given by the fact that no G8 country has appropriated funds to support the initiative. The merit of the initiative resides in its attempt to engage the Arab world, which knows that it has to change, is concerned on how to go about this, and fears that an opening of democratic space may carry the risk of ceding power to Islamic parties. The region is also against US interference.[17]

Amre Moussa, the current Secretary-General of the Arab League, immediately set upon the proposed program, challenging even the legitimacy of its earlier name "The Greater Middle East Initiative." Referring to the Palestinian question, Moussa, subtly but clearly, indicated that he does not support the US proposals for reform in the Middle East. Responding to the same question as Ottoway, he sketches the Arab World's suspicions about the United States' proposal:

> None of us opposed proposals for renovation, change, and innovation. The opposition voiced in the region stemmed from the confusion regarding the meaning of 'greater' Middle East, and the nature of Western security concerns. When the [US proposal] first came out this was a package badly put together, of which we were informed through the press. But I don't think that the notion of change itself was rejected. I believe that reform is the tallest order of today. It should happen independently from any other consideration. Naturally, we believe that a just and fair solution for Palestine is imperative.[18]

Moussa was politely suggesting that the United States mind its own business and not force reforms at a pace that Arab League members do not want and do not welcome. At another level, it is also clear that the region's political economy and society include many factors that are not conducive to civil society and democracy in the Western pattern. The strong electoral success of movements like the Muslim Brotherhood,

---

17   "Interview with Marina Ottoway," *Shoulder to Shoulder*, Publication of the Center for Trans-Atlantic Relations, Johns Hopkins University 2/2 (July 2004), 4.

18   "Interview with Amre Moussa," *Shoulder to Shoulder*, Publication of the Center for Trans-Atlantic Relations, Johns Hopkins University 2/2 (July 2004), 3–4.

Hamas, and Hezbollah suggests that democratization will be accompanied with increasing Islamization of political life and, therefore, result in further restrictions on civil society, women and religious minorities. If fact, the problem may be deeper than a mere cultural proclivity against democratization. In the words of Lawrence Rosen, an eminent anthropologist, Western-style freedom may be seen as vices in the Arab world:

> Such moments [sic. Saddam's fall] pose exceptional dangers, since chaos, not freedom, is seen by many Arabs as the real alternative to tyranny. 'It is worse to make a man live in chaos than to kill him', goes one saying. 'Better to live in tyranny than chaos', goes another. Just as the Quran repeatedly warns against social disorder, common sense urges a person back into the game so that he can keep alive the flow of mutual indebtedness that prevents the system itself from falling to pieces.[19]

Perhaps even more threatening to the established order in the Arab world is the idea of women's equality which is an important part of MEPI's program and agenda. For better or for worse, this idea directly contradicts some of the foundations of Arab society and as a result, MEPI is not likely to meet success in this area. In the words of Lawrence Rosen:

> At such times, women may appear as a special threat to orderliness. Whether it is their irrepressible sexuality or men's vulnerability to it, to many Arab men, women, as holders of men's good opinion of themselves, threaten relationship itself by confuting particular ties. Lacking an indispensable ritual place in the practice of Islam, women nevertheless test its central requirement—the maintenance of a unified community of believers. To bind women to inferior social roles is therefore not merely to express male dominance; it is to focus on one of the central sources—along with ignorance and irreligious passion— of societal disruption.[20]

Rosen quotes a Moroccan judge who states plainly that the role of civil society is unwelcome because civil society brings a questioning of social roles and boundaries. "What we call chaos is what you call civil society."[21] Of course, non-Muslim minorities such as Jews and Christians had their assigned subsidiary social roles to which they were expected to conform. Challenges to these assigned roles implied a disruption of order—thus the Arab street's incapability of coming to terms with non-Muslim power in Palestine or elsewhere. While well-intentioned and perhaps a necessary learning process for the United States, the MEPI program needs to remain very modest in role and scope; it needs to look at dialogue between the Arab world and the United States at a societal level as one of its primary goals rather than the transformation of the Middle East into a zone of democracy. Democracy in the Middle East may be possible, but it will not have the "look and feel" of any of the democracies in the Western world. At best, it will resemble the confessional democracy that existed, and may exist today, in Lebanon.

---

19   Rosen (2005), "What we got wrong: how Arabs look at the self, their society, and their political institutions," *American Scholar* 74/1, 42–51.

20   Ibid.

21   Ibid.

Arab League's non-cooperation, if not direct opposition to MEPI, is premised on some deeply held beliefs on how to organize society and polity. The United States and its MEPI program cannot possibly begin to address these issues. The Arab world will need to undergo a deep, grass roots transformation, perhaps even a reformation. The good news in the midst of the crises in Iraq and elsewhere is that the Arab world may be undergoing the same processes today that Europe underwent before the Enlightenment.[22] To that end, MEPI may be useful in starting a conversation with the Arab world, but it should not be expected to yield the results its founders have attached to it. At one level, the Bush administration's proposals concerning MEPI and related programs, and the negative reaction they engendered, led to the adoption of some of its contents, especially those concerning human rights, development and democratization.[23]

Iraq

The normative and perceptive gaps associated with MEPI are reflected in the latest Iraqi war and the subsequent occupation of that country. Ironically, Iraqis may be the least hostile Arab population to the United States, at least with regard to the removal of their previous government, if not the occupation of their country. The lack of a nation-state at the heart of most of the populations' political allegiance and loyalty makes it very difficult for Arab states to explain their positions to their populations. Unlike other regions of the world where the state is the primary locus of political loyalty, Arab populations tend to view political conflict through the prism of identity. Ironically, it is precisely the Arab street's support for Saddam and the "resistance" that followed his regime's collapse that may have alienated many Iraqis, especially the Shiite, from the Arab world and into the waiting arms of the Iranians. Elie Podeh, a professor of Middle Eastern Studies at the Hebrew University of Jerusalem, poses that the Iraq's invasion was seen not as a war between two foreign states, but as a problem that deeply touches and influences Arabs far away from the conflict:

> The Iraqi occupation, just like the 1990-91 crisis, invigorated—if temporarily—the political Arab identity as well, deepening the existing gulf between 'we' (the Arabs) and 'them' (the West). The US expedition to Mesopotamia, as Fouad Ajami called it, resulted in conquering Iraq, demolishing its regime, and instituting another—acts reminiscent of twentieth century Western imperialism. Unable to stand to this challenge, Arab leaders and societies once more felt humiliated by their subjugation. Though most detested Saddam Hussein, Arabs sympathized in general with the Iraqi people (as well as with the Palestinians), thus creating a common ground based on a shared Arab identity.[24]

---

22   Zakaria, F. (2007), "Islam's Road to Reformation", *Newsweek,* February 12, available at http://www.msnbc.msn.com/id/16960410/site/newsweek.

23   *The Declaration of the Summit Presidency on the Work of the Committee for the Follow-Up and Implementation of the Sharm al-Shiakh Summit Decisions*, (Tunis: The Arab. League); Arab. League Summit Decisions, May 22–23, 2004, 40–59, available at http://www. arableagueonline.org/las/arabic/details_ar.jsp?art_id=2690&level_id=202#.

24   Podeh, E. (2005), "Between Stagnation and Renovation: the Arab System in the Aftermath of the Iraq War," *Middle East Review of International* Affairs 9/3, 66. Podeh cites

The Iraq War was a blow to the Arab League, because its members lacked consensus on what position to take and because the leadership of the various Arab states was seen as ineffective and irrelevant. However, the Arab League did hold a summit before the United States-led invasion of Iraq and hammered out a declaration that tried to stand against the war, while supporting the Kuwaiti demands for inspections, the return of the Kuwaiti prisoners and Iraqi adherence to United Nations resolutions concerning weapons of mass destruction.[25]

Overall, it was not a bad position to take, but it also meant that the leadership of the Arab world was facing two very difficult choices: either support the United States and risk a popular backlash or support Saddam Hussein and risk American ire. Consequently, the Arab League adopted a position that seemed to grant Kuwait its demands without approving the war. Of course, the price of this bit of indecision was that the war was bound to discredit and embarrass the Arab League's system. Yet embarrassment may have been the cheapest price to pay to find a way out of the dilemma the League faced. Arab intellectuals and public opinion did not share the above evaluation. *Pan*-Arabist scholars like Fawaz Gerges argued that the whole system is discredited beyond repair:

> The Iraqi crisis has discredited and weakened the Arab League. More important, it has shattered old myths regarding Arab solidarity and unity, the role of public opinion, and the meaning of 'Arabness." Arabs were not only deeply divided, but they, or many of them, tacitly consented to the invasion and occupation of a sister state by a foreign power. Arab rulers stand naked in the eyes of their restive people, and the latter are pointing accusatory fingers at each other for failing Iraq and Iraqis. Iraqis reproach their fellow Arabs for their silence regarding Saddam's crimes against humanity: three hundred thousand Iraqis disappeared during the twenty-four years of his rule.[26]

To Gerges' credit, he recognizes that many Iraqis have a "nuanced view" of the American invasion, deploring it but also accepting that its removal of the Baathist government was a positive aspect that could, should the current troubles be overcome, lead to an improved political atmosphere in the country, if not democracy. Unfortunately, many, if not most other Arabs, do not see the invasion through these nuanced sights. The news, as it is carried on the ultra-popular *Al Jazeera* channel, routinely depicts the United States as the aggressor, occupier and defiler of Iraq. This material is broadcast to populations suffering from widespread illiteracy and to elites feeling hopeless and marginalized in a world that seems to have had all the boundary lines broken. The results are deep antipathy towards the United States, reflected in the decisions of the Arab League which seem to often strive to shield Arab states

---

Fouad Ajami (2003), "Iraq and the Arabs' Future," *Foreign Affairs* 82/1, 2. He also refers to As'ad AbuKhalil (1992), "A New Arab Ideology? The Rejuvenation of Arab Nationalism," *Middle East Journal* 46, 22–36.

25   *Summit Decision at the Normal Level*, Arab League Summit Decisions, Sharm El Shaikh, March 1, 2003, available at http://www.arableagueonline.org/las/arabic/details_ar.jsp?art_id=3105&level_id=202.

26   Gerges, F.A. (2004), "Rudderless in the Storm," *Dissent*, available at http://www.dissentmagazine.org/article/? article=378.

from United States criticism or accountability, as with Iraq in the recent past and with Syria currently.

Fortunately for the United States, the League exists for purposes other than to antagonize it, and the League's communiqués and declarations are mainly for meeting a purpose other than politics. The Arab League is ultimately about Arab identity and not politics. As such, it can afford to be embarrassed, it can afford failure, and it cannot afford, and perhaps even be boosted by, humiliation and marginalization. Podeh captures its primary objectives in their pure unadulterated essence:

> The League has been under attack since its foundation in 1945. Yet, while celebrating its sixtieth anniversary this year, scholars, instead of announcing its demise time and again, should consider what has made the League so durable in spite of the many setbacks it has suffered. The Iraqi crisis gave a partial answer: states and leaders are still unwilling to relinquish their pan-Arab identity, which is reflected in this institution. Moreover, any foreign interference or steps perceived as attempts to replace the existing Arab order—such as the Greater Middle East Project—are bound to reinvigorate the calls for retaining—and even reforming—the existing order.[27]

Conclusion: The United State and the Arab League

Recent Arab League Summit decisions have emphasized economic development, the enlargement of Arab political space, human rights and a variety of other concerns such as an Arab common market. The politics do remain in place, and the latest significant document, the Tunis Declaration, includes the usual litany of Arab identity-driven political demands from Israel and the United States, but these demands are a far cry from the Khartoum summit's pronounced hostility to the Western world. They also indicate that at the leadership level, at least, many Arabs are now resigned to accepting and dealing with Israel as long as the Palestinian people can be allowed to form a viable state within reasonable borders. Yet, one should not regard these demands as one-sided, because they do point to the League's willingness to co-exist with other states in a world where social and political boundaries are being challenged, erased and sometimes removed altogether. To that extent, the Arab League is beginning to embark on a process of slow, gradual change that is bound to lead it towards improvement, if not clockwork predictability and efficiency.

For many American observers, it is sometimes too easy to be dismissive of the Arab state and the Arab League. The gross over-politicization of life, the human rights violations, the abuse of women, the suppression of religious and ethnic minorities, the rentier economics, the widespread corruption, and the fake elections create an array of present vices. However, few Western observers appreciate the dilemmas facing any state construction project, and by extension, a transnational project like the Arab League. At the domestic level, the Arab state confronts immense competition from local, regional and sub-national identities. It also faces the demands that an Islamic identity imposes on its citizens. The implication of this stance is that religion is placed above country, and the nation becomes a vehicle for

---

27   Podeh, 68.

the religion rather than vice versa. Very few Western states have had to deal with these pressures and demands on their citizens' allegiance and loyalty since the Treaty of Westphalia. Add to this the deeper cultural concerns with boundaries, order and chaos and a clearer picture of the true success of the Arab state and the Arab League in surviving and even carrying out some of the tasks expected of decent governments becomes increasingly obvious.

The challenge for the United States is not to lose sight of the fact the Arab states, and their Arab League based system, are very young. Morocco can claim to be the oldest, having achieved its current extent under the ruling Alawite dynasty during the Mid-seventeenth century. Of the remaining states, only Egypt has developed a strong sense of national identity. Jordan, Palestine, Syria, Iraq, and Saudi Arabia are fairly recent geographic constructs. While these states can claim the heritage of Islamic civilization, they are very recent and are bound to make all the mistakes suffered in Europe as well as in the new world. American policy towards the region must take into consideration a deep sense of patience and magnanimity, even in the face of terrorist activities like 9/11.

The alternative to the Arab state system is network of Islamist systems. Such an outcome may accompany the premature introduction of democracy to the region without having carried out the deeper cultural and social changes required to sustain it, even if it were a local form thereof. Radical Islamization will mean increased friction with the United States, more wars with Israel, and perhaps the entry of Turkey and Iran into the Arab world for defensive reasons that could evolve into a re-run of the Ottoman-Safavid wars over the region. America should also keep in mind that Westphalia was a direct result of three decades of vicious religious warfare, and it should help the Arab League as much as possible to avoid a replay of such a "reformation" in the Middle East.

Help may entail additional aid to the poorer Arab states, but it also means pushing for a final, peaceful and complete resolution of the Palestinian dispute along the lines that the Palestinian leadership can reasonably "sell" to its people. Such a development would remove a great deal of pressure from the Arab political scene and, while it will not be a panacea that will cure all the region's ills, it will improve the image of the United States in the Arab world and deprive al-Qaeda of its best recruiting sergeant. The United States will also need to develop a deeper understanding of Arab society and the role of "face," personal ties, boundaries and taboos in the formulation of political opinion. Special attention must be paid to the ways with which different interpretations of Islam compel people to take political stances that are often against their personal and national interests. This means that at some stage, Arab society must internalize Westphalia and understand its full implications. Hopefully, such internalization could take place through education instead of three decades of warfare. The Arab League can be used as a form to justify United States assistance and it can also be used as a means of helping the Arab state make the difficult transition towards modernity. Should modernity gain hold in the Arab world, 9/11 would finally be relegated to history and the death of so many people would not have been in vain.

Chapter 14

The United States and the United Nations: Partnership for Peace?

Tom Lansford

Since its creation in 1945, the United Nations has shared with the United States many of the same interests and goals in the Middle East. Both the international body and the US, the world's primary economic and military power, have sought to maintain stability and peace in the region and, at various times, to promote democracy and human rights. Although the United States was able to use the UN to legitimize various interests and goals in the immediate post-Second World War era, the increasing bipolar rivalry of the Cold War, combined with Arab nationalism, diminished the utility of the world body for successive US administrations. The UN has also served as a forum for states, particularly Arab nations to criticize US policy.

The result is that the United States has used the UN when there has been a convergence of interests. For instance, at the onset of the Cold War, the administration of Harry S. Truman used the UN to lend legitimacy to efforts to counter Soviet attempts to gain influence in Iran. The US also utilized the organization to secure recognition for Israel in 1948 and garner support for the liberation of Kuwait during the 1991 Persian Gulf War. At other times, the US has largely ignored the organization in Washington's pursuit of national goals, including containment of the Soviet Union and unilateral support for Israel. The United States has also been at odds with the UN General Assembly over the US dual containment policy toward Iran and Iraq, as well as the 2003 Iraq War. Through the often contentious relationship between the world body and the world's sole remaining superpower, the two actors have consistently cooperated on a range of initiatives and programs designed to promote peace and stability in the region.

The US, the UN and Global Interests

The United Nations was created as the result of efforts by Franklin D. Roosevelt who sought to overcome the inherent flaws of the League of Nations and create a global collective security organization that could prevent the reoccurrence of worldwide war. The UN Charter was ambitious in scope and depth, yet it was constrained by the contemporary international system. The UN's most powerful agency, the Security Council, included the five great powers of the day, China, France, Great Britain, the US, and the USSR, each of which had veto authority. Nonetheless, the UN was able to achieve consensus on and endorse a range of initiatives in the Middle East in its early years, sometimes at the expense of the great powers and, on other occasions, at their request.

Article 55 of the UN Charter pledged that the organization would "promote higher standards of living, full employment and conditions of economic and social progress and development."[1] The United Nations launched a range of development and humanitarian programs to achieve those goals. These initiatives were backed by the United States and complimented the broader efforts by the Truman administration to promote democracy and economic liberalization. Under Truman, the United States prompted the creation of a range of agencies to further these goals. For instance, the UN Technical Assistance Program was based on similar American programs and subsequently served as the basis of later United Nations agencies and efforts.[2] For Truman and other US leaders, the UN was perceived as a means to spread the principles and values of New Deal programs throughout the world.[3]

Nevertheless, as the Cold War intensified, consensus at the United Nations was more difficult to achieve. In addition, American support for Israel often created conflicts with other US interests in the region. Washington's repeated use of the veto to prevent the adoption of resolutions condemning Israel was especially controversial in the eyes of regional allies. However, the United States government regularly justified its use of the veto to create "balance" in the Security Council and General Assembly. Washington asserted that resolutions condemning Israel seldom were accompanied by measures deploying terrorism against the Jewish state.[4] General tensions between the US and the UN over issues such as America's financial contributions to the world body and efforts by Congress to link domestic interests to United Nations policies and activities, often eroded the ability of the superpower and the organization to work harmoniously. The end of the Cold War initiated the most promising era of US–UN Middle East cooperation, but that period proved to be short-lived. Differences over, and criticisms of, both the US and UN Iraq policy ushered in a new period of strain which were exacerbated by the 2003 Iraq War.

Outside of the issue of Israel (and later Iraq), US and UN interests were remarkably intertwined. Throughout the Cold War period and beyond, successive administrations sought stability in the Middle East, a goal shared in principle by the UN, in spite of the actions of individual member states. Consequently, the United States repeatedly turned to the United Nations for diplomatic support or as a forum to gain global endorsement for its actions and policies. The first such endeavor occurred over Iran at the very dawn of the Cold War; the US would make use of the UN in other cases as well. The United States also sought to engage the world body in a range of

---

1   UN, *Charter of the United Nations, San Francisco*, available at http://www.un.org/aboutun/charter/chapter9.htm.

2   Owen, D. (1959), "The United Nations Expanded Program of Technical Assistance: A Multilateral Approach," *Annals of the American Academy of Political and Social Science* 323, 26.

3   Ekbladh, D. (2006), "From Consensus to Crisis," in Francis Fukuyama (ed.), *Nation-Building: Beyond Afghanistan and Iraq*, Baltimore: Johns Hopkins University Press, 22.

4   "US Opposition to Measures Condemning Israel," *The American Journal of International Law*, **98**(3), July (2004), 591.

peacekeeping missions in the Middle East. The very first UN peacekeeping mission, the UN Truce Supervision Organization (UNTSO), was deployed to the Middle East in 1948. Later, the United States endorsed United Nations operations as a means to avoid deployment of American forces, especially in light of the experiences of US participation in UN peacekeeping operations in the region, such as Lebanon in the 1980s.

UN agencies undertake a range of humanitarian missions that contribute to regional peace and stability. The world body operates disease prevention programs, economic development enterprises, and education initiatives. Although the United States subsidizes these programs through its annual dues, the benefits for Washington far exceed the payments. The US contributes a portion of the costs, but gains the full advantages of UN actions. Nonetheless, corruption, fraud and inefficiency in some programs resulted in varying degrees of criticism by American officials and a series of congressional investigations.

Washington, New York, and the Birth of the Cold War

For the United States, the end of the Second World War did not translate into the desired reduction in global tensions. Truman noted later in his memoirs that the "surrender of the Axis powers did not bring any relaxation or rest for our people."[5] Instead, the country found itself locked into a new global conflict with the Soviet Union. The resultant Cold War may have had its roots in the division of Europe between East and West blocs, but the early potentially explosive crises occurred in the Middle East. The 1947 Truman Doctrine provided more than $430 million in military and economic aid to Greece and Turkey, combating Soviet influence in Europe and the Middle East. Meanwhile, during the Second World War, but reflecting the Cold War divisions in Europe, Iran was divided into a Soviet zone in the north, an autonomous region in the central, and an area controlled by the US and the British in the south. When the Second World War ended, the British and Americans withdrew, but the Soviets stayed and supported separatist movements in an attempt to create pro-Moscow states from Iranian territory. Tehran sought assistance from the United States in regaining control over its northern regions.

Truman suggested the Iranians take their grievance to the UN in an early test of the effectiveness of the world body in countering Soviet expansion. With US backing, Iran appealed to the UN for assistance in resolving the conflict. In January 1946, the second resolution adopted by the new UN Security Council called for a negotiated withdrawal of Soviet forces from northern Iran by March 19. The Security Council subsequently adopted two other resolutions demanding the departure of Soviet troops.[6] To reinforce the seriousness of the US in supporting the resolutions,

---

5   Truman, H.S. (1965), *Memoirs, Years of Trial and Hope, 1946–1952*, New York: Signet, 134.

6   The Soviet representative was absent and, therefore, unable to veto second of these measures (UN Security Council Resolution 5) which on May 8, 1946 declared that the body would enact "further proceedings" against the Kremlin if Soviet troops were not withdrawn; United Nations. Security Council Resolution 5, May 8, 1946.

Truman ordered Secretary of States James F. Byrnes to "send a message to Stalin 'if he doesn't get out we'll move in'."[7] The president also dispatched American forces to the region. In April 1946, Iran and the Soviet Union signed an oil agreement and in May, all Soviet forces were withdrawn.

The incident contributed to the growing mistrust between the US and the Soviet Union.[8] In addition, US support for Iran solidified an alliance that would remain in place until 1979. The use of the UN to counter Soviet expansionism provided legitimacy to US actions and ensured global support for Washington's goals and interests. The Truman administration would continue to utilize the world body to enhance diplomatic backing for its initiatives, as would other US administrations. Nor was the US alone in efforts to use the UN to resolve conflicts in the region.

The Creation of Israel

In the aftermath of the Second World War, fighting between Arabs and Jews in the British colony of Palestine led London to turn to the United Nations for assistance in developing a settlement. The British sought a UN recommendation to serve as the basis for a lasting peace agreement, including the creation of a Jewish state. Truman endorsed the British attempt to utilize the world body to resolve the crisis and insisted on a Jewish state. The US backed a UN proposal to create two states, Israel with 57 percent of the territory and Palestine with 43 percent (along with UN oversight and administration of Jerusalem). The US understood that the UN proposal would not necessarily end fighting in the area. Truman wrote that he was "fully aware of the Arabs" hostility to Jewish settlement in Palestine.'[9] However, he believed that the proposal was the most practical solution for the region. Truman also faced significant domestic pressure for American support for a Jewish state. Truman wrote in his memoirs that "The White House, too, was subjected to a constant barrage. I do not think I ever had as much pressure and propaganda aimed at the White House as I had in this instance. The persistence of a few of the extreme Zionist leaders—actuated by political motives and engaging in political threats—disturbed and annoyed me."[10]

The Truman administration launched a broad diplomatic campaign to garner international support for the UN plan, applied pressure and offered incentives to allies in Europe and the Middle East. Undersecretary of State Sumner Welles subsequently described the US diplomatic initiative:

> By direct order of the White House every form of pressure, direct and indirect, was brought to bear by American officials upon those countries outside of the Moslem world that were known to be either uncertain or opposed to partition. Representatives or intermediaries

---

7   Truman, H.S., "Interview Summary: Foreign Policy Notes on Marshall Plan, Iran and Western Union", Memoir Files, Truman Presidential Library.

8   Philipp Rosenberg (1979), "The Cheshire Ultimatum: Truman's Message to Stalin in the 1946 Azerbaijan Crisis," *The Journal of Politics* 41/3, 937.

9   Truman, *Memoirs*, 133.

10   Ibid., p. 158.

were employed by the White House to make sure that the necessary majority would at length be secured.[11]

The General Assembly passed the two-state solution proposal on a vote of 33 in favor and 13 opposed. However, on May 14 1948, when the British withdrew, Truman immediately granted diplomatic recognition to Israel, without the corresponding Arab state. He imposed an arms embargo on Israel and the surrounding Arab states. As Loy Henderson, chief of Near Eastern and African Affairs at the State Department noted, without a prohibition on US arms sales to the region, "the Arabs might use arms of US origin against Jews, or Jews might use them against Arabs. In either case, we would be subject to bitter recrimination."[12] Truman removed the embargo on August 4, 1949, after Israel signed armistice agreements with the Arab states involved in its independence struggle.

US support for Israel gained the country a lasting ally in the region, but significantly undermined relations with Arab states (although tensions were ameliorated over time and following the enunciation of the Eisenhower Doctrine, combined with US pressure for the withdrawal of Anglo-French-Israeli forces during the 1956 Suez Crisis). For the UN, management of the Arab–Israeli conflict provided one of the greatest continuing tests of the world body and a recurring source of tension with the United States.

Israel, US Policy and the UN Veto

United States attempts to mediate the Arab–Israeli conflict during the Cold War were generally opposed by the Soviet Union which sought to capitalize on strife in the Middle East in order to undermine Anglo-American primacy in the region. As a result, the Soviets supported the Arab nationalist movements throughout the area, while the US was seen as the endorsing the status quo, including Israel and the Middle East's monarchical regimes. Jerome Slater notes that Washington's mistrust of the Kremlin, led successive US administrations to perceive that "Soviet ambitions were antithetical to the prospects for a settlement of the conflict that would protect the legitimate security interests of Israel, America's principal regional ally."[13] One result was that American peace efforts usually were unilateral. Washington, in fact, rejected a series of proposals by the Soviet Union for superpower disengagement from the Middle East even though the Soviets began to tie arms transfers to states such as Egypt to a political settlement.[14] US mistrust of the USSR was reinforced by Soviet vetoes of early peace or multilateral initiatives.

---

11   Welles, S. (1948), *We Need Not Fail*, Boston: Houghton Mifflin, 63.

12   Henderson, L. (1971), "The Near East, South Asia, and Africa," *Foreign Relations of the United States, 1947*, 5/2, Washington, D.C.: GPO, 1249.

13   Slater argues that US policy was actually based on misperception and that the Soviets equally sought a resolution of the conflict. From the late 1960s onward, he contends that the USSR wanted peace and stability in order to prevent a conflict in the region from escalating into an international war; Slater (1990/91), "The Superpowers and an Arab–Israeli Political Settlement: The Cold War Years," *Political Science Quarterly* 105/4, 557.

14   Ibid., p. 568.

The main consequence was that the US typically worked outside of the framework of the UN to resolve regional disputes. The main exception to this trend was UN Security Council Resolution 242, enacted in November 1967. The Resolution was the culmination of a series of negotiations between the US and the USSR which established the broad outlines of the measure prior to its introduction before the Security Council. The Resolution called for the Israeli withdrawal from territories captured in the 1967 war, in exchange for formal peace agreements with the Arab states. Both Israel and the Arab states rejected most of the Resolution, although both sides used portions of the Resolution to justify their respective positions. The United States subsequently rejected Soviet proposals based on Israeli withdrawal and the creation of demilitarized zones since the initiatives did not provide guarantees for lasting Israeli security.

From the 1970s onward, the United States was increasingly on the defensive in the United Nations as Washington was forced to veto, or threaten to veto, successive resolutions by the Security Council, General Assembly and other UN bodies condemning Israel. In 1992, the US issued a veto in the UN to block a resolution condemning Israeli attacks on Syria and Lebanon following the massacre of Israeli athletes at the Munich Olympics. The veto was cast by then US Ambassador to the UN (and future president), George H. W. Bush who criticized the measure for failing to condemn terrorism. In explaining the rationale for his vote, Bush declared that "We [the US] are implementing a new policy that is much broader than that of the question of Israel and the Jews. What is involved is the problem of terrorism, a matter that goes right to the heart of our civilized life."[15] Hence, the Nixon administration and later US governments, adopted the stance that the use of the veto was justified as a means to balance anti-Israeli measures that did not also criticize or call for an end to terrorist action against the Jewish state.

Between 1972 and 1997, the US vetoed or otherwise blocked 32 resolutions pertaining to Israel. From 1998 to 2006, there were additional nine vetoes. In 27 of the measures, the United States was the only country to vote against the resolution, although some states abstained in various cases. In 1982, alone, the US vetoed six separate resolutions pertaining to Israel, including individual resolutions sponsored by France, Spain and the Soviet Union, respectively, on the Israeli invasion of South Lebanon. Between 1990 and 1995, the US temporarily reversed its position. As part of the broader effort to gain and maintain consensus among the anti-Iraq coalition, America joined other UN members in six resolutions condemning Israeli action against the Palestinians. For instance, Resolution 672 (October 12, 1990): "2) Condemns especially the acts of violence committed by the Israeli security forces resulting in injuries and loss of human life; and 3) calls upon Israel, the occupying Power, to abide scrupulously by its legal obligations and responsibilities under the Fourth Geneva Convention, which is applicable to all the territories occupied by Israel since 1967."[16] However, the US also ensured that the measure declared

---

15   Alden, R. (1972), "Policy Shift by US at UN," *The New York Times*, September 12, **10**.

16   United Nations, Security Council, Resolution 672, New York, October 12, 1990, available at http://www.un.org/Docs/scres/1990/scres90.htm.

that any "just and lasting solution" to the conflict could only be achieved "through an active negotiating process which takes into account the right to security for all States in the region, including Israel, as well as the legitimate political rights of the Palestinian people."[17] In 1995, the Clinton administration restored previous US policy and began again shielding Israel from Security Council measures with two more vetoes, followed by nine in the Bush administration. For instance, in opposing a March 25, 2004 measure that condemned an Israeli attack on Hamas leaders, the US officially declared that the Security Council resolution was "silent about the terrorist atrocities committed by Hamas; because it [the resolution] does not reflect the realities of the conflict in the Middle East; and because it will not further the goals of peace and security in the region."[18]

The United States has also frequently criticized the relative ease with which Arab states are able to garner support for anti-Israeli measures, while efforts to fashion resolutions condemning terrorism in the Middle East are rare. In October 2003, a suicide bomber killed 19 at a restaurant in Haifa, Israel. The UN Security Council refused to debate a measure condemning the attack. However, when the Israelis launched a military strike in response, the Council took the unusual step of meeting on a Sunday (which also happened to be Yom Kippur, the Jewish holy day) to consider a Syrian measure to criticize Tel Aviv. Israeli UN Ambassador Daniel Gillerman summarized the incident in the following manner: "The mere fact that Syria, which everybody recognizes as one of the main perpetuators of terror in the world, can get fourteen other members of the Security Council to disrupt their holiday, to hold a meeting on the holiest of the Jewish holidays, is another manifestation of the terrible hypocrisy at the UN."[19] Many domestic critics in the United States point to such episodes as evidence of an anti-Israeli, and by extension, and an anti-US bias at the world body. Conservative correspondent and pundit Eric Shawn summed up the anti-UN Middle East position among Americans in the following way: "The United Nations, by permitting itself to be used as a platform by terrorists and terrorist-supporting states-inadvertently-tacitly condones their goals while officially condemning their methods."[20] Nonetheless, Arab states and even America's allies have criticized the United States for hypocrisy for not taking stronger action to punish Israel following incidents such as the massacres at the Sabra and Shatila refugee camps in which hundreds of Palestinians were killed by pro-Israeli militia groups during the 1982 invasion of Lebanon.[21]

---

17   Ibid.

18   *Explanation of the Position by Ambassador John D. Negroponte, US Representative to the United Nations, on the Situation in the Middle East, Including the Palestinian Question, in the Security Council*, (New York: U S Office of the UN Ambassador) (March 24, 2004).

19   Quoted in Shawn, E. (2006), *The UN Exposed: How the United Nations Sabotages America's Security and Fails the World*, New York: Sentinel Books, 18.

20   Ibid., p. 19.

21   Even in the official investigation of the massacres by Tel Aviv, the government conceded that the Israeli Defense Forces were "indirectly responsible" for the attacks and that the military failed to control the actions of its Lebanese allies operating in areas under Israeli control; Israel, *Report of the Commission of Inquiry into the Events at the Refugee Camps in Beirut*, February 8, 1983, available at http://www.mfa.gov.il/MFA/Foreign%20Relations/

The US position on UN measures toward Israel has undermined the perception of Washington as an "honest broker" in the efforts to settle the Arab–Israeli conflict and created a perception of bias among Arabs in the region. For example, Saudi Foreign Minister Prince Saud Faisal contended in 2004, that the US has a "bias toward Israel" and that "the Arab peoples cannot fathom why these guarantees are transformed into unrestricted backing of unrestrained Israeli policies contrary to international legality."[22] American actions have further alienated some within the bureaucracy of the UN because of US support of Israel despite attacks on United Nations positions in Lebanon in 1982 and 2006. US Vetoes also sparked retaliatory action. For example, following a November 2006 US veto of Security Council action against Israel for a military incursion into Gaza following a suicide bombing, Arab governments ended their support for a financial embargo on the Hamas-led government of the Palestinian National Authority. Then US Ambassador to the UN, John Bolton, stated that the resolution was "biased against Israel and politically motivated" and that it did "not display an even-handed characterization of the recent events in Gaza, nor does it advance the cause of Israeli-Palestinian peace to which we aspire and for which we are working assiduously."[23] Nonetheless, American actions to protect Israel at the world body reaffirm the special relationship of the two countries. The US position also routinely provides political cover for states such as Australia, Japan, Germany the United Kingdom, and a range of other European states which routinely abstain from votes against Israel and rely on the United States to defeat the measure without these countries being forced to vote "no." For instance, since 1983, the UK has abstained from 14 anti-Israeli measures, while Denmark abstained from six votes during two terms on the Council, and Australia, Germany had four abstentions each.

The End of the Cold War and the Persian Gulf War

In the waning days of the Cold War, the United States sought to utilize the United Nations to a degree unmatched since the early period of the organization. The demise of the Soviet Union seemed to usher in a period of potential great power collaboration, free from the rivalries that marked the bipolar world. Furthermore, states that had previously voted in compliance with Moscow, ranging from the Czech Republic, to Hungary, to Poland, now backed the United States on many initiatives. For instance, on the Palestinian question, columnist Thomas Friedman summed up the transition in this manner: "Since 1948, the Palestinians had been able to count on the Soviet Union, its Eastern Bloc allies, and the Third World to support virtually any position

Israels%20Foreign%20Relations%20since%201947/1982-1984/104%20Report%20of%20th e%20Commission%20of%20Inquiry%20into%20the%20e.

22   Quoted in Kessler, G. (2004), "Arab Officials Criticize US Support of Israel," *Washington Post*, December 11, 2004, available at http://www.washingtonpost.com/wp-dyn/ articles/A57342-2004Dec11.html.

23   "Arabs Lift Blockade of Palestinians in Response to US Veto," *USA Today*, November 12, 2006, available at http://www.usatoday.com/news/world/2006-11-11-resolution-israel_ x.htm?csp=24.

they put forward at the United Nations, whether it was that Zionism equaled racism or that the world was flat. They had an automatic majority in the General Assembly for isolating Israel."[24] This majority was broken apart by the end of the Cold War.

The 1991 Persian Gulf War was the first test of the post-Cold War order in the Middle East. The conflict also marked the high point of international cooperation in the region. In response to the August invasion of Kuwait by Iraq, the United States was able to secure quick action at the United Nations. In Resolution 660, the UN Security Council voted 14–0 to condemn the invasion and order an immediate Iraqi withdrawal.[25] In his memoirs, future US Secretary of State Colin Powell noted that the invasion was not dealt with "as another East-West confrontation, with the Soviet Union willy-nilly lining up behind its onetime friend Saddam."[26] The Bush administration launched a diplomatic offensive to gain global support for military action against the Saddam regime. With this stance, Washington effectively utilized the world body to legitimize its policy objectives.

As the grand coalition developed, the Bush administration dispatched officials around the world to bargain with various leaders and governments. As aforementioned, Washington was willing to compromise on UN resolutions toward Israel in order to secure good will among Arab capitals. In addition, the administration offered financial incentives for coalition members. For instance, in September 1990, the US announced that it would forgive Egypt's $7 billion debt.[27] The US was also able to garner financial backing for military action from Arab states such as Saudi Arabia and Kuwait, as well as countries such as Germany and Japan.[28] The US also compromised in the series of resolutions which followed UNSCR 660. Most importantly, the Bush administration compromised on the language of the resolution authorizing the use of force. Secretary of State James A. Baker, III, initially proposed a measure that included the precise phrase "the use of force" in the case of Iraqi non-compliance. However, the US conceded on the phraseology of the resolution and included one final opportunity for Saddam to withdraw. The resulting resolution ordered the Iraqi regime to "comply fully with resolution 660 (1990) and all subsequent relevant resolutions," and stated that the Council "decides, while maintaining all its decisions, to allow Iraq one final opportunity, as a pause of goodwill, to do so."[29] Resolution

---

24 Friedman, T. (1995), *From Beirut to Jerusalem*, New York: Anchor Books, 533.

25 The language of the Resolution was direct. In the measure, the Security Council specifically ordered "that Iraq withdraw immediately and unconditionally all of its forces to the positions in which they were located on 1 August 1990"; UN, Security Council Resolution 660, S/RES/660, August 2, 1990.

26 Powell, C. with Persico, J.E. (1995), *My American Journey*, New York: Random House, 463.

27 Tyler, P.E. (1990), "Bush to Forgive $7.1 Billion Egypt Owes for Military Aid," *Washington Post*, September 1; Claiborne, W. (1990), "Mubarak Sets Summit, Seeks All Arab Force," *Washington Post*, August 9, 1990.

28 See Riding, A. (1990), "US Officials Begin Tour to Seek Financial Backing for Gulf Force," *The New York Times*, September 5; Tyler, P. and Hoffmann, D. (1990), "US Asking Allies to Share the Costs," *Washington Post*, August 30; "Making 'Em Pay", *The Economist* (January 26, 1991), **18**.

29 UN, Security Council Resolution, 678, S/RES/678 (November 29 1990).

678, passed on November 29, 1990, allowed Saddam to meet all of the clauses by January 15, 1991. Otherwise, the Council authorized "all necessary means to uphold and implement resolution 660."[30] Twelve members of the Security Council voted to support the resolution (Cuba voted against it and China abstained).

The US was also able to rebuff an effort by Saddam to link withdrawal of his forces from Kuwait to the removal of Syrian and Israeli troops from Lebanon, as well as the withdrawal of Israeli forces from the West Bank and Gaza. The result of US efforts was, as Gary G. Sick and Lawrence G. Potter point out, the "largest and most capable international military coalition in a generation" that included troops, ships or aircraft from more than 60 nations.[31] The coalition provided more than 200,000 ground troops, from 26 countries, including 50,000 forces from Arab states such as Egypt, Syria, and the United Arab Emirates. Military operations commenced on January 17, 1991 and ceased on February 27. Arab states and entities that did not support the coalition, such as the Palestine Liberation Organization and Jordan, were marginalized in the aftermath of the liberation of Kuwait.

Over the next few years, the US continued to utilize the UN to pursue national interests in the Middle East. For example, in November 1975, the UN General Assembly enacted Resolution 3,379 that declared Zionism to be "a form of racism and racial discrimination."[32] The vote was 72 in favor, 35 opposed and 35 abstentions. However, in December 1991, the Assembly rescinded the measure with Resolution 4,686 on a vote of 111 in favor, 12 opposed and 13 abstentions. The US also maintained the coalition to carry a series of resolutions supporting the sanctions regime on Iraq, as well as the creation and maintenance of the Northern and Southern no-fly zones in the country. The international sanctions formed the core of the US containment strategy toward Iraq.

The 2003 Iraq War and the UN

While the Persian Gulf War demonstrated the utility of US–UN cooperation in regional security, the 2003 Iraq War created deep rifts between the world's superpower and the world body. The administration of George W. Bush initially followed the model of his father in attempting to fashion a broad coalition. On September 12, 2002, Bush even spoke before the United Nations in an effort to garner support for military action against Saddam.[33] Initially, Bush's efforts achieved tangible results. The UN Security Council adopted Resolution 1441 on November 8, 2002. The measure declared that Iraq "has been and remains in material breach of its obligations under relevant resolutions ... in particular through Iraq's failure to cooperate with United

---

30   Ibid.

31   Sick, G.G. and Potter L.G. (1997), "Introduction," in Gary G. Sick and Lawrence G. Potter (eds), *The Persian Gulf at the Millennium: Essays in Politics, Economy, Security, and Religion*, New York: St. Martin's, 1.

32   UN, General Assembly, Resolution 3379, New York, November 10, 1975.

33   Powell was instrumental in convincing Bush to speak before the world body; Woodward, B. (2002), *Bush At War*, New York: Simon and Schuster, 334.

Nations inspectors."[34] The Resolution also stated that Iraq would "face serious consequences as a result of its continued violations of its obligations."[35] The measure passed unanimously.

However, the administration proved unwilling to make the concessions and compromises that had marked the earlier grand coalition. Many of the memberstates that voted for 1441 assumed that another resolution would be necessary to authorize the use of force, as 678 had done in the Persian Gulf War. US-led efforts to craft a second measure were met by resistance from Russia and traditional American allies, France and Germany. When agreement on a resolution specifically endorsing force failed, the US declared that it did not need another measure, but instead could act under 1441 and in the face of Iraqi non-compliance with previous measures. The Bush administration also criticized the opponents of military action, especially the growing economic ties between Iraq and France, China, Egypt and Russia (Iraq's main trade partners in 2002).[36]

The US led a smaller coalition of allies in the Iraq War which began in March 2003. Washington was charged with unilateralism and ignoring the United Nations. The inability of the world body to prevent, or at least constrain the US, undermined the standing of the UN. It also confirmed the inability of the organization to prevent action by the great powers of the day. Nonetheless, in the aftermath of the invasion and the overthrow of the Saddam regime, the US successfully gained UN endorsement on a range of issues. For instance, in May 2003, in Resolution 1483, the Security Council recognized the United States as the occupying power and ended sanctions on Iraq, as well as resuming UN operations in the country. It also appointed a special representative to Iraq to oversee UN assistance programs. In 1483, the UN also authorized the transfer of funds from the oil-for-food program that had operated during the sanctions period to the interim Iraqi Government. However, following the attacks on the UN headquarters in Baghdad in August 2003 (which killed the UN special representative, Sergio Vieira de Mello and 16 others) the UN reduced its presence in Iraq but continued to provide limited humanitarian funds, medical support and technical assistance.[37] The UN has resisted repeated calls from the United States to increase its presence in Iraq.

Relations between Washington and New York deteriorated in the aftermath of comments by UN Secretary General Kofi Annan on the US-led invasion and revelations of corruption in the oil-for-food program. For instance, in 2004, in an interview with the BBC, Annan described the invasion as "illegal" on the eve of US presidential elections.[38] In 2006, Annan followed his comments with an assertion that life for average Iraqis was much better under Saddam, a suggestion bitterly

34   UN, Security Council, *Resolution*, 1441, New York, November 8, 1991.

35   Ibid.

36   Post, J.M. and Baram, A. (2002), "Saddam is Iraq: Iraq is Saddam," *Counterproliferation Papers: Future Warfare Series* 17, 57.

37   For an overview of UN activities in Iraq, see "UN–Iraq Humanitarian Update, August 2005," August 2005, available at https://www2582.ssldomain.com/uniraq/documents/HU%20August%202005.pdf.

38   "Iraq War was Illegal, says Annan," *BBC* (September 16, 2004), available at http://news.bbc.co.uk/1/hi/world/middle_east/3661134.stm.

denounced by Iraqi leaders, especially in the Kurd and Shiite communities.[39] In response, Iraqi National Security Adviser Mouwaffaq al-Rubaie declared: "Doesn't Kofi Annan differentiate between the mass killing of Iraqis by the security and intelligence apparatus of Saddam Hussein and the present indiscriminate killings of civilians, Iraqi civilians, by the al-Qaeda terrorists in Iraq" and questioned the failure of the UN to support efforts to end sectarian violence in Iraq and fight terrorist groups.[40] Many US officials assert that Annan's departure at the end of his term in May 2006 could lead to improvements in US–UN relations.

Peacekeeping and Conflict Resolution

While Washington's Israel policy has created rifts with the Security Council and other UN bodies, the United States and the United Nations have a long, although often complicated, history of collaboration and cooperation on peacekeeping missions. The UN peacekeeping missions were initiated, as Laura Neack points out, as a means to avoid the "political deadlock between the USA and the USSR in the Security Council while allowing the UN to fulfil its charter obligations regarding the maintenance of international peace."[41] Key to the success of UN mission was the principle of neutrality. UN peace missions could not be perceived as favoring one or another side in a conflict, and participants in peacekeeping missions were not supposed to pursue unilateral interests. The UN peacekeeping operations in the Middle East, although often maligned by combatants, have generally followed these principals. However, the line between UN peacekeeping missions and UN sanctioned operations has sometimes been hazy and led to criticism of the world body. For instance, following the 1991 Persian Gulf War, the UN authorized the deployment of a multilateral force to enforce no-fly zones over northern and southern Iraq. Led by the United States, the forces deployed in Operations Northern and Southern Watch did "not wear the blue helmet of the UN"—the missions were not formal UN peacekeeping missions.[42] However, the tendency for the media and common citizens to confuse formal UN missions with UN-authorized operations has led to criticism of the world body and charges that efforts such as Northern and Southern Watch were simply extensions of US foreign policy, legitimized by the UN.[43]

Despite tensions over Iraq, the US repeatedly turned to the UN to take the lead in peacekeeping and conflict resolution in the Middle East. The world body also served as a means to pursue US objectives in a multilateral forum. For instance, in 2004, in Resolution 1559, the Security Council called for the withdrawal of all Syrian forces from Lebanon and the dismantling of militia groups. The UN also endorsed free and

---

39   "Annan: Iraq Was Safer Under Saddam," *Guardian Unlimited*, December 4, 2006, available at http://www.guardian.co.uk/Iraq/Story/0,,1963612,00.html?=rss.

40   Ibid.

41   Neack, L. (1995), 'UN Peace-Keeping: In the Interest of Community or Self?' *Journal of Peace Research* 32/2, 182.

42   Ibid.

43   Ibid.

open presidential elections.[44] Syria subsequently withdrew its 20,000 troops from Lebanon in 2005. The US also turned to the UN to manage the investigation of the assassination of former Prime Minister, and outspoken critic of Syria, Rafik Hariri on February 14, 2005. The world body created the UN International Independent Investigation Commission (UNIIIC) through Resolution 1595 (2005)[45] which implicated Syrian intelligence in the attack.

The UN was also instrumental in ending the Hizbollah-Israeli conflict in Lebanon in 2006. Israel invaded southern Lebanon in July 2006 in response to the capture of two Israeli soldiers and attacks by Katyusha rockets. On July 18, Annan called for the creation and deployment of a peacekeeping force to end the conflict. US, European and Arab leaders met intermittently over the next months to craft a solution. One faction, led by France, sought the withdrawal of Israeli forces and the restoration of Lebanese sovereignty, while the other faction, led by the US, supported an Israeli withdrawal only in conjunction with the disarmament of Hizbollah and other militia groups. On August 11, the US and France reached agreement on a draft resolution which called for the end to hostilities and the deployment of UN peacekeeping troops. The resultant measure, Resolution 1701, was adopted unanimously by the 15-member Security Council. The UN agreed to create a 15,000-troop peacekeeping force and ban the transfer of arms or weapons to nongovernmental militias. The Resolution also established a buffer zone between the combatants. The UN force was charged "to ensure that its area of operations is not utilized for hostile activities of any kind, to resist attempts by forceful means to prevent it from discharging its duties under the mandate of the Security Council."[46] The example of Lebanon in 2006 demonstrated the utility of US–UN cooperation in the Middle East.

Conclusion

The creation of the UN was a foreign policy priority for the US. Throughout its history, the US sought to utilize the world body to advance its interests in the Middle East. The Truman administration successfully used the United Nations to help mediate the Soviet–Iran conflict in the post-world war era and to ensure the creation of Israel. However, during the Cold War, tensions between the US and the

---

44   The Resolution was based on a Franco-American proposal and passed on a vote of nine in favor with six abstentions, including China and Russia (in a show of support for Syria, one of Moscow's few traditional allies in the region); see "Security Council Declares Support for Free, Fair Presidential Election in Lebanon: Calls for Withdrawal of Foreign Forces," UN Press Release SC/8181, September 2, 2004, available at http://www.un.org/News/Press/docs/2004/sc8181.doc.htm.

45   The third report of the UNIIIC is available at: United Nations International Independent Investigation Commission, *Third Report of the International Independent Investigation Commission*, March 15, 2006, available at http://www.tayyar.org/tayyar/unreport3.pdf.

46   *Security Council Calls for End to Hostilities Between Hizbollah and Israel, Unanimously Adopting Resolution 1701,'* (UN Security Council); *Press Release SC/8808* (August 11, 2006), available at http://www.un.org/News/Press/docs/2006/sc8808.doc.htm.

USSR generally precluded multilateral action on major issues in the Middle East, especially the Arab–Israeli conflict. By the 1970s, the US was forced to repeatedly veto anti-Israeli resolutions in order to protect one of its main allies in the region, a trend that continued through the Reagan administration in the 1980s, but was briefly interrupted during the Persian Gulf War.

The Gulf War marked the high point of US–UN cooperation in the Middle East in the post-Cold War era. Both the world body and the world's remaining superpower pursued the same goal—Iraqi withdrawal from Kuwait. In order to maintain the grand coalition, the United States limited its end goal to the removal of the Iraqi forces, and not regime change. The main lesson for future US policy from the war was that the extraordinary measures undertaken by the administration of George H.W. Bush, including the willingness to compromise on a variety of fronts, returned significant dividends in the form of broad, multilateral support. Under Bush, the US was able to gain a succession of resolutions that enhanced Washington's own coalition-building initiatives. Conversely, the administration of George H.W. Bush was frustrated in its efforts to gain UN support for military action against Saddam. The inability of the second Bush administration to secure a resolution specifically authorizing the use of force undermined international support and was a reflection of the divisiveness of the conflict. Tensions between Bush and Annan continued throughout the remained of the Secretary-General's tenure.

Nonetheless, as demonstrated by US–UN cooperation over Lebanon, the world body continues to play a major role in the region and serve as a useful partner for the pursuit of American foreign policy. Both the United States and the United Nations seek to promote democracy and stability in the region, even if those goals are impeded by the actions of individual member states. The continuing ability of permanent UN Security Council members France, China and Russia to block US initiatives requires ongoing great power's cooperation to achieve objectives, forcing future administrations to seek compromise and consensus. The United States is unlikely to again have the power or clout employed by the Truman administration and, therefore, must use the George H.W. Bush administration as the model for future UN interaction.

Index

Tables are indicated by italic page numbers.